FROM CHIEFDOM TO STATE IN EARLY IRELAND

This book tracks the development of social complexity in Ireland from the late prehistoric period into the Middle Ages. Using a range of methods and techniques, particularly data from settlement patterns, D. Blair Gibson demonstrates how Ireland evolved from constellations of chiefdoms into a political entity bearing the characteristics of a rudimentary state. This book argues that Early Medieval Ireland's highly complex political systems should be viewed as amalgams of chiefdoms with democratic procedures for choosing leaders rather than as kingdoms. Gibson explores how these chiefdom confederacies eventually transformed into recognizable states over a period of 1,400 years.

D. Blair Gibson is a professor in the Department of Anthropology at El Camino College and the director of the college's Anthropology Museum. He has published articles in a number of journals, including the *Journal of Anthropological Archaeology* and the *Proceedings of the Harvard Celtic Colloquium*. He is the editor of two books, *Tribe and Polity in Late Prehistoric Europe* (with Michael Geselowitz) and *Celtic Chiefdom, Celtic State* (with Bettina Arnold).

Oblique aerial photograph of the trivallate cashel of Cahercommaun showing associated field boundary walls and enclosures. Photo: J. K. S. St. Joseph. Copyright reserved. Cambridge University Collection of Aerial Photography.

FROM CHIEFDOM TO STATE IN EARLY IRELAND

D. BLAIR GIBSON

El Camino College

CAMBRIDGE
UNIVERSITY PRESS

CAMBRIDGE UNIVERSITY PRESS
Cambridge, New York, Melbourne, Madrid, Cape Town,
Singapore, São Paulo, Delhi, Mexico City

Cambridge University Press
32 Avenue of the Americas, New York, NY 10013-2473, USA

www.cambridge.org
Information on this title: www.cambridge.org/9781107015630

First published 2012

Printed in the United States of America

A catalog record for this publication is available from the British Library.

Library of Congress Cataloging in Publication Data
Gibson, D. Blair.
   From chiefdom to state in early Ireland / D. Blair Gibson.
      p.   cm.
   Includes bibliographical references and index.
   ISBN 978-1-107-01563-0 (hardback)
   1. Ireland – Politics and government – To 1172.   2. Ireland – History – To 1172.
   3. Chiefdoms – Ireland – History.   I. Title.
   JN1408.G53   2012
   941.501–dc23   2011032285

ISBN 978-1-107-01563-0 Hardback

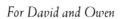

For David and Owen

Contents

Contents

Illustrations

Preface

The Irish chieftains of old established their claims to rule, and the political stature of their polities, through the creation and recitation of genealogies. This project possesses a genealogy as well, and, like the medieval Irish genealogies, it is constructed in part through a retrospection of the past from the standpoint of the living subject, and in part through the conflation of previous genealogies that may not necessarily represent a true blood link to the present but attain such through the manipulation of the remains of the past by those living in the present.

Cahercommaun is a large, ancient settlement site defined by three concentric walls of limestone flags, perched on the edge of a ravine in the Burren region of northern Co. Clare in western Ireland (Figure 1.1). It was excavated by Hugh O'Neill Hencken of the Harvard Peabody Museum over a period of six weeks in the late summer of 1934 with a crew of Irish and American students (including Joseph Raftery, future director of the National Museum of Ireland, and J. O. Brew, future director of the Harvard Peabody Museum) and workmen recruited from the area's farms.

The excavation, one of many undertaken by Hencken in Ireland, proved Cahercommaun to be rich in occupation remains. Cattle bones predominated in the site's inventory. The material remains found were common to the Early Medieval period. The only closely dateable find, a silver brooch, placed at least a part of the site's occupation at around 800 AD (Hencken 1938:2–3, 27–30). Hencken, however, did not stop at the mere description and dating of the settlement. On the evidence of differences in the size, spatial location, and artifactual content of the remains of huts found at the site, he ventured determinations as to the differing social positions of their occupants (ibid.:17–20). On the basis of the large size of the site relative to other similar cashel-type homesteads in the area, Hencken determined that Cahercommaun was the center of a chieftain of northern Clare (ibid.:1).

The Cahercommaun excavation was part of the Third Harvard Expedition to Ireland. Taking part in this expedition were a number of distinguished faculty members from Harvard: Halam Movius Jr., who was the first to do a purposeful and detailed examination of the Irish Mesolithic (1942), and Conrad Arensberg and Solon Kimball, who wrote a now-classic ethnography on the small farmer of Clare (1940). Ironically, much like the famed Central Asiatic Expedition of Roy Chapman Andrews to the inner reaches of Mongolia, which had the questionable objective of locating a non-African place of origin for the human race but instead found the first dinosaur eggs, the Harvard expedition was conceived as part of E. A. Hooton's Harvard Irish Survey – a project that had as its goal the development of a system of European racial classification (Hooton 1940; Hooton and Dupertuis 1955). Needless to say, the prodigious results of the work of Hencken, Movius, Arensberg, and Kimball had no tie-in to Hooton's questionable undertakings.

Hencken and Hooton were far from my mind when I first viewed the site in 1980 in the company of a friend from Germany with whom I was attempting to circumnavigate Ireland by hitchhiking. Indeed, I was unaware of the existence of the latter progenitor. My first year as a graduate student in Ireland was behind me, during which time I had read the report of the excavation in the course of preparing for my qualifying exams.

Later, while I was coming to grips with the Irish law texts for my master's thesis, I came in contact with the work in social anthropology of Raymond Firth, Marshall Sahlins, and Timothy Earle. I was awakened not only to the explanatory potential of the chiefdom concept for the material from the earliest period of Irish history, but also to the possibility that social organization viewed from an evolutionary and ecological perspective may constitute a first principle for the explanation of the existence of a myriad of early Irish social institutions and practices. The Irish law texts describe in fairly elaborate detail the structure of Irish society in the eighth and ninth centuries AD down to the smallest social unit, and lay out the rights and privileges of each social class. I was awakened to the potential of matching this explicit emic social structure to its concrete manifestation in the archaeological record. The payoff could work in two directions: the written sources could render the archaeological record coherent and meaningful, and the archaeological record could illustrate those aspects of social organization left unsaid by the texts, providing it with a "real" structure.

Cahercommaun then presented itself to me in a new guise as the plausible center of a chiefdom-type polity. A further factor enhanced the choice of this site as an object of study over other comparably large, excavated sites of the Irish Late Iron Age. On the basis of its size and defensive siting, Barry Raftery included Cahercommaun in his discussion of Irish hill-forts of the Early Iron Age (1972:51–53). Identification of Cahercommaun with sites of the hill-fort class would make it a remnant of a type of site that had gone out of vogue in the British Isles (with the exception of Wales) in the century after the birth of Christ.

Hill-forts elsewhere in Europe are obvious and dominating features of the landscape that have long exercised a magnetic influence on archaeological investigators. They are distributed from Portugal to Poland and were built by various peoples from the Bronze Ages through the Early Middle Ages. The archaeological literature of Europe is long on published excavations of hill-forts, but sadly, with only a few exceptions (see Crumley and Marquardt 1987; Palmer 1984), the settlement structure and hence the structure of the societies behind construction of hill-forts have not been examined. Cahercommaun then seemed to offer up the novel possibility of documenting in detail the social structure of a European society at the level of development associated with hill-forts.

This kind of project would not be possible if it were not for the richness and variety of sources available in Ireland to the scholar with an interest in prehistoric lifeways and long-term social processes. Ireland probably has the most complete archaeological record of any European country. The density of obvious sites per square kilometer in this country is perpetually astonishing. And though site destruction is proceeding at an alarming rate in the Burren, as in the rest of the country, in many parts of the Burren it is still possible to encounter intact prehistoric landscapes covering many millennia of activity. This is due to the unsuitability of much of the region for plow agriculture on account of the frequently inclement weather, hilly terrain, and large stretches of exposed bedrock and bog. A by-product of this state of affairs for the field worker is that traces of nearly all past structures can be noted on the ground surface, a phenomenon enhanced by a practice of the local inhabitants throughout prehistory and history simply to abandon past habitations and move on rather than destroying or building over them.

The historical record of Ireland constitutes a resource of immeasurable value that allows the investigator to gaze deeply into the distant past of the country through the eyes of its inhabitants. Gaul fell before Julius Caesar's armies without any of the many complex Gaulish polities having left behind a single text. Similarly, no document remains from any of the British chiefdoms of the pre-Roman period. However, Ireland, which received writing along with the Christian tradition commencing in the fourth to sixth centuries AD, enshrined its multifaceted traditions to an amazing extent due to the labors of the men of learning both within and without the Christian tradition.

The Irish historical record is at once socially comprehensive and extensive. The earliest documents of note were composed in the seventh to eighth centuries AD, but sources such as annals, sagas, and saints' lives enshrine earlier oral traditions that probably extend as far back in some instances as the Late Bronze Age. From the corpus of Irish law texts, one can glimpse, often in minute detail, the social structure of eighth-century Ireland and the rights, prerogatives, and situational and invariant obligations and responsibilities of the socially distinct members of the island's chiefdoms. The genealogical materials and the annals allow one to reconstruct the political history of the country and the political and social dynamics of chiefly succession. On account of this immense historical corpus there is probably no other place in the world where chiefdoms can be examined in such great detail.

Taken together, these two records, the historical and the archaeological, make Ireland one of the world's great laboratories for diachronic studies of long-term social processes. This book utilizes both records to arrive at an understanding of the nature and structure of protohistorical Irish chiefdoms in the Burren region of northern Co. Clare. It must be admitted that the inspiration for picking this particular region came initially from the archaeological qualities of this region rather than from a consideration of the historical sources. However, as will later become apparent, due chiefly to the greater length of time that Clare was spared the disruption of foreign hegemony, the historical sources are more plentiful and reflect indigenous Celtic cultural and social institutions more accurately than is the case elsewhere in Ireland.

Acknowledgments

Given that this text stems in part from archaeological fieldwork carried out in northern Co. Clare over a decade and analyses of historic materials that went on in between and for many years after the campaigns in the field had ceased, there are a large number of persons and institutions to which I owe a debt of gratitude.

The program of archaeological research was variously known to its participants and benefactors as the Chiefdoms of County Clare Project, the Cahercommaun Archaeological Research Project, or, more simply, the Cahercommaun Project. The sponsor of this project in its initial stages was Professor George Eogan of the Department of Archaeology of University College, Dublin, Ireland. I would like to thank him for his support and advice. I would also like to express my appreciation to my PhD committee at UCLA, consisting of Timothy Earle, Dwight Read, the late James Hill, Joseph Nagy, and Charles Bennett, for guidance and inspiration in the early stages of this project. Thanks also to the late Peter Danaher, the former Chief Archaeologist of the National Parks and Monuments Branch of the Irish Office of Public Works, for his interest in the project's research program.

The lion's share of the funding for the project in both its 1985 and 1986 field seasons was provided by Earthwatch, and I would like to acknowledge Jane Flaherty of Earthwatch for her patient assistance to the project and to its greenhorn P.I. The project benefited from grants from the Graduate Division of UCLA in 1984 and 1986. The grant of 1986 was conferred by the Department of Anthropology, UCLA, and went to finance radiocarbon analysis. Research grants were also awarded to the Cahercommaun Project by the UCLA Friends of Archaeology. Additional data were gathered in 1990 while the author was a crew chief on Sinéad Ní Ghabhláin's Churches of Kilfenora Project. The author is grateful for the opportunity

Dr. Ní Ghabhláin afforded to return to the Burren, and I wish also to thank those participants in her project who volunteered to accompany me on weekend mapping trips. The Cahercommaun Project returned to the field for a final season of survey in 1993, this time generously supported by the late lamented University Research Expeditions Program. I would like to thank Jean Colvin and Anne Forrest for all that they did to make this field season a success. The composition of the final draft of this text was largely enabled by the granting of a single-semester sabbatical by my employer, El Camino College in Torrance, California.

The crew chiefs of the first season's work of the Cahercommaun Project were Keith Johnson, Michael Geselowitz, and Judith Carroll, and they deserve special commendation for working under very trying circumstances. Patrick Jones was the project's botanist. The crew chiefs of the second field season were Kevin McGimpsey, Una MacDowell, Mary Anne Murray, Ellen McCallig, and the late Wade Richards. The crew chiefs for the 1993 season were Maura Smale and my wife Susan Saul. The latter deserves copious praise for tolerating my frequent and prolonged stints of isolation while I wrote and rewrote the text of this book.

I extend thanks to the following Earthwatch volunteers, whose financial contributions and labor were vital to realizing the project's goals: 1985 – Forrest Bucher, Mary Dahl, Margaret Decker, William Disher, Russell Duino, Marvin Ellenbaas, Ruth Eubank, Ermine Gartley, Barry Haff, Joy Jackson, Donna Kucia, Mary Ludes, Elizabeth Meehan, Margery Norton, Carol Polzer, Carolyn Scheck, Pamela Stross, Janet Sullivan, Sheila Sweeny, Elizabeth Waddell, and Joshua Zimmerman; 1986 – Nora Alverez, Cecil Clennon, Catherine Colleran, Lillian and Al Eisberg, Jacquelyn Engle, Maria Ferraro, Glenn and Donna Franklin, Mary and Richard Freiburg, Mark Gideon, Carol Hayes, Margaret Heindl, Molly Lowell, John Magerlein, Irene Mullen, Christina Ringelstein, Anne Schepp, Joanne Tisei, Nancy Wagner, Tracey Whitesell, Cindy Wolfe, Peter Wangell, and Rosy Zachow. The UREP volunteers from 1993 were Deborah Baker, Gayle Calhoun, Marjorie Chang, Hollister Finch, Matt Forister, Jim and Lewayn Gilchrist, Doreen Griffin, KimBerly Johnson, Kathleen Logue, Barbara Robey, and Betsy Wertheimer.

I would like to thank Michael and Filomena Hines and family for the hospitality they showed me when I stayed with them in Carron in 1984. Tomás and Maureen O'Dea were the caretakers of the cottages in Coskeam where we were headquartered during the 1986 season. Many thanks for use of her telephone and for the homemade goat's cheese. In 1993 we used the Corofin Village Hostel, and I would like to thank Jude and Marie

Neylon for keeping me apprised of the turbulent local political situation that awaited our arrival that year. I would like to thank the following local scholars for their help and interest in the project: Mr. Richard Cronin who runs the Dysert Castle Center, and the late Tomás Coffey who photographed and drew some walls for me after the cessation of formal field activities. Thanks also to the late Tina Conole for her keen interest in the project, and for her assistance with mail and phone calls. Finally, I would like to thank Mr. Gerald McGann, Mr. Eamon MacMahon, Jane and Thomas Gutherie, and the other farmers of the Burren who tolerated the presence of our survey crews on their land. Thomas and Jane Gutherie granted permission to the project to excavate what turned out to be an Early Bronze Age habitation site located on their land. Mrs. Gutherie also gave members of the project shelter in her house when they were caught in rain squalls on the plateau, and presented us with much-appreciated homemade bread.

In working with the medieval documentary sources that shed light on Co. Clare, I would like to acknowledge the invaluable and tireless assistance of Joseph Flahive of University College Cork with Irish texts and Thomas O'Donnell of the University of York for translations of Latin texts. Ultimately, the fault for all errors of translation, and I am sure there are many, lie with me. I would like to thank the then–Assistant Keeper of Antiquities of the National Museum (Dublin), Michael Ryan, for allowing radiocarbon dating to be undertaken on samples of bone from the museum's collection of material from Cahercommaun. Finally, I would like to thank Built Heritage, Northern Ireland Environment Agency, for supplying Figure 3.3, the Royal Society of Antiquaries of Ireland for extending permission to reproduce plates II and VI (Figures 5.1 and 5.5 in this book) from Hugh O'Neill Hencken's Cahercommaun report, the Royal Irish Academy for extending permission to publish figure 2 (Figure 5.2 in this book) from Hull and Comber's excavation report for Caherconnell, and Brian Lacey and the Discovery Programme (Ireland) for supplying the image of Dún Aonghasa.

Notes on Irish Names and Spellings

The reader who is unacquainted with Irish culture, history, and language will no doubt experience some confusion with the Irish names and terms that appear in the body of this work. This study spans three periods in the development of the Irish language, so personal names, names of peoples, and terms are differently rendered in the sources, depending upon their period of origin. This problem is compounded by the fact that personal names in Irish exhibit both nominative and genitive forms, and also by the fact that it wasn't until 1948 that the Irish language was standardized, and so the spelling of words varies greatly between texts, especially in texts of the Middle Ages. To ease some of the confusion, I have included a glossary of personal names later in this section, and a glossary of Irish terms in the back of this volume.

To help the reader keep track of the plethora of historical personages that appear throughout the body of this work, I have assembled a number of genealogies of the leading aristocratic kin groups in an appendix. As the names of individuals of these ramages appear in the text, they are linked to their appearance in a genealogy by a number (e.g., Brian Bóroimhe [6]). This should assist the reader in recognizing a name even where a genitive form or alternate spelling is given.

A NOTE ON THE SPELLING OF NAMES

Given the substantial chronological sweep of this book, it has proven enormously challenging to maintain consistency in the spelling of names of peoples and places, especially given my limited competence in the various stages of development of the Irish language. Starting with Chapter 3, I render the names of composite chiefdoms and chiefdom confederacies in Old Irish. However, throughout the book, place-names are often rendered either in their Anglicized forms or in Modern Irish.

A GUIDE TO THE MOST COMMON IRISH
NAMES IN THIS TEXT

Old Irish	Middle, Modern Irish	Name as frequently rendered in English
—	Brian gen: Briain	Brian
Blat gen: Blait	— gen: Bloid	—
Cass gen: Cais	—	—
Conchobor	Conchobhar, Conchobur gen: Conchobhair	Conor, Connor
Diarmait	Diarmuid, Diarmaid gen: Diarmada	Dermot
Donnchad	Donnchadh gen: Donnchaidh	Donough
Domnall	Domhnall gen: Domhnaill	Donnell, Donall, Donald
Fermac	Fearmac gen: Fearmaic	—
Máel Sechnaill	Maolsheachlainn	Malachy
Mathgamain	Mathghamhain gen: Mathghamhna	Mahon, Mahony
Muirchertach	Muircheartach gen: Muircheartaigh Murchad, Murchadh gen: Murchaidh	Murrough, Murtagh, Murchad
Tadc	Tadg, Tadhg gen. Taidg, Taidhg	Teig, Teigue
Tairdelbach gen: Tairdelbaich Toirdhealbhaigh	Toirdelbach, Toirdhealbhach gen: Toirdelbaig,	Turlough
Uaithne	Uaithne	Owney
Uí	Ua	Ó

Abbreviations

ACl	*Annals of Clonmacnoise*
ACon	*Annals of Connacht*
AFM	*Annals of the Four Masters*
AI	*Annals of Inisfallen*
ALII	*Ancient Laws and Institutes of Ireland*
AU	*Annals of Ulster*
BB	*The Book of Ballymote*
BM	*The Book of Munster*
CGrG	*Cogadh Gaedhel re Gallaibh*
CGH	*Corpus Genealogiarum Hiberniae*
CGSH	*Corpus Genealogiarum Sanctorum Hiberniae*
CT	*Caithréim Thoirdhealbhaigh*
DIL	*Dictionary of the Irish Language*
IMC	*Irish Manuscripts Commission (Books of Survey and Distribution)*
JCHAS	*Journal of the Cork Historical and Archaeological Society*
JRSAI	*Journal of the Royal Society of Antiquaries of Ireland*
Lec	*The Yellow Book of Lecan*
LL	*The Book of Leinster*
NMAJ	*North Munster Antiquarian Journal*
PRIA	*Proceedings of the Royal Irish Academy*
TRIA	*Transactions of the Royal Irish Academy*
UJA	*Ulster Journal of Archaeology*

CHAPTER ONE

Theoretical Considerations

Reduced to its bare essentials, this work is a study of human social organization, or the manifold ways in which humans structure their relationships (see Gibson and Geselowitz 1988:15). Over the course of the last century, two perspectives have evolved on the analysis of social organization. The older tradition, with roots in British functionalism and structural-functionalism, is interested in the modalities by which humans group themselves in varying contexts (e.g., family, extended family, hamlet, lineage, clan) and the reasons for these groupings. By contrast, the interactionist perspective, best exemplified by the work of Fredrick Barth, concerns itself with the dynamic qualities of human relationships and the ways in which roles and groupings are negotiated.

While an interactionist perspective has considerable merit, the dynamic qualities of social structures and the arcs of individual careers are difficult to resolve with the ethnohistorical and archaeological source materials of Early Medieval Ireland. However, even though this case study utilizes the formal analytical categories of social organization developed by the functionalist anthropologists, it is ultimately concerned with social dynamics of people living in groups and, more specifically, with whether or not these groups change in their configurations and why.

In recent decades, some archaeologists have taken up the topic of the stability of chiefdoms – their propensity to either collapse or evolve into primitive states (Anderson 1994; Anderson, Cleaveland, and Stahle 1995; Bogucki 1999: chap. 7; Carneiro 1981; Earle 1987; Flannery 1995, 1999; Kirch 1984; Kristiansen 1982, 1991; Milner 1990; Scarry 1996; Wright 1984). The chiefdoms of America, Africa, and Polynesia that were observed by Europeans in the seventeenth to nineteenth centuries lacked written histories. As these societies came in contact with the industrial nation-states of Europe and the United States, they were exposed to new technologies, new diseases, and both military and economic pressure. They exhibited a variety of responses ranging from collapse to rapid expansion and to absorption into colonial empires.

Ireland provides a stark contrast to the experiences of non-Western chiefdoms. The intelligentsia of Early Medieval Irish society attained literacy several centuries before the onset of foreign invasions. And when Ireland was attacked by Vikings beginning in the eighth century, and invaded by Anglo-Normans in the twelfth century, large swaths of the island managed to remain somewhat aloof from the direct impact of these incursions. Until the sixteenth century Gaelic polities endured outside the areas usurped by foreigners for towns and estates. Thus, one is enabled to study changes in the organization of Irish society over a period of almost 1,000 years through both historical records and archaeological remains.

This very long span of documentation allows the researcher to form solid judgments about the structure of Irish chiefdoms, how the organization of these chiefdoms was sustained, and whether or not these political systems were stable. The question of the stability of chiefdoms leads naturally to the larger issue of the evolutionary potential of these systems. In an earlier publication, I proposed that a state emerged in Munster in the twelfth century AD (Gibson 1995). This study will examine the inevitability of this development – whether the state of Muirchertach Uí Briain was the product of autochthonous forces or was promoted by external stimuli. This examination of historical Irish social organization is thus motivated by an overarching interest in human social evolution.

There are a number of competing paradigms within the social sciences that are expressly evolutionary, including Marxist, structural Marxist, cultural ecological, cultural materialist, selectionist, political economist, and so forth. This study is an outgrowth of the substantivist model of cultural evolution (Gibson and Geselowitz 1988). The substantivist model, in its latest avatar, is an amalgam of the cultural ecology and multilineal evolutionism of the anthropologist Julian Steward (1979) and the substantivist approach of the economic historian Karl Polanyi (1971) to the study of economic systems. Social organization occupied a position of primary importance in the approaches of both scholars to the study of human behavior. Polanyi's work propounded the primacy of behavior in its "instituted" form in the analysis of economic behavior (ibid.). By instituted behavior, Polanyi meant social institutions as they were held to dictate the individual economic values and actions of the social actors. Social institutions are considered to be integrated forms of human behavior and can be diverse in form – examples include the practices surrounding chieftaincy, honor-price, clientship, periodic markets, gift exchanges between elites, or even raiding (Polanyi 1971:249–250). They constitute any instance in which humans are brought together in a predictable set of relationships,[1] corresponding to roles for purposes of social (including economic) action.

Julian Steward devised a body of theory that sought to explain the social structure and economic behavior of a group by reference to the group's specific ecological adaptation and its achieved level of social complexity. These two bulwarks of his thought system have become distilled into the school of cultural ecology on the one hand, and the evolutionary heuristic tool of levels of sociocultural integration on the other. This latter construct bears an isomorphic relationship to Polanyi's "forms of integration" concept (1971:250) to which Polanyi attributed a determinative role with respect to configuring a society's economic institutions. In Steward's thinking, levels of sociocultural integration constituted a methodology for the study of social evolution, and indeed were directly comparable to taxonomic practice in biology (1979:51). He defined them simply as "organizational types" (ibid.) in a continuum of cultural development that proceeded, following his explication by example in *Theory of Culture Change*, from simple to complex.[2]

Over the latter part of the twentieth century, refinements to Steward's original levels of sociocultural integration have been advanced by influential evolutionary anthropologists such as Elman Service, Marshall Sahlins, Allen Johnson, and Timothy Earle (Johnson and Earle 1987; Sahlins 1963; Service 1971, 1975). While both evolutionary anthropology and cultural ecology have lost favor within mainstream anthropology, the products of these schools, not surprisingly, were taken up with great enthusiasm by archaeologists in America and, to a lesser extent, in the United Kingdom. However, criticism has also been leveled by archaeologists at the employment of evolutionary stages on grounds ranging from a perception that they divert attention from the dynamic qualities of social change to charges that levels of sociocultural integration may function as value-laden labels that could be used to deprive indigenous groups of their rights (Feinman and Neitzel 1984; Kehoe 2004). But as Kent Flannery has recently countered, the stages of sociocultural integration are a part of a *methodology* for the study of social evolution, not a description of evolution itself (Flannery 1995; see also Marcus and Feinman 1998:5). Biologists do not waste time repudiating the tools of taxonomy, and anthropologists should not waste time on analogous efforts either.

In the present context, a level of sociocultural integration describes the maximal social entity within which members acknowledge a common allegiance and organize their roles in correspondence to the organizational dictates of the unit. It does not refer to social subunits within a larger polity or to larger social units of sporadic occurrence.

Different levels of sociocultural integration are distinguishable through qualitative structural dichotomies (Gibson 2004). For instance, big-man societies are marked by a segmentary structure of lineages and entrepreneurial leadership, while chiefdoms are characterized by lineages linked together by genealogical relationships into a broader social construct. These lineages are further arrayed in a hierarchy reflecting putative kin relationships between their founding ancestors with respect to the ancestor of the principal line (Sahlins 1958:140–142). The office of leadership is permanent, with succession often constrained to a single sept. As we shall see in Chapter 9, however, succession to office within the complex chiefdoms of Ireland was more open-ended than it was in precontact Polynesia.

Within the bounds of a level of sociocultural integration, there is an appreciable amount of variation with respect to organizational complexity. Ranking societies by the dimensions of spatial extent or population size (scale) does not yield consistent results across cultures; a large number of case studies amply demonstrate that societies of similar organizational complexity may vary greatly in these dimensions due to differences in yields between subsistence technologies and the distribution of productive resources (Gibson 1988, 1995, 2004, 2008b). It is, therefore, more beneficial to compare societies by reference to their organizational complexity (Carneiro 1981:47–48; Earle 1987:288–289; Gibson 2004). Distinctions of scale in this work thus refer to the number of hierarchical levels of authority within a polity. These are the number of superimposed political units within a polity headed by an individual of authority, such as a lineage leader, subchieftain, or paramount chieftain (see Carneiro 1981:46; Drennan 1987; Feinman and Neitzel 1984:47–48; Flannery 1998; Gibson 1982:75–82, Fig. 5; Gibson and Geselowitz 1988:18; Johnson 1978:10; Upham 1987).[3] These levels of authority within a polity are of course synonymous with the number of nested social units within a polity, as will become clearer as this examination proceeds.[4]

The social formations and institutions that characterize different levels of sociocultural integration give rise to specific cultural institutions. These are belief systems and associated rituals practiced commonly by the members of a social unit that serve to objectify and justify the social order and reinforce or regulate social behavior. Cultural institutions, in effect, fulfill a multitude of roles in the framework of social analysis offered here. In a primary sense, they serve to define the level of sociocultural integration by the fact of their presence or absence. For instance, the chiefdom level of sociocultural integration is partially defined by the existence of the office of chieftain and by the presence of many corollary institutions such as inauguration rituals, promulgation of aristocratic genealogies, and ancestor veneration (Sahlins 1958:140–142). Social and cultural institutions are thus corollary indices of the level of social complexity of any given social group.

Though there are organizational features that are universal to chiefdoms, certain institutions reflect the economic-ecological posture of the group. For instance, centralized storage is a universal characteristic of the palace economies of early agrarian states, and clientship is a social institution specific to the agropastoralist chiefdoms and states of Africa and northern Europe (Buxton 1963; Gibson 1988; Patterson 1981; Webster 1990). The institution of centralized storage reflects the physical suitability of cereal crops for long-term storage under varied climatic conditions. A secondary consideration is the fact that early agrarian states tended to arise in areas whose topography presented minimal obstacles to bulk transport or was even conducive to it (e.g., plains, river valleys). The association between clientship and agropastoralism is an outgrowth of many factors specific to a pastoralist economy, including a pattern of dispersed settlement, the risks associated with cattle raising (e.g., disease, human and animal predators), the relatively slow growth rates of cattle herds and consequent length of time necessary for herd replacement in the case of calamity, and the need for protection (Gibson 1988; Webster 1990).

Of significance to the archaeologist are those institutions, cultural and social, that generate highly survivable material correlates in the archaeological record. In Ireland, chieftainship leaves its material imprint in varied forms: inauguration mounds, ostentatious brooches, and sizable homesteads. These archaeological expressions of leadership are supplemented in Ireland by further diagnostic survivals in the historical record, such as the genealogies and descriptions of chiefdom social structure contained in the legal texts. Since, in Ireland, both archaeological and written resources are so abundant for the Early Middle Ages, the deficiencies in the archaeological record can be filled out by historical information, and the biases and deficiencies of the historical record can be checked against archaeological remains. These factors make Ireland a provident laboratory for the social analysis of the past.

Paramount to the various institutions of a society is the glue that binds them together into a coherent system: the social structure. The social structure is here conceptualized as the totality of relationships between individuals that channel social action. Of course, these relationships vary from those that are situational and sporadic to those that are permanent and incessant, and, in complex societies, social relationships are multifaceted and hierarchical. In the substantivist framework of analysis, the relationships of import are those that order individuals and institutions and enhance the predictability of the outcomes of social interactions. These relationships fall within two overlapping categories with respect to the traditions of social science research: kinship and political systems.

Systems of kinship bring individuals together into social units defined by linkages of descent and marriage. The quantity and quality of these linkages vary greatly between groups and across cultures, and can be extended to include an entire polity of several hundred individuals. The political system differs from the kinship system only insofar as linkages between individuals are contractual – roles are vested with varying degrees of power and may possess the additional dimension of leadership over a group. These intertwined systems provide the structural principles that order roles and institutions, and social scientists have ascribed to them a primary place in explanations of social evolution.

THE CHIEFDOM LEVEL OF SOCIOCULTURAL INTEGRATION

Raymond Firth provided the first extensive descriptions of the social organization and economics of chiefdoms in two now-classic works: *The Primitive Economics of the New Zealand Maori* (1929) and *We, the Tikopia* (1936), though the term "chiefdom" was first coined by Kalervo Oberg in his survey of the social organization of the lowland indigenous peoples of Central and South America (Carneiro 1981:38; Oberg 1955). In the decades since these early works, usage of this term to describe societies of intermediate social complexity has spread to additional cultural regions, and the examination of societies attributable to this class has intensified (see Carneiro 1981; Earle 1987; Feinman and Neitzel 1984 for reviews).

Service defined chiefdoms as redistributional societies with a central agency of coordination (1971:34). Sahlins detailed the organization of Polynesian chiefdoms through the enumeration of an entire checklist of social traits (1958:4–9), though he viewed ramage social structure as the chief organizing principle (ibid.:139–151). More recently, Earle (1978:3, 1987:279) and Carneiro (1981:45) have come to represent chiefdoms simply as social entities comprising multiple communities under the leadership of a chief, though to be fair to these authors, they go on to present the social attributes of these polities.

It is crucial to return to Steward's practice of prioritizing the features that define a sociocultural level of integration. However, I deviate here from his practice of basing these diagnostics upon core features related to subsistence activities, as these are certain to vary from one ecological setting to another. What has come out of cross-cultural comparisons since his initial work is the understanding that the higher levels of sociocultural integration, from segmentary systems on up, possess a suite of characteristics that do not vary across different ecological settings in the same way that the social organization of hunter-gatherers and primitive horticulturalists does. These characteristics lie in the realm of social organization.

All chiefdoms, irrespective of their specific ecological adaptations, exhibit the ramage social structure described by Gifford for Tonga (1929) and Firth for the Tikopia (1963:299–329; see also Sahlins 1958: chap. 8). This fact is important, as it establishes a universal core definition for chiefdoms and predicates a structure that sets out the characteristics of other dependent institutions. The ramage system of Polynesia consisted of ambipatrilineal lineages bound together into a single structure through a belief in descent from a common original ancestor. The concept of social ranking is implicit in this system, as lineages within the most inclusive ramage are ranked through genealogical proximity to the original line of descent. Hence, as cadet lineages branch off of the main line of descent, and as further branching takes place off of these lineages, the ranking of individuals within these cadet lineages becomes correspondingly lower.

This description of the ramage system is as applicable to Ireland as it is to Polynesia (Patterson 1994:26). I have found the ramage concept to have greater utility in the Irish context than the rival terms "conical clan" (Kirchoff 1955) and "status lineage" (Goldman 1970:chap. 20). Since chiefdoms are composed of lineages of comparable structure that are conjoined and hierarchically arranged, a ramage can be taken to describe either the entire assemblage of related lineages or any of its constituent subunits. The other terms do not lend themselves to such ease of manipulation.

In Ireland there were in all likelihood three hierarchically ordered social levels to the ramage concept. In describing these levels, I adapt to the Irish situation the terminology that Raymond Kelly utilized in his study of the social organization of the Nuer of Sudan (R. Kelly 1985:169). The maximal ramage refers to all genealogically related lineages that maintain some degree of political cohesion. In Ireland, this is manifested in a number of ways, among the most obvious being a patronymic identifying the apical ancestor (e.g., Uí Lochlainn [descendants of Lochlaind]). The name of the leading ramage is, of course, not often the same as the name of the chiefdom, which in most cases either refers to the dominant ramage at an earlier stage of its existence or to a formerly dominant people of the territory. A second manifestation of the political cohesion of a maximal ramage is the ramage's control of a territory with clearly established boundaries. This quality of a maximal ramage eliminates the blurring caused by the ancient practice of extending group patronymics to ratify the membership of a chiefdom confederacy, such as the *Connachta* (descendants of Conn) or the *Éoganachta*, (descendants of Éogan). This practice led to a number of maximal ramages that bore the same patronym, albeit with a geographical qualifier (e.g., *Éoganacht Locha Léin*), but that controlled noncontiguous territories.

Next in social inclusiveness is the major ramage, termed *slíocht* in the Medieval period Irish sources and *derbfíne* (true family) in the earlier (seventh to eighth century AD) legal texts, and often translated into English as "section" (Gibson 1995). This was a single aristocratic lineage within those that together composed a maximal lineage. From an analysis of the social constitution of the sixteenth-century O'Lochlainn chiefdom in the Burren, it seems that the section was a corporate landholding unit and maintained a distinctive political identity, manifested by a principal residence that I have termed the "section capital" (Gibson 1995, 2000). Some intermediate ramages probably had their origins in the progeny of the former chieftains of a chiefdom.

The legal text *D'fodlaib cineoil tuaithi* (On the divisions of the lineage in the chiefdom) establishes the existence of a sublineage within the *derbfíne* called the *gelfíne* (white or bright kindred) (Charles-Edwards 1993:55; F. Kelly 1988; McLeod 2000). The color symbolism may refer to that segment of the *derbfíne* out of which future leaders emerged by virtue of proximity to the principal line of descent.[5] One may also surmise on the basis of the five households that were said to make up this grouping that the term indicates the lineage leader and his adult male offspring. This hypothesis is supported by a rule that seems to preclude claims on the property of the *gelfíne* by more distant kinsmen (Charles-Edwards 1993:515). The legal texts are clear, however, that the *derbfíne*, not the *gelfíne*, was the true corporate group (Ó Cróinín 1995:143).

The major ramage or section was a subdivision of the maximal lineage. It in turn presided over lineages of free commoners. By analogy with African chiefdoms and segmentary societies, one may surmise that section territories were also populated by nonaristocratic lineages that did not share the patronym of the leading ramage (Buxton 1963; Evans-Pritchard 1969:212). Those lineages unrelated to the maximal ramage may have even constituted the majority of the population of an Irish chiefdom. As the ethnohistorical legal texts that have come down to us were composed under aristocratic patronage, the social structure of the nonaristocratic sector of the population is not clearly discernible. Archaeological evidence, to be discussed later, will enable the first steps toward filling this gap.

Settlement evidence allows us to discern the existence of an even smaller, spatially distinct, though certainly not autonomous, social unit: the single household. Individual farms and farmers form the basis of discussion in legal texts dealing with relations between neighbors (*Bretha Comaithchesa*) and inheritance (Charles-Edwards 1993:47; F. Kelly 2000:413), though the social constitution of a household is not detailed. The settlement evidence to be detailed in the present study indicates only limited residential autonomy for what may be presumed to have been extended families or kindreds.

In addition to ramage social structure, there are a number of social and cultural institutions that one may expect to encounter in any chiefdom. Naturally, the most important social institution is the office of chieftain. This office exists independently of the current holder – that is, it is conceived as something to be filled or occupied after the last occupant's demise (Johnson and Earle 1987:220).

The chiefly office is consistently invested with several cultural institutions relevant to the chief's roles as leader, adjudicator, source of largess, and sacred personage. The chief was considered to be an intermediary between the supernatural realm and the natural world. One inevitably finds among societies of the chiefdom level that the ancestors of the chiefly lineage are religiously venerated (Firth 1963; MacAnany 1995; Sahlins 1958:142). In Ireland, medieval ancestor veneration has left varied traces. In the textual realm the deeds of ancestors were the focus of the mythic cycles, most prominent in this regard being the Historical Cycle. These myths served to apotheosize a maximal ramage's founding ancestor. Select monuments on the landscape, such as standing stones inscribed with a dedication in the ogam script, served as constant reminders to the citizens of a chiefdom of the significance of chiefly ancestors. Important walled settlements often bear the names of individuals, and we can presume these place-names refer to the settlements' putative founders (e.g., *Cathair Commáin* [The Dwelling Place of Commáin]). Some inauguration mounds, such as Carn Mhic-Táil (The Mound of Mac-Tál), were held to be the final resting place of ancestors. Taking an oath of office while standing on top of the burial place of an ancestor was seen as the ultimate test of the legitimacy of a chieftain-elect, as it was thought that the ancestor could signal immediately if the presumptive ruler were illegitimate. Ancestor veneration extended from the preservation of the relics of famous ecclesiastics associated with the various ramages and their display in times of crisis to the invocation of an ancestor's name at the commencement of battle. Ancestor veneration was the principal source of legitimacy for the chiefly ramage and provided a key element for forging a common identity among a chiefdom's membership.

A natural adjunct in a society in which social position and political relationships were contingent upon the relations between ancestors was the keeping of genealogies. Numerous genealogical texts, containing the names of thousands of chieftains, survive from medieval Ireland (O'Brien 1976; Ó Cróinín 1995:63). This corpus of material was produced by genealogical specialists, who are likewise typically encountered in chiefdom societies.

In chiefdoms, generosity is axiomatic to the definition of social status (Firth 1929:118, 288–289, 1965:219–222, 230; Goldman 1970:18–19; Sahlins 1958:xi, 3–4). This cultural institution is a corollary to the chief's role in the mode of economic circulation that is typically associated with the political economy of chiefdoms – that is, redistribution. Questions were raised in the 1970s and 1980s as to whether redistribution at the chiefdom level is indeed really redistributive in nature (see Carneiro 1981:58–63; Earle 1978; Peebles and Kus 1977; Rosman and Rubel 1978). A recurrent critique of the redistributive model was that not much actually reverts to the producer; the bulk of the revenue to the chiefly household stops with this institution (Carneiro 1981:60–63; Earle 1978:180–185; Peebles and Kus 1977). Beyond the percentage taken to support the chief's household, most goods are converted into prestige items or used to attract followers.

The problem with this debate is that it is unfocused with respect to the level of sociocultural integration.[6] In his earliest writings, Firth was clear that even the chieftain of the simplest polity enjoys unequal access to the means of production (1963:333–342), and that wealth accumulation by a chief is important to establishing and expanding his status (1929:118–121). To stereotype the institution of redistribution as a simple quid pro quo circulation of goods is simply missing the point.

The problem is not one of factual error, but of incomplete characterization. A redistributive economy *is* a political economy (see Johnson and Earle 1987:15, 208; Sahlins 1972:139–140). If Polanyi committed any sin in formulating the concept of redistribution, it was that he focused unduly on the mechanical aspects of this mode of economic circulation – on appropriation, storage, and allocation:

Redistribution obtains within a group to the extent to which the allocation of goods is collected in one hand and takes place by virtue of custom, law or *ad hoc* central decision. Sometimes it amounts to a physical collecting accompanied by storage-cum-distribution, at other times the "collecting" is not physical, but merely appropriational, i.e., rights of disposal in the physical location of goods. Redistribution occurs for many reasons, on all civilizational levels, from the primitive hunting tribe to the vast storage systems of ancient Egypt, Sumeria, Babylonia or Peru. In large countries differences of soil and climate may make redistribution necessary; in other cases it is caused by discrepancy in point of time, as between harvest and consumption. (1971:253–254)

The existence of rituals of redistribution in societies with social ranking is beyond question; these rituals are the tangible expression of the political economy at the big-man level of integration, crystallized in the potlatch of the indigenous cultures of the Pacific Northwest. Similarly, the chieftains of New Zealand and the Trobriand Islands sponsored massive displays of foodstuffs that were consumed at large-scale feasts (with political objectives). Significant at the level of the chiefdom are gradual changes in the character of redistribution. In big-man societies and simple chiefdoms, the political economy takes the form of sporadic goods amassment realized through the labor of the kinsmen of the big man. The produce is mobilized as a result of his entrepreneurial efforts, and is contributed out of respect of the populace for the chief (Firth 1965:190–191; Sahlins 1972:130–137). The political economy of complex chiefdoms exhibits a shift to systematized and regular accumulations of goods backed by coercive force (Earle 1978:186–190). Stealing a cue from Polanyi (1968), Timothy Earle and Terrance D'Altroy have called the latter mode of goods accumulation staple finance (1982; D'Altroy and Earle 1985). In its outward manifestations the system of staple finance is certainly redistributive, and the redistribution concept is apt in describing the gross mechanics of the system: goods flow to the chiefly center and are in return dispensed by the chieftain (Johnson and Earle 1987:208). The redistributive mode of economic circulation likewise provides a theoretical foundation for the maxim of Firth that the chieftain gains in prestige through his role as a conduit of goods (Firth 1929:274, 289, 423). However, the concept of staple finance is better at highlighting the constraints on the circulation of goods and the rationale behind the system.

THE CHIEFDOM CONCEPT IN EUROPEAN PREHISTORY

Chiefdoms have been an explicit focus of discussion by archaeologists in Europe for as long as they have been in any other culture area of the world outside of Polynesia. However, analyses of the social organization of European chiefdoms have been underway only within the last thirty years, and have been limited to the British Isles and Scandinavia (Byock 1988, 2001; Charles-Edwards 1993; Foster 1989; Patterson 1994; Roymans 1990; K. Smith 2004). Though European archaeology has had a largely humanistic bent, British and Scandinavian scholars have shown a greater interest in exploring the social dimensions of their data.

On the continent, the archaeologists who have been most attracted to the identification of chiefdoms in the archaeological record are those involved with the Neolithic, Chalcolithic, and Early Bronze Age periods (e.g., Milisauskas 1978; Milisauskas and Kruk 1984; Rowlett 1991; Shennan 1982; van de Velde 1979). The objective of this work has been to establish the presence in western Europe of societies of an intermediate scale of social complexity at an early point in time. Those archaeologists working on the later periods have only used the chiefdom concept as a point of reference by which the relative level of complexity of the archaeological period of a region is characterized, analogous to a kind of peg on which one can hang one's hat (see, for instance, Barker and Rasmussen 1998: chap. 2; Collis 1984; Frankenstein and Rowlands 1978; Kristiansen 1982).

Colin Renfrew can be credited with being the first to apply the chiefdom concept to the archaeological record of the British Isles. Early on, he put forward the idea of a qualitative shift in the nature of chiefdoms in Britain from the communally organized "group oriented" chiefdoms of the Late Neolithic to the "individualizing chiefdoms" of the Bronze and Iron Ages, characterized by individual burial and prestige display (1974). Renfrew also produced detailed examinations of the territorial and religious organization of the chiefdom polities of Neolithic Wessex (1973) and the Orkney Islands in the Early Bronze Age (1979). However, in his explicit use of formal social models in archaeology, Renfrew is something of a lone voice in Britain, confirmed by the fact that chiefdoms receive only passing mention in Richard Bradley's *The Social Foundations of Prehistoric Britain* (1984).

ETHNOHISTORICAL IRISH CHIEFDOMS

In addition to what has been said above about the eminent suitability of Ireland for the study of social process, Ireland can also rightly be called a laboratory for the study of chiefdoms. One can identify chiefdoms in the Irish ethnohistorical sources over the entire course of the Early Middle Ages (200–1170 AD) as well as during the High and Late Middle Ages up until the destruction of most of the Gaelic polities by the armies of Oliver Cromwell in 1646–1651, and by William of Orange in 1689–1691. Recently, several excellent in-depth examinations of Early Medieval Irish social structure based on the legal texts have appeared in print (e.g., Charles-Edwards 1993; Patterson 1994), so the sketch of the organization of Early Medieval Irish chiefdoms presented in this chapter is merely a starting point for the framing of the hypotheses to be tested against the archaeological record.

The sources that shed light on the earliest periods of Irish history, the legend cycles transcribed in the Early Middle Ages, portray the culture of aristocrats within a stratified heroic society. Many Irish social institutions that were to persist for many centuries, such as fosterage and clientship, were documented at the earliest instance in these myths. The fullest early descriptions of early Irish social institutions are to be found, however, in the corpus of Irish legal texts, the brehon laws, which were commuted to writing beginning in the seventh century AD (ALII; Binchy 1978). Of these texts, *Críth Gablach*, *Uraicecht Becc*, and *D'fodlaib Cineoil Tuaithi* of the *Senchus Már* have the most direct information on social organization (see ALII vols. I, II, IV, V; Binchy 1941, 1958; Charles-Edwards 1993: Appendix C; F. Kelly 1988; MacNeill 1923; McLeod 2000).

Commensurate with what is understood about ramage social structure, the Irish of the Early Middle Ages perceived the social structure of their polities as the branching through time of a single large family, called the *fine* (Gibson 1982:38–39). This conception of political relations as family relations was carried all the way up to the pinnacle of the political system. The legal texts describe the social order as having been stratified into three primary tiers of authority represented by named leaders of social units that are arranged into a scalar hierarchy. Proceeding from lowest to highest, as has been stated above, the *gelfine* sublineage provided leadership for the *derbfine* major ramage. The head of the *gelfine* portion of the lineage was known as the *áighe fine* (pillar of the family) or the *cenn fine* (family head) (Gibson 1982:30–31, 54–57).

The next level higher in the Early Medieval Irish social order was the *túath*, the most elemental Irish chiefdom. In theory, all individuals within a *túath* traced their descent to an original ancestor, by whose name the aristocrats of the *túath* identified themselves (e.g., Uí Briain = the descendants of Brian, after Brian Bóroimhe [6] [d. 1014 AD]). At the pinnacle of the *túath* was the *cenél*, a *derbfine* within the *túath* that owed its superior social position to its direct descent from the founding ancestor (Patterson 1994:29). The male representative of this sept, the *rí*, ruled the *túath*. In contrast to the chiefdoms of Polynesia, early Ireland had no rule of primogeniture and so the *rí* could be any male from within the *derbfine* bounds of descent, a fact that promoted the factional infighting characteristic of Irish succession.

The *mór thúath*, or great *túath*, consisted of a number of *túatha* united through ties of kinship and/or military domination by a single *túath* into a composite chiefdom (Gibson 1995). At the head of the *cenél* of this *túath* was the *rí ruirech*, or paramount chieftain. Composite chiefdoms possessed constitutions in the form of genealogies that presented the relationship of each chiefdom of a *mór thúath* to the others by tracing the kin relations of founding ancestors. Often, origin legends detailed the exploits of the ancestor of the entire named group and listed his sons. Each *túath* within the *mór thúath* would possess an individual genealogy for its *cenél*, tracing back the line of the ramage to one of the lesser sons of the founding ancestor. Naturally, much of the content of these genealogies was fictive – genealogies were frequently altered to reflect and support the existing political relationships and circumstances.

Several legal tracts on status present multiple levels of chieftains, each denoted by a separate term, but the texts are inconsistent as to terminology (Jaski 2000:99–102). *Rí ruirech* is the most commonly attested term for a superior chieftain. The lawyers may have been influenced by numerology to create additional chieftain statuses in order to conform to a scheme involving multiples of three. However, as will be detailed in a subsequent chapter, the lawyers may also have been trying to describe the complex hierarchies of chieftains that resulted from the expansion of composite chiefdoms into chiefdom confederacies and the creation of alliances between these confederacies.

KINGS, TRIBES, AND CLANS

Within works by historians on Early Medieval Ireland, one frequently encounters terms such as "king," "tribe" or "tribal," "clan," and "lordship." Readers who are familiar with the historical literature on Early Medieval

Ireland may be disconcerted by the fact that this book departs from the conventions of usage of this social terminology. There are a number of points of justification for skirting these terms, or, in the case of the word "king," restricting its usage (Gibson 2010). The simplest justification is simply that this book is not a work of history; it is an anthropological study written by an anthropologist. Practitioners of anthropology themselves are not entirely consistent in their use of social terminology – see the statements above concerning ramage and conical clan. However, it is a long-standing convention that when an anthropologist uses a social term, unless its meaning is universally agreed upon, the term is defined by delineating the qualities of the social structure or social institution. Considerations of tradition and linguistics loom more prominently for historians of Early Medieval Ireland.

The first case in point is the Old Irish word *rí*, which is conventionally rendered as "king" in translation. The ground offered for translating *rí* as king is its linguistic affinities with other early European terms for a leader or ruler, such as Gaulish *rix*, Latin *rex*, and Sanskrit *raj* (Jaski 2000:38; McCone 1998). The unspoken argument is that since Latin *rex* is translated into English as "king," Old Irish *rí* deserves the same treatment. This line of reasoning presents a substantial problem. These terms may jointly derive from a common Proto-Indo-European source, but that is no guarantee that the descendant institutions to which these derivatives refer are isomorphic. The joint Indo-European ancestor of *rí*, *rex*, and *raj* may have been a root *(H)rēǵ-/(H)reǵ-* meaning "direct" or "rule" (McCone 1998; cf. Mallory 1989:125). Following the spread of Indo-European speakers across Europe, derivatives of this root came to refer to Italic, Roman, and Irish leaders. To translate both *rí* and *rex* as king has the unfortunate repercussion of equating the leader of an Irish *túath* with the leader of a Mediterranean *polis*, even though the scale and qualitative aspects of the organization of these polities were in all likelihood vastly different.

In modern usage the English word king itself describes leaders of such disparate levels of power as George III of England, who reigned at the pinnacle of an empire, and the nineteenth-century king Kabarega I of Ankole, a leader of a formerly independent primitive state that now lies within modern Uganda. King, then, is an English word that sorely lacks specificity in the vernacular. In anthropological literature the word king is typically reserved for the apical leader of a state with a monarchical form of central government (Possehl 1998:264). The least complex type of society over which a king would rule would be a primitive or archaic state. It will become clear (hopefully) in subsequent chapters that Irish polities did not approach state-level complexity until the twelfth century. Therefore, the word king will not come into play in this volume until Chapter 8, in which the origins of the primitive state in Munster in the twelfth century are discussed.

Daniel Binchy, the preeminent twentieth-century scholar of Early Medieval Irish political institutions, sought to reduce the apparent contradictions between Early Medieval Irish kings and their shortcomings with regard to their administrative and jural capacities by stating that Irish kings were "tribal kings" (Binchy 1970). This line of reasoning, in its modern manifestation, rests upon the translation of the word *túath* as "tribe" (Byrne 2001:8). To an anthropologist, this constitutes another poor choice of terminology, as the word "tribe" has become almost completely moribund within the discipline, again due to its lack of specificity. F. J. Byrne does not really help matters any as he defines the word tribe simply as a "distinct political entity" (ibid.). The Roman Republic and British Empire were distinct political entities, but no one calls them tribes and their rulers are not referred to as tribal kings.

Nerys Patterson has recently proposed the rehabilitation of the word "clan" to describe the largest-scale political units of the medieval Irish (1994:29). This would seem to be a sensible way to escape the traps of calling the Irish political systems kingdoms or tribes, since clan is a term both used by anthropologists and derived from the Irish word *clann*, meaning "offspring." *Clann* had the further connotation of referring to an aristocratic lineage. Though Patterson cites a 1940 definition of clan from Evans-Pritchard's *The Nuer* as a "collection of lineages," which agrees with her application of the concept (though the clans of the Nuer are not really analogous to an Irish maximal ramage), the word has since come to be applied by anthropologists strictly to a single unilineal descent group "whose members trace their descent to an unknown ancestor or, in some cases, to a sacred plant or animal" (Scupin 1998:365). Its application has been invariably restricted to segmentary societies. Though as a social scientist I am sympathetic with Patterson's desire to revive usage of clan, it is not an appropriate choice for medieval Ireland.

More recently, the terms "petty kingdoms" and "lordships" have been applied to medieval Gaelic polities. The term lordship seems to be especially preferred by scholars as a descriptor for the Gaelic polities of the later Middle Ages, possibly out of discomfort with their small size when compared with the medieval English state, which had intruded into Ireland in the twelfth century. While it is certainly not in error to refer to a *túath* or *mór thúath* as a lordship, as these were most certainly ruled by lords, there is no analytical gain in doing so either. No qualities have been put forward by which someone may distinguish a lordship from any other kind of polity, and the term takes no heed of the scalar differences that existed between Irish polities that the terms *túath* and *mór thúath* encompass.

SETTLEMENT STRUCTURE AND SUBSISTENCE ECONOMY

To prepare the reader for the subsequent discussion of Irish political systems, it is necessary to briefly lay out the information that is available from the ethnohistorical sources and excavations on the economic orientation and settlement structures of Irish society in the first millennium AD. The overall cultural history of Early Medieval Ireland is far too complicated to relate here, and the reader is referred instead to several good works of general introduction (see Charles-Edwards 2000; de Paor and de Paor 1978; Edwards 1990, 2005; Mac Niocaill 1972; Ó Corráin 1972, 2005; Ó Cróinín 1995, 2005).

Over fifty years ago Daniel Binchy famously described Ireland of the period of the law texts as "tribal, rural, hierarchical, and familiar" (Binchy 1954:54). Archaeological and geographical studies of Irish settlement during this period have found nothing to contradict this pronouncement. Towns and villages were certainly foreign to the Irish before the establishment of coastal emporia by the Vikings in the ninth century AD, and nucleated settlement remained by and large foreign to them to the millennium's end.[7]

The dominant domestic settlement of the Early Medieval period was the enclosed homestead. There are several categories of enclosed homestead that crop up in the medieval literary sources and survive as components of place-names and in the technical vocabulary of archaeologists: a *ráth* or *lios* is a homestead defined by an enclosing bank of earth. These are collectively referred to as raths by archaeologists. Cashels are similar sites, except that the enclosing wall was of unmortared stone, and they lacked ditches. A *crannóg* (Angl. crannog) is a homestead established upon an artificial island in a lake or marsh built of deposits of brushwood, surrounded by a palisade. The unusual wealth and diversity of craft products that crannog excavations have uncovered, taken with known historical associations of some sites, indicate that crannogs were exclusively the residences of Irish chieftains (Edwards 1990:41; Gibson 1982:274, 1988:54; O'Sullivan 1998:136–137).

Though all of these settlement types vary in setting and construction materials, they are equivalent with respect to layout. The remains or traces of circular (or later subrectangular) huts are usually found within the enclosure. The number of huts present depends upon the size and importance of the settlement. Even the ecclesiastical settlements displayed this same layout, though showing greater elaboration in the morphology of the buildings and internal divisions into different zones of use (see Fanning 1981:150; Lawlor 1925).

Though sometimes several raths have been found situated close to one another (e.g., Cush, Co. Limerick, for which see Ó Ríordáin 1939–1940; Lisleagh, Co. Cork, for which see Monk 1988, 1995, 1998), more often they stand spatially removed from other like sites. This characteristic of Irish settlement extends all the way up the social hierarchy to the very pinnacle. To date, several settlements have been excavated that are the known historical centers of regional chiefdoms: Lagore crannog, a ninth-century center of the southern Brega Síl nAedo Sláine branch of the Uí Néill (Hencken 1950); Knowth, the center of the northern Brega Uí Néill from the ninth century to the Norman invasion (Eogan 1968, 1974, 1977); and Uisneach, the center of the Clann Cholmáin Uí Néill from the sixth to the twelfth centuries (Macalister and Praeger 1928). These sites differ from the ordinary rath in that they are larger, more elaborate (more huts and enclosing banks present), and richer in evidence of craft production and consumption (Gibson 1982:chap. 5). Fundamentally, they were just homesteads on a grand scale, and not the focus of any sort of nucleated pre-urban foundations.

The balance of ethnohistorical documentation portrays Ireland as preponderantly given to cattle pastoralism (Lucas 1989). The centerpiece of the great national epic *Táin Bó Cuailgne* is a raid by the ancient Connachta to capture a great bull of the Ulaid. The most common units of value in the legal texts are cows. Wealth accumulated to the aristocracy through their investment of cattle in clients, who delivered in return the increase in their herds in calves (Gerriets 1983; F. Kelly 1988:29–33, 2000:446–447; Patterson 1981). As Kenneth Nicholls has remarked, the obsession with cattle in the texts tends to obscure those aspects of the Irish economy not devoted to cattle husbandry (Nicholls 1972:114).

The food lists of the *Senchus Már* do, however, communicate that vegetable foods and products from other species of livestock were significant to the early Irish domestic economy. Strips of woolen cloth, such as those that have survived at Lagore crannog, demonstrate the importance of sheep to the domestic economy (Start in Hencken 1950:203–224). Finds of spindle whorls and sheep bones in the inventories of all sites of this period that have yielded bones reinforce this impression. Pigs must have also been kept in some number, as salted joints were a part of the requisitions of the chieftains. Frequent references to the state of mast crops are also made in the annals.

Due to the dampness of the climate, barley and oats were the principal cereals grown, the latter species predominating (Monk, Tierney, and Hannon 1998). Oat cakes figure in the tribute lists, and oat porridge crops up in the ecclesiastical sources (Sexton 1998). Rotary querns are also found on every domestic site of this period, providing an indirect witness to the cultivation of grain. Scholars of the Irish Early Medieval subsistence economy describe it as a mixed-farming system (Patterson 1994:62; Proudfoot 1961). By this term they mean that both livestock rearing and cultivation were pursued. Cultural ecologists refer to an economy in which livestock and crop production are jointly pursued, but in which the livestock sector is dominant, as agropastoral (Gibson 1988:44). The importance of livestock versus cereals in the Early Medieval Irish diet is difficult to judge, but the attention paid to cattle in the surviving literature and the sizable bone collections that have come from Early Medieval settlements with alkaline soils show a preponderant focus on livestock (F. Kelly 2000:27). Cattle were even more important in areas of Ireland with heavier rainfall and heavy soils, such as obtains in the north and west of the country.

THE OBJECTIVES OF THIS STUDY

The law texts, genealogies, annals, and other written sources of the Early Middle Ages contain an emic representation of Irish society – the perspective originates with the actors themselves. In the case of the law texts, there is an aristocratic slant, since not only were chieftains the patrons of the literati who created these books, but the literati were also themselves members of aristocratic ramages (Ó Corráin 1978). Beyond these inherent biases the texts present other significant limitations to achieving an understanding of the outlines of Early Medieval Irish society. More to the point, they present us with the outlines of social and political systems but give no indication of the physical constitution of these systems. That is, we have little idea how the actual structure of Irish society at this time coincided with the theoretical structure presented by the texts. For instance, we may assume that the *derbfine* was a kinship group, but was it a residential group as well? How big was a *túath*? Was the *túath* politically homogeneous? What kind of social stratification existed inside it? Where did the *rí* live?

The present study surveys the available archaeological and ethnohistorical evidence for a specific region in Ireland, present-day County Clare,

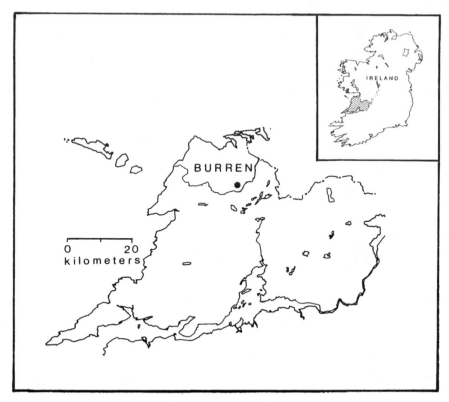

Figure 1.1. Map of County Clare, Ireland, showing the location of Burren Barony and Cahercommaun cashel (dot).

with the intention of reconstructing and assessing the properties of its protohistorical political systems. The framework of the analysis will proceed from the distribution of individual households within a simple chiefdom or *túath* to view how simple chiefdoms became the building blocks of larger political systems: composite chiefdoms, chiefdom confederacies, and alliances between confederacies. One of the elementary questions with which this study will grapple is when a state, and true kingship, can be said to have emerged in the province of Munster for the first time, and how it may be distinguished from the complex nonstate systems that preceded it.

It is possible to reconstruct chiefdoms in northern Clare in far greater detail than elsewhere in Europe due to its extensively preserved archaeological landscapes, historical records, and abundant place-names and topographical folklore. It is highly likely that a full realization of the organization of Irish chiefdoms will add to an understanding of the structure of the Celtic polities that blanketed Europe prior to the Roman conquest, especially those that constructed simple hill-forts. When they are distilled into a spatial model, the organizing principles of Irish chiefdoms should provide a basis for exploring the organization of prehistoric polities in other European locales. This study should at the very minimum help to set standards of appropriateness for the questions that archaeologists ask of the archaeological record when attempting to reconstruct the configurations of regional polities.

CHAPTER TWO

The Climate and Geology of Clare

Cattle raising has been the focus of Irish economic life during all historical periods up to the introduction of the potato in the eighteenth century. It is a thesis of this work that the early political systems examined here owed their character and specific institutions to the agropastoralist subsistence base of Ireland's medieval inhabitants. Ultimately, the prominence accorded to livestock in the medieval subsistence economy is traceable to the limitations placed on cereal cultivation by the climate and soils of Ireland. The geographical structure of the political units of early Ireland was also dictated by the distribution of land forms and soils. It is, therefore, worthwhile to summarize the salient features of the climate and geography of Ireland and of Co. Clare, the study region.

Due to its location west of Britain facing the north Atlantic, Ireland is the first body of land to intercept the frequent rain and storm fronts that move east toward England. As a consequence, a precipitation cline shades from northwest to southeast in the country, with rainfall ranging from 1,400 mm on average annually in the southwest to 700 mm in the east (Mitchell 1976:88). As the naturalist Frank Mitchell has pointed out, the volume of precipitation alone is not as consequential to the practice of agriculture as is the number of days on which it rains, since this factor affects the rate of evaporation. The number of rain days ranges from over 200 per annum in the extreme western highlands to less than 150 in the southeast. The frequent spells of rain, taken together with Ireland's cool climate, result in a low rate of evaporation. These conditions produce podzolization in the soils, which in many areas of the country are the breakdown products of granite, sandstone, or shale, and are hence highly acidic to begin with. Much of the land of Ireland is thus unsuitable for cereal or other cultivation due to high acidity, leaching, poor drainage, and consequent saturation. Up to the modern era,

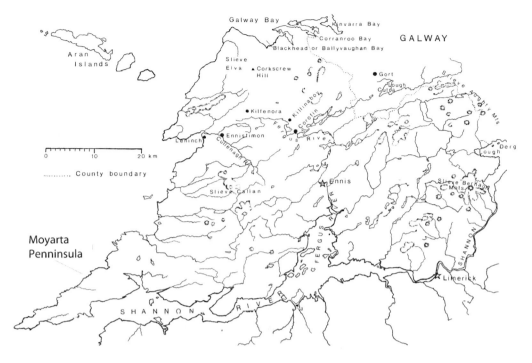

Figure 2.1. Physical map of Co. Clare.

a large portion of the countryside was also covered by extensive tracts of bog.

The county of Clare lies along the rainy west-central seaboard of Ireland (Figures 1.1, 2.1 and 2.3). To the extreme north, the county border is the southern coastline along Galway Bay. The boundary between Clare and Galway counties begins in Aughinish/Corranroo Bay and follows the northwest edge of the Burren limestone massif. The boundary leaves the massif at Slievecarran and dips south to trace a wide circumference around the town of Gort and Lough Cutra before joining and skirting two southern peaks of the Slieve Aughties. The southern and eastern boundary of Clare is the Shannon River, Ireland's largest and longest waterway. The fact that Clare is nearly entirely surrounded by water gives it the physical and cultural characteristics of an island. Cultural developments that swept through Ireland, such as Christianity, reached Clare last. Its geographical isolation also provided benefits to its populations in the form of affording some protection from invasion.

Eons of sedimentation, depression under glacial icecaps, and subsequent uplifting have produced a convoluted landscape in Clare. In the extreme northern part of the county is the Burren (Figure 2.2), a Carboniferous seabed that had been uplifted and then extensively carved by glaciers.

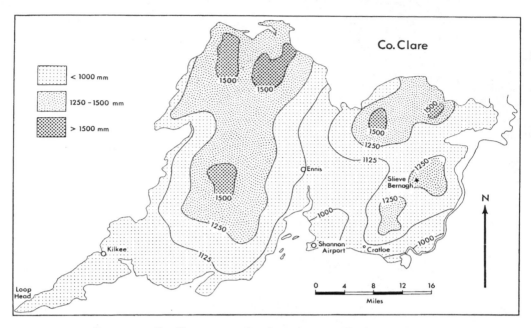

Figure 2.2. Co. Clare – general geological regions (Finch 1971, Fig. 9).

Clearance of the Burren's forests by Neolithic farmers led to soil loss and accelerated dissolution of the limestone, so that the Burren has been a karst topography for the last 3,000 years (Crabtree 1982; Drew 1982, 1983). In the eastern portion of the Burren the landscape is characterized by hills and high tilted beds of bare, horizontally bedded limestone pavement with a maximum elevation of 305 m (Figure 2.2). Interspersed between these hills and plateaus are a number of glacial valleys and ravines that exhibit a general north-south orientation. While soil cover on the hills and plateaus is thin or absent, the valley soils are relatively deep, consisting of a rich glacial till mixed with limestone boulders and sandstone erratics. The western Burren, while also mountainous, has large stretches of bog land.

The Burren is one of the wetter regions in Clare. Rainfall averaged between 1,472 mm for Ballyvaughan on the northern coast and 1,656 mm on Corkscrew Hill in the central interior over a thirty-year period (1951–1980; data supplied by the Irish Meteorological Service). Overall, annual precipitation for the Burren is 1,500 mm (see Figure 2.3). Despite the heavy rainfall, there are few streams in the Burren because the water is chiefly carried away underground through a system of caves. Turloughs, or disappearing lakes, also owe their existence to the porous limestone.

Directly south of the Burren is a lower-lying, convoluted land of hills, rivers, drumlins, and lakes. The River Fergus marks the demarcation between

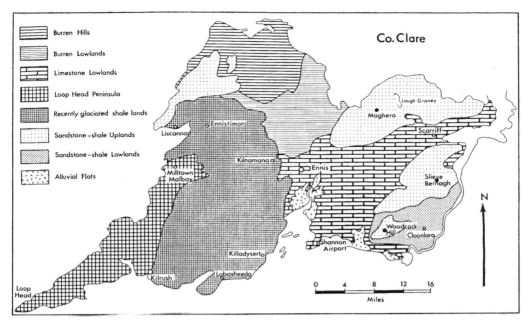

Figure 2.3. Rainfall distribution in Co. Clare on an average annual basis (Finch 1971, Fig. 10).

the Burren lowlands on the east and the sandstone/shale uplands to the west (compare Figures 2.1 and 2.2). The Burren lowlands are essentially a continuation of the aforementioned limestone beds at a lower elevation broken by numerous drumlins and lakes. The town of Corofin lies in the west of this region near Inchiquin Lake (directly to the west of Corofin in Figure 2.1). To the west of Corofin between the Burren and the shale uplands is a valley that was an ancient line of communication between the interior of Clare and the seacoast. Within this valley are the Dealagh, Clooneen, and Inagh rivers and the western headwaters of the Fergus. The regionally important towns of Killinaboy, Kilfenora, and Lehinch are located along this valley from east to west (Figure 2.1). The town of Ennistimon is located at the junction of this valley and the valley of the Cullenagh River, which bisects the west-central shale uplands in a north-west-southeast direction, leading eventually to Ennis, the county seat.

The best lands for tillage in Clare lie in the sward of land that is situated between the southern Slieve Aughties and Slieve Bernagh in the east. Not only is the land composed of rich calcareous soils by virtue of the underlying Carboniferous limestone parent rock, but it also receives a lower level of rainfall, 920–1,125 mm annually (see Figure 2.3). The last region of note is the Moyarta Peninsula that has land composed of lower-lying podzolics, gley soils, and peat.

CHAPTER THREE

Clare's Chiefdoms at the Dawn of History

Even though the earliest Christian missions arrived on Ireland's shores in the fourth century AD, writing, to judge from the earliest surviving texts, did not become commonplace until the seventh century. However, the authors of both secular and ecclesiastical documents often felt compelled to project the temporal reach of their works back to the time of Saint Patrick in the fifth century, and at times even beyond that period to the time of Christ. Thus, at the center of the prologue to the *Senchas Már* is an anecdote wherein Saint Patrick endorses the creation of the later secular legal texts contained within it. The reach of the Annals of Ulster is back to year 1. The hundred or so lives of Irish saints describe the doings of churchmen who putatively lived in the fifth and sixth centuries AD, though these texts were composed up to several centuries after their deaths.

These indigenous records purporting to describe Ireland before the seventh century are in general not trusted by historians, and up to the last decade have been analyzed chiefly to reveal the authors' belief systems and motivations. Each set of "historical" records that reflect on the period between the birth of Christ and the seventh century AD has its own manifold problems, and so every reconstruction of Irish society of these times, including this one, is inescapably speculative. This chapter will examine the historical sources of information bearing upon the political constitution of Co. Clare during what might be called the protohistorical period – the period during which there are no direct historical records from Co. Clare. The early peoples of Co. Clare do figure in historical sources created outside the confines of Thomond, but these are meager and ambiguous and so must be used with caution.

IN THE BEGINNING . . . THE ANTIQUITY OF
IRISH CHIEFDOM CONFEDERACIES

There is only one source that historians believe may name a few of Ireland's Late Iron Age political bodies with some degree of accuracy, and that is the description of Ireland contained in Ptolemy's *Geography*. Since the *Geography* stems from c. 150 AD, and since Ptolemy drew upon the work of previous geographers, principally Marinus of Tyre, his description may be said to date to the early second century AD (Freeman 2001:66).

Ptolemy and other Classical geographers were dependent upon merchants for their information concerning Ireland and other lands beyond the Mediterranean. This fact would dictate that only those groups that came into intercourse with merchants would become known to the writers, and one would expect that this select group would tend to be those who were near navigable waterways and sheltered harbors, and so the *Geography* is biased toward coastal populations. Ptolemy lists sixteen groups within Ireland; twelve of these are located along the eastern and southeastern coasts, which one imagines would be the areas of Ireland most accessible to the coast-hugging merchantmen of the time.

Only a few of the groups listed by Ptolemy can be matched with populations known from other historical sources, and none of these peoples are on the western coast. Indeed, the western coast of Ireland is the most poorly represented area in Ptolemy's description, so that even the location of the groups of this region is highly uncertain. A reasonably certain match can be made between the *Senu* River of Ptolemy and the Shannon (Old Ir. *Sinann*), and the group between this river and what may be Galway Bay are the *Auteinoi* (Freeman: 2001:74–75; Mac an Bhaird 1993:7). This could perhaps be an approximation of Uaithne Tíre, a group that in the tenth century was located on the eastern side of the Shannon River in County Tipperary (Figure 3.1).

From the second to the fourth centuries AD, there is a gap in the historical record until the appearance of dedicatory stones with inscriptions in ogam script. These stones are concentrated in the south of Ireland with an especially heavy concentration in the Dingle Peninsula of County Kerry, but none have been found in Co. Clare, which underscores the isolation of this region from Munster at this time. This drawback notwithstanding, the wording of the earlier dedications does reveal something of the way groups within Ireland were organized.

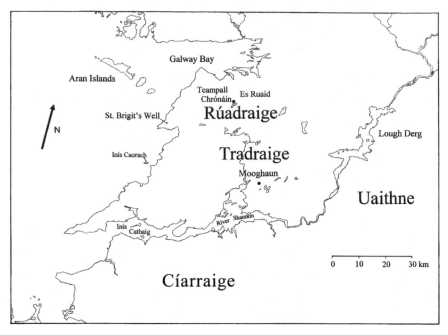

Figure 3.1. Co. Clare in the Late Iron Age.

Thomas Charles-Edwards has done the most recently to classify the various patronymic terms found in the ogam inscriptions and establish their significance with regard to the structure of Irish society in the protohistorical period. His methodology rests upon examining the ogam inscriptions against information from the Early Medieval Latin *vitae* (saints' lives), which are presumed to be earlier than those written in the vernacular. His views are worth examining in this context. Ogam inscriptions are generally brief, usually specifying a male by reference to his father (e.g., MOINENA MAQI OLACON [Moinena son of Olchu]) (Edwards 1990:103). More rarely, the name was expanded to reference the group to which the individual belonged by naming the god/deified ancestor from which the group claimed descent (e.g., BIR MAQI MUCOI ROTTAIS [Bir son of the descendants of Roth]) (ibid.; MacNeill 1911–1912). Among the numerous ogam inscriptions from the Dingle Peninsula in Co. Kerry are a handful that read "MAQQI MUCCOI DOVVINIAS." Charles-Edwards identified Dovinia as a goddess whose name in the Old Irish period became Duibne, the ancestor of the historical Corcu Duibne (Seed of Duibne), who inhabited the eponymous Corkaguiney Barony of Dingle Peninsula. He concluded then that the kinship term *muccoi* identified the person memorialized on the ogam stone as a member of a ruling lineage of a chiefdom – a class of persons referred to in the Old Irish sources by the word *cenél* (Charles-Edwards 1993:147–156). Given the fact that ogam stones were erected over a period of four hundred years, and that there are roughly four hundred surviving examples, it is clear that only a small proportion of the population was memorialized by these monuments.[1] It is, therefore, highly probable that all inscribed stones were erected for aristocrats, whether the inscription identifies the maximal ramage or not.

The ogam stone inscriptions are not so long and detailed as to allow one to identify higher levels of political organization. However, from the distribution of the names of maximal ramages on ogam stones in the two Decies baronies in County Waterford, and from the description of the constitution of the historical Déisi in their origin saga, Charles-Edwards deduces the existence of a composite chiefdom (*mór thúath*) that was possibly dominated by the Nia-Segamon (Charles-Edwards 1993:152–154). Another branch of the Déisi that would emerge in the historical period in Munster as the Dál Cais likewise exhibited a composite structure.

Did chiefdom confederacies also exist in this early period? The saga *Táin Bó Cuailgne*, believed to reflect the pre-Christian past of central and northern Ireland, poses a strong argument in the affirmative, as the action transpires against the backdrop of hostility between the allied confederacies of the Connachta and Laigin against the Ulaid of the north. The substance of such a struggle is borne out by the existence of monumental earthworks and palisades along the presumed southern border of the Ulaid, such as the Black Pig's Dyke and the Dorsey. These defenses have been excavated and have been found to date to the Iron Age, having been constructed between 200 and 100 BC (Mallory and McNeill 1991:150–153).

The construction of the Iron Age defensive system in Ulster was contemporary with the establishment of a ritual structure/inauguration mound at *Emain Macha*, identified in the Ulster Cycle of tales as the capital of the Ulaid leader Conchobar Mac Nessa. Navan Fort is the modern Anglicized place-name for Emain Macha, and excavations were carried out there by Dudley Waterman in the 1960s. Waterman's excavations revealed that between the third and second centuries BC, a series of three large round buildings succeeded one another, followed by the erection of a ritual structure consisting of concentric rings of posts (Warner in Waterman 1997:189).

One may deduce from medieval traditions revolving around sites such as Tara and Cruachan that a capital site was invariably associated with a chiefdom confederacy. It is highly likely that as chiefdom confederacies were geographically extensive and were largely voluntary assocations, ritual centers provided these groupings an organizational and ideological focus. They were also simple extensions of the fact that all Irish medieval and Iron Age polities had ritual foci. Ptolemy lists ten towns (*poleis*) in his *Geography*, and given the lack of urban centers in pre-Viking Ireland, these were most likely the ritual centers of chiefdoms and chiefdom confederacies. There is agreement among scholars that the *Woluntioi* of Ptolemy's map are the historic *Ulati*, or Ulaid, and some maintain that *Isamnion Cape* of Ptolemy's map was Emain Macha (Mac an Bhaird 1993:10, 12). The excavations carried out at Emain Macha and other hilltop centers such as Dún Ailinne and Ráith na Ríg, Tara, known to be the ritual foci of protohistorical groups, offer indirect evidence that chiefdom confederacies in Ireland date to at least the Iron Age (Roche 1997; Wailes 1976, 1990; Waterman 1997).

The Connachta were a confederacy of chiefdoms spanning central Ireland that succeeded in seizing Meath and the associated ceremonial center of Tara in the early fifth century AD from the Laigin, and southern Ulster from the Ulaid around the same time (MacNiocaill 1972: 21–22; Mallory in Waterman 1997:200; Ó hÓgáin 1999:165). Their founding ancestor was held to be Conn Cétchathach (Conn of a hundred battles), but recent scholarship indicates that their name was originally *Condos*, meaning "headship" or "supremacy" (Ó hÓgáin 2002:204; Sproule 1984:32). That they were a confederacy of chiefdoms is indicated by the huge expanse of the territory that they dominated – too large to have been controlled by a single leader. Indeed, this territory shortly split into three smaller confederacies – the territories of the Airgialla, Uí Néill, and the remaining Connachta in the west, all of which also exhibited decentralized leadership. That these descendant political entities were chiefdom confederacies is also indicated by a lack of a central leader or dominant chiefdom within them.

The qualities of a chiefdom confederacy are more clearly realized from the records pertaining to a slightly later example, the confederacy of the Éoganachta of Munster. David Sproule's brilliant article on this group reveals that this confederacy was born in imitation of the Connachta confederacy to the north. Whereas the Connachta concocted Conn Cétchathach as their apical ancestor, the Éoganachta came up with an equivalent in Éogan Mór Mug Nuadat (Éogan the Great, Slave [Follower] of [the god] Nuadhu). This supposed paramount chieftain may have been derived from a god *Ovogenos* (Ó hÓgáin 2002:204). Most of the member chiefdoms of the Éoganacht confederacy claimed a common ancestor in Corc mac Luigthig. The name of this ancestor could be a transposition of the name of a chiefdom. Under this theory, the point of origin of the name *Corc* would have been the word *corcu* (seed of), the first element of several chiefdoms' names in the west of Ireland (e.g., *Corcu Baiscind*). In their origin legend, the name of the Corcu Duibne chiefdom was transformed into an ancestor Corc Duibne (Byrne 2001:166; Ó hÓgáin 1999:113), and indeed there was a chiefdom, Corcu Loígde, whose former territory was preserved in the territory of the diocese of Ross located along the coast in modern-day Co. Cork.

The foregoing discussion sets out one of the defining elements of a chiefdom confederacy. Chiefdom confederacies consisted of chiefdoms that allied themselves to one another and adopted a common identity, promulgated by a name such as Connachta or Éoganachta. This group name expressed the fiction of a common origin of the ancestors of each member chiefdom's ruling elite from a shared apical ancestor or set of ancestors (Gibson 1995:123). In the Early Middle Ages, genealogies were created that explicity described the consanguinal ties that supposedly linked the ancestors of the maximal ramages of each member chiefdom of a confederacy to one another.

What was the raison d'etre of the Éoganacht confederacy? Propagandistic texts have them waging war against the weaker peoples at the fringes of Munster and alternating rule over Munster between three maximal ramages, only one of which actually had within its boundaries the putative seat of the paramount chieftain: Cashel (Byrne 2001:204–207). Sproule indicated the substantial difficulties with accepting these circumstances, supposedly dateable to the seventh century AD. He demonstrates that the leading Éoganacht ramages had other identities prior to the seventh century, and that they invented the common ancestor Corc mac Luigthig to link themselves to each other (Ó Buachalla 1952:67–68; Sproule 1984:33–34). Sproule's own theory was that belonging to the Éoganacht confederacy was tantamount to joining a country club – it was a mechanism whereby already powerful groups enhanced and promulgated their prestige (Sproule 1984:34).

However, it would seem from the other early salient examples of chiefdom confederacies that confederacies were fundamentally alliance systems for the promulgation of warfare. The coordinated construction of defenses around Ulster and Emain Macha, and the successes of the Connachta against their enemies, demonstrate the significance of the military dimension to alliance formation between chiefdoms. However, there is an Early Middle Irish text that had been copied from a late Old Irish exemplar from the Laud 610 corpus, nicknamed by historians "West Munster Synod," that introduces another dimension of chiefdom confederacies. Mac Ardae Meic Fiataig is a chieftain/ancestor diety of the Cíarraige Lúachra who, to presume from what is known of the other personae dramatis of the text, is represented as living in the late sixth century. He initiates an alliance with the chiefdoms of the Altraige, Múscraige, and Corcu Óchae with the objective of resisting the "heavy hand" of the paramount chieftain of *Irmumu* (West Munster) who was the chieftain of the Éoganacht Locha Léin (Byrne 2001:216–217; Meyer 1912:315–316). One can draw the inference from this text that Irish chiefdoms formed alliances not only to promulgate warfare, but also to resist or break away from the domination of oppressive powerful polities.

COUNTY CLARE'S PROTOHISTORICAL CHIEFDOMS: A SOMEWHAT SPECULATIVE RECONSTRUCTION: 200–750 AD

In southern Co. Clare, there is a hill-fort called Mooghaun (possibly from Ir. *Múchán* [ruins (of stone)], situated 3.5 kilometers to the east of Dromoland Lake (see Figure 3.2). Some time ago, Barry Raftery classified Mooghaun as a hill-fort and placed it within his IIa class, sites with widely spaced multivallate defenses (1972:45–46). On present evidence generated by a campaign of survey and excavation carried out by the Discovery Programme, it is to be strongly doubted that Mooghaun's walls were built for military reasons (Grogan 2005:219). This immense site consists of a hill fully circumscribed by three concentric walls that were most likely meant to define the hilltop as a sacred precinct (Figure 3.1). The outer wall has a mean diameter of c. 400 m, and defines an area 11 ha in extent. It originally consisted of a bank that averages 12 m in width and an outer ditch 5.8 m wide (Bennett and Grogan 1993; Grogan 2005:233). The middle enclosure wall ranges from 7.3 to 13 m wide. It was constructed as a series of five stepped linear compartments, the second from the inside being the highest and most substantial. The inner enclosure alone has a mean diameter of 111 m and varies from 8.5 to 10 m in width (Grogan 1996b:51; Grogan 2005:231; Westropp 1902:112). There is a trigonometrical station on the summit of the hill within the inner enclosure that had been placed on top of what may be a prehistoric cairn (Condit and Grogan 2005: 122; Grogan 1995:58). Ironworking, bronze-making, and quern-making debris dating to the Iron Age was recovered from the summit (Grogan 2005:137). Two cashels had been built on top of the site's outer and middle enclosure walls, and were therefore secondary in date to them (Bennett and Grogan 1993). In and around the site are the numerous remains of other enclosures and *fulacht fiadh* (heaps of stone from communal cooking rituals) (Grogan

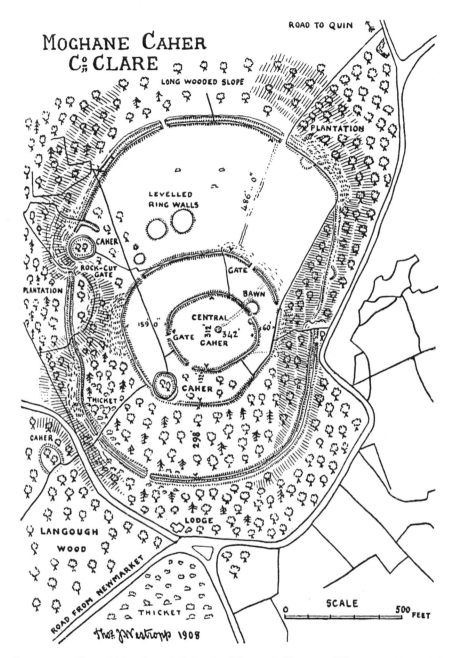

Figure 3.2. Plan of Mooghaun hill-fort by Thomas J. Westropp (Westropp 1907–1908, Plate IX).

et al. 1995; Grogan 1996a: Fig. 22). The largest hoard of Late Bronze Age gold objects ever to be found in Ireland was discovered in 1854, 700 m to the northeast of Mooghaun hill-fort in what used to be a part of Mooghaun Lough (Eogan 1983: No. 58; Grogan et al. 1995:51; Grogan 2005:70–73).

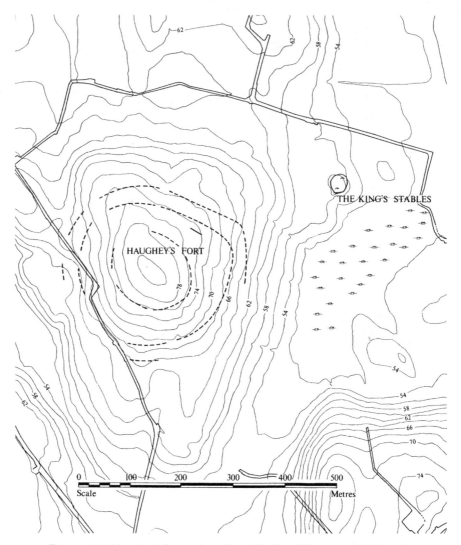

Figure 3.3. Haughey's Fort and the King's Stables (Waterman 1997; Fig. 2).

On the basis of several radiocarbon dates, including one from beneath the outer rampart wall, Eoin Grogan has concluded that the enclosing walls were constructed in the final two decades of the tenth century BC (Grogan 2005:240). Dates from the occupation deposits of Area C show activity in the areas excavated lasting not much longer than sixty years after the walls were built. By comparison, radiocarbon dates from Navan Fort show potential Late Bronze Age activity beginning not before the ninth century BC, followed by the construction of large timber buildings between the third and second centuries BC (Warner in Waterman 1997). The multi-ring timber structure was then erected and destroyed on the site c. 100 BC. One may reasonably conclude, then, that Navan Fort and

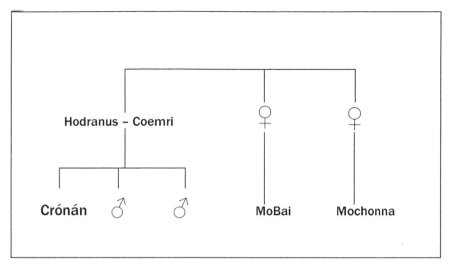

Figure 3.4. Kinship diagram of St. Crónán's family from *Vita St. Cronnani Abbatis de Ros Cré.*

Mooghaun were not erected within the same time frame. However, as at Mooghaun, Navan Fort was one site of a complex of ritual establishments that included a pond (the "King's Stables") and a hill-fort ("Haughey's Fort"). The remains excavated from the King's Stables indicate that ritual sacrifices of animals, humans, and weapons were carried out there (Lynn 1977). Dates from Haughey's Fort and the King's Stables indicate that they are contemporary, having been constructed at the beginning of the first millennium BC (Lynn 1977; Mallory 1988). The Navan complex taken as a whole, then, is broadly contemporary with Mooghaun.

Both Mooghaun and Navan Fort are large, enclosed sites situated on a hill. Both hills are surmounted by a mound, or cairn. In the case of Emain Macha, this mound is assumed to have been a ritual structure figuring in the inauguration of paramount chieftains of the Ulaid confederacy (Lynn 1997:229). Like Mooghaun, Haughey's Fort was circumscribed by three concentric ditches enclosing an area 340 m in diameter (Mallory 1988). Both Mooghaun and Haughey's Fort were located in proximity to bodies of water at which sacrificial rites were carried out (Figure 3.3).

Given that both Mooghaun and Emain Macha/Haughey's Fort were Bronze Age ritual centers of considerable importance and physical scale, and given that both apparently continued to attract attention into the first half of the first millennium AD, I propose that both continued to function as the conceptual capitals of chiefdom confederacies – Emain Macha as the ritual capital/inauguration site of the *Woluntioi/Ulati/Ulaid*. Mooghaun was constructed during the Late Iron Age on a scale to have

similarly functioned as the ritual capital/inauguration site of a chiefdom confederacy. The extent of this confederacy is unknown, as is its
name, though at a minimum it probably took in the southern half of
Co. Clare.

PAGAN GODS FROM LATIN SAINTS' LIVES

Historians of the Irish Early Middle Ages, with ample justification, have
generally disparaged the genealogies and saints' lives as untrustworthy
sources of information, as truthfulness and historical accuracy were not
the primary goals of the compilers of these documents. However, these
texts do preserve, albeit in a highly corrupt form, shreds of the cosmology
and origin legends of Ireland's many chiefdoms. With eyes wide open as to
the deficiencies and problems of the sources, one may peruse this information to construct hypotheses concerning the cosmology of protohistorical
Irish chiefdoms.

It is possible that a sketch of the origin myth of the principal gods of
the chiefdoms of Co. Clare may be pieced together from evidence contained in the Latin *vita* of St. Crónán, the genealogies of the Cíarraige
Lúachra, Corcu Baiscind, and Corcu MoDruad, and the *Corpus Genealogiarum
Sanctorum Hiberniae* (Ó Riain 1985). The *vita* of St. Crónán is potentially
the oldest source of information and may therefore contain the least corrupt version of the origin myth. Though the lives of Irish saints cannot be
dated with much accuracy, those in Latin are thought to have been written
before the ninth century AD (Sharpe 1991:22–23). According to his *vita*,
St. Crónán of Ros Cré had a father of the Éle, who were located in what is
now Co. Tipperary, and a Corcu Baiscind mother. His mother was one of
three sisters, each of whom gave birth to a son, and all of these sons eventually became saints as well. The names of Crónán's cousins were MoBai
(Ir. *Mobáe*, also variously *Báetán* and *Báeth* in *CGSH*) and Mochonna. The
twelfth-century *CGSH* expands this group to five and makes these saints
the sons of a common father named Sinell (Ó Riain 1985:22:129).[2]

Further along in the *vita*, St. Crónán (§2) pairs himself with Mochonna
and leaves his family for the wilds of Connacht, eventually coming to a
whirlpool called *Ruaid* (in the original text, *Ruayd*, Heist 1965:274–275).
Ruaid is at first identified as a whirlpool (*gurgitem*) and in §2 as a lake (*laci*).[3]
In the Burren there is a small stone church dedicated to St. Crónán located
close to what the Irish call a *turlough*, or disappearing lake. At *Teampall
Chrónáin* (Crónán's Church), there are two tent-shaped tomb-shrines and a
small stone oratory standing within the grounds of what may have been a

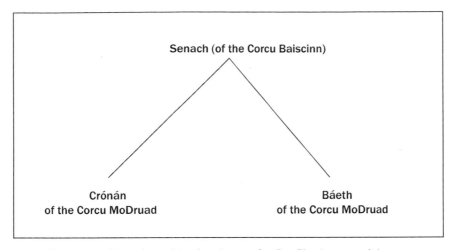

Figure 3.5. Hypothetical kinship diagram for Co. Clare's ancestral deities.

small monastery (Figures 3.6, 3.7). The site is situated upon a ridge over-looking the turlough that lies at the bottom of the Carron depression imme-diately to the south of the site. The turlough fills with water when it rains heavily, but when it ceases to rain, the water gradually drains out through the Burren's porous limestone and a network of subterranean passages to the sea (Figures 3.8 and 3.9). Though in the Middle Ages Co. Clare was part of a region called North Munster (*Tuadmumu*, Anglicized Thomond), in the Early Middle Ages what is now Co. Clare was considered to lie within Connacht. It lies within the realm of possibility, then, that the whirlpool of *Ruaid* was this disappearing lake.

Another significant dimension of §2 is that it describes the foiling of an execution by St. Crónán. A local chieftain has sent a bound prisoner to the lake to be drowned. When the man is thrown into the lake, St. Crónán appears in the water and clasps the man to him and thus prevents his drowning. There are deep religious undertones to this story. The Celts held bodies of water to be portals to the otherworld. The practice of water sacrifice to deities is amply attested in Ireland not only by finds of substan-tial numbers of elite metal objects in lakes and rivers, but also by entries in annals and sagas detailing the sacrificial killing of enemies by drowning, most famously the execution of the Viking Turgesius in the saga *Cogadh Gaedhel re Gallaibh* (Todd 1965:227). If one interprets the act of drowning the prisoner as a sacrificial act, the question of the identity of the god or goddess on the receiving end then arises. The place-name of the lake, Ruaid, could simply indicate the color red (*rúad*) or the god to whom the lake is dedicated. *Rúad* crops up in Gaul in the names of warlike gods such as *Rudianus* and *Rudiobus* (Green 1992:181), as the color red connotes

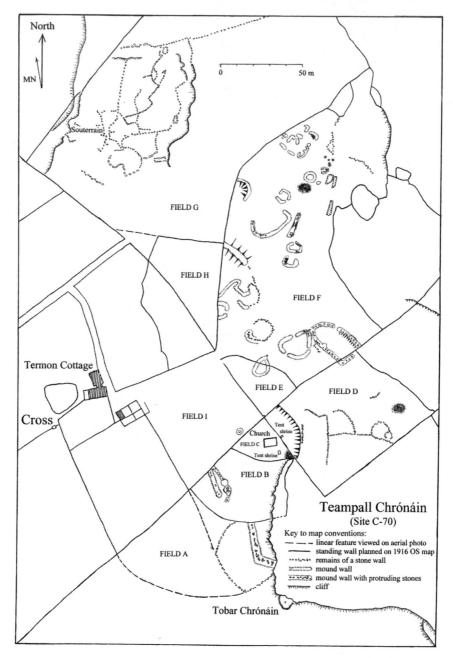

Figure 3.6. Teampall Chrónáin – plan of site and environs.

warlike valor. Rúad crops up on ogam stones in its Primitive Irish form both as a proper name (RODDOS) and as an element in compound names (?MAQI-RODAGI "Devotee of *Rúadáin*"), which attests to the existence of a god named Rúad in Ireland (McManus 1991:107,109).

There is a deeper significance to Crónán's intervention in the act of sacrifice. On a superficial level, St. Crónán's miracle subverts a pagan

Figure 3.7. Teampall Chrónáin – photo of the church and a tent-shaped shrine taken from the south (photo: Blair Gibson).

Figure 3.8. The Carron turlough as it usually appears in the summer, photographed in 1985 (photo: Blair Gibson).

Figure 3.9. The Carron turlough in August 1985 after a period of prolonged rain (photo: Blair Gibson).

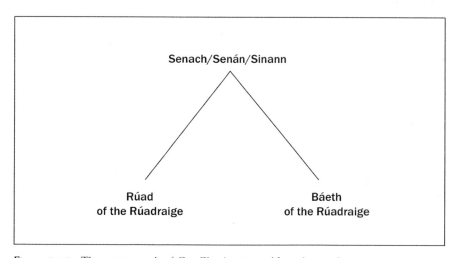

Senach/Senán/Sinann

Rúad
of the Rúadraige

Báeth
of the Rúadraige

Figure 3.10. The origin myth of Co. Clare's principal Iron Age gods.

ritual and represents a triumph of Christianity over paganism. On another level, St. Crónán may be viewed as a substitution or transmogrification of the divinity, Rúad. The name Rúad means "(brownish) red," and this linguistic fact may indicate a connection between this Celtic god and St. Crónán. Crónán's name could be translated as "crooning," but *crón* also means "reddish-brown." The substitution of Crónán for Rúad marks the Christianization of this god, and the erection of Teampall Chrónáin on the edge of the turlough would signify, then, a rededication of a pagan cult place to Christianity.

The former name of the Corcu MoDruad and their former allegiance to Rúad are explicitly indicated in the genealogy from the Rawlinson B 502 manuscript. *Rudraige* is listed as the apical ancestor of this group, occurring seven generations earlier than Me-drui in the list of chieftains (O'Brien 1976:155 a 2). This bit of evidence confirms that originally the Corcu MoDruad called themselves the Rúadraige. It is, therefore, all the more likely that the Carron turlough was formerly called *Es Rúaid* (Mod. Ir *Eas Rúaid*), and that this was their sacrificial pool – one of the sacred centers of their composite chiefdom.

The genealogies offer further evidence that MoBai and Crónán were figures whose significance spanned the ecclesiastical and political realms. The Book of Leinster version of the Corcu MoDruad genealogy lists a chieftain Báeth [48] who was a grandson of a chieftain named Senach Mór [47] (Senach the Great), and the Rawlinson B 502 version of the Corcu MoDruad genealogy includes Crónán as a member of this ramage and lists him as the offspring of Senach ("Fox").[4] Báeth is a legendary chieftain associated in several instances with the Corcu MoDruad. He appears in the life of St. MacCreiche as Baeth-brónach (Báeth the Sad), and is also indicated as the father of a saint associated with a monastery in Killinaboy parish, *Cill Inghine Baoith* (Church of the Daughter of Báeth) in northern Co. Clare (Plummer 1925:56–57).

Senach appears as an early ancestor in the chieftain lists of several peoples of the coastal southwest of Ireland, such as the Cíarraige and the Corcu Loígde of Co. Cork. The name Senach is also to be equated with the name of the famous Irish saint Senán (see *CGSH* under Mosenóc), who is said to have founded monasteries on islands in the River Shannon on Inis Luinghe, Inis Caorach (Mutton Island), and, the most famous, on Inis Cathaigh (Scattery Island; Figure 3.1). These islands circumscribe the Shannon boundary of the Corcu Baiscind as it was following the eighth century AD. St. Senán was the principal saint of the Corcu Baiscind, but the location of the monastic foundations attributed to him lie in the Shannon, and the isomorphism of his name with that of the river (Old Ir. *Sinann*) makes it all but certain that the saint was derived from the pagan god, or rather goddess, associated with the river.

These correspondences between the genealogies of the chieftains of the Corcu MoDruad and the lives and genealogies of the saints of Co. Clare exist because, as I will argue, they derive from a single source. An ancestor deity, Senach, fathered two early ancestors of the Corcu MoDruad: Báeth and Rúad. It seems clear from this and the foregoing discussion of Báeth that Rúad and Báeth should be regarded as tutelary deities of the forerunners of the Corcu MoDruad, the Rúadraige.

The arguments presented earlier posit that the genealogy of Crónán's family contained in his *vita* and in the *CGSH* was appropriated from an origin myth of the Iron Age gods of County Clare. This myth would seem to establish the precedence of the Corcu Baiscind or their Iron Age forerunners over the Corcu MoDruad as Senach, Crónán, and Báeth are Corcu Baiscind in origin and the principal deity of the Corcu Baiscind is the progenitor of the two deities of the Corcu MoDruad, who then migrate north and establish themselves among these people. This myth could be seen as a grandiose claim of dominance put forward by the Corcu Baiscind, or it could be viewed as reflecting an ancient alliance that existed between the principal composite chiefdoms of Co. Clare, with the Corcu Baiscind as the dominant party. The massive scale of their ritual center at Mooghaun could be seen as buttressing this interpretation.

While it seems certain that the Corcu MoDruad originally called themselves the Rúadraige, can the former name of the Corcu Baiscind be discerned? No easy clues are forthcoming from their Early Medieval name or chieftain lists, but place-name evidence may hint at their former identity. In the Early Middle Ages, *Tradraige* was the name of a territory located between the Shannon and Fergus rivers in southeastern Co. Clare. Significantly, the ritual complex of Mooghaun is located within its borders.

By virtue of its *-raige* ending, meaning "people of," the name Tradraige belongs to those collective names with roots in the Iron or Bronze Age, as such an ending is typically paired with the name of a pagan god, totem, or color, as in the names Osraige (Deer People) or Cíarraige (Black People) (Mac Niocaill 1972:3). "Trad" does not appear in O'Brien's collection of genealogies as a personal name, and only makes a single appearance in the Middle Irish text *Cóir Anmann* (The Fitness of Names) as Trad mac Taissach, the son-in-law of Delbaeth of the Túatha Dé Danann (Arbuthnot 2005:95). In this instance the name Trad is likely to have been concocted to explain the place-name.

It is otherwise possible that "trad" in Tradraige may be a geographical reference; evidence for this interpretation comes from an Irish saint's life written in Latin. While St. Brigit is most famously associated with Kildare, she is attested on the western coast of Ireland as St. Briga, sister of St. Brénainn moccu Altae in *Vita Altera St. Brendani Abbatis Clonfertis* from the Codex Salmanticensis (Brendan the Navigator, d. 577 or 583 AD). St. Brénainn addresses his sister at the end of this life prophesying her resurrection "... not here ... but you shall rise in your own country, that is, of the Tragei" (*"non hic ... sed in tua, silicet Trageorum, terra resurges"* (Heist 1965:331). The Old Irish word *traig* means "coast." The case can be made that the territory referred to is that of the Tradraige. Place-name evidence places St. Briga in Clare as well, though admittedly in the northern rather than the southern half of the county. A short distance inland from the famous Cliffs of Moher, Co. Clare, is the elaborate shrine built around St. Brigit's well.

Briga is also linked, albeit indirectly, to the Tradraige and, more specifically, to Mooghaun in a tract in the *CGSH* that the editor has entitled "On the Mothers of the Saints." The passage fixes Briga within an aristocratic sept of the Airgialla, and further identifies her as the mother of the otherwise unknown saint Luchthigern mac Lugdach, of whom it is stated *Is e fil i Tuaim Findlocha i Tratraige* (It is he who is in Tuaim Findlocha in Tradraige) (*CGSH* 1985:181). Tomfinlough is the parish in Bunratty Barony that contains both the townlands of Mooghaun North and Mooghaun South. The name Luchthigern mac Lugdach (Shining Lord son of Lugdach) hints at a former association of the Mooghaun ritual center with the pagan god Lug – fitting given its hilltop site.[5]

One further scrap of information can be cited in support of my hypothesis concerning the Tradraige. Though major early monasteries associated with Irish saints for which there are *vitae* are absent from Thomond, there are a number near Thomond's borders, so Saint Columba of Tír Dá Glas in northern Tipperary on Lough Derg would not have had to travel far to walk in country of the Tradraige (*Columba ambularet in regionibus Tradrigi*, Heist 1965:230).

From these meager and ambiguous historical and place-name scraps of information I extract the hypothesis that during the Iron Age, there were initially two composite chiefdoms occupying Co. Clare: the Tradraige in the south and the Rúadraige in the north, and these possessed corresponding ritual centers at Mooghaun and Eas Rúaid. The origin legend extracted from the *vita* of Crónán of Ros Cré suggests that these two composite chiefdoms were bound together into a confederacy, with the Tradraige as the dominant partner. The preeminence of the Tradraige would have been directly manifested in the massive scale of the archaeological remains at Mooghaun in stark contrast to the lack of visible early remains in the vicinity of the Carron turlough. I shall therefore term the political union of these two composite chiefdoms the Tradraige confederacy.

THE POLITICAL FORTUNES OF THE TRADRAIGE
CONFEDERACY

As Donnchadh Ó Corráin has pointed out, the Corcu MoDruad attain prominence in the annals in the early to mid-eighth century, the period of their decline, fighting what was to become a string of losing battles against the invading Uí Fidgeinti of Co. Limerick and a ramage originally of the Déisi chiefdom confederacy, In Déis Tuaiscirt (The Northern Déisi) (Ó Corráin 1972:7–8, 1975:21). The Uí Fidgeinti genealogies first appear in the twelfth-century Rawlinson B 502 manuscript, grouped together with the genealogies of the Éoganachta, and the overlap of the gods in the mythological portion of their genealogy with those listed in the genealogy of the Éogananacht Caisil, and the fact that later chiefdoms founded by Uí Fidgeinti ramages claimed to be Éogananacht, demonstrates that, post-invasion, they considered themselves to be members of this confederacy.

However, the previously mentioned ninth-century text "West Munster Synod," concerned with the formation of an alliance by the Cíarraige Lúachra with other chiefdoms in western Munster in the Laud 610 compilation, points in another direction. The leaders of the focal chiefdom of the Cíarraige Lúachra in this text are Mac-Ardae mac Fitaich and his half brother St. Cíarán of Clonmacnoise. This Cíarraige chiefdom is shown to have been allied with the Altraige through Bréndán mac Uí Altae (Byrne 2001:216; Meyer 1912:315). A chieftain named *Arade* (*Meic-Arda* in the Yellow Book of Lecan and the Book of Ballymote) appears in the Rawlinson B 502 manuscript as an ancestor of the Uí Fidgeinti (O'Brien 1976:152 a 7), and, in fact, Fiacach Fhidgenid, the eponymous ancestor of the Uí Fidgeinti, appears four generations before Mac Ardae in the Uí Fidgeinti chieftain list. Mac-Ardae, then, probably appears in the text as an ancestor-deity of this group. Therefore, it is highly likely that originally the Uí Fidgeinti evolved from one of the ramages making up the Cíarraige Confederacy. An eighth-century text places the Uí Fidgeinti on an equal footing with the Éoganacht Raithlind and the Éoganacht Locha Léin (Bhreathnach 1999:85). Entries in the annals demonstrate that leaders of this maximal ramage were asserting themselves in military conflicts remote from their territory since the early seventh century (ibid.).

An entry in the Annals of Ulster for 744 records the destruction of the Corcu MoDruad at the hands of the Déisi. This could be taken as an indication that the Corcu MoDruad were once situated in southeastern Co. Clare, where the descendants of the In Déis Tuaiscirt, the Dál Cais, were to subsequently possess lands (Ó Corráin 1972:30). Following this line of reasoning, the Corcu MoDruad could have fled to northern Co. Clare, to Corcomroe and Burren baronies where their descendant chiefdoms were situated in the twelfth century.[6] Alternatively, it is equally possible that they were always situated in the north of Clare, and that the annalist either mistakenly labeled the Corcu Baiscind as the Corcu MoDruad, or that as leaders at the time of the Tradraige confederacy, the defeat was attributed to them. Some historical facts seem to undermine this latter hypothesis.

An entry in the Annals of Ulster for 721 cites a battle between the Connachta and the Corcu Baiscind in which an unnamed chieftain of the Corcu Baiscind, the son of Thalamnaig,[7] was killed. This is the first entry in the annals to name the Corcu Baiscind, and their relatively shallow genealogy in the Book of Leinster would seem to indicate that they had not emerged long before that time. Compared to other West Munster chiefdoms, however, the leaders of this group appear fairly frequently in entries in the Annals of Innisfallen for the late seventh and early eighth centuries AD. Their chieftains also entered the annals earlier and far more frequently than those of the neighboring Corcu MoDurad. Further evidence of the early prominence of the Corcu Baiscind in Co. Clare is to be found in the *Vita St. Cronnani Abbatis de Ros Cré*. The *vita* attributes the origins of the other principal saints of Co. Clare – Senán, Mo-Báe, and Crónán – to the Corcu Baiscind.[8] It is hard to escape the conclusion that Corcu Baiscind was the leading chiefdom of the Tradraige alliance in the seventh and early eighth centuries AD.

The genealogies hint that the original Corcu Baiscind ramage or *cenél* may have been replaced by a ramage of the Cíarraige Luáchra as early as 721 AD, for both Corcu Baiscind genealogies in the Book of Leinster list a chieftain named Rechtabra, a name that appears a bit earlier in contemporary Cíarraige genealogies (Table 3.1). This could be interpreted as a case of telescoping, as Rechtabra *rí* Corcu Baiscind died in 774 AD (AI). However, there is a Cíarraige chieftain named Rechtabra mac Máel-Tuile whose grandfather's name is Aithlech (O'Brien 1976:327 c 53). This parallelism strongly suggests that the Cíarraige had usurped the chieftainship of Corcu Baiscind by 721 AD. This presumption is reinforced by the fact that numerous lineages of the Uí Decci *cenél* of Corcu Baiscind claimed a chieftain named Rechtabrat as an apical ancestor (O'Brien 1976:381–382). The Uí Decci genealogies would have been compiled between the middle and end of the ninth century. This Rechtabrat is absent from an early ninth-century genealogy of the Corcu Baiscind on page 380 of O'Brien's corpus. This point will be discussed more extensively later. In 762 AD, the Annals of Ulster record a battle between the Uí Fidgeinti, Corcu MoDruad, and

Table 3.1. Concordance of names of chieftains from the genealogies of three ramages from the Book of Leinster. Names in bold are found in the annals, but not in the genealogies.

Corcu MoDruad	Corcu Baiscind	Cíarraige
Amargin (father of Conal Cernach, son-in-law of Cathbad the druid)	Mogán	Dairthecht/Retha
Senach Már	Donnán	Senach
Fuilíne	Báetán	Áedlug/Aithlech
Báeth	Laidcenn ('mac Báeth Bonnach' d. 661 AD, AI)	Máel-Tuili
Dub-dá-crich	Talamnach d. 665 AD (AI)	Rechtabra
Mac-Láech	Aithechdai / Áed (Rón) died 721 AD (AU) 723 AD (AI)	Colmán

Rechtabra   Torpaid   Dub-da-lethi   Flann   Gallchobor   Mael-Tuili   Dub-durlais

Corcu MoDruad	Corcu Baiscind	Cíarraige
Dub-dá-crich	**Flann** died 725 AD (AI)	Flann Féorna* died 741 AD (AI)
Rechtabra	**Rechtabra** died 774 AD	
Torpaid d. 769 AD (AI)	**Torpaid mac Aithechda** died 788 (AI)	
	Áed Rón died 812 (AI)	

Corcu Baiscind. The battle of 762 AD probably marked a culmination of a second wave of assaults perpetrated upon the Cíarraige-derived ramages at the head of both the Corcu Baiscind and Corcu MoDruad on the part of the Uí Fidgeinti. As we will see in subsequent chapters, the swath of chiefdoms spawned by the Uí Fidgeinti would stretch from the Shannon in the south almost to Galway Bay in the north.

THE POLITICAL GEOGRAPHY OF NORTHERN CLARE PRIOR TO THE NINTH CENTURY: THE HEROIC BIOGRAPHY OF MAC CREICHE AND THE COMPOSITE CHIEFDOM OF CORCU MODRUAD

Mac Creiche is the only saint of the Corcu MoDruad for whom we possess a *vita*. The highly corrupt text of the life is in Middle Irish, a fact that places the date of its composition after the tenth century AD. Based on internal evidence, it was most likely written in the eleventh or twelfth century. In the life, the chiefdom of the Corcu MoDruad, called *Corcumruadh Ninois* (Corcu MoDruad of the Waves), is restricted to the northwestern corner of *Tuadmumu* (North Munster, Anglicized Thomond), co-terminous with the modern barony of Corcomroe. This was the state of the Corcu MoDruad chiefdom following its fission into the two chiefdoms of *Corcu Mruad* (Corcomroe) and *Boireann* (Burrren) in the twelfth century. Mac Creiche was presumed, however, to have lived in the late sixth century (Plummer 1925:8–10).

Mac Creiche is a descendant of the god Ercc, who is presented in the Rawlinson B 502 chieftain list of the Corcu MoDruad as a chieftain named Mac Ercc.[9] His Corcu MoDruad father possessed the non-Irish name Pesslan, and his mother was of the Cíarraige (O'Brien 1976:154 d 54; Plummer 1925:13; Ziegler 1994:34). Mac Creiche's name translates as "Son of Plunder." One may deduce from his travels in a chariot with a trusted companion, Mainchin, and his practice of single-handedly confronting and overcoming groups hostile to the Corcu MoDruad and Cíarraige that he was originally the Corcu MoDruad's equivalent of Cú Chulainn. I think it is highly likely that *Betha Meic Creiche* was, in its original form, a saga concerning the exploits of a pagan hero, born of a god and a mortal woman, who engaged in single combats against enemies of the Corcu MoDruad and also battled a monster. This hypothesis would go a long way toward explaining why the life has faithfully preserved a number of facts of regional political history over a period of 400–500 years.

The place-names from within Corcu MoDruad from *Betha Meic Creiche* that can be identified with modern counterparts are all in northern Clare and fall within the modern adjacent baronies of Corcomroe, Burren, and Inchiquin (Figure 3.11). The Life has Mac Creiche beginning his ecclesiastical career in a hermitage that can be located in the far northwestern corner of Burren Barony in the valley of the Caher River, formerly called the Eidnech River (Figure 3.11). The life then describes the circumstances surrounding the foundation of Kilmacreehy Church (*Cill Meic Creiche*) in the extreme southwest of Corcomroe Barony. Following a display of the saint's holy stature, the Corcu MoDruad chieftain Báeth (Middle Ir. *Baeth-brónach*) makes a grant to him of his own seat of *Clúain Dirair*. Given that the residence is described as being by the sea, the church that was founded upon it may be Drumcreehy (*Droim Críoche/Creiche?*) church in Burren Barony.[10] Geographically, this would square with the Life only if *Fid Inis*, the starting point for the saint's trip before proceeding west to

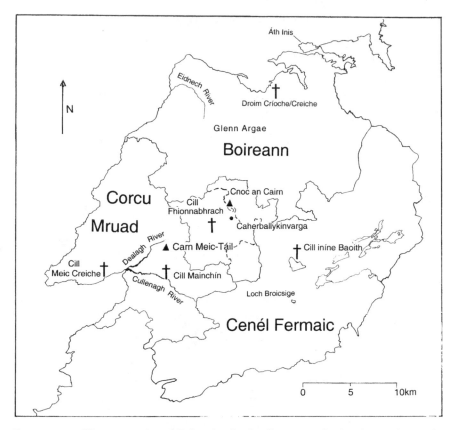

Figure 3.11. The geography of *Betha Meic Creiche.* Crosses mark churches and triangles mark cairns.

Clúain Dirair, is modern *Áth Inis* on the modern Clare/Galway border. James Frost, however, locates the residence, or *dún*, of Baeth-brónach on a hill in the townland of Lissatunna in Corcomroe Barony. If so, then the church that resulted from his grant would have been Killmanaheen (*Cill Mainchín*), which is dedicated to Mac Creiche's protégé (Frost 1978:111; Figure 3.11).[11] This identification fits with the westerly direction taken by Mac Creiche's party to reach Clúain Dirair, and St. Ailbe's subsequent westward departure from there over the ocean to *Tír Tairngire* (the Land of Promise).

At the end of the Life, Mac Creiche is summoned by the saints of *Cenél Fermaic* to battle a monster dwelling in Lough Raha (then *Loch Broicsige*) in Inchiquin Barony (Figure 3.11). Inchiquin Barony is, in fact, the modern territorial descendant of the Medieval period chiefdom *Cenél Fermaic*. The Cenél Fermaic saints had been unsuccessful against the monster, but Mac Creiche prevails by means of his bell and skullcap. This episode of holy men banishing monsters from bodies of water crops up often in saints' lives, and in some instances may mark a kind of exorcism or reconsecration of formerly pagan sacrificial sites. Loch Broicsige, then, may have formerly been the sacrifical lake of the *Uí Dedaid* or whoever preceded them as leaders of Cenél Fermaic, as its central location within Cenél Fermaic would seem to indicate. The greater point of this story, however, was to demonstrate the superiority of the saint of the Corcu MoDruad, and by extension the superiority of the Corcu MoDruad chiefdom itself, over Cenél Fermaic.

Betha Meic Creiche lays out the belief on the part of the Corcu MoDruad that in the seventh century they were located in the north of Co. Clare (*Tuadmumu*), and argues that they were the leading chiefdom of all of *Tuadmumu*. Mac Creiche's life also assumes that the territory of Corcu MoDruad took in Corcomroe and Burren Baronies, and, further, that the Corcu MoDruad dominated a people whose territory was adjacent to theirs, *Cenél Fermaic*. When these three baronies are combined, the resultant territorial entity has the appearance of a rough circle (Figure 3.11). This is the characteristic shape that an Irish composite chiefdom assumes.

The story of Baeth-brónach and Clúain Dirair seems at first reading to be a later interpolation in the Life, reflecting the circumstances of Corcu MoDruad following its fission in the eleventh century into two chiefdoms, Corcu Mruad and Boireann. Both of these daughter chiefdoms had chiefly seats that were in valleys facing the sea: Corcu Mruad at the confluence of the Dealagh and Cullenagh rivers and Boireann in Gleann Argdae. However, the capitals of Irish chiefdoms are usually situated at the center of the polities they govern, so if the three baronies of the Life of Mac Creiche together composed the extent of the early composite chiefdom of Corcu MoDruad, then the most likely candidate for its capital would be the large cashel site of Caherballykinvarga (Gibson 1995: Figure 3.12).

CAHERBALLYKINVARGA: CAPITAL OF
THE CORCU MODRUAD

Apart from its central location, there are other factors that lend support to the argument that Caherballykinvarga was the original capital of Corcu MoDruad. To begin with the weakest line of reasoning, Westropp claims that this site can be identified with Caghir Loglin (*Cathair Lochlainn*) in the seventeenth-century *Books of Survey and Distribution*, and was called Caherflaherty (*Cathair Flaithbhertaigh*) in the mid-nineteenth century (*IMC* 1967:189; Westropp 1897:121–122). Hence it carried at a late date the names of two

Figure 3.12. Caherballykinvarga (photo: J. K. S. St. Joseph. Copyright reserved Cambridge University Collection of Aerial Photography).

historical chieftains of the Corcu MoDruad.[12] A much stronger indication of its former significance is its location very close to the chief religious center of the chiefdom, *Cill Fhionnúrach* (Kilfenora), the seat of the bishop of the diocese of the same name (Figure 3.11). A third line of reasoning revolves around the splitting of the chiefdom of Corcu MoDruad into two polities in the twelfth century. When Corcu MoDruad was divided, an effort was made to locate the common border very close to Caherballykinvarga, perhaps because the idea of a unified chiefdom persisted after the split and neither the O'Connor chieftains of Corcomroe nor the O'Lochlainn chieftains of Burren would relinquish their symbolic claims to the chieftainship by relinquishing possession of the former capital site outright.

Caherballykinvarga's preeminence is also substantiated by its great size and singular appearance. Though the site possesses a thick and high enclosure wall of quarried limestone laid in courses, it is also surrounded by a

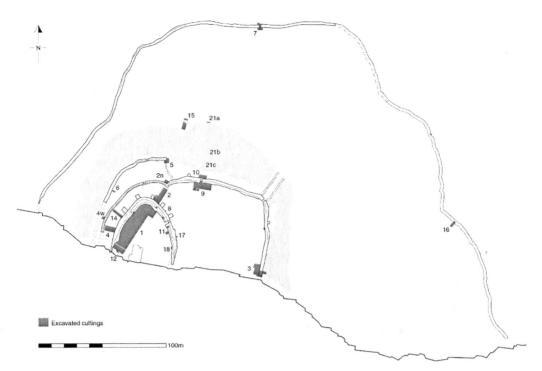

Figure 3.13. Excavation plan of Dún Aonghasa, Inis Mór, Co. Galway (from Cotter 1996: Fig. 1).

double-belt of *chevaux-de-frise* (Figure 3.12). *Chevaux-de-frise* are a field of stone orthostats propped upright that surround a site. Stylistically, the enclosure wall of slabs laid in courses at Caherballykinvarga dates to the Early Medieval period (the dating to be discussed further later). *Chevaux-de-frise*, however, is a feature common to Bronze Age and Early Iron Age settlements of Spain, and so, by analogy, this could be an ancient feature of the site.

Another settlement in the region with a combination of *chevaux-de-frise* and coursed-stone walls is Dún Aonghasa on Inis Mór of the Aran Islands (Cotter 1995, 1996; Jones 2004:172–176; Westropp 1902: Fig. 19; Figure 3.13). The recent excavations carried out at Dún Aonghasa discovered that the *chevaux-de-frise* were simply propped upright on the original ground surface, and so could not be dated (Cotter 1996). There is slight evidence that it predates the latest remodeling at the site, as two radial walls connecting the outermost enclosure wall (Wall 4) with the middle enclosure wall (Wall 2a) cross over it (ibid.; Ó Ríordáin 1979:49, Plate 14). However, the *chevaux-de-frise* do not seem to date to the Late Bronze Age period of the site as their distribution seems to align with Walls 2B and 3 dating to this period (Jones 2004:172). In conclusion, it remains an open question as to exactly when the *chevaux-de-frise* were erected, but it would be dangerous to assume that they are of necessity prehistoric.

A fact that substantiates Caherballykinvarga as a capital site above all else is its proximity to the cathedral of the diocese of Kilfenora, *Cill Fhionnúrach*. The cathedral is the second element of what I have called the "capital set," the three elements that composed the capital of an Irish medieval polity (Gibson 1995:116–117). The three elements of the capital set are the principal homestead of the chiefly ramage, the principal ecclesiastical establishment patronized by this ramage, and the inauguration mound or cairn. The concept of the capital set was developed to characterize a capital in a non-urban context where the three elements viewed as essential to the expression and reproduction of leadership would be spatially discrete. Though the number of elements composing the capital set for Ireland remains fairly steady at three throughout the Middle Ages, in earlier periods the number and elements composing the set would be expected to vary. For instance, whereas churches and inauguration mounds were a part of the Irish sacral landscape in the Early Middle Ages, their Iron Age counterparts would have been hilltop shrines and sacrificial ponds or lakes, as discussed previously with reference to Mooghaun, Emain Macha, and Loch Raha.

The sacral primacy of Caherballykinvarga and Kilfenora over, respectively, the secular and religious components of the social structure of the Corcu MoDruad composite chiefdom made their physical proximity to one another inevitable, as inevitable as was the foundation of the Vatican in the Roman capital. The complementary sanctity of these two sites set off their common district as hallowed ground. In Figure 3.8, I have marked out a putative central territory of the Corcu MoDruad chiefly ramage. It would have consisted of what became after the twelfth century three Medieval period parishes: Kilfenora, Noughaval, and Kiltoraght (Gibson 2000; Ní Ghabhláin 1996). A cairn can be found, which fulfills the third leg of the capital set. In full view of Caherballykinvarga is a large, obviously man-made cairn on a prominence fittingly called Knockacarn (*Cnoc an Carn* [Mountain of the Cairn]), 1.4 km north-northwest of the site.[13] In *Betha Meic Creiche*, Carn Meic Táil (Mod. Irish *Carn Mhic-Táil*), a large cairn that was thought to be the burial mound of a revered ancestral chieftain named Mac-Táil [46], was the point of assembly of the Corcu MoDruad (FitzPatrick 2004:89–90; Figure 3.14). It is located at a distance from Caherballykinvarga but is close to the center of the twelfth-century O'Connor chiefdom of *Corcomruad*. This factor does not, however, rule out Carn Mhic-Táil as the Early Medieval inauguration mound of Corcu MoDruad. Of all the elements of the capital set, the location of the inauguration mound tends to be the most variable (Gibson 1995:117).

Figure 3.14. Carn Connachtach (Carn Mhic-Táil), Ballygheely, Co. Clare (photo: Blair Gibson).

THE CÍARRAIGE CONQUEST OF CO. CLARE

Working from a basis of myth and the chance sharing of a name between the maximal ramages of two chiefdoms, a late (post-eleventh century) genealogical poem propounds a common origin for the Corcu MoDruad and the Cíarraige, who in the eighth century were occupying a territory in northern Co. Kerry along the southern shore of the mouth of the Shannon:

Sliocht Ir Mic Míleadh (The lineage of Ir Mac Míl [43])
Do chraobhsgaoileadh Sleachta Ir mic Mileadh annso:
Dias do shliocht Ir ar a bhfuil sliocht i nEirinn
go prínsiopálta, mar áta Conall Cearnach, agus Fearghus Mac
Róigh. ó Chonall Chearnach atá Mac Aonghusa, agus
Mac Cairteáin, agus O'Mórdha. ó Fhearghus atá
O'Conchubhair Ciarraighe, agus O'Conchubhair Chorcamruadh,
O'Lochlainn Bóirne, agus Síol bhFearghail gona ngabhlaibh geinealaigh.

The dissemination of the line of Ir mac Mil here:

There were two men of the line of Ir which was the principal lineage of Ireland, namely Conall Cernach, and Fergus Mac Roich. Descended from Conall

Cernach are Mac Aengusa, and Mac Carteáin, and O'Morda. Descended from Fergus was O'Conchubair Ciarraige, and O'Conchubair Corca Mruad, O'Lochlainn of the Burren, and Síl Fergail having a forked genealogy (pedigree). (O'Donnchadha 1940:250)

This poem is premised upon the body of mythology created by the Irish "synthetic historians" of the ninth century onward in their efforts to present a common origin myth for the diverse polities of Ireland (Mac Neill 1981:6, chap. 3). Though the author's logic and facts in this instance can be dismissed, the poem does reflect a belief among the Irish intelligentsia of the Middle Irish period in the existence of a historical relationship between the Corcu MoDruad and the Cíarraige. This belief in their common kinship is also strongly expressed in another late source, *Betha Meic Creiche*.

In the Christian era, saints superseded tutelary gods and deified ancestors as the source of the spiritual power of the chiefdom. Brénainn moccu Altae was the patron saint of the Cíarraige Lúachra and his Latin Life states that his sister St. Briga was of the Tradraige – a clear statement of the existence of an alliance between these higher-level chiefdoms expressed in terms of kinship between tutelary saints (Heist 1965:331). The pattern of the descent of St. Mac Creiche can also be seen as a manifestation of the beliefs pervasive among the inhabitants of Corcu MoDruad in the twelfth century concerning their past political relationships. Not only does Mac Creiche have a Cíarraige mother, but he is also summoned to the Cíarraige in the hopes that he may be able to recover cattle and three of his kinsmen abducted by a raiding party led by the three sons of Crimthann mac Cobthach, the sixth-century chieftain of the Éoganacht Locha Léin, a chiefdom located directly to the south of the Cíarraige in what is now Co. Kerry.[14] That the identities of Crimthann, his sons, and his grandson from this story match the king lists in the genealogies of the Éoganacht Locha Léin lends substance to the reality of an alliance between the Cíarraige and the Corcu MoDruad.

Crimthann mac Cobthach of the Éoganacht Locha Léin possibly figures in another story that focuses on the antagonistic relationship between the Éoganacht Locha Léin and the Cíarraige, the "West Munster Synod" in the Laud 610 collection. This document is nearer chronologically to the political situation in Clare in the eighth century, as elements of the language place it in the ninth century at a minimum (Joseph Flahive, pers. comm. 2008; Byrne 2001:220). In this story, the Cíarraige Lúachra are led by Mac Ardae mac Fitaich, though it seems that the shots are being called by St. Brénainn moccu Altae and half-brother St. Ciarán of Clonmacnoise (Byrne 2001:216). In response to Éoganacht Locha Léin aggression, they put together an alliance with chiefdoms of the Múscraige and Corcu Oché. The chieftain of the Éoganacht Locha Léin is in this text identified as *Crimthann Odor* (Crimthann the Swarthy). The text is fascinating insofar as it designates some chiefdoms as *fortúatha* — that is, chiefdoms ruled by ramages "not descended from the ancestors of the ruling stock in the territory they inhabit," meaning that the original ramage has been replaced by one imposed by an outside chiefdom (*DIL*1983). Later on the text refers to *forslointe* (sing. *forslondud*), which are the replacement ramages, and names a string of chiefdoms that were located on the fringes of the Cíarraige/Éoganacht Locha Léin heartland in Kerry, Limerick, and Cork to the north, west, and south: "*Corco Bascind* and *Corcomruad* (Corcu Modruad) and *Ui Fidgente* and *Corco Luigde* (Corcu Loigde)…. and *Uí Echach.*" (Meyer 1912:316). Though it is not made explicit that these are the *fortuatha* that the text had earlier referred to, evidence will be detailed below that, in the eighth century, the Corcu Baiscind and Corcu MoDruad fit this description.

Also fascinating is the prominent role attributed to clerics as both organizers of the alliance and guarantors of each chiefdom's participation in it. All of the clerics involved were saints, and so they are standing in as totemic representations of the monasteries within the chiefdoms with which these were associated. It is conceivable, however, that in reality clerics (and, earlier, druids) did play this role in the creation of intrachiefdom alliances. Shamans played an analogous role as alliance instigators among the Nuer of Sudan (Evans-Pritchard 1969:121).

Of all the diverse categories of historical evidence stemming from the Early Middle Ages, the genealogies, or lists of chieftains, are easily the most problematical. Like the histories kept by the Aztecs, they were periodically rewritten to accommodate changes in the political landscape. As a matter of fact, one could state with some assurance that one of the principal reasons they were composed in the first place was to confer gravitas upon a given political order through its supposed antiquity (Ó Murchadha 2004). This is especially true in the case of the genealogies of later chiefdom confederacies such as the Dál Cais and the Éoganachta, where it is obvious that the founding ancestors of disparate chiefdoms have been made into sons of a common father (Sproule 1984). For chiefdoms of a smaller scale, it has been claimed that genealogies have been concocted against a vacuum of genealogical facts with the objective of weaving the most powerful families together in a way that reflects an already existing hierarchy (Ó Corráin 1975).

The deficiencies of the genealogies are most apparent when they are compared against the annals. Prominent individuals cited in the annals are frequently missing from the genealogies and vice versa. The reasonable explanation for this pattern is that as maximal ramages lost power and faded into obscurity, they were expunged from the genealogies in favor of ascendant groups. For this reason, and also due to the well-known occurrence of telescoping in materials of this sort, one cannot therefore simply count back through the lists of chieftains in order to make estimates as to the timing of a reign of a particular individual (Ó Murchadha 2004).

Given these severe deficiencies, are the genealogies of any use in historical research? The answer to this question is a highly qualified yes, as there are names occurring in the genealogies that *do* appear in the annals, demonstrating that there are tangible facts strewn among the inventions. Furthermore, there are regularities in the data of the genealogies that can be exploited to a limited degree. The first regularity is the constancy in the status of a chiefdom's often eponymous founding ancestor. In the case of the chiefdoms of the Early Middle Ages that possessed roots extending back past the Viking invasions, it is a certainty that the ancestor will have been a tutelary deity. An example of this is Dovinia, the eponymous ancestor of the Corcu Duibne.

The second regularity in the genealogical data is redundancy and regionalism in name preference among aristocratic ramages. Examination of any aristocratic pedigree will reveal names that were used repeatedly, reflecting the manner in which living generations venerated those that had come before them. One would also expect that names would be bestowed upon aristocratic offspring that would set their lineage apart from those of other maximal ramages, especially those of groups that were looked upon as hostile.

The various Corcu MoDruad genealogies present disparate traditions, but seem to sort themselves into two camps: on the one hand are the genealogies preserved in the Book of Leinster, probably dating to the early ninth century. On the other hand there are other later sources such as Rawlinson B 502, Book of Lecan, Book of Ballymote, Book of Munster – Rawlinson B 502 dating to the twelfth century (Ó Murchadha 2004). The Book of Leinster genealogies for the Corcu Baiscind chieftains end with Lennán mac Catharnaich, who ascended in 898 AD following the death of his brother Flann (*AI*). The genealogies of the Book of Leinster are therefore presumed to be more reliable for the eighth century.

Evidence from the genealogies suggests a link of some sort between the Cíarraige to the south of the Shannon and both the Corcu Baiscind and the Corcu MoDruad prior to the twelfth century. First of all, the Book of Leinster places the Corcu MoDruad genealogy among the Cíarraige genealogies (O'Brien 1976). In the Book of Leinster pedigree the first ancestor of the Corcu MoDruad was Messen-Sulad [44] (Fosterling of Súla). Mac-Táil [46] occurs four generations following Messin-Sulad and is the link between the Corcu MoDruad genealogy and the genealogy of the Dál Cais. The god Senach (discussed previously) is the first link between the genealogies of the Cíarraige and Corco MoDruad in the Book of Leinster. In the Cíarraige genealogies of both Rawlinson B 502 and the Book of Leinster Senach precedes a chieftain named Rechtabra by either three (LL) or four (Rawl.) generations.

Rechtabra occurs two generations above Flann Féorna in the Book of Leinster chieftain list, which may place his period of activity in the late seventh or early eighth century AD, as Flann Féorna died in 741 AD. At this time, there is strong evidence of violent disruption to the Corcu Baiscind and Corcu MoDruad. For 705 AD, the Annals of Ulster record a Battle of Corcu MoDruad, which seems to have involved a conflict with a ramage of the Uí Fidgeinti (to be discussed at greater length later). Prior to that, Talamnach of the Corcu Baiscind dies in 665 AD in the battle of Loch Fén *eter Mumain ocus Chonnachtu* (between Munster and Connachta). This entry provides evidence that the chiefdoms of Co. Clare were allied with the Connachta chiefdoms, or at least assumed to lie within their social sphere. Loch Fén is present-day Loughfane, which lies in the Barony of Lower Connello on the banks of the Shannon. In the seventh century this would have been the territory of the Uí Fidgeinti. The Corcu Baiscind were then unsuccessfully attacking the Uí Fidgeinti on their own turf. Talmanach's son is then said to have died in 721 AD, fifty-six years following the death of his father.

Significantly, following Talamnach in the lists of chieftains in the Book of Leinster is Aithechdai (vassal). It is highly unlikely that a chieftain would have borne this name, so it should be regarded as a social designation or editorial comment by the genealogist, probably to connote a chieftain of foreign origins. That Aithechdai mac Thalamnaich is said by the Annals of Innisfallen to have died in 723 AD, a full fifty-eight years after the death of his supposed father, strengthens doubts about his relation to the aboriginal Corcu Baiscind ruling lineage. His successor, bearing the name Flann, dies a mere two years after he does. Flann is a name common to both Cíarraige and Corcu Baiscind genealogies as evidenced by the near contemporary chieftain Flann Féorna of the Cíarraige.

I would suggest that the chronological gap in the chieftain list for Corcu Baiscind following the death of Talamnach, which ends with the appearance of Aithechdai in the list, is due to a catastrophic defeat incurred by the Corcu Baiscind, followed either by reduction of their ramage to vassal status and/or expulsion of their ramage and replacement by a ramage of the Cíarraige or of the closely-related Uí Fidgeinti.

The successors to Áed in the Corcu Baiscind chieftain lists do not appear in the annals, and the names that do, Flann, Rechtabra, and Torpaid, do not appear in the chieftain lists of the Corcu Baiscind until Áed Rón, who died in 812 AD (AI). Thereafter, there is greater correspondence between the annals and genealogies, though the picture is not necessarily one of stability. If the *Genelach hÚa nDécce* of the Corcu Baiscind in the Book of Leinster is to be trusted, further turmoil is indicated with names seeming to be aboriginal, such as Talamnach (d. 853 AD), Máel-Brigte, and Cermait mac Cathrannach (d. 864 AI), alternating with another sequence of Aithechdai-Rechtabra-Áed, to end with the unique names of Carthanach and Lennán. This last chieftain assumed office in 898 AD.

The first leader of the Corcu MoDruad to appear in annals is Torpaid [54] (d. 769 AI), whom the later annals confuse with the Cíarraige chieftain Flann Féorna. The name Torpaid does not appear in the Corcu MoDruad genealogies, but it is a common name in the genealogies of the Cíarraige, with five entries in CGH. It also appears in the genealogy of the Corcu Baiscind following their late seventh-century defeat at the hands of the Uí Fidgeinti (Table 3.1). Torpaid is, therefore, also likely to have been of Uí Fidgeinti/Cíarraige origins. He has a place-name reference in the Burren in the site of Dún Torptha in Glennarraga (Figure 3.15). This is a rath-type homestead site on the valley floor and the appearance of *dún* designates it as a chieftain's seat. The valley within which it is located, *Glann Argae*, references the name of an ancestor deity not only of the Corcu MoDruad, but also, and probably originally, of the Cíarraige named Argddae or Mac Ardae, who appears in the West Munster Synod text (Appendix).

These data gathered from the genealogies and annals provide the background story to the relationship between the Corcu MoDruad, Corcu Baiscind, and Cíarraige represented in Middle Irish texts such as the "West Munster Synod" and *Betha Meic Creiche*. Indeed, the Corcu Baiscind and Corcu MoDruad could have been subordinate chiefdoms within an alliance led by the Cíarraige, as described in the "West Munster Synod," due to the fact that they had been conquered by aristocratic lineages deriving from either the Uí Fidgeinti alone or both the Uí Fidgeinti and Cíarraige Lúachra in the late seventh/early eighth century. This alliance may have existed down to the time of Flann Féorna, who may have imposed one of his own sons, Rechtabra, on the Corcu Baiscind (Table 3.2). Rechtabrat and Flann Feórna, moreover, are found in the genealogies of all three

Table 3.2. A section of the Cíarraige Lúachra genealogy from Rawlinson B 502.

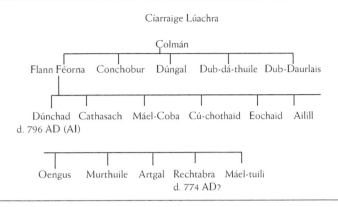

Cíarraige Lúachra

Colmán

Flann Féorna   Conchobur   Dúngal   Dub-dá-thuile   Dub-Daurlais

Dúnchad   Cathasach   Máel-Coba   Cú-chothaid   Eochaid   Ailill
d. 796 AD (AI)

Oengus   Murthuile   Artgal   Rechtabra   Máel-tuili
d. 774 AD?

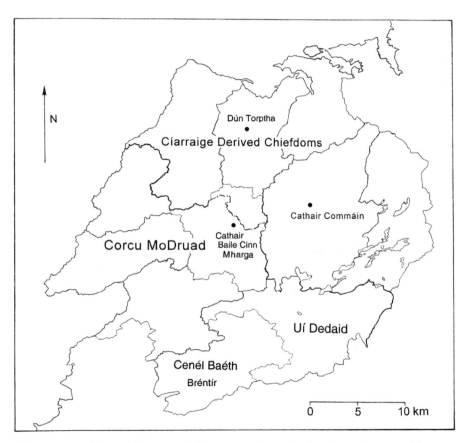

Figure 3.15. Map of Burren and Corcomroe baronies showing primary parishes as reconstructed in Chapter 10, Figure 10.10, and Ní Ghabhláin 1995, 1996. The boundaries of Inagh parish within Inchiquin Barony, containing *Bréntír*, are shown, as are sites bearing the names of individuals referred to in eighth-century annal entries.

chiefdoms, and Flann died within half a decade of the destruction of Corcu MoDruad by In Déis Tuaiscirt in 744 AD (*AU*), who had at some time prior to this point entered and occupied southeastern Co. Clare. In so doing, they had to have displaced the Corcu Baiscind from their heartland, in essence driving a wedge between the Uí Fidgeinti and Cíarraige Lúachra and the chiefdoms they had spawned in Co. Clare. The death of Flann Féorna in 741 AD then marked the end of the fortunes of the Cíarraige and their allies (Charles-Edwards 1993:125).

CO. CLARE, 750–800 AD

The invasion of Clare by the Cíarraige, Uí Fidgeinti, and In Déis Tuaiscirt of Munster during the seventh to eighth centuries AD led to tangible results in the form of chiefdoms that were established by them in eastern, central, and northern Co. Clare (Bhreathnach 1999; Figure 3.16). The domination of Clare by Munster groups would eventually lead a name change for the region as a whole, as it would come to be referred to by the annalists as Tuadmumu (North Munster). The first such reference to the region occurs in 927 AD in the *Annals of Innisfallen*.

As stated previously, the Cíarraige may have overthrown and replaced the ruling ramage of the Corcu Baiscind, at least temporarily. The Uí Fidgeinti, on the other hand, seem to have been responsible for establishing a string of chiefdoms that extended northward from the Fergus estuary with the Shannon all the way north to Corcu MoDruad, to possibly even take in the Aran Islands (Bhreathnach 1999). One such chiefdom created by the Uí Fidgeinti was that ruled by Uí Chormaic. The chiefdom of the Uí Chormaic was possibly co-terminous with present-day Islands Barony, though James Frost thinks they may have originally occupied the territory that was later to become the chiefdom of Uí Caissín. The ancestor from whom they derived their name, Cass mac Conaill Echluaith [33], would become the common ancestor of the Dál Cais chiefdom confederacy, and the territory of the Uí Caissín contained the important ritual center of Magh Adhair, at which was located the inauguration mound and sacred tree (*bile*) of the Dál Cais. It is perhaps significant that this ritual center was located due north of Mooghaun, the former ritual center of the chiefdom confederacy displaced by these interlopers (Figure 3.16).

Betha Meic Creiche implies that the maximal ramage of Cenél Fermaic was alien to the Corcu Modruad; this inference is supported by the genealogies

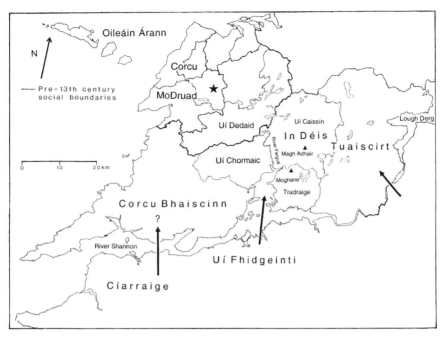

Figure 3.16. Co. Clare in the eighth century AD, showing the direction and impact of invasions by the Cíarraige, Uí Fidgeinti, and In Déis Tuaiscirt. The star indicates the location Caherballykinvarga.

of two of the three ramages occupying Cenél Fermaic found in the twelfth-century Rawlinson B 502 manuscript, those of the Uí Dedaid and Clann hIffernáin (Appendix). However, the genealogy of the third and weakest ramage of Cenél Fermaic, Cenél Báeth, does betray affinities with Corcu MoDruad.

According to the genealogy of Cenél Fermaic under its old name *Aes Iar Forgus* (The People West of the Fergus), the senior branch of this chiefdom was the Cenél Báeth. Little is known of this ramage, but a portion of the late fourteenth-century topographical poem of Giolla-na-Naomh Ó hUidhrín described their contemporary location:

Ceinél mBaoith nach beag fine,
gasraidh bhreaghdha Bréintire;
Uí Mhaoil Mheadha fheilmghil fhinn
an fheadha um Eidhnigh aoibhinn.
    (Carney 1943:57)
Cinel Baith, of no small chiefdom,
The fine tribe of Brentir,
O'Maoilmeadha of the fair land,
His [are] the woods about the delightful Eidhneach.[15]

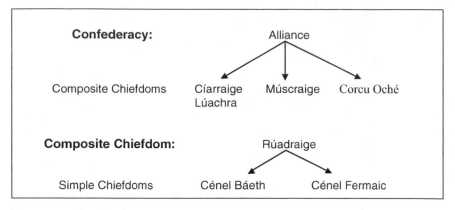

Figure 3.17. Levels of political organization in Co. Clare and West Munster in the Early Middle Ages. The examples have been drawn from the discussion in the text for heuristic purposes and are not specific to any one century. Modeled after Heider 1991: Diagram 4.

This poem tells us that in the fourteenth century the Cenél Báeth was led by the O'Maoil Mhuaidh, and that they made their home in the Bréntír district of Cenél Fermaic in modern-day Inagh (Eidneach) parish. Far from being a "fair land," Bréntír was a place of forests, swamps, and mountains, as indicated by its name, which translates as "Rotten Land" (see Figure 3.15). In the saga *Caithréim Thoirdealbhaigh*, it was a place of temporary refuge for Toirdhealbhach Uí Briain [22] and his followers (O'Grady 1929 I:13, II:14). One wonders what ancient calamity befell Cenél Báeth to have been permanently exiled to this desolate locale – why the most senior branch of Cenél Fermaic was banished to the most marginal area of the territory.

The name Báeth is itself of interest to this discussion. As previously mentioned, it figures in the *Life of Mac Creiche* as the name of the contemporary chieftain of the Corcu MoDruad. In the Corcu MoDruad genealogies in the Book of Leinster there are two occurrences of the name: first as the second son of Oscar [45] in the mythological portion of the genealogy from the Book of Leinster (O'Brien 1976: *LL* 161 a 25), and second as a son of Cullén or Fuilne in a Corcu MoDruad genealogy from the Rawlinson B 502 manuscript [47] (O'Brien 1976: *LL* 327 e 20). Báeth's appearance as a ramage ancestor in these mythological sources and on ogam stones confirms what has been stated above concerning Báeth's status as a pagan deity, perhaps a fertility god or Bacchus-like god, given his name ("Foolish") and his association with crops in the *Life of Mac Creiche*.

More prolific than references to Báeth are those to a daughter of Báeth, or *Ingen Báeth*. The first mention of this daughter is in the Dál Cais genealogy from the Psalter of Cashel, where she is listed as having an origin in

Óengus Cenn Aittinn [34] (O'Brien 1976: 152 a 50). The Book of Uí Maine fleshes this identification out, identifying this saint as Findclú (white or fair renowned) and making her, paradoxically, the daughter of the mysterious Fer Domnach [42] (Macnamara 1907). I have little doubt that Ingen Báeth was stated to have come from Óengus Cenn Aittinn [34] (Oengus of the Gorse Mountain or, less likely, Oengus Furze Head), the founding ancestor of Clann hIffernáin, due to the physical location of a church dedicated to her in Clann hIffernáin territory. This is Killinaboy church, or *Cill Inghine Baoith*, the principal church of Killinaboy parish in the Middle Ages (Figure 3.8).

Killinaboy church stands at the terminus of the *Bóthar na Mac Ríg* (Road of the Chieftain's Sons) between Corofin and Killinaboy. It was obviously an important ecclesiastical establishment in its day, probably monastic due to the fairly large size of the church, the existence of the ruins of a round tower on the premises, and extensive *termonn* lands around it (Westropp 1909a). The boundaries of these lands were marked by stone crosses, one of which, located a little over 2 km to the west of Killinaboy, is still in existence (ibid.). This famous cross, which has the tau form with two filial arms in the form of human heads, is named *Cros Inghine Baoith*. Across the road is *Suíochán Inghine Baoith* (Seat of Báeth's daughter), a stone chair renowned as a cure for backaches.

The oldest tradition places the progenitor of Ingen Báeth, Fer Domnach, in Cenél Báeth, and the patronym of this saint strongly identifies her with this ramage as well. Therefore, Ingen Báeth was originally most likely the patron saint of Cenél Báeth, and Cill Inghine Baoith was their principal ecclesiastical establishment. Invoking the logic of the capital set, one would then expect that the capital site of the Cenél Báeth formerly would have been located somewhere in the neighborhood of this monastery. If this represents a true reconstruction of the social constitution of Killinaboy parish, it stands to reason that the Cenél Báeth were displaced from this territory by the Uí Chuinn and Uí Dedaid, and so were forced to move southwest to the refuge of Bréntír. The genealogies were then altered to reflect these new circumstances, insofar as Ingen Báeth was said to descend from the founder of Clann hIffernáin. The location of the wells dedicated to Ingen Báeth reinforces the identification of this saint with Killinaboy parish and may show in a rough way the extent of the former hegemony of the Cenél Báeth.

Given the genealogical seniority of its ramage in the Cenél Fermaic genealogies, and the extent of the influence of its cult, Cenél Báeth was, in all likelihood, the dominant ramage of a territory taking in Cenél Fermaic and the eastern Burren. The appearance of the name Báeth in the pedigree of the Corcu MoDruad, and the folklore concerning a chieftain of the same name of this chiefdom, suggests the hypothesis that Cenél Báeth was at one time a section of Corcu MoDruad. Some tangential evidence can be invoked to support this assertion: St. Mo-Báeth is named for *Cluain Fhionnabhair*, a place-name linked to *Cill Fhionnúrach* (Kilfenora), in the Martyrology of Donegal (Westropp 1900:110)[16] and Mo-Báeth aka Mo-Báe aka Báetán appears as a son of Senach, an ancestor god appearing in the genealogies of the Cíarraige, Corcu Baiscind, and Corcu MoDruad (Table 3.1). Thus, the pagan god Báeth was given a Christian identity for the new era, and could become simultaneously an ancestral chieftain for a ramage of the Corcu MoDruad, and later, a tutelary saint of one of their principal ramages.

Keeping in mind that Kilfenora, the place-name of the cathedral of Corcu MoDruad, is Cill Fhionnúrach, it would seem that a father–daughter relationship existed between these ecclesiastical establishments as Westropp's statements about Ingen Báeth would seem to indicate (1900:109).[17] The asymmetrical symbolic kin relationship between these two churches may have in turn reflected the quality of the political relationship that existed at one time between the western and eastern halves of the presumably composite chiefdom of Corcu MoDruad. These two chiefdoms were linked, but the western section represented by Kilfenora exerted political dominance over Cenél Báeth, represented by Killinaboy.

The cult of Ingen Báeth was still flourishing at the start of the fourteenth century, for *Caithréim Thoirdhealbhaigh* states that in 1317 the army of Diarmuid Uí Briain "held from Ruane as follows: they just grazed Barnakilleen and the pathetic grave of famed O'Lochlainn's daughter" (*ó ma[i]gh na poll puballglan, agus do bhernaidh craebtorthigh í Chaillín, agus do lecht laomscarcraidhech ingine í Lochlainn*) (O'Grady 1929, 26:98, 27:89). Ruan (*Ruadhán*) is situated a little over 1 km to the northwest of Dromore Lake in the east-central portion of Cenél Fermaic. As Westropp has pointed out, this passage is somewhat confused, as it would seem to have the army marching from the east *toward* Ruan: "straight on still into upper Clancullen and to the causeway of Achrim" (*Echdroma*; this is on the Fergus to the southeast of Ruan) (O'Grady 1929, 27:89; Westropp 1903:154). However, the rest of the passage seems consistent with a march from Ruan to Corofin: "with left-hand towards.... Tulach O'Dea, across Bescnat's streaming banks to Macaburren's causeway" (*carraidh mic amboirend*, at the Kell's bridge 1 km south of Lough Cullaun). This passage is of interest, for "O'Lochlainn's daughter" can be no other than Ingen Báeth, whose grave site was thus held to be located in the vicinity of Ruan in eastern Cenél Fermaic. The greater significance of this testimony of medieval folk tradition is that it links the Ingen Báeth with the Uí Lochlainn branch of the Corcu MoDruad, not with the Dál Cais as the Psalter of Cashel genealogy purports. Though one should not make too much of this ambiguous bit of evidence from a late period, the logical extension of the above interpretation is that it can be taken as an indication that, in the regional folk memory, Cenél Báeth were considered to have been of the Corcu MoDruad.

If Cenél Báeth had been shunted aside within their former district, it is logical to assume that Uí Dedaid and Clann hIffernáin were responsible for its demise. In their genealogies both ramages claimed an affinity with the Dál Cais, a chiefdom confederacy that was to emerge in the tenth century. However, the Éoganachta confederacy genealogy establishes the affinity of the Uí Dedaid with this earlier confederacy by listing their ancestor Dedad as a grandson of the founder Éogan Mór (O'Brien 1976:148 a 17). On top of that, the same genealogy positions Dedad as a brother of Fiachu Figenid, the eponymous ancestor of the Uí Figcinti. Their other brothers in this same section of the Éoganachta genealogy are founders of groups of Cíarraige derivation, and it was most likely out of the Cíarraige that the Uí Dedaid and Uí Fidgeinti originally came.

DISCUSSION

It is necessary to intone again that due to the meagerness of the historical sources for Ireland prior to the eighth century, much of what has been said in this chapter is conjectural. The reconstructions that are offered here of the early political landscape of Co. Clare and environs are hypotheses awaiting testing, principally through the collection of archaeological data, though there may be unpublished texts that could also contribute to the resolution of the questions that were raised in this chapter. Subsequent chapters will examine archaeological data from Co. Clare, but the focus will be on the political landscape of Tuadmumu in the eighth century and later.

As early as the time of composition of Ptolemy's map of Ireland, in the mid-second century AD, Irish political systems were of the same magnitude of complexity as those of the early Middle Ages. Simple chiefdoms were organized into composite systems under the authority of a preeminent chiefdom's maximal ramage. It is difficult to know what the internal organization of these composite chiefdoms was like; it may have been structured like a flower with the territories of the constituent chiefdoms arrayed around the territory of the leading ramage, or composite chiefdoms may have had a dual system whereby a territory was split between two ramages. It may have been this factor that led to the Tradraige territory being split between an Uí Fidgeinti group and In Déis Tuaiscirt, and the greater portion of the territory of the Corcu MoDruad being taken over by several ramages of interlopers.

The data further indicates that, in turn, composite chiefdoms were bound into confederacies, which in the case of the Tradraige involved mutual defense against hostile chiefdoms. In the case of Co. Clare, the confederacy of the Tradraige bound together the composite chiefdoms Corcu Baiscind and the Corcu MoDruad, with the former seeming to have played a leading role in the eighth century. This dual organization seems to have been a typical feature of Irish chiefdom confederacies. The Déisi of Munster was composed of the Déis Tuaiscirt and the Déis Deiscirt, and as indicated above, the Cíarraige were to split into the Cíarraige Lúachra and Uí Fidgeinti, possibly an indicator of preexisting dual organization.

In the Iron Age, the chiefdom confederacy was promulgated through the creation of a ritual center involving a mound/temple on a hill and associated sacrificial pond. The important role played by these temples in the political life of Irish chiefdom confederacies is ironically attested in the scornful references made to them by clerics, for instance in the famous exchange that occurred between the cleric Múra and supposed seventh-century chieftain Áed Alláin when the former was trying to deduce the reason God had inflicted a mortal illness on the latter:

"Indisfead," ar an rí, "an ní búdh dóigh leam do crádh an Coimdeadh. Ra fhuabhras," ar sé, "fir Éireand do thinól dochum an tsléibhe si thair, .i. Carrláogh, dá chomarduccadh thúas, ocus teach dimór do dheanamh ann, ocus as eadh rob áil, go faicstea tene an tighi sin gach trá[th] nóna i mBreathnaibh oc i n-Airiur Gaoidhiol, ocus ra fheadar roba diomas mór sain."

"Rab olc sin," ar an cleireach. . . .

"I shall relate," said the chieftain, "that which I think likely to have offended the Lord. I attempted," said he, "to gather the men of Ireland to this mountain to the east, that is, to Carrlóeg, to build it up, and to construct a huge house on it, and I wished that the fire of that house might be seen every evening in Britain and Argyle; and I know that that was great arrogance."

"That was evil," said the cleric. . . . (Radner 1978:6–7)

The results of excavations at Navan Fort, Mooghaun, and Freestone Hill seem to show that in the Iron Age wooden temples gave way to mounds, which probably functioned as places for the inauguration of the confederacies' leaders. The association between tutelary deities and mountains persisted in Clare at least into the Christian era. Evidence for this is to be found in the genealogies of the Uí Dedaid and Clann hIffernáin of Cenél Fermaic, where their founding ancestors display the appellations Óengus Cenn Nathrach [41] (Oengus Snake Mountain) and Óengus Cenn Aittinn [34] (Óengus Furze Mountain).

At a later period, there are strong indications of alliances – alliances between chiefdom confederacies whose territorial reach spanned large sections of the island. How far back in time these alliances existed is a matter for future research. To judge from the Ulster Cycle, the Ulaid, Laigin, and Connachta confederacies extended back beyond the historical period, and these alliances left strong traces in the archaeological record. Certainly there were structures that could be construed as temples on the tops of the hills of Temuir (Tara) and Emain Macha (Navan Fort), the centers of the Laigin and Ulaid, respectively, as early as the Late Bronze Age, and the Black Pig's Dyke that marks a portion of the boundary of the Ulaid dates to the Iron Age. However, the earliest documented historical successes of the Connachta against the Laigin and Ulaid do not appear until the fifth century AD.

These alliances came late to Munster, which is a good thing from the standpoint of historical reconstruction, as the sources are ethnohistorical rather than purely mythological or archaeological. On the one hand, in the seventh century a number of powerful chiefdoms in Munster's interior started calling themselves the Éoganachta, and composed genealogies to place their gods into relations of kinship and descent (Sproule 1984). In the following century, the Cíarraige put together an alliance with surrounding composite chiefdoms and with the ramages spawed by the Cíarraige/Uí Fidgeinti invasion of Co. Clare in opposition to the Éoganacht Locha Léin (Byrne 2001:170).

There is ample evidence that alliances were not long-lasting political systems – all of the alliances discussed so far were destined to break apart. The Laud 610 account of the formation of the Cíarraige alliance explicitly demonstrates that these alliances came into being in the face of an external military threat. They were consciously promulgated and voluntarily entered into. The Irish expression for entering into an alliance, "making brotherhood," implies a kind of equality between its members. The Laud 610 text and others signal the existence of an overall leader or leading ramage, an *ard rí* or paramount chieftain. The Laud text even goes on to identify the Éoganacht Airthir Cliach leader as the paramount chieftain of *Caisel* and overlord to both the Éoganacht Locha Léin and Cíarraige. However, these claims come centuries after the fact and are the products of literati writing for specific patrons – in the case of the Laud

610 text, most likely later leaders of the Cíarraige Lúachra. Modern historians point out that apart from titles bestowed by annalists and boasts contained in texts generated by literati in the employ of the claimants, there is scant evidence for the institutionalization of confederacy leadership. The office of *rí ruirech* (paramount chieftain) was unaccompanied by accoutrements of the state such as a bureaucracy, a standing army, a system of taxation, and jural or legislative authority (Davies 1993). In the context of alliances, then, *rí ruirech* should be thought of as an honorific title, not as an office.

E. E. Evans-Pritichard established a set of key concepts in 1940 with the publication of *The Nuer* that are relevant for understanding the alliance systems of Irish confederacies. The Nuer were acephalous agropastoralists with rudimentary technology, yet they possessed social systems encompassing tens of thousands of individuals. Evans-Pritchard advanced the concept of complementary opposition to explain how these complex social formations came about and were sustained. "Each segment is itself segmented and there is opposition between its parts. The members of any segment unite for war against adjacent segments of the same order and unite with these adjacent segments against larger sections" (Evans-Pritchard 1940:142).

The same type of social formations were encountered by Karl Heider among the Dani of the Grand Valley in highland New Guinea, in which neighborhoods were united into confederations, and these in turn were linked by alliances uniting several thousand individuals (Heider 1991:68). These alliances took the name of their most prominent leader, but were otherwise not institutionalized, as they held no joint rituals. It is clear from Heider's analysis that warfare was the motivation for their formation (ibid.).

The confederations and alliances of the Irish in the Early Middle Ages departed from those of the Nuer and Dani in two key respects: the Irish were organized into chiefdoms and their confederacies and alliances were larger in scale. They attempted to institutionalize their political units at nearly every level – chiefdom, composite chiefdom, and chiefdom confederacy – by establishing a church and inauguration mound under the aegis of a chiefly lineage at that level. The same was attempted with alliances – the Éoganachta promulgated a common ritual center at Cashel and the associated concept of an *ard rí Caisiul* (high chieftain of Cashel). Though there is scant evidence for tangible central leadership of the Éoganacht alliance, and no evidence that Cashel was more than a ritual center, the institutionalization of the alliance was apparently successful in the short run in recruiting a large number of adherents so that, in the eighth century, not only was all of *Mumu* (Munster) carpeted by Éoganacht chiefdoms, but chiefdoms of the alliance – the Déis Tuaiscirt and Uí Fidgeinti – also felt free to attack former allies in Co. Clare. This was probably the primary benefit of joining an alliance: converting an enemy such as the Éoganacht Locha Léin into an ally freed up a chiefdom's military resources for offensive action against neighboring nonallied chiefdoms.

CHAPTER FOUR

An Early Medieval Chiefdom of Northern Clare: Archaeological Investigations

This section is concerned with the period preceding the advent of the Anglo-Normans in Co. Clare. The geographical focus here narrows as the Burren and environs in northwestern Co. Clare become the center of interest for detailed analyses. However, the disciplinary scope of the examination becomes much wider as the archaeological record, local ecology, and aspects of the ethnohistorical record come under scrutiny. It will eventually become clear that the Burren's geographical position at the periphery of both Thomond and Munster provides a unique vantage point for the elucidation of the social and cultural history of the province of Munster as a whole.

THE PHYSIOGRAPHY OF THE BURREN

When one conjures forth a mental image of an Irish landscape, it is not the Burren's physiography that typically comes to mind. Indeed, the Burren is a locale unique to Ireland given the striking juxtaposition of karst geology, the presence of rare species in the local plant communities, and the extensively preserved archaeological landscapes from various cultural periods. As the geology, climate, and plant communities of the Burren have had an impact on the past social and subsistence adaptations in this region, it is worthwhile to outline the relevant dimensions of the Burren's physiography. I will not bore the reader with a thorough recitation of the cultural history of the Burren here, much of which lies beyond the scope of this work. Rather, I will discuss the level of preservation of the archaeological remains in this locale and describe briefly the variety of monuments one encounters in the field from the different cultural periods.

The present-day visitor to the Burren is left with an impression of desolate solitude, as the panorama he or she is confronted with is largely treeless, consisting in the main of towering bare white limestone hills and cliffs. The descriptions of the Burren made by Edmond Ludlow, Cromwell's general who visited the region in 1651, and the semipoetic description of the area left by Mac Craith in *Caithréim Thoirdhealbhaigh* in the fourteenth century leave the reader with the impression that the Burren has remained physically unchanged over the last 500 years:

… he cast about to shift for himself and so took a precipitate eastward course to the skirts of the Burren, that is hoary and slippery with her crag. Over wide Burren's naked hills … (O'Grady 1929, 26:103)

In this guise they made their way in the edge-stoned huge-rocked rough-hilled land of Corc; through Burren's uncouth ways, narrow gaps, crooked passes, rugged boulders, and high sharp crests … (ibid.:115)

… of which it is said (of the Burren) that it is a country where there is not water enough to drown a man, wood enough to hang one, nor earth enough to bury him, which is last so scarce that the inhabitants steal it from each other, and yet their cattle are very fat, for the grass growing in turfs of earth of two or three foot square, that lie between the rocks, which are of limestone, is very sweet and nourishing. (Ludlow in Frost 1978:381)

However, this impression of geographical and ecological stability gives way under closer scrutiny. To begin with the more recent lines of evidence, photographs and drawings of the Burren's archaeological sites made in the course of the surveys carried out by T. J. Westropp and George Macnamara in the late nineteenth century show a landscape almost completely devoid of bushy or arboreal vegetation. Today, many of the same sites illustrated by these energetic scholars are covered by thick copses of hazel, sloe, blackthorn, and blackberry brambles rendering complete penetration of some of these areas impossible. Over the course of a century, a tremendous amount of regrowth has obviously occurred. The dramatic drop in the numbers of the Burren's inhabitants since the Famine, coupled with a switch to oil, gas, electricity, and turf purchased in the nearby towns, has relieved pressure on the local vegetation to supply the fuel needs of the region. The consequent regrowth of bushy scrub forced the farmers to use bulldozers to reclaim pasture land in the lower areas in the 1980s.

Recent geological and botanical studies in the Burren show changes of a similar or greater magnitude to have occurred in the prehistoric past. A pollen core from the turlough in the Carron Depression examined by Keith Crabtree revealed that prior to the clearance of vegetation by humans in the Late Neolithic, the Burren possessed a forest cover of pine trees with an undergrowth of hazel (1982:111). This forest cover would have required a more extensive soil cover than exists today (ibid.:112–113; Jones 1998:32).

The conclusion drawn from the pollen evidence that ancient forests once existed in the Burren has been corroborated by two independent lines of evidence. Soil profiles from two contexts have been examined by David Drew: deep fissures weathered into the surface of the limestone clint called grikes, and soil preserved underneath monuments of the Late Neolithic/Early Bronze Age periods (1982, 1983). In the former environment rich mineral soils were found that showed characteristics of having been deposited there subsequent to grike formation. The coring or excavation of chambered tombs of the Neolithic and Early Bronze Age, which are presently situated in areas of bare limestone pavement, were found to be resting upon a thin layer of rendzina mineral soil (Drew 1983:116–122). Moreover, a comparison of the configurations of solution marks, or karren, on protected and unprotected slabs in megalithic monuments demonstrated that the former had been covered by a soil covering prior to having been incorporated into the prehistoric structures (Drew 1983:122–123; Plunkett Dillon 1983).

The explanation for the prehistoric loss of soil in the Burren is rather straightforward. The loss of forest cover following clearance for agriculture resulted in a greater exposure of the soil to wind, desiccation, greater light intensities, and water run-off (Crabtree 1982:113; Mitchell 1976:138). The cumulative effect was that the increased run-off and changes in soil chemistry induced by the removal of vegetation promoted the erosion by solution of the underlying limestone bedrock. The thin soil cover was then simply washed down into the expanding grikes, hollows, and caves leaving the limestone clint exposed – a fact that further promoted bedrock erosion and changes in local hydrology, producing the austere landscape visible today (Drew 1982:115–119).

> The evidence from the preserved and colluviated soils and from karren morphology suggests that for at least part of the prehistoric period the Burren had an extensive cover of mineral soil, sufficient to support a tree-dominated vegetation cover. The loss of soil and consequent vegetation regression to the present-day plagioclimax of poor pasture probably occurred within a relatively short space of time during the latter part of the Bronze Age. (Drew 1983:124)

ARCHAEOLOGY

Clare's prominent position in Irish historiography and archaeology is due in no small part to the fact that so many prominent scholars hailed from the county. The well-known seventeenth-century scholar Dubaltach MacFirbisig received part of his training at the O'Davoren school at Cahermacnaghten. Other Claremen who have made important contributions to our understanding of the history and folklore of the area include Eugene O'Currey, Standish Hayes O'Grady, Thomas J. Westropp, George Macnamara, and John Hunt.

The Burren's archaeological monuments were first approached through several extensive surveys. The earliest systematic work was undertaken during the first half of the nineteenth century by the Ordnance Survey, upon which George Petrie, John O'Donovan, and Eugene O'Currey were at times engaged. The maps produced by this survey provided the basic site inventory from which all subsequent surveys have proceeded. The surveyors mapped the more visible of the archaeological sites. The Irish language scholars O'Donovan and later O'Currey recorded place-names, made detailed accounts of the folk and historical associations of archaeological and historic sites, and provided Anglicized versions of names for the maps (Herity and Eogan 1977:7–9).

Thomas J. Westropp and George Macnamara made up the second team of archaeological surveyors to work in the Burren. Westropp was an engineer by training and Macnamara was a physician. During the latter part of the nineteenth century and the first decades of the twentieth, Westropp surveyed almost every known archaeological site type in Clare, publishing them in several dozen papers and tracts. He was especially attracted to the Burren due to its richness of well-preserved sites, of which the cashel habitation sites of the Early Middle Ages were the most prominent. The archaeological term cashel refers to the still standing remains of the stone enclosing walls that encircled the yard and buildings of a habitation site. It is a rendering in English of the Irish word *caiseal* (Old Irish *caisel*), which is cognate with the Latin *castellum*. Locally, such sites are referred to by the Irish term *cathair*. This word forms a common prefix to the place-names of these sites, such as Cahercommaun, which originally was *Cathair Commáin* (Dwelling-place of Commáin). It is typical of place-names incorporating the *cathair* element that *cathair* is followed by a personal name. Westropp's publications included not only drawings and plans of multitudes of cashel sites, but also theories concerning their derivation.

Archaeological surveys undertaken in the decades following Westropp's work have been narrower in focus. Under the direction of Ruadhrí de Valera and Seán Ó Nualláin, the Megalithic Survey of Ireland has published a catalogue of all known Megalithic monuments in Clare (1961). The 1980s witnessed the debut in the Burren of systematic field surveys of archaeological remains. These surveys moved beyond the practice of recording sites in isolation. The geographer Emma Plunkett Dillon undertook a survey of the Burren's ancient field boundary walls, principally through the examination of preexisting aerial photographs (Plunkett Dillon 1985). Sinéad Ní Ghabhláin conducted a field survey of the ecclesiastical sites of Corcomroe and Burren Baronies (1995a, 1995b, 1996, 2006), and Carleton Jones and Christine Grant have undertaken intensive mapping projects of locales in the Burren possessing well-preserved field boundary walls, habitation sites, and chambered tombs (C. Grant 1995; Jones 1997, 1998; Jones and Walsh 1996).

THE EARLY MIDDLE AGES

This era's appearance of distinctiveness is due to the advent of Christianity in Ireland during the fourth to fifth centuries AD. Christianity established new avenues of communication between Ireland and the rest of Europe through which ideas and goods flowed. An accompaniment of the introduction of writing to Ireland was the Latin concept of the keeping of annals. Though record keeping in Ireland did not really commence in a big way until the eighth century AD, memories of many earlier events that had been maintained by a vigorous oral tradition were transcribed onto vellum at that time.

Medieval settlement remains are profuse in the Burren, and the architecture of these sites is preserved to the extent that on the larger Early Medieval period habitation sites, enclosure walls still stand to a height of over 2 meters. Further, the foundations of buildings inside enclosures can frequently be made out. Over the years, Irish archaeologists have developed a morphological typology of settlement types partially grounded in ethnohistorical references to sites. For that reason, the typology consists of Irish terms, and it may be helpful for the nonspecialist reader to briefly review the terminology, especially as it departs in some instances from the local vocabulary of Co. Clare.

The earthen equivalent of the cashels are termed raths. The original Irish word from which this is derived, *ráth*, has much the same connotation as the word *cathair*. Another Gaelic word describing the same sort of site, *lios*, is a more common component of place-names in the Burren. Linguistically, the word *ráth* refers to the enclosing earthen bank of the settlement, while the word *lios* refers to the habitation area so enclosed. The Cahercommaun Project, directed by the author, made a systematic survey of settlements of these types in the eastern portion of the Burren in 1984–1986 and 1993.

Crannogs are a third habitation site-type of the Late Iron Age. The word *crannóg* refers to a structure composed of wood. They are dwellings established upon artificial islands of brushwood in lakes or marshes. Scholars in the past have equated crannogs with rath-type settlements. Most crannog excavations have yielded rich artifact inventories and prolific evidence for specialized craft production, demonstrating that these sites were established by chieftains in the Early Middle Ages (Gibson 1982:chap. 5; Gibson 1988:54; O'Sullivan 1998:136–141). Due to the paucity of permanent bodies of water, very few sites of this type have been located in the Burren proper.

The last type of site deserving mention in this section are the ecclesiastical establishments. There are a number of different religious site-types of this period; including holy wells and burial grounds for unbaptized children called killeens (*cillín*). The two most substantial varieties of ecclesiastical site are monasteries (including abbeys and friaries) and churches. The structure of the ecclesiastical sphere of Irish life in northern Co. Clare has been the subject of several recent surveys (Mytum 1982; Ní Ghabhláin 1995b, 1996, 2006; Sheehan 1982).

THE MEDIEVAL PERIODS

Social and political aspects of Thomond during the Middle Ages will be discussed in Chapters 8 and 9. Here, I would like to make a few comments concerning the chronological terminology to be used in the remainder of this work. Beyond the failed establishments at Bunratty and Quin, the Anglo-Normans were never able to establish themselves as a lasting presence in Thomond. For this reason, modifications in the cultural history of the Burren probably took a gradual course. Evidence will be offered in subsequent chapters that cashels and raths continued to be constructed after the thirteenth century AD in the Burren. This should hardly be surprising, as it is certain that a few were inhabited up to the seventeenth century.

THE CAHERCOMMAUN PROJECT: THE STRATEGY OF RESEARCH

A principal assumption made by the Cahercommaun Project was that the tri-vallate cashel site Cahercommaun was the capital site of a chiefdom of unknown scale and internal structure. Authorship for this assumption must be properly attributed to Hugh O'Neill Hencken, who excavated the site under the auspices of the Third Harvard Archaeological Expedition in Ireland in 1934:

> In the early part of IX a chief of North Clare, whose name is not known from historical record, built a stone fort on the edge of a ravine four and a half miles north of the modern village of Corofin. In County Clare little stone forts are to be counted in thousands and most of them must have been mere homesteads … Cahercommaun, being one of the very few larger ones, presumably corresponded to a castle. (Hencken 1938:1)

As chiefdoms are social systems that are regional in scale, the program of research geared to revealing the organization and extent of the chiefdom polity associated with Cahercommaun would have to be regional in scope. The Cahercomaun Project, as originally conceived, was to consist largely of a systematic field survey including the mapping of known settlement sites of potential Early Medieval date. The survey was to be supplemented by test excavations and soundings to gather carbon samples by which a site chronology could be constructed. It transpired that the soundings and excavations that were undertaken were to be of only marginal significance to the project's goals. Therefore, the chief body of evidence for the resolution of this project's objectives was generated by the two-fold program of survey to be described later. Though additional survey and excavation would be desirable, the survey work so far accomplished has achieved much in the way of laying the groundwork for the interpretation of the Burren's Early Medieval social systems. Excavations that have been carried out in the Burren upon two cashels since the last time that the Cahercommaun Project formally took to the field in 1993 have provided valuable chronological data that have enabled a more precise seriation of the Burren's medieval aristocratic settlements (M. Fitzpatrick 2001; Comber and Hull 2010).

THE INTENSIVE SURVEY

A two-fold survey strategy was employed that encompassed three desiderata of the Cahercommaun Project. An initial goal of the project was to determine the extent of the Cahercommaun polity through the discrimination of its former boundaries within patterns in the distribution of Early Medieval settlements and field boundary walls. Among historical geographers, there is a long-standing supposition that the spaces between Irish chiefdoms were thinly populated waste areas of forest and bog (see Ó Riain 1972; Smythe 1982:26). This idea seems logical in light of the fact that chiefdom polities were frequently at war with one another and so would presumably wish to isolate themselves from neighboring polities with natural barriers. It was thought, then, that border areas of Irish chiefdoms might manifest themselves as areas where Early Medieval settlements and associated field boundary systems dropped off sharply in frequency.

In order to gather the relevant data, an intensive survey was undertaken of Early Medieval settlements and features that proceeded outward from the region's focal point, Cahercommaun. Unfortunately, it never proved possible to put the boundary effects hypothesis to a test, as the area that was intensively surveyed proved to be of insufficient extent to do so. This deficiency has been overcome in this study by an analysis of the relationships of the boundaries of historic territories, both secular and ecclesiastical, to Early Medieval settlement in the study region.

Secondly, it was desired to explore in detail the internal social organization of the Cahercommaun polity as manifested through its settlement remains. It was assumed at the outset that the social complexity of any polity would be reflected in the degree to which a polity was internally stratified, that is, in the number of levels of authority that existed within a chiefdom. Social stratification in turn would be expressed in rank-size differences between households as manifested in differences in the size and elaborateness of their settlements. Attaining this goal would entail gaining some idea of the variation in the size of Early Medieval households and the distribution of households with respect to the location of Cahercommaun. An intensive survey of the townlands within 3 km of this site was undertaken to meet the demands of this portion of the research program (Figure 4.1).

The third desideratum was to reconstruct the structure of the political system of Cahercommaun, and to gain some understanding of the place of this polity within the larger region of Thomond. It was assumed that large Early Medieval settlements would be the former residences of aristocratic families. The size of any one residence was held to correspond to the size of the labor pool an aristocrat would have mobilized to construct it. Labor in Early Medieval Ireland was mobilized though a system of clientship (Gerriets 1983; F. Kelly 1988:29–35; Patterson 1981). One would reasonably expect that, under these conditions, an aristocrat's status in the social hierarchy would be commensurate with the number of clients he could call upon to construct his residence. As the Irish aristocracy was internally stratified, the internal complexity of the Cahercommaun polity would be expressed in the rank-size variation exhibited by these residences.

To extend the above logic further, it is expected that the number and relative status ranking of the various chiefdom polities of northern Co. Clare

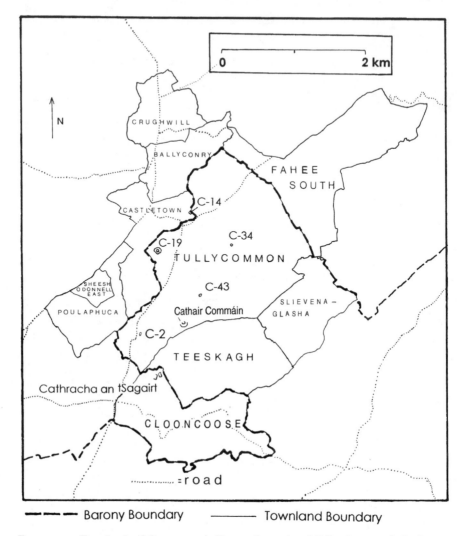

Figure 4.1. Townlands of Carran parish (Burren Barony) and Killinaboy parish (Inchiquin Barony) selected for intensive survey. The position of some cashels and enclosures are noted.

would be reflected in the relative size and distribution of their former chieftain's principal residences. In order to gain an understanding of the variation in the size of aristocratic residences, an extensive survey of the larger presumed Early Medieval settlements of the Burren and neighboring regions was undertaken (Figure 4.2). The sites were located on Ordnance Survey six-inch maps, and teams were then sent out to map the settlements and record details of their standing architecture. This extensive survey was expansive in design with no predetermined maximum limits. The limiting factor was the amount of time that could be devoted to this portion of the survey within the 1985 and 1986 field seasons (two weeks). Survey teams

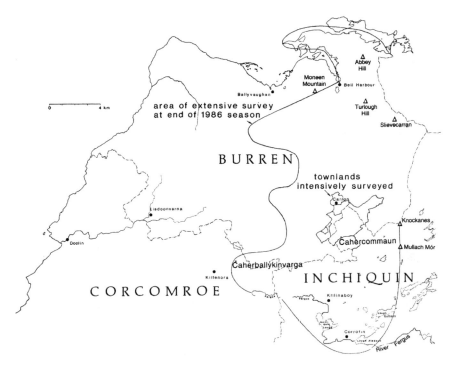

Figure 4.2. Northwestern Co. Clare, showing the extent of the area that had been extensively surveyed by the Cahercommaun Project by the end of 1986.

began by recording the settlements nearest to Cahercommaun and then proceeded to progressively map sites at a greater distance.

The social structure of the Cahercommaun polity would be expected to have dictated aspects of the organization of economic behavior, just as the economic adaptation of the local population would be expected to have influenced the kinds and sizes of social units in the region (Gibson 1988). Understanding the structure of the local economy through the study of archaeological remains related to subsistence was therefore another goal of the project. This aspect of the research program met with only limited success due to the fact that the two sites chosen for excavation by the project turned out to be prehistoric (Gibson 2004, 2008a).

Acting upon inspiration derived from Carole Crumley's project concerned with the Adeui polity of protohistorical Gaul (Crumley and Marquardt 1987), it was decided to adopt a survey design that did not establish predetermined boundaries to the study area. Since the approach adopted by the Cahercommaun Project had as its goal the detection of social boundaries, care was taken not to prejudge or obscure the location of these boundaries by establishing definite limits to the research area. Instead, a strategy of continuous expansion of the survey outward from the focal center, Cahercommaun, was adopted. The survey would commence in the fields near Cahercommaun and expand outward, hopefully taking in the boundaries of Cahercommaun's polity. The ultimate spatial limits of the survey would lie wherever the survey teams found themselves at the termination of the project.

Naturally, practical considerations dictated that the operation of the survey could not be completely open-ended, and indeed, the organization of survey work must be carried out under strict guidelines to ensure that survey teams record data uniformly and also to ensure that the study region is systematically covered. Each survey team was assigned to investigate blocks of territory with fixed boundaries. A characteristic of the historical geography of modern Ireland is the subdivision of the landscape into small territorial units of variable size called townlands. Within the Burren's townlands are fields defined by stone boundary walls. Indeed, the borders of townlands in northern Clare are also delimited by stone boundary walls, often of greater than usual height.[1] Given these preexisting territorial and physical demarcations of the landscape, it was decided to organize the operation of the survey utilizing townlands and fields as the basic spatial units.

The size of the study region and the complexity of the region's topography and archaeological record worked to preclude a total survey, and one might think then that some sort of sampling approach would be appropriate. However, there are strong factors that lessen the potential value of random sampling in the context of the Burren. First of all, all techniques of random sampling for survey known to the author (cf. Redman 1974) employ basic sampling units of standardized size and orientation. Uniform sampling units are necessary to ensure even coverage of the study region, preventing sample bias. The efficiency of field crews is increased when the sampling units are of uniform size and orientation. Sampling units of uniform size also place less of a burden on the statistician in that less effort is needed to generate a sample, and the areal coverage of the sample can be more easily calculated.

However, regions where random sampling techniques have been employed possess the qualities of being only loosely or nonuniformly compartmentalized by human activity. They are also regions where such land divisions such as field boundaries may exist, but have not been systematically printed on maps. Random sampling is thus valuable for imposing organization and regularity upon an environment that, from the scientist's perspective, is irregular and of uncertain dimensions.

Ireland's landscape is almost completely anthropogenic. In the Burren, all land, including mountains and barren expanses (with the exception of bogs), has been compartmentalized into fields by often substantial stone boundary walls. In Ireland, field boundaries, while not impervious to change, are not often modified and have been accurately and repeatedly mapped since the mid-nineteenth century. To impose an arbitrary survey sampling grid onto the preexisting field divisions of the Irish landscape has little practical value. Survey crews would be requested to clamber over innumerable walls, often to record only portions of fields.

The torturous Burren landscape, with its many cliffs, deep ravines, dense thickets, and high, rugged hills, poses additional complications to any survey employing a random sampling strategy. It was felt that much valuable time would be lost in tackling the physical challenges of the Burren's landscape under a strategy that did not acknowledge them. In this situation, a nonrandom approach utilizing preestablished survey units was selected. In the words of Zvelebil et al., "The practical benefits of using ... fields rather than arbitrary grids or transects are obvious since the Irish landscape is broken into landtracts that can be easily identified on the Ordnance Survey Maps" (1987:16).

Another prime consideration in devising a survey strategy is the physical dimension of the sites composing the archaeological record. Random sampling strategies are often favored in the study of the archaeological remains of hunters and gatherers and primitive horticulturalists, as the sites and settlements of these peoples are physical isolates. There are no roads or other man-made structures that connect them. In the British Isles it is now obvious that since the Neolithic period, settlements in many, if not most, areas, were often physically integrated into enormous complexes by expansive systems of fields and roads. These systems incorporated homesteads, fields, roads and droveways, ceremonial centers including burial monuments, and defensive features. I believe that it is difficult to comprehend a regionally integrated system by viewing its parts in isolation. This is especially true with respect to field systems. Field systems can reveal the extent of a regionally integrated community and give information on the structuring of the subsistence economy. One cannot hope to reap this harvest of information from small isolated segments of field systems.

I decided then to survey the fields within the selected townlands intensively and systematically in toto, recording all sites and field systems. Tullycommon townland was selected for survey as it contained Cahercommaun. The next two townlands closest to this site, Castletown to the northwest and Teeskagh to the southeast, were also chosen as a part of the initial area to be intensively surveyed (see Figure 4.1).

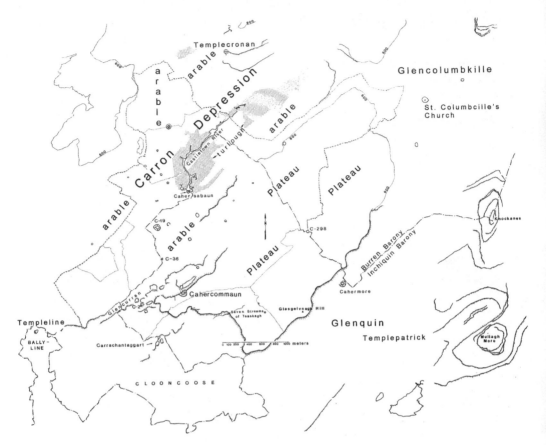

Figure 4.3. The townlands selected for intensive survey by the Cahercommaun Project, viewed against local topography.

These three townlands offer a good mixture of topography (see Figure 4.3). A high plateau is to be found in the southern and western portions of Tullycommon townland. This plateau extends into Teeskagh townland to the south, and to the west into the townlands of Slievenaglasha, Knockans Upper, Cappaghkennedy, and Fahee South. To the east, Tullycommon dips to take in Glencurran, a wild ravine, and the grassy eastern slopes and bottom of the Carron depression. In the north, the bare limestone of the depression's bottom gives way to the Carron turlough east of the Castletown River.

Castletown townland has an odd shape, making one suspect that other townlands have been cut from it or added onto it in the past. It covers the greatest part of the southern portion of the Carron depression, including the southernmost part of the Carron turlough (just north of the Castletown tower-house). The northern portion of Castletown contains arable land, while the southern part (to the south of the townland name

Figure 4.4. Clooncoose (*Cluain Cuais*) viewed from Teeskagh townland (photo: Blair Gibson).

on the map, Figure 4.1) has only scattered soil and much exposed bedrock. Interestingly, this latter area was covered by a dense network of abandoned field systems. Sadly, following the 1985 field season, these were cleared by bulldozer after only a portion of them had been surveyed.

Teeskagh townland is windswept and desolate in appearance. The portion of the plateau that lies within it is bisected by a semisubterranean stream, the "Seven Streams of Teeskagh," named for the number of waterfalls that appear after a good rain where the stream cascades over the edge of the plateau. This stream then flows to the west along the plateau's base. There is a spring near the Carrachantaggart enclosure immediately to the south of the townland border. The central and western portion of Teeskagh is a limestone shelf. The shelf is tilted, and is higher in elevation in the south. The southern townland boundary wall marks the point of demarcation between this shelf and the steep northern slope of Clooncoose (*Cluain Cuais* [the meadow of the hollow]), a narrow, steep-sided grassy valley (Figure 4.4). This southern higher portion of the shelf in Teeskagh is nearly devoid of any soil. By contrast, the portion of the shelf at the base of the plateau is covered with dense thickets. Up to the second half of this century this latter area was the sole focus of human habitation in this townland.

A favorable aspect of these three townlands from the project's perspective is that they are positioned astride the boundary between Inchiquin and Burren baronies (Figure 4.1). Teeskagh and Tullycommon townlands lay in Inchiquin Barony, and Castletown in Burren Barony. Political systems and social groupings often express themselves through the demarcation of land, and so it was important to gain some idea of the antiquity of County Clare's historical territorial divisions: the townlands, parishes, and baronies. It was hoped that the boundaries would reveal their age through patterns in the distribution of archaeological sites, and in the extent of the ancient field boundary walls associated with these.

THE INTENSIVE SURVEY: PROCEDURE AND RESULTS

The intensive survey was conducted over the span of four summers from 1984 to 1986, and 1993. Work was initiated with a pilot survey undertaken in August and September in 1984. With the assistance of a local boy, I surveyed a portion of the bottom of the Carron depression extending from Crughwill townland along the eastern side of the turlough proceeding south in the direction of Cahercommaun (see Figure 4.5). In this manner the central portion of the townland of Ballyconry was surveyed, taking in sloping arable land at the western side of the depression.

Full-scale survey operations commenced in the summer of 1985. Three survey teams were employed, each consisting of three persons and a crew chief. In Ireland all open soil areas are covered by a grass mat, making artifact scatters invisible to the naked eye. However, the rough and uneven terrain and the small size and slight remains of some sites such as clocháns (stone beehive huts), huts, and mound walls (prehistoric walls so eroded so that only a slight mound remains) demanded that the survey crew work as a compact unit. Crew members lined up and spaced themselves close enough to each other so as to be able to see clearly the ground surface between them. The intervals between crew members varied with the vegetation cover and the size of the field surveyed, but they were generally less than 10 m.

The survey of each townland was begun in the northwesternmost field. The crews surveyed townlands moving through strips of fields proceeding gradually south and east. Two standardized recording forms were used to record data: a site recording form and a wall architecture recording form for both the structural walls on sites and field boundary walls. On the site recording form the crews were asked to classify the sites and features encountered under a known Irish type (e.g., cashel), or form (e.g., hut

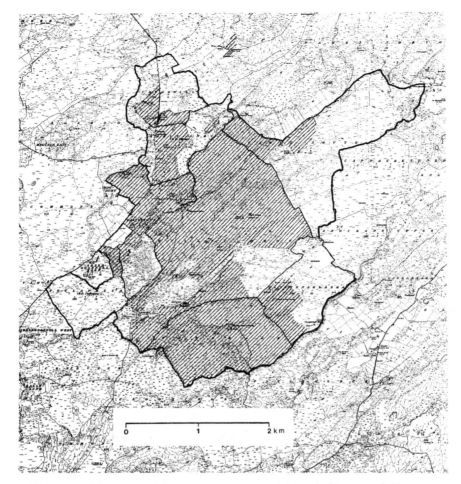

Figure 4.5. The extent of the intensive survey as of the end of the 1993 field season.

foundations), or to otherwise describe it. Late Neolithic and Early Bronze Age burial structures were not recorded in detail, and only the positions of cairns were noted.

The crews mapped each site that was encountered using a Brunton pocket transit mounted upon a tripod, and tapes. The surveyors prepared drawings of elevations of sections of the surviving architecture of the sites on separate forms. The layout of all field boundary walls and traces of field walls were recorded on field copies of sections of the Ordnance Survey maps showing the townlands, and elevations were made of a section of each field boundary wall that was encountered for purposes of determining whether chronologically sensitive stylistic changes in construction could be detected.

The survey did not proceed as quickly as hoped. Crews were hindered by three principal factors. The ruggedness of the terrain presented considerable difficulty. Crews were instructed to survey all of the land in their path, including large expanses of nearly impenetrable hazel thickets containing a profusion of three species of thorny plants. Even though each crew was supplied with machetes, they returned in the evening with clothing torn to shreds. The Carron turlough in Tullycommon also presented survey problems. It was difficult to gain a sure footing in the marshy sediments, and one crew chief nearly disappeared into a deceptively deep pool. Record rainfall marked both the 1985 and 1986 seasons, and many days were lost waiting out rainstorms. Finally, the survey crews encountered a tremendous profusion of sites and field boundary walls, roughly 300 of each. Often individual areas were very complex, containing a dense concentration of sites and field systems necessitating many days to record them.

Figure 4.5 shows the amount of land that had been intensively surveyed by the end of the 1993 field season. It was possible to completely survey all of Teeskagh townland; however, time did not permit the completion of the survey of Castletown and Tullycommon townlands. This was particularly unfortunate in the case of Castletown townland as the portion that was not completed was subsequently cleared by bulldozer. In addition to the initial three townlands that were selected for survey, small sections of Poulaphuca, Sheeshodonnell East, Fahee South, and Slievenaglasha townlands were also surveyed. They were surveyed for reasons as varied as proximity to routes of access to areas to be surveyed within the initial three townlands, confusion on the part of crew chiefs over the position of townland boundary walls, or the desire to record the continuation of field systems associated with a site lying within a selected townland.

THE EXTENSIVE SETTLEMENT SURVEY

It was perceived at the start that the intensive survey would not be capable of covering an area large enough to gather settlement data sufficient in quantity and diversity to allow insight into the structure of the regional political system of the Cahercommaun polity, let alone its place in the ancient political order of northern Clare. To judge from the fact that the only apparent rival chiefdom capital in the Burren, Caherballykinvarga, was located at a linear distance from Cahercommaun of nearly 8.5 km, it was thought likely that, at a minimum, the Cahercommaun polity would have encompassed a territory of over 50 sq. km. The initial goal for the first season of intensive survey was to cover an area with a diameter of 6 km, taking in 28 sq. km. The intensive survey would therefore not begin to approach the presumed boundaries of the polity for several seasons and, as it would eventually transpire, not at all. For this reason, a concurrent strategy of selective large settlement mapping was adopted. It was hoped that the rank-size distributions of these sites might alone inform on the degree of social stratification within the Cahercommaun chiefdom, and that the physical distribution of these sites would indicate roughly the location of political boundaries.

In essence, this aspect of the survey design only acknowledged and expanded upon the previous survey work carried out by the Ordnance Survey and T. J. Westropp. As a result of their efforts, the location and plain dimensions of many prehistoric sites were known prior to commencing work. Indeed, so thorough was the Ordnance Survey that probably every enclosed Early Medieval period site 30 m in diameter and larger can be assumed to have been recorded by them. It only remained to comb their maps and select the largest Early Medieval sites for data collection.

Crews visited these sites in order to map them and collect data on aspects of the sites not covered by the earlier surveys, such as the architecture of standing site enclosure walls and their thickness. The larger sites possessed substantial standing dry-stone architecture, and it was hoped that patterns in the style of construction of the walls of these settlements would allow for the creation of a seriation scheme for the cashels. Therefore, it was necessary to record a fair number of the walls of these settlements to allow statistical analyses to be undertaken.

The extensive survey was run somewhat like the intensive survey in that it proceeded outward from the core townlands centered upon Cahercommaun. Those large sites nearest to Cahercommaun were recorded first, followed by sites progressively farther away in all directions. As can be seen from Figure 4.5, the survey was carried as far north as Finavarra and Aughinish Island, and as far south as just beyond the southern bank of the Fergus River in Inchiquin Barony. The county boundary between Clare and Galway constituted the eastern boundary of the extensive survey region, and in the west, the survey was brought roughly and incompletely to an imaginary line running between the towns of Ballyvaughan in the north and Kilfenora in the south. This strategy was pursued with the most vigor during the 1985 field season. During the 1986 field season, the only sites that were mapped outside of the intensive survey area were those ecclesiastical sites immediately surrounding Cahercommaun. Only a few additional secular sites were mapped and these lay within the territory already covered in 1985.

CHAPTER FIVE

Reconstructing the Social Order of Irish Chiefdoms through Settlement

In the following two chapters, it is intended to examine patterns of settlement size, distribution, and morphology in the Burren in order to arrive at some conclusions about Irish social organization and political systems during the Early Middle Ages. A problem crops up immediately in that the Irish Early Middle Ages lasted for 800–900 years, a fact that makes discussion of change in aspects of the material culture of the period awkward. The problem is compounded by the fact that so much of the material culture of Early Medieval Ireland is notoriously difficult to date closely. Several archaeologists have offered schemes for subdividing the Early Middle Ages into phases for purposes of facilitating discussion of change in material culture. In the past, I have favored the chronological scheme of Brian Scott (1976), as its terminology lays stress on continuity with the preceding Iron Age (Iron Age I, IIa, IIb, IIc, IId). However, in the last two decades a consensus has emerged among scholars of the period to call the period that begins with the introduction of Christianity to Ireland and attendant appearance of written sources the Early Medieval period. Raghnall Ó Floinn, an expert on Early Medieval decorative metal objects, has offered a finer subdivision of the Early Medieval period into four phases (1999). However, his phases lack specific beginning and ending times (e.g., "EM3: Later seventh-eighth century") and do not reach to the end of the Early Middle Ages (1200 AD). Therefore, with a prayer that I do not make a bad situation even worse, I offer my own synthesis of Scott's and Floinn's systems:

Iron Age I   200 BC–200 AD
Iron Age II   200 AD–400 AD
Early Medieval I 400 AD–550 AD
Early Medieval II 550 AD–650 AD

Early Medieval III   650 AD–800 AD

Early Medieval IV   800 AD–1000 AD (Period of Viking Influence)

Early Medieval V   1000 AD–1200 AD (ends with Anglo-Norman invasion)

Medieval   1200 AD–1450 AD

Late Medieval   1450 AD–1600 AD

In subsequent discussion touching on chronology, I will be abbreviating the Early Medieval period as EMP.

SERIATING THE BURREN'S MEDIEVAL SETTLEMENTS

It is important that some idea be gained of the chronology of the Burren's settlements so that assessments made of the changing configurations of Early Medieval society in the Burren have some semblance of truth. A problem is presented insofar as only three of the Burren's many cashel sites, Cahercommaun (C-1, Figure 5.1), Caherconnell (C-66), and Cahermore in Ballyallaban townland (C-79; Figures 5.3, 5.4), have been excavated (Comber and Hull 2010; Fitzpatrick 2001; Hencken 1938). Fortunately, these excavated sites possess well-preserved standing stone architecture, and radiocarbon determinations show a good chronological spread between them. Caherconnell postdates Cahercommaun by at least a century, and Cahermore would seem to be younger than Cahercommaun by about 500 years. These sites will figure prominently in a technique to be explored in this chapter of dating medieval homesteads with stone enclosure walls using pattern recognition analysis.

CAHERCOMMAUN

It is proper to commence the exploration of the seriation problem with a chronological reassessment of Cahercommaun, which for years was the only Early Medieval settlement in the Burren to have been extensively excavated. Cahercommaun has an enclosed habitation area 30 m in diameter, defined by a wall that was still nearly 4 meters high and 9 meters wide at its thickest section at the time of excavation (see Figure 5.1). Two further substantial concentric walls surrounded this inner enclosure. Cahercommaun is situated at the edge of a ravine southwest of the Carron Depression on the southwestern projection of the plateau, which culminates at Glasgeivnagh Hill (see Figure 4.3). Due to its siting at a relatively high altitude at a location with great military defensive potential,

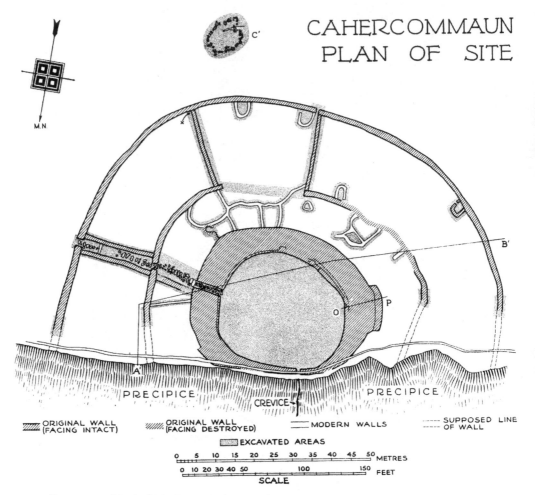

Figure 5.1. Hugh O'Neill Hencken's plan of the Cahercommaun cashel (Hencken 1938: Plate II; Reproduced by permission of the Royal Society of Antiquaries of Ireland ©).

Barry Raftery has classed Cahercommaun as a cliff-top hill-fort of his class IIb variety (sites with widely spaced, multivallate defenses, Raftery 1972:51–53).

The site was excavated during the months of July and August in 1934 by Hugh O'Neill Hencken of Harvard in what today would be considered to be an extremely short space of time, seven weeks, enabled by a large crew of thirty-seven laborers (Hencken 1938:3). In his day, Hencken was considered to be a meticulous excavator, though this perception may have been influenced by the standards of excavation technique current in Ireland that preceded him (Cotter 1999:64; O'Sullivan 1998:21). The proveniencing of the finds produced by the excavation left a lot to be desired. Most of the finds were reported without specific provenience, often being provenienced to a quarter of the enclosure's interior only. Occasionally,

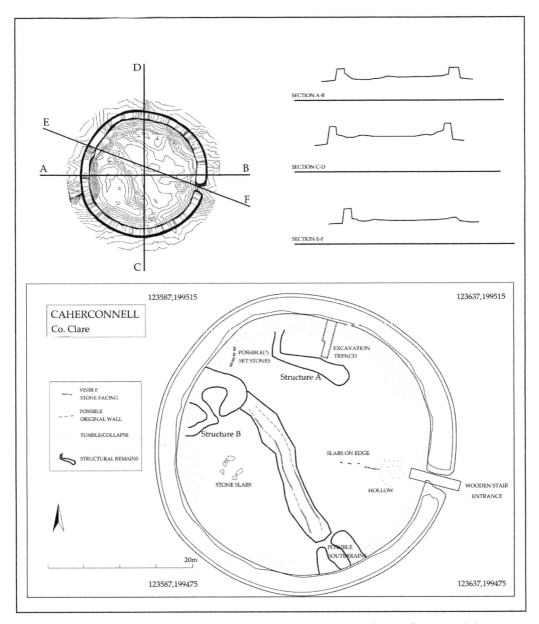

Figure 5.2. Plan of Caherconnell (Hull and Comber 2008. Fig. 2. Reproduced by permission of the Royal Irish Academy ©).

the provenience was narrowed down to a structure, and the description of the vertical provenience of an object was rare.

Though Hencken found a considerable depth of midden in the central enclosure, like most Early Medieval period habitation sites, Cahercommaun yielded only a few of the decorated objects, principally jewelry, normally used at the time to make a chronological assessment. Hencken anchored

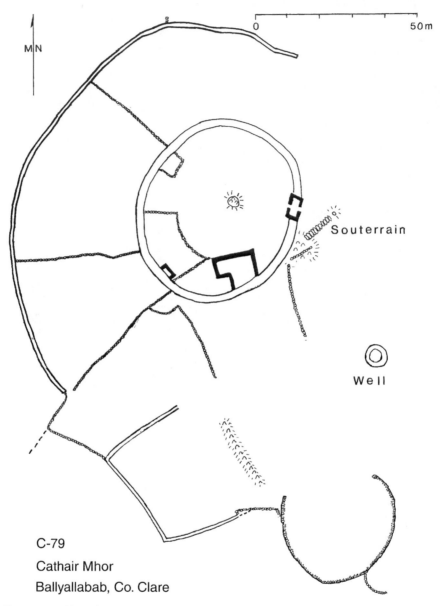

MN

0   50m

Souterrain

Well

C-79
Cathair Mhor
Ballyallabab, Co. Clare

Figure 5.3. Plan of the enclosure of C-79, Cahermore, Ballyallaban townland.

the occupation of Cahercommaun in the early part of the ninth century AD on the basis of a comparative analysis of the decoration of a silver brooch found at the bottom of a layer of ash and bone within souterrain B (1938:1, 27–30).[1] This is one of the few objects for which Hencken provided an exact provenience. In doing so, he downplayed the significance of some items of material culture that could indicate that the occupation of the site may have begun several centuries earlier (Ó Floinn 1999; Raftery 1972:51–53). These include a bronze brooch with zoomorphic terminals

Figure 5.4. Cahermore from the air. Note the other nearby enclosures (photo: J. K. S. St. Joseph; copyright reserved Cambridge University Collection of Aerial Photography).

(Hencken 1938:33–34, cat. no. 372), flint end scrapers (nos. 580, 767, 478), shale stone axes (nos. 364, 407, 445, & 564), keeled rubbing stones, and saddle querns (58–60). In his reappraisal of the jewelry assemblage from Cahercommaun, Raghnall Ó Floinn also added the iron penannular brooch (no. 72) and iron pins with looped heads to the list of pre-ninth-century objects (1999:74–75).

The zoomorphic bronze pennanular brooch is plain, with pronounced eyes, ears, and snout. In the scheme of the principal typologist of Irish brooches, H. E. Kilbride-Jones, this brooch would be considered an "initial form," and hence one of the earliest brooches of the series. In his corpus Kilbride-Jones dates brooches of this type to the third century AD (Kilbride-Jones 1937:410, 1980:67). Hencken is rightly critical of Kilbride-Jones's brooch chronology (Hencken 1938:33). Kilbride-Jones sought to tie the brooches to the presumed occupation span of the major Early Medieval political centers (1980:75–78) to the neglect of contrary evidence. Indeed, the Cahercommaun brooch is not mentioned in his 1980 corpus. Hencken interpreted the presence of this brooch at Cahercommaun as the final appearance of this brooch type in the Irish archaeological record (1938:34). Ó Floinn acknowledges the brooch's atypical aspects and surmises that it might date to the sixth or seventh century (1999:75).

Hencken cited the presence of rubbers like those found at Cahercommaun on English Early Iron Age sites, but determined that the mates for these rubbers, the saddle querns, were coeval with the rotary querns found at Cahercommaun on the basis of stratigraphic association (1938:58–60). He also noted that polished stone axes, though in use in Ireland from the Mesolithic to the Early Bronze Age, are commonly found on sites of the Early and Late Iron Age in Britain, and accepts the possibility of their use in later periods (55–57). Though the continued manufacture of polished stone axes in the Irish Early Medieval period cannot be discounted, recent excavation and survey carried out on the plateau in the neighborhood of Cahercommaun has shown that the site was established in proximity to a number of Early Bronze Age hamlets (Gibson 2004). It is therefore possible that the axes, flints, and saddle querns were picked up or dug out of these sites. The test excavation of a Late Neolithic/Early Bronze Age settlement located within 150 m of Cahercommaun, C-221, yielded a sizable number of fragments of sandstone querns and numerous small scrapers of black chert.

The body of the material assemblage recovered from Cahercommaun seems to fit Hencken's estimation of an early ninth-century placement for the settlement, though it is only loosely diagnostic in chronological terms. An iron axe-hammer was found (Hencken 1938:Fig. 31, no. 336) that is identical to specimens recovered from both Lagore (Hencken 1950:Fig. 40, A) and Lough Faughan crannogs (Collins 1955:Fig. 11, 71). Lagore has been dated to between the late seventh and late tenth centuries AD (Hencken 1950:6–7). The iron knives and rotary quern stones from Cahercommaun are of the pre-Norman variety (cf. Gibson 1982:104–105, 116–120). Glass beads and bracelets were also found at the site. These were in currency in the later first millennium AD. Finally, Andy Halpin has identified the "iron tool with small tang" (Hencken 1938:no. 728) as a tanged leaf-shaped arrowhead of ninth-century date or later (Cotter 1999:71).

To fix the placement of Cahercommaun more firmly in time, it was decided at the outset to attempt to obtain radiometric dates from some of the bone from the site that had been retained in the collections of the National Museum of Ireland. Hencken reports that 9,223 lb. of animal bones were excavated from within the cashel's inner enclosure (74–75). Naturally, it is not to be expected that all of this would be retained in the collection. However, a sample of bone from the site had been maintained in the Irish National Museum of Natural History, and permission was granted to subject a portion of these to radiocarbon dating.

Table 5.1. Radiocarbon Dates for the Burren's Cashels

Site and locus	Material number	Laboratory	Uncalibrated date	Calibrated date[a]
Cahercommaun (C-1)				
Unprovenienced	Bone: Bos Distal end of humerus	QL-4048	720 ± 70 AD	781 AD 681–886 AD
Unprovenienced	Bone: Bos Humerus	QL-4127	740 ± 120 AD	790 AD 670–970 AD
Caherconnell (C-66)				
Deposit 65	Animal bone Vertebra fragment	UBA-8564		1021 ± 32 AD 989–1027 AD one sigma
Deposit 62	Charred Hazelnut	UBA-8563		944±44 1029–1054, 1057– 1154 one sigma
Cahermore (C-79)				
"… directly below the gatehouse."	Scallop shell deposit	UB-4592		1308 AD

[a] References for datasets [and intervals] used: (Stuiver and Pearson 1986; Pearson et al. 1986).

A total of five bones of cattle were obtained, consisting of two complete metapodials, two humeri, and the proximal end of a femur. Unfortunately, the first and largest sample, a complete metapodial, was entrusted to a laboratory (UCLA) that proved to be untrustworthy due to faulty processing of the sample – the bone was destroyed for a date that had to be discarded. The second and third samples were sent to the radiocarbon laboratory at the University of Washington and they provided the dates displayed in Table 5.1. The amount of collagen present in the fourth and fifth samples was too small to be dated by conventional means. Though only two in number and from bones that lack precise provenience, the dates support the original determination of Hencken, placing some part of the occupation of Cahercommaun in the late eighth or early ninth century AD.

To summarize this review of the chronological evidence from Cahercommaun, modern assessments of the items of material culture recovered from Cahercommaun by this author and Claire Cotter et al. have not dramatically altered the initial assessment by Hugh Hencken that Cahercommaun was occupied in the late eighth and early ninth centuries AD. The radiocarbon dates from bone samples from the excavation lend support to this finding. It is likely that some, if not most, of the items of prehistoric material culture were picked up and reused by the cashel's occupants. Still, one cannot totally exclude the possibility that Cahercommaun was a focus for settlement prior to the eighth century AD, and additional radiocarbon tests on old samples from the original excavation, or on new material excavated from the base of the cliff, would probably reward the effort.

Caherconnell, in a townland of the same name, is a univallate cashel a portion of which has been excavated by a team led by Graham Hull and Michelle Comber. The presence of what appeared to be the remains of the walls of a structure with a rectangular outline (Structure A) suggested that the cashel postdated the Early Medieval period (Gibson 1990:253–254; Figure 5.2), Excavation has shown this building to be Late Medieval, but also that the cashel itself was constructed at the beginning of the eleventh century (Comber and Hull 2010).

The settlement complex at Cahermore in Ballyallaban townland is bisected by the modern route of the road from Ballyvaughan south to Leamaneh Castle. The road was moved to its present course in the late nineteenth century. Westropp observed the dismantling of portions of the archaeological remains at Cahermore for stone in 1898 when the road was put through the site (Westropp 1901a:284, 1915:269). However, it is still possible to make out the configurations of an impressive complex consisting of a bi-vallate cashel, attached rectangular enclosure, and two secondary cashels linked together by stone walls. The principal cashel possesses a building with rectangular, mortared foundations and a rectangular gatehouse, leading Westropp to conclude that the cashel belonged to the Late Middle Ages (1896b:150).

The complex at Cahermore was mapped by the Cahercommaun Project in 1985 and 1990. It was later surveyed by Martin Fitzpatrick and Kieron Goucher in 1995 and 1998–1999 on contract from Dúchas, The Heritage Service, and the gatehouse was excavated in 1999 in advance of stabilization and reconstruction work. The excavation recovered a seventeenth-century coin from a grike to the east of the entrance (Fitzpatrick 2001:53). The gatehouse was revealed to have been a later insertion into the earlier cashel wall. A radiocarbon date on shell from midden soil from underneath the gatehouse produced a date of "approximately 1308 AD" (Fitzpatrick 2001:53). The excavator estimated that the cashel was occupied from the fourteenth to as late as the seventeenth century (ibid.:57–58).

THE SERIATION OF THE BURREN'S CASHELS BY ARCHITECTURAL ANALYSIS

Cahercommaun, Caherconnell, and Cahermore are the only cashels from the Burren that can be dated with any degree of certitude. For the rest of the sites, we are forced to rely on two lines of evidence to estimate their ages: (1) chronologically diagnostic aspects of site morphology known from excavated sites elsewhere in Ireland, observable in the Burren's unexcavated sites, and (2) patterns of change in certain dimensions of site morphology amenable to techniques of relative seriation.

Commencing with site morphology, in the last three decades archaeologists have begun to realize the dating potential in the variation within the structural morphology of settlements of the Early Middle Ages (cf. Lynn 1978). So far, discussion of chronologically diagnostic aspects of site morphology has been restricted to the presence or absence of souterrains on sites (Cotter 1999:68; Gibson 1982:120–121), and to the ground plan of the internal structures (Gibson 1982:112–115; Lynn 1978, 1982). Souterrains are underground passages and chambers frequently found on Irish sites of this period. They are not terribly useful as chronological markers. Though found in Iron Age contexts in Great Britain and on the continent, the earliest radiocarbon dates from an Irish souterrain are from the sixth century AD (Power et al. 1997:281). On the scanty radiocarbon evidence, most would seem to have been built between the eighth and tenth centuries with their span of use, if not construction, extending into the Middle Ages (Clinton 2001:89–95). Within the long period of souterrain construction few chronologically diagnostic structural changes have been noted.

The ground plan of domestic structures seems to offer greater utility for settlement seriation. Houses of the EMP in Ireland were typically of wattle and thatch construction, though in the extreme west, foundations or walls of stone have been encountered. Prior to the advent of radiocarbon dating, houses with rectangular, subrectangular, and round ground plans had been found in excavations of settlements, sometimes on the same site. Since the artifact assemblage for this period was thought to exhibit little change over the centuries, no discernible chronological patterns of change in house form were detected. This situation began to change with the slow accumulation of excavations incorporating radiocarbon dates in their reports, so that a temporal sequence of changes to Irish EMP house form could be discerned.

It is evident that prior to the tenth century AD, the typical Early Medieval house was closely similar to the houses of the British Early Iron Age. That is, it was a circular post and wattle structure with a conical thatched roof. On an average rath site the principal house was placed near the center of the enclosure, sometimes accompanied by additional circular or rectangular buildings located along the enclosure's periphery. Evidence from the rath of Feerwore (Raftery 1944) and from the excavation of a cashel on

Aughinish Island (Eamonn Kelly, pers. comm.) shows this to be a pattern extending back into the Later Bronze Age, if not farther.

On some sites the predominant house form was subrectangular. Examples of this are Antiville, Co. Antrim (Waterman 1971); White Fort, Co. Down (Waterman 1956); Carraig Aille II, Co. Limerick (Ó Ríordáin 1949); and Leacanabuaile, Co. Kerry (Ó Ríordáin and Foy 1941).[2] Even though there are no radiocarbon dates for most of these sites, selected artifacts from some of them would tend to place them late in the EMP. A single radiocarbon date of 1050±120 AD from the subrectangular dwelling at White Fort, Drumaroad, Co. Down (Waterman 1971:75), calibrated to 1160 (1010–1260) AD (Stuiver and Pearson 1986), dates this dwelling to EMP V.

Several sites show clearly the transition from round to subrectangular forms (see Lynn 1978: Table 2 for a complete list). The earliest examples to be noted are the houses uncovered at Carrigillihy, Co. Cork, by O'Kelly (1951). Here, a subrectangular house nearly identical to the house at White Fort was found superimposed upon an oval house. A round house was found to have been succeeded by a rectangular house in a rath at Lisduggan North, Co. Cork, excavated in 1972 (Twohig 1990). More recently, excavation at the raised rath of Rathmullan in County Down has revealed a building with a rectangular ground plan clearly following a round wicker structure in stratigraphic succession (Lynn 1982). This rectangular structure was associated with a souterrain, where its predecessor was not. The rectangular building can be broadly dated to the tenth century AD on the basis of a radiocarbon date (1982:156, 1985:Table 1).

One need not go far to discover the impetus to the change in house form. Scandinavians were raiding and, what is of greater significance, establishing emporia along the Irish seaboard during the ninth and tenth centuries AD. County Down, in the north of Ireland, was particularly exposed to Norse contact, as its coastline is the closest point between England and Ireland, and so was an obvious stopping place along the sea route from Scandinavia to western England and eastern Ireland via Scotland and the Hebrides. Excavations of the Norse settlements in York and Dublin show the Vikings to have lived in smallish rectangular houses (cf. Gowen and Scally 1996; Ó Ríordáin 1971; Simpson 1999; Wallace 1992). No doubt, the Irish rectangular and subrectangular house forms represent the influence of Scandinavian settlers. They signify the beginning of a trend whereby subsequent developments in Irish domestic architecture such as moated sites, raised raths, castles, and tower-houses

Table 5.2. Larger Burren Cashel Sites with Visible House Foundations

Site no.	Type	Mean enclosure	Structure shape		Posited date
		Wall thickness[a]	Central	Peripheral	
C-1	Cashel	6.2 meters	Round	Rectangular	8th/9th
C-2	Cashel	3.1	Round		Early
C-19	Cashel	3	Rectangular?	Round	Late
C-34	Cashel	5.7	Round	Round	Early
C-66	Cashel	3.1		Round & rectangular	10th–11th/ 15th
C-69	Cashel	2.9	Round		Early
C-73	Cashel	3	Round?	Rectangular[b]	Early?
C-79	Cashel	2.5		Rectangular	14th
C-80	Cashel	4.4	Rectangular		Late
C-81	Cashel	—		Round	Early?
C-82	Cashel	6.2	Round	Rectangular	Early
C-93	Cashel	3.0		Round & rectangular?	Early?
C-111	Cashel?	—	Rectangular		Late
C-118	Cashel	2.5	Rectangular?		Late
C-298	Cashel	2.3	Round	Round	Early

Note: There are radiocarbon dates for cashels with numbers in bold type.
[a] Of the inner enclosure wall in the case of multivallate cashels.
[b] There is a large rectangular structure just *outside* the cashel wall.

occurred in Ireland on the heels of acculturative influences stemming from foreign contact.

In the context of archaeological survey, in any other region of Ireland except the Burren, knowledge of a change in house form in the tenth century would be of little use, as one must excavate to recover house floor plans. However, in the Burren, the foundations of domestic structures were often established in stone, and if the soil cover is thin enough, they are visible without excavation. Even in the valleys and soil-covered hill-slopes it is sometimes possible to trace the outline of buildings as a patch of darker-colored grass.

Table 5.2 lists those cashels thought to fall within the EMP with visible house foundations, and gives a relative estimate of their age. Here "early" means pre-tenth century, and "late" tenth century or later. For a number of sites with visible remnants of internal structures, it is often not possible to determine the original configurations of the building(s). These have not been listed. Also, on several sites, the outlines of both round and rectangular buildings could be seen. It is useful in this respect to make a distinction between *central* and *peripheral* structures, as those in the center are more likely to have been used for domestic habitation.

CAHERCOMMAUN
PLAN OF INTERIOR

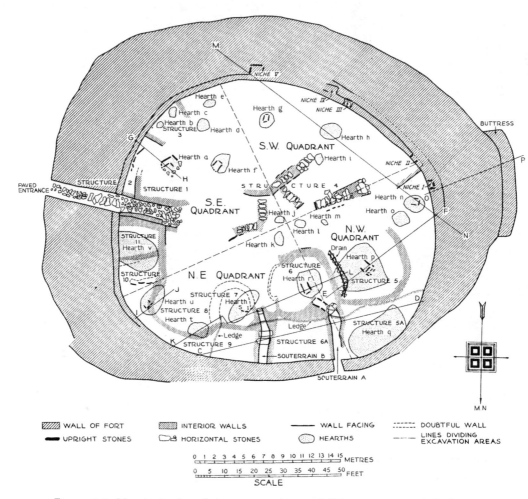

Figure 5.5. Hencken's plan of the inner enclosure of Cahercommaun cashel, showing features revealed by excavation (Hencken 1938: Plate VI; reproduced by permission of the Royal Society of Antiquaries of Ireland ©).

From Hencken's plan and description of the excavated central enclosure of Cahercommaun (Figure 5.5), it is possible to determine that the huts closest to the center of the enclosure, nos. 5 and 6, were "roughly round" in configuration (1938:20). Judging from the distribution of hearths and other interior features, structure 4 may have been circular as well, but no floor plan remained (1938:18). However, of the discernible foundations of structures placed up against the inner face of the central enclosure wall, the two buildings that displayed any coherent floor plan, 10 and 11, were definitely rectangular (1938:26). This pattern is mirrored in the plan of

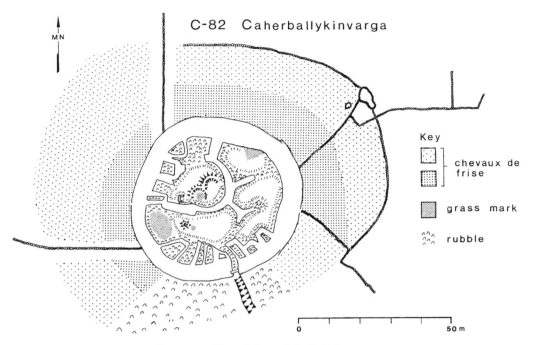

Figure 5.6. Plan of C-82, Caherballykinvarga.

the unexcavated interior of Caherballykinvarga (C-82, Figure 5.6). Both Westropp's plan and the plan made by the Cahercommaun Project imply that the central structures were circular, while the outlines of the foundations of the buildings against the wall of the central enclosure display angular corners.

A further complication is introduced by the fact that on some suspected late-period settlements, the most substantial structural remains are often located at the periphery of the enclosure. At C-66, Caherconnell, the wall foundations of a rectangular building along the northern interior section of the enclosure wall can be seen in large slabs that have been laid on end in a double row (Figure 5.2). This is an uncommon technique for Early Medieval domestic architecture, and excavation has now shown this structure to have been built between the fifteenth and seventeenth centuries AD (Hull and Comber 2008:Table 11; Comber and Hull 2010:158). An identical example of this building technique is exhibited by the foundations of a large quadrilateral building at C-80, Caherscreebeen. C-79, Cahermore, provides the strongest illustration of this trend. The mortar and stone foundations of a rectangular building, undoubtedly the principal dwelling, are at the southern periphery of the central enclosure and the cashel has been dated by radiocarbon to the fourteenth century AD (Fitzpatrick 2001).

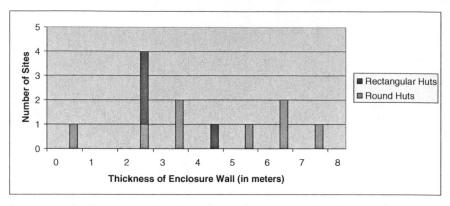

Figure 5.7. Graph comparing the shape of house foundations with enclosure wall thickness.

Another attribute of cashels that may have a chronologically diagnostic value is the thickness of the innermost enclosure walls. From an examination of the plans and features of the larger cashels surveyed by the project, it seemed that the walls of the cashels considered on architectural grounds to be later in date had thinner walls. The means of the thicknesses of inner enclosure walls were calculated where the circumstances of preservation permitted. These measurements were then segregated based upon the relative age estimates derived from the shape of the outline of buildings in the center of the cashel, and are presented in a stack-bar graph (Figure 5.7). Though the numbers of sites in the sample used in this procedure is small, the graph would seem to support the hypothesis of the enclosure walls of the Burren's cashels becoming progressively thinner over time. The three cashels for which there are radiocarbon dates buttress this conclusion, as the mean thickness of the inner enclosure wall diminishes progressively from 6.2–3.1–2.5 meters (Table 5.2). It also emerges that the walls of the "earlier" cashels are more variable in thickness than those of the "later" cashels. However, there are several other circumstances that may have influenced the thickness of an enclosure wall besides stylistic considerations.

Some cashels such as C-298, Mohernacartan, were established upon knolls, and the enclosure walls were built upon a slope as a consequence. At C-298, there was little effort made to establish an inner face to the enclosure wall, and so the cashel wall is thinner than it might have been if it had been built upon more level ground. However, a knoll-top location is not so easily reducible to a single effect. C-2 Cashlaungarr (Ir. *Caisleán Gearr*) and C-80 Caherscreebeen are also positioned upon knolls, and their walls are 3.1 and 4.4 m thick, respectively. The political status of a cashel was possibly a more significant variable. Caherballykinvarga C-82 was the political capital of a composite chiefdom, and so the greater thickness of its walls may be an outgrowth of the larger pool of labor that was available to the paramount chieftain. This may have also been the case with Cahercommaun. However, there is an example that runs counter to this reasoning. C-79 Cahermore was also the likely capital of a composite chiefdom and its enclosure wall is among the thinnest of the sample.

MEDIEVAL AND LATE MEDIEVAL PERIOD CASHELS

During the Tudor period (sixteenth century), tower-houses were the dwellings of the major and minor Gaelic aristocracy – the chieftains and leaders of aristocratic lineages. The common people apparently lived in hamlets in houses with a rectangular floor plan like the example excavated by Ó Ríordáin and Hunt at Caherguillamore, Co. Limerick (Ó Ríordáin and Hunt 1942). A hamlet that probably belonged to this period (C-18) was mapped by the Cahercommaun Project's survey. It is situated just a few hundred meters to the south of the tower-house at Castletown (C-169), and just north of the cashel C-19 (Figures 5.8; 5.9; Figure 5.25).

An interesting facet of this village was the fact that many of the homes had been erected within one or possibly two ruined cashel-like enclosures. Historical sources and archaeological remains indicate that cashels were still being occupied in the Burren into the sixteenth and seventeenth centuries. The best-known and documented example is the O'Davoren center and law school at Cahermacnaghten, mentioned in the previous section. Another obvious example is the site of Ballygannner (Baile Uí Dhanair) in the southern portion of Noughaval parish. This site consists of a tower-house occupying a portion of a cashel. The castle is mentioned in several of the Inchiquin manuscripts of the late seventeenth century (Ainsworth 1961:nos. 1120 & 1176), though there is no indication that it was occupied at the time. It was also not enumerated in a list of the Burren's castles of the late sixteenth century. However, Frost states that the castle does appear on the 1580 list, and that it was in possession of the O'Lochlainns (1978:29).

Only a few settlements potentially of the Late Medieval period were examined by the project, including Cahermore (C-79) (see Figure 5.3). C-111 in Teeskagh townland is another potential example of a Late Medieval settlement (Figure 5.10). The project's surveyor described it as a hill-fort, while the local landowner called it "the castle." Both descriptions seem to apply, though on a humble scale. The site occupies a low prominence in the townland. A modern field wall, XXII, transverses and circumscribes this site. The surveyor was certain that this field wall lay on

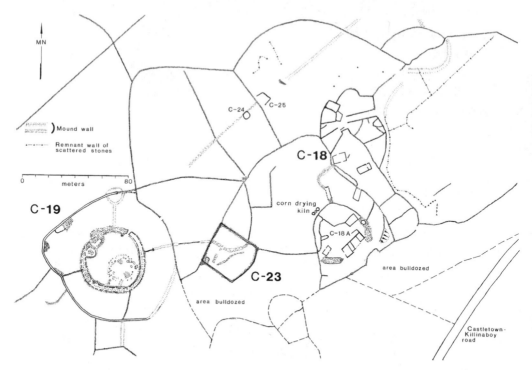

Figure 5.8. Plan of a multicomponent area of archaeological remains in Tullycommon townland.

top of the rubble of an earlier enclosure wall. Inside the site were copious remains of human occupation, including intact portions of the walls of one, if not two, rectangular buildings. The wall of one building still stood to a height of 1.3 meters.

SERIATION BY PATTERN RECOGNITION ANALYSIS OF CASHEL WALL ARCHITECTURE

Another avenue for determining the relative ages of the Burren's cashels lies in the patterns of stone size, shape, and placement within the façades of their enclosure walls. Generally, the enclosure walls of cashels are constructed of an inner and outer face of stacked slabs and chinking stones that retain a stone rubble core. The hypothesis to be explored here is that at any given point in time, there were stylistic norms that guided how the slabs were shaped by the masons and how they arranged them within the outer façade of cashel enclosure walls. If this hypothesis is true, then the possibility exists that there also may have been uniform style changes in slab shaping and arrangement over time that could serve as a tool in settlement seriation.

Figure 5.9. Aerial photo of site C-19 (bivallate cashel) and associated archaeological remains in Tullycommon townland (photo: J. K. S St. Joseph; copyright reserved Cambridge University Collection of Aerial Photography).

The inspiration to look upon patterns of stone arrangement in the walls of buildings as a potential relative dating technique came from another cultural region where the construction of settlements in stone was typical, the aboriginal American Southwest. Since the 1930s, investigators working at Chaco Canyon, New Mexico, have recognized that there are various distinctive patterns in the arrangement of stones within the walls of the enormous pueblo-type buildings there. Dendrochronology dates from the wooden roof support beams (*vigas*) of the rooms within these pueblos

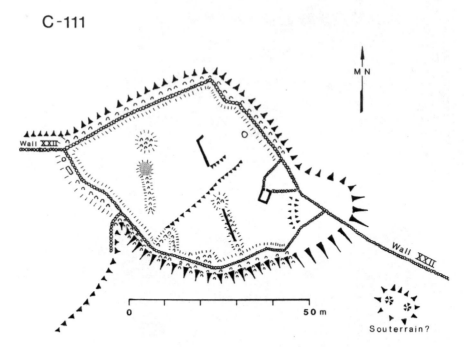

Figure 5.10. C-111, Teeskagh townland.

provided dates for these wall-building styles, and showed them to be uniform for a given period across different pueblos. The stone arrangement styles could then be used independently to date constructional sequences at different pueblos (Lekson 1984).

While pointing the way to the utility of pattern recognition analysis as a means of seriating stone architecture, architectural studies at Chaco Canyon have not established any particular technique for the identification of patterns in stone wall construction. The styles were recognized simply through the perceptiveness of the investigators who described them in words and drawings. This is fine where ancient building styles exhibit great distinctiveness. However, it cannot be expected that all stylistic variation in stone walls can be distinguished solely by eye, especially when not much care was taken by the masons in dressing the stones. A rigorous study was undertaken of stylistic patterning in the architecture of Byzantine brick buildings and architectural fragments in Anatolia (Mitchell et al. 1982). The periods of construction of many important Byzantine buildings were known through historical sources, but there were also a number of structures and architectural fragments of unknown date. The goal of the study was to see if styles in the patterns of the brickwork of walls of Byzantine buildings and structural fragments could be established so that unknown buildings could be related to known structures, and so arranged in a chronological sequence.

The study of Mitchell et al. utilized discriminant analysis to achieve this goal. Byzantine architecture provides an ideal setting for the application of this particular statistical technique, for most methods of discriminant analysis require predetermined classes into which the data are likely to fall as a result of the application of the procedure. In this instance, the building dates of many churches and other civic buildings were known beforehand, so chronological classes could be established against which various variables were evaluated as to their ability to discriminate between walls of different periods. Radiocarbon dates were available for only a single cashel at the time this seriation study was first undertaken, so it was not possible to apply discriminant analysis. Now that there are three dated cashels with considerable chronological separation between them, it may be possible to attempt an analysis along these lines.

Whereas the walls of the Chaco Canyon pueblos are of stone bonded with adobe, and the bricks of Byzantine church walls are bonded with mortar, the walls of the Burren's cashels are entirely of dry-wall construction. Slabs of limestone bedrock were pried up and roughly dressed for this purpose. Given this somewhat more casual approach to wall construction, there was naturally some apprehension as to whether pattern recognition techniques would work. Other considerations also shed doubt upon the outcome. Local differences in the physical characteristics of the limestone rock might influence stone shape to a degree exceeding the variation attributable to human agency. For this reason, it was considered important to consider the geographical dimension of the variation within the distribution of building styles in order to see if buildings from the same local area showed stylistic homogeneity or heterogeneity.

The data for this test were collected as a part of the Cahercommaun settlement survey. Volunteers were instructed to make drawings with uniform dimensions of the walls of any structure with extant standing architecture that they encountered. There was uncertainty at the outset as to how large a section of wall should be sampled. Initially, crews were given instructions to draw stones within a column 50 cm wide and up to 4 meters high. It was discovered part way through the first field season that the *mean* length of stones in the lower levels of many structures exceeded 50 cm, and so the width of the column was increased to a meter. There was not sufficient time to send crews or individuals back to re-record all of the walls planned with a 50 cm column, and these data are consequently of marginal use. However, the walls of a few key sites were re-recorded in 1990. During the 1986 field season, a 2 x 2 meter sample planning column was used. When the collected data were subjected to analysis subsequent to the fieldwork, the conclusion was reached that for cashel sites a sampling column 2 meters wide was the minimum area that could be expected to yield a sample of stonework that would be reasonably representative of the wall as a whole. Smaller stones were disproportionately represented in narrower columns as the larger stones were often truncated. Still, even a sampling column 2 meters wide often yielded a sample size of fewer than ten stones. To obtain the most representative sample, a recording column 2.5–3 meters wide would have been optimum.

Initially, photography was not required in this particular study, as there were concerns about the effects of distortion and about the reliability of, and consistency between, individual photographers. For instance, a photographer might not shoot directly straight toward the wall face every time, and individual shots might be ruined for a number of environmental reasons. The experiences in the field largely justified these concerns. Lighting conditions changed rapidly and rainy squalls were frequent, causing periodic camera failure and detrimentally affecting many individual shots. Cashel walls were often built upon steep slopes, forcing the cameraman to tilt the camera upward to take in the entire height of wall, introducing substantial vertical distortion. The sheer height of some surviving walls alone introduced substantial vertical distortion. Further problems were caused by the use of black and white film. In a dry-stone wall, stones project outward from the face and others are recessed, and so these are masked by shadow. This is especially true for chinking stones, which tend to disappear in the photos. There are many sizable fissures and cracks in limestone that has been exposed to the elements for up to 1,000 years, making it difficult to distinguish between individual stones in photographs. Moss, bushes, and grass add to these problems.

Though crews were not asked to photograph wall sections, in a number of cases, photos accompanied the drawings, and despite initial trepidations, these proved to be an invaluable resource for checking the accuracy and representativeness of the drawings. The drawings were conversely helpful in estimating the amount and kinds of distortion in the photos. Optimally, photos and sketches should be used together, one serving as a check or guide to the other. The photographer should also be given specific training and instructions on the way in which walls are to be photographed. This will not eliminate distortion, but training may at least ensure consistency.

THE PROCEDURE AND RESULTS OF
WALL-STYLE ANALYSIS

The procedure utilized in the test was largely patterned after the study of Mitchell et al. (1982). Naturally, the conditions of the test were somewhat altered, as the potential variation in stone patterning within a single dry-stone wall could be expected to exceed that of a mortared brick wall. The kinds of variation one would expect in a dry-stone wall fall into three categories:

1. Variation in the vertical and horizontal dimensions of the slabs or blocks within a wall sample. Included in this category of variation is variation in the mean dimensions of building stones between vertical sections of a single sampling column.
2. Variation in the sizes and numbers of chinking stones that were used relative to the major building stones.
3. Variation in the degree to which the stones have been dressed. This third variable was not examined in this study.

The sample recording column was divided into one-meter-high sections. Each stone was numbered on the drawings/photos and then two dimensions were measured: the maximum horizontal length, and the maximum vertical thickness. In the case of truncated stones in the drawings or photos, the nontruncated dimension was recorded only if it was fairly certain that the dimension recorded was indeed shown at its maximum (this was easy to ascertain with respect to length in the case of stones resting in the soil, often difficult with stones cut off on the sides). To resolve the problem of stones that fell between two vertical sections, a horizontal line was established 10 cm below the section junction. All stones intercepting or touching it were recorded in the lower sample frame. Those stones above the line and clear of it were included in the next higher sampling section.

Photographs were trickier to use for the reason, stated previously, that substantial vertical distortion was introduced by high sloping walls. The distortion was corrected by estimating the photographer's distance from the wall when he or she made the shot, and estimating the angle at which the camera was tilted. This involved taking a camera outdoors, finding a wall with the ground sloping away from it, marking the height of the prehistoric wall on the modern wall, and then pacing away from the wall while viewing it through the camera lens until the distance was reached where the wall's image filled the lens to a degree equal to the original photo. In a future study, this exercise could be eliminated by marking on a recording form the distance from the wall at which the photo was made.

THE RESULTS OF THE WALL-STYLE EXAMINATION

The superficial impression that one comes away with upon viewing the building stones used in the medieval structures of the Burren is that, in the main, they were simply rough slabs of limestone that had been pried up from the underlying bedrock and then heaved straight away onto the growing stack of a wall's façade. However, as the following analysis will reveal, the slabs were produced and dressed more systematically than this. Moreover, the guiding hand of master builders, who appear from time to time in the Irish laws, will become apparent in the stonework of the larger and more complex building projects.

Though not as massive as the largest cashels, the ecclesiastical establishments of Early Medieval Ireland placed the greatest demands on the skills of stonemasons. In contrast to the dry-stone technique of building the walls of the cashels, mortar was employed in the construction of churches and the various structures found at monasteries. The stones used in ecclesiastical buildings such as oratories and churches were dressed to a high degree, resulting in a tight fit between stones. Ornamental stonework was employed around doorways and windows, and stone sculptures, often in the form of human heads, were placed in the walls beginning in the twelfth century.

Ecclesiastical settlement in the diocese of Kilfenora (which includes Corcomroe and Burren baronies) has been the subject of a survey conducted by Sinéad Ní Ghabhláin (1995a, 1995b, 1996, 2006), and there have been other earlier surveys reaching back to Westropp (1900). Most of the stone churches and chapels of the Burren that were studied by Ní Ghabhláin are presumed on architectural grounds to be Medieval period or Late Medieval period in date (see Leask 1955:53; Ní Ghabhláin 1995:82–83; Westropp 1900:130–135).

Ní Ghabhláin has recently published her seriation analysis of the churches of the diocese of Kilfenora. Her methodology was similar to the methodology used here but departs from it in some significant aspects. She gathered data on the length and thickness of the building stones within a 2 x 2 meter sample section of a church's wall, or walls if it seemed that the building had undergone multiple building phases. She then looked for clusters in the data and applied tests of association that resulted in the isolation of three masonry styles. These three styles were thought to succeed each other in time though they have not been tightly dated. Style 1 includes examples of cyclopean architecture – large thin slabs laid on their narrow sides with a rubble infill, such as found at the church at the monastic site of Oughtmama: Oughtmama 1. This style was held to date to the Early Medieval period. The presence of Romanesque decorative elements allowed Ní Ghabhláin to assign buildings of Style 2 to the twelfth or early thirteenth century, whereas Style 3 was adjudged to be Later Medieval (Ní Ghabhláin 2006:152–154).

Two churches near Cahercommaun, Temple Cronan (C-70, Anglicization of Teampall Chrónáin) located 3.5 km NNE of Cahercommaun.and Templeline (C-72) situated 2.3km WSW of Cahercommaun, fell within her masonry Style 2 class. Ní Ghabhláin, echoing O'Keeffe, states that the present church at Temple Cronan was rebuilt in the twelfth century, reusing large stones from an earlier church that were mixed with smaller stones (2006:164; O'Keeffe 1991). A doorway inserted into the south wall is an alteration of the fifteenth century, showing continued use of this building up to this century (Jones 2004:138). These are the only ecclesiastical sites located in proximity to the project's intensive survey region to have been surveyed by the Cahercommaun Project. Both were churches that were at the heart of complexes of fields and the ruins of structures.

Elevations were drawn of sections of the preserved walls of the churches at Templeline and Temple Cronan, and these were also photographed. Though a team was not sent to record the monastic site at Oughtmama (*Ucht Máma*) 11.6 km NNW of Cahercommaun, Harold G. Leask surveyed the site and published elevations of several structures there in his corpus of ecclesiastical buildings (1955). Stonework data were extracted from a 6 m-wide section of an elevation of a wall of the western church (Oughtmama 1, in Ní Ghabhláin 2006, 1958:Fig. 26).

The means of the length and thickness of the stones in the walls of the churches at these three sites are plotted in Figure 5.11. Even without a regression line, it is clear that the means of the variables of stone size show a linear distribution, though it is easy to overstate the significance of this with only three sites in the sample. Is it possible that the regression line describes a trend of increasing or decreasing stone size through time? A close dating of medieval ecclesiastical stone buildings is highly problematic given the typically long period of use of these structures, dotted with episodes of remodeling and rebuilding. If the trend in slab size in church architecture progressed in the same direction as that which will be evidenced in domestic architecture, with slabs becoming larger rather than smaller over time, Templeline would be the earlier site.

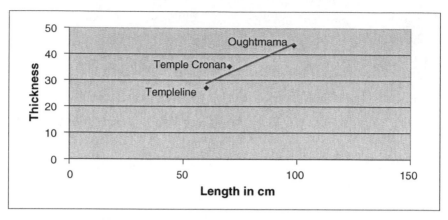

Figure 5.11. Regression graph of the dimensions of stones within the walls of three ecclesiastical buildings found within the survey area.

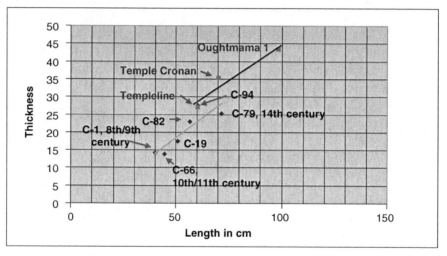

Figure 5.12. Comparison of mean stone dimensions: cashels and churches. Cashels are indicated by diamonds, churches by squares.

If Templeline had been constructed in the twelfth century, assuming a linear trend of change in stone shape commensurate with the trend that will be put forward for the cashels, Temple Cronan would have been constructed some time after the fourteenth century AD (Figure 5.10). This date would be not only at variance with the Romanesque elements of the church, thought to be of the twelfth century, but of the architectural elements that are held to be even older, such as the sealed lintelled west doorway.

From her data, Ní Ghabhláin argues that the trend in church architecture is the reverse of what will be proposed here for the cashels – builders started out in the Early Medieval period using the cyclopean technique, which over time degenerated to a more haphazard style of mixed large and small stones in the twelfth and thirteenth centuries, to then give way to walls built exclusively of small stones in the later Middle Ages. If true, then the parallelism and overlap in dimensions of stones used in secular and religious buildings, displayed in Figure 5.10, is coincidental, or a reflection of two classes of builders influenced by each other's efforts, arriving eventually at a common style from opposite directions. Troublesome to this view of things is the fact that cyclopean construction is seen not only in a number of the Style 2 buildings such as Temple Cronan, but in at least one Style 3 building as well (Jones 2004:132; Ní Ghabhláin 2006:165–166). Radiocarbon dating of churches of cyclopean construction and with flat-lintelled doorways on the Aran Islands shows them to have been erected in the twelfth century AD (Berger 1995:165–166). Therefore, one should not exclude the possibility that the Temple Cronan and Oughtmama 1 churches were built in the Medieval period.

Even though the regression lines are roughly parallel for the two classes of structures, this fact may not reflect exact chronological parallelism, especially if Ní Ghabhláin is right about chronology of her masonry styles. The only means to judge the calibration of the two classes of sites at present is by obtaining material by which the churches can be independently dated.

SERIATION OF THE BURREN'S CASHELS BY PATTERN RECOGNITION ANALYSIS

In Figure 5.13, markers representing the means of length and thickness of the stones making up the 0–100 cm level of the façades of the enclosure walls of all the cashels of the sample are shown. A regression line has been calculated for this distribution. The correlation coefficient is not terribly high, and there is a significant amount of variation, especially in the thickness dimension. However, focusing on the three cashels for which there are dates (C-1, C-66, C-79), a linear trend may be evident. The marker for the oldest dated cashel, Cahercommaun, is in the lower left position within the scatter, and the marker for the youngest cashel, C-79, is both higher and to the right within the scatter. Therefore, with the passage of time, the stones making up the lower portion of the outer façade of a cashel wall might have become longer and thicker. The marker for C-66, however, is only slightly to the right of that for Cahercommaun, which does not falsify the assumption of a linear chronological change in stone dimensions, but it does seem to indicate that the rate of change was not gradual, but rather discontinuous. Another potential problem for this approach crops

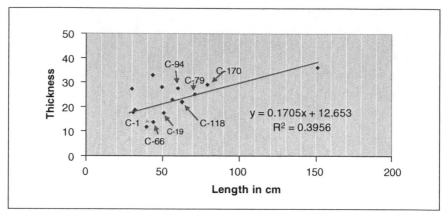

Figure 5.13. Regression of mean stone dimensions 0–100 cm. The marker for Cahercommaun is the triangle to the right of the label.

up when one notes that the marker for cashel C-170 is to the right of that of C-79, indicating that it is potentially younger than C-79. A wall associated with the cashel but at a distance from the inhabited enclosure was excavated in 1985, and a radiocarbon determination made on bone found underneath the wall centered on the late ninth century AD (Gibson 2008a:19). If this date was associated with the cashel, it would make it 500 years older than C-79, but the context cannot be reliably linked to the cashel itself. C-170 belongs to the smallest class of cashels to be encountered by the Cahercommaun Project's survey, and was probably built and inhabited by a nuclear family of commoners. As the inhabitants supplied their own labor, it is not likely that a master mason such as guided the construction of chieftain's residences was involved. To see if this is potentially true, it is worthwhile to sort the cashel database into classes reflecting the social status of the inhabitants.

These classes are chiefdom capitals, the presumed residences of the chieftains of composite chiefdoms, section capitals, the seats of the leaders of the various major ramages making up the maximal ramage, and the homesteads of lineage leaders and commoners. These site classes will be discussed at length in a subsequent section, but suffice it to say at this juncture that they are distinguished by the mean external diameter of the outermost enclosure wall (Table 5.3).

Figure 5.14 presents the data sorted into the four site classes with a regression line that has been calculated for the chiefdom capital sites only. The slope of the regression line that has been fit onto the data in Figure 5.11 is less steep than that for the capital sites alone, which stems from the elimination of the greater variation found in the stonework of the

Table 5.3. Enclosure Wall Diameter Ranges for the Burren's Early Medieval Settlement Classes

Site class	Range of mean external wall diameters
Capital sites	126–92.5 m
Section capitals	80–40 m
Lineage leaders	39–30 m
Commoner homesteads	27–10 m

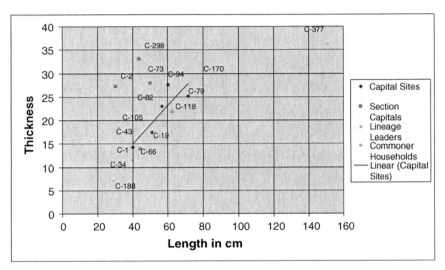

Figure 5.14. Cashel mean stone dimensions. 0–100 cm. The cashel sample sorted into four social classes, with a regression line fit onto the data from chiefdom capital sites.

other cashel classes. Oddly enough, the greatest spread is found within the section capital class. For instance, the lower courses of the enclosure wall of C-298, a univallate cashel located a little over 2 km to the northeast of Cahercommaun on the same plateau, were composed of slabs that were twice as thick. The same is true for C-2, Caisleán Gearr, only 700 m distant from Cahercommaun. Could these sites' location on rocky prominences have been a factor? Another explanation is that, in the earlier periods, the lesser nobility within a chiefdom did not often employ the same master builders employed by the chieftain.

The sample size of cashels with walls that can be sampled at the 100–200 cm level is smaller (N = 13) than the sample at 0–100 cm (N = 17), and becomes restricted almost exclusively to cashels of the chiefdom and section capital classes. When plotted, the data show a correlation coefficient of .04 and a regression line with only a slight slope (Figure 5.15). Obviously, much less care went into the masonry at the higher levels of cashel wall façades, with differences in stone thickness flattening out. The positions

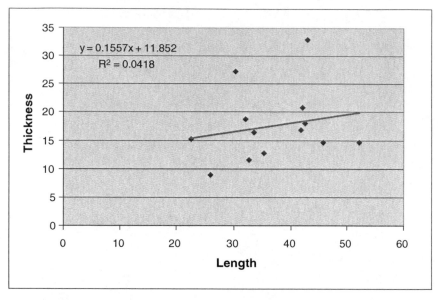

$y = 0.1557x + 11.852$
$R^2 = 0.0418$

Figure 5.15. Mean cashel stone dimensions: 100–200 cm. Regression graph of the means of the dimensions stones within the central enclosure walls of a sample of the cashels of the study region at the 100–200 cm elevation.

of the cashels in respect to the regression line are only very roughly preserved from the previous scatterplot.

CHINKING STONES

Chinking stones (or "spalls" in Ní Ghabhláin 2006) are small stones used by the builders of both cashels and churches to fill in gaps between the always irregularly shaped building stones, or to level them. The bar graphs show the lengths of all stones in cashel wall samples and illustrate the relative proportions of chinking stones to major stones in the walls (see Figures 5.16–5.17). Chinking stones seem to consistently average about 11 cm in length, though the range in size variation does seem to expand slightly with the passing of time. The proportions of stones deemed to be chinking stones of the cashels from which these data could be recorded are listed in Table 5.4. Assuming C-1 to be representative of the earlier cashels in this group, and C-118 and C-79 to be younger cashels because of the presence of houses with a rectangular ground plans at these sites, there would seem to be a weak temporal shift toward the use of a higher proportion of chinking stones in the walls of the cashels with the passage of time. The sites deemed to be early due to the presence of structures with a round ground plan average 27.2% chinking stones in the 0–100 cm level,

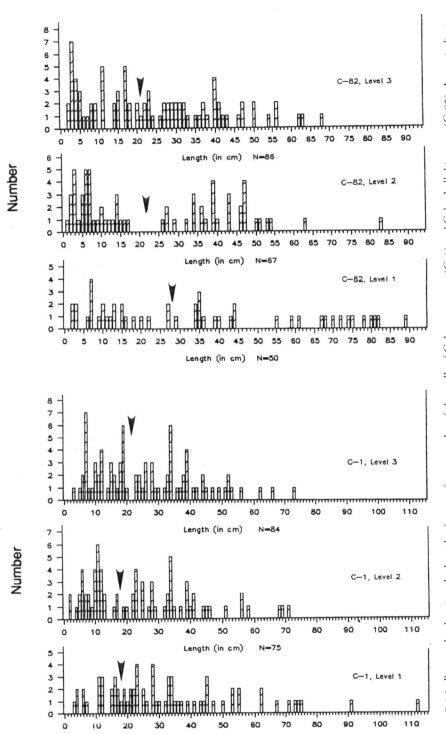

Figure 5.16. Bar graphs showing the length of stones from samples of the walls of Cahercommaun (C-1) and Caherballykinvarga (C-82). Arrow indicates demarcation between chinking and building stones.

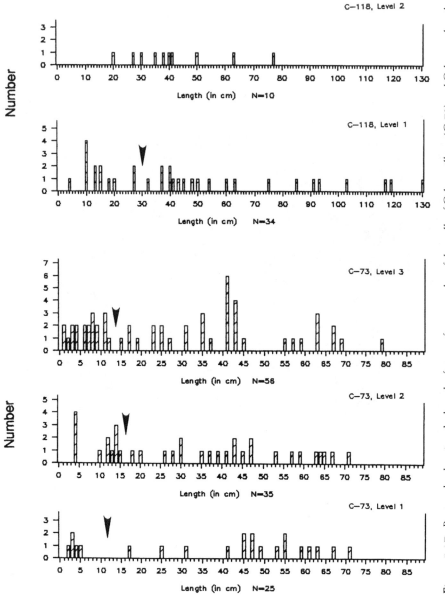

Figure 5.17. Bar graphs showing the length of stones from samples of the walls of Cahergrillaun (C-73) and Cahermackerrila (C-118). The arrow indicates the demarcation between chinking and building stones.

Table 5.4. Percentage of Chinking Stones in Cashel Enclosure Walls

Site		Level	% Chinking stones	Sample size	Date (est.)
C-1	Cahercommaun	1	28	72	8th/9th cent.
"		2	40	75	
"		3	42	53	
C-2	Caisleán Gearr	1	29	21	
		2	32	22	
		3	50	30	
C-19		1	18	3	I
C-66	Caherconnell	1	44	43	10th/11th cent.
"		2	69	88	
"		3	59	152	
C-73	Cahergrillaun	1	28	25	
"		2	38	33	
C-79	Cahermore	1	54	13	14th cent.
		2	47	32	
C-82	Caherballykinvarga	1	46	50	I
"		2	51	67	
C-94	Cahermore	1	59	37	
"		2	69	131	
C-118	Cahermackerrila	1	34	35	L
Small cashels					
C-43	Cahereenmoyle	1	24	21	
C-298	Mohernacartan	1	8	24	
"		2	14	21	

I = intermediate in date; L = late in date.

while those cashels deemed to be late average 37.5% chinking stones in their walls.

In Figure 5.18, these data are plotted on an xy graph using building stone length as the independent variable and the percentage of chinking stones in the 0–100 cm level as the dependent variable. As expected, the correlation coefficient between these two variables is not especially high at .358, and the correspondence with the previous results from the examination of building stone length and thickness is not strong. C-1, C-2, and C-43 are at the low end of the regression line, fulfilling the prediction of the hypothesis of lower frequencies of these stones at earlier cashels, and C-94 and C-79 are at the uppermost end of the regression line. Some differences with the building stone scatterplot are personified by C-82 Caherballykinvarga, which has the third highest frequency of chinking stones in its wall, and C-19, with the second lowest frequency of chinking stones, though this might be due to the degree to which the wall of this site has been ruined. To conclude, chronological trends seem to be present

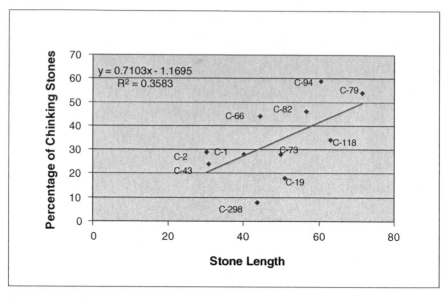

Figure 5.18. Regression comparison of the percentage of chinking stones in cashel enclosure walls against mean stone length at the 0–100 cm elevation.

in the chinking stone data; however, the percentage of chinking stones in a cashel wall is probably not a consistent indicator of age.

INNER ENCLOSURE WALL THICKNESS

Cahercommaun differs markedly from Cahermore and every other cashel site in the Burren in the thickness of its inner enclosure wall (Table 5.5). Obviously, just for defensive purposes, it is not necessary to erect a wall that is over six meters thick in a context where cannon are lacking. The wall's thickness is likewise superfluous to provide a windbreak. Its significance must therefore lie in the social need to display prestige, possibly as a way of demonstrating control over a sizable labor force. The thickness of the inner enclosure wall can be taken, then, as a reflex of the position of a cashel's occupants in the region's social hierarchy. Table 5.5 lends support to this theory, as the cashel with the second thickest inner enclosure wall in the sample is C-82 Caherballykinvarga, presumed to have been the capital of the composite chiefdom of the Corcu MoDruad.

Variation in enclosure wall thickness alone cannot have any temporal significance. Figure 5.19 demonstrates this fact, showing what seems to be a general progression toward thinner enclosure walls as time, represented by lengthening building stones, progresses. However, the overall correlation between these variables is weak. In order to determine whether or not this variable does possess chronologically sensitive variation, one

Table 5.5. Wall Thickness of Cashels

Site	μ Wall thickness at the base (in meters)		
C-1	6.2	C-82	5.75
C-2	3.4	C-94	3
C-19	3	C-105	.95
C-34	5.7	C-118	2
C-43	3.4	C-170	1.6
C-66	3.1	C-188	"thin"
C-69	2.9	C-298	2.3
C-73	3	C-360	1.25
C-79	2.5	C-377	.7
C-80	4.4		

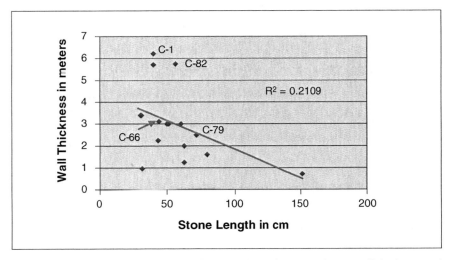

Figure 5.19. Regression comparison of the variables of inner enclosure wall thickness and stone length within a sample of the study region's cashels.

has to sort the cashels into the categories of social rank discussed above: chiefdom capitals, section capitals, etc. Building stone length will again function in this test as the dependent variable, and cashel wall thickness as the independent variable. Before proceeding further, however, a caveat of the analysis should be brought up. Optimally, one would like to calculate the mean of the thickness of a cashel's wall from measurements taken in a minimum of four places due to the substantial variation in thickness that cashel walls exhibit. Cahercommaun is a case in point, as the range of thickness in its inner enclosure wall ranges from 1.2 to 9 meters due to its cliff-edge siting and the erection of a buttress against the wall to the east. It is probably an extreme example; however, since these cashels have stood where they were built for up to 1,000 years or more, their walls are ruined

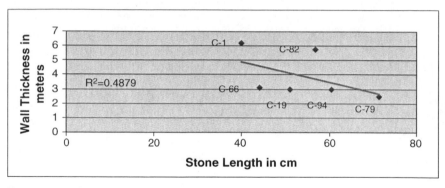

Figure 5.20. Regression comparison of the variables of wall thickness and stone length restricted to the chiefdom capital sites and Caherconnell.

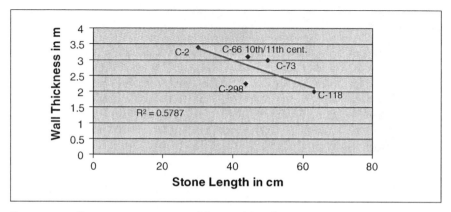

Figure 5.21. Regression comparison of the variables of mean stone length and thickness at the 0–100 cm elevation of the enclosure walls of the study region's section capitals.

to varying degrees. Therefore, multiple measurements of the walls of some sites were not possible.

Taking chiefdom capital sites first, the slope of the regression line is not as steep as that for all cashels taken together, and the correlation coefficient is much stronger (Figure 5.20). Both graphs show a distinction between a small group of cashels with very thick walls and those with enclosure walls that range between 3.2 and 2.5 meters in thickness. In both groups there seems to be a trend of increasing stone length and declining wall thickness over the 500 years between Cahercommaun and Cahermore.

The correlation coefficient is slightly stronger for the relationship between stone length and enclosure wall thickness for the section capitals, as there is no separate class of cashels with significantly thick enclosure walls in this group (Figure 5.21). One would predict that C-2 Caisleán Gearr, a cashel near Cahercommaun, would be the oldest cashel within this class and it does have the thickest enclosure wall, but its wall is not markedly thicker

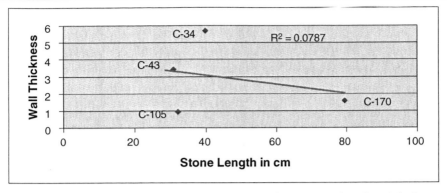

Figure 5.22. Regression comparison of the variables of mean stone length and thickness at the 0–100 cm elevation of the enclosure walls of homesteads thought to have belonged to lineage leaders.

than those of either C-66, Caherconnell, or C-73 Cahergrillaun. C-298, Mohernacartan, which is not far from Cahercommaun, has an unusually thin enclosure wall – a reflection of the fact that the wall lacks an internal facing. C-118, Cahermackerrila, as expected from other indications, seems to be the latest site in the sample. One comes away with the overall impression that section capital sites conform to the trends in construction noted in the walls of the chiefdom capitals. It is, therefore, quite possible that the owners of these cashels also engaged master builders to oversee the construction of the enclosure walls of the cashels of this class.

The thickness of the enclosure walls of homesteads presumed to have been occupied by the leaders of lineages is so variable as to show no correlation with building stone length (Figure 5.22). Given the outcomes of the above two tests, this result was to be expected, as the walls of these homesteads were most likely constructed by the members of the lineage without the input of a master mason or builder. Another factor to consider, however, is that two of the sites in this category may belong to an earlier period. Apart from a similarity in diameter, a common characteristic of sites of this class is that they are situated close to commoners' homesteads, but are not linked to them physically. When I visited C-105 and C-188, I suspected from their appearance that they might be pre-ninth century in date, and C-188 would be the oldest site on the building stone length and thickness regression line and would predate Cahercommaun if the norms of wall building that have been extrapolated for the aristocratic residences applied to settlements of this class. It differs most strongly from the other EMP III cashels in the thinness of its enclosure walls and building stones. C-34 tests closest to Cahercommaun on the stone size scatterplot and also has the thickest enclosure wall of sites of this class, similar in thickness to Cahercommaun and Caherballykinvarga.

COMMONERS' RESIDENCES

There are only two commoners' residences, C-360 and C-377, in the architecture sample, though in retrospect I am grateful to have any at all. Through three seasons of survey by the Cahercommaun Project, sites of this class were unrecognized as such, chiefly due to the fact that their remains are so slight that they were apparently easily destroyed or overbuilt. It was only during the 1993 field season that two reasonably intact commoners' residences were encountered that had not been subsequently overbuilt with later field boundary walls. Their discovery allowed a number of similar sites to be retroactively recognized among the ruined field systems surrounding Cahercommaun that were surveyed in 1985 and 1986.

The enclosure walls around commoners' residences are slight and were apparently not built with great care – the surviving portion of the wall that survives around C-377 consisted solely of large long slabs of limestone bedrock roughly stacked upon each other to a single stone's thickness. The wall of C-360 was little better than a haphazard jumble of irregularly shaped slabs and stones. No more than the labor of a single household was mobilized to build walls of this sort. One's concerns would be legitimate, then, especially given the sample size, that the stylistic attributes considered in this analysis would apply to the sites of this class.

Looking at the attributes of stone length and thickness, C-360 would appear to be a late site, given the almost perfect overlap of its stone size means with those of the consistently late site of C-118. C-360 is located on the Glasgeivnagh plateau 1.15 km distant from Cahercommaun – close enough that its field boundary wall systems interact with those emanating directly from Cahercommaun. Though the field boundary wall data are difficult to interpret, they also indicate that C-360 was established on the plateau at a later date.

C-377 would appear to be in a class by itself by virtue of the enormously long and thick slabs that make up its enclosure wall. However, the lower courses of the enclosure wall of another cashel of the section capital class, C-69 in Poulanine townland, have the same character. Only the two lowest courses remained of the portion of the wall that was sampled, and it was sampled using the 50 cm wide column. However, of the three stones that fell within this column, one was 193 cm long, and the other was 190 cm long. The average thickness of the three stones was 43 cm, which would make them the thickest stones in the cashel sample but nearly equal in thickness to the stones in Oughtmama 1.

If C-377 and C-69 are not aberrant examples, then, there is the question of where they fit in chronologically. Traces of central huts were noted at both sites, and in both cases they were circular – pointing to an Early Medieval date.

SUMMARY: RESULTS OF THE EXAMINATION OF CASHEL WALL STYLE

This study of patterning in the construction of the walls of cashel-type sites of the Burren has demonstrated that norms of stone preparation and arrangement existed, even though the walls are entirely lacking in mortar. Two crosscutting factors are probably responsible for the variation in two attributes of style so far examined in this study, the shape of the major stone blocks and the proportion of blocks to chinking stones. These factors are the passage of time on the one hand, and the size class of site on the other.

Of all the variables considered so far, building stone length, internal structure shape and enclosure wall thickness have yielded results that seem consistent across the sample of settlements. Building stone thickness and the percentage of chinking stones proved to be less reliable predictors of a structure's age. Following upon the tests that have been carried out, a rough chronological scheme is offered below in Table 5.6 for the cashel walls that have been analyzed.

It may come as a revelation to some archaeologists that the cashel remained popular as a settlement type in the Burren well into the Middle Ages, though it really should not. Medieval period features such as mortar-built buildings (e.g., the rectangular house and gatehouse at C-79 Cahermore) had been published and commented upon by Westropp in the late nineteenth century, and cashel-like enclosure walls surround some tower-houses in the Burren and on the Aran Islands.

There is no firm evidence from the Burren that any of the churches predate the earliest cashels, and ample evidence from the Burren that the construction of dry stone enclosure walls around dwellings extends back to the Bronze Age and beyond (Jones 1998, 2004:60–61). Therefore, it is tempting to see the techniques that had been applied to the foundations of the cashel's walls being extended to the walls of churches. The hypothesis that elements of architectural style in stonework were transferred across site types is strengthened when one considers the one aspect of style not treated here so far, the degree to which the stones are dressed. The church buildings show an almost Inka-like attention to the shape of the stones

Table 5.6. Seriation Scheme for the Burren's Cashels

Early Medieval II 550–650 AD

Site		Estimated date	Basis for estimation
C-105		7th century?[a]	Stone length & thickness, enclosure dimensions

Early Medieval III 650–800 AD

C-1	Cahercommaun	8th century	**Radiocarbon dates**
C-2	Caisleán Gearr	8th century	Stone length, chinking stones, wall thickness
C-34		8th century	Length/thickness, wall thickness
C-43	Cahereenmoyle	8th century	Length/thickness, chinking stones, wall thickness
C-188		8th century?	Stone length & thickness, enclosure dimensions, proximity to C-1

Early Medieval IV 800 AD–1000 AD

Site		Estimated date	Basis for estimation
C-170		9th century?	Radiocarbon date, upland location
C-298	Mohernacartan	9th century	Stone length, internal structure shape
C-66	Caherconnell	10th century	Radiocarbon date, length/thickness, chinking stones, wall thickness
C-360		10th century?	Hut shape, stone length, thickness

Early Medieval V 1000 AD–1200 AD

Site		Estimated date	Basis for estimation
C-19		11th century	Length/thickness, rectangular structure, wall thickness
C-73	Cahergrillaun	11th century	Length/thickness, rectangular structure, wall thickness
C-82	Caherballykinvarga	11th century	Length/thickness, wall thickness
C-118	Cahermackerrila	12th century	Length/thickness, rectangular structure, chinking stones, wall thickness
C-94	Cahermore	12th century	Length/thickness, chinking stones, wall thickness

Medieval 1200 AD–1450 AD

Site	Estimated date		
C-79A & B	Cahermore	13th/14th century	Radiocarbon date, length/thickness, rectangular structure,
C-66	Caherconnell	15th century	Radiocarbon date (reoccupation)

[a] A question mark indicates that the attribution of a site to a time period is little more than a guess.

and their fit. The sides and ends of each individual slab were squared to a considerable extent before these were added to the wall, though perfect rectilinearity was not sought. A block was selected and shaped to fit snugly among its neighbors in the walls. Like the churches, the walls of the Later Medieval cashels consist of thick long slabs with squared ends. By contrast, in the walls of Early Medieval cashels the slabs are shorter, thinner, and the slab ends are only roughly dressed. It has to be borne in mind, however, that churches differ greatly from cashels in the shape of the buildings, use of mortar, the orientation of the facing slabs in the wall, the continuance of fine construction all the way to the top of the walls, and the practice of ornamental stone carving. Excavation of church structures will have to be undertaken with the objective of seriating them before the question of the stylistic relationships between them and the cashels can be investigated.

Master builders, as are mentioned in the law texts, were involved in the construction of church structures: "viz. a stone church and a wooden oratory. He (the master builder) receives twelve cows for these i.e. six cows for each and there is taken into account his superintendence over the other art from these out ..." (gloss, *Uraicecht Becc, ALII* II:95).

Master builders were also probably employed in the construction of the residences of aristocrats, though some sites that have been classified as section capitals, such as Mohernacartan (C-298), show idiosyncratic features more in line with a lineage leader's residence and should perhaps be classified as such despite their greater circumference. The lineage leaders and the commoner occupants of the smallest cashels would seem to have relied entirely on the labor and skills available within their family.

FITTING MEDIEVAL IRISH SOCIETY ONTO THE SETTLEMENT DATA

Chiefdoms are internally stratified social systems. The various constituent social units of chiefdoms, ranging in scale from individuals, households, lineage segments, and the sections themselves, are ranked. More information concerning the factors that generate social ranking can be gained through an examination of ethnographic and ethnohistorical sources than through a perusal of archaeological materials, no matter how profuse these latter may be. However, archaeological settlement data from prehistoric or protohistorical chiefdoms can be expected to reflect the degree to which a chiefdom was stratified. Simply put, the more medieval domestic settlements are found to vary with regard to size, complexity, and details of their layout, the more stratified one would expect the chiefdom to have been. One hopes that given a large enough sample of prehistoric settlements from a specific region, the sites would sort themselves into classes of size and morphology, and that these settlement classes would in turn reflect the tiers in the internal social order of a protohistoric chiefdom. The Burren region provides an optimal setting to put these assumptions to a test, as chiefdoms are known from the historical sources to have existed in the region.

Medieval Irish chiefdoms possessed capitals, and the analysis of historical materials reveals that the seats of chieftains can be identified by their central spatial position within the chiefdom territory, and by the spatial proximity of ritual and religious sites near the principal homestead of the chieftain – all sites together constituting the capital set (Gibson 1995). It remains to be seen just how Early Medieval Irish chiefdom capitals are physically distinguished from other contemporary settlements, and whether the same sorts of spatial relationships that were observed to exist between capital sites and subsidiary settlements of chiefdoms in the Late Medieval period in Co. Clare also obtained in the Early Medieval periods (Gibson 2001). It will be of considerable interest to see whether a capital set can be identified in the archaeological remains of the Burren, and, if so, just what its elements were in the earlier period.

THE DETERMINANTS OF SETTLEMENT SIZE

At the outset, one would expect that the size of a settlement would correspond to two variables: (1) the number of inhabitants and (2) the social prominence of the principal occupant. It is entirely possible in a society in which, from a jural perspective, a lineage is the most important corporate group, that households could be composed of multiple nuclear families, especially if the prevailing subsistence strategy was agropastoralism (Gibson 1988). However, it is certain that the variable of household constitution will be crosscut by considerations of the social status of the principal occupant. An aristocrat's residence can be expected to be larger irrespective of the size of his household due to his need to communicate his status through ostentatious display (Earle 1987:291). An aristocrat would be able to draw upon a larger than usual pool of labor to this end (Arnold and Ford 1980:716).

Cashel sites, and raths to a lesser degree, are often imposing sites that required considerable labor for their construction. There is evidence in the law texts that indicates that one of the obligations of a client to his aristocratic patron was to assist in the construction of his residence. That section of the *Senchus Mór* entitled *Cáin tSóerraith*, the section detailing the contractual obligations between patrons and *saer* clients, begins:

Cáin tSaorraith cid ara neiparenar?

Cia measom do cain tsaorraith

Manchuine ocus ureige.

The Law of *Saerraith*, what is said of it?

What is the worst (condition) of the Law of Saerraith?

Manual labor and homage.

This text is accompanied by a gloss. The following section is relevant to this discussion:

Manchuine, .i. fer cacha somhuine, do derumh a dúine, no a meithle, .i. an dún, no asluaighedh lais, ocus ní feghtur fris turcluide im manchuine.

Manual labor, that is, a man for all services, to the making of his *dún* (the capital site of a chieftain), or of his working party, that is, the *dún*, or his hosting with him, and he does not contemplate an exchange of *turchluide* for manual labor.[3] (*ALII* 2:194–195)

The sense of these passages is that from an early period (eighth century AD), a *saer* client was expected to supply labor to the patron on a periodic basis as a part of his clientship obligation. The later gloss specifies the construction of a chieftain's residence as a task for which the labor obligations were invoked (see also F. Kelly 1988:30). Though *Cáin Aigillne*, the law tract dealing with the inferior *daer* class clients, makes no specific allusion to obligations to assist in the construction of the patron's residence, it does frequently refer to the *daer* client's obligation to perform unspecified *somaíne* (services) for the patron as a part of his contract. It may be assumed from these passages, then, that the labor pool of aristocratic patrons was larger than that of households farther down the social scale. Therefore, the size of a residence was linked to the social rank of its occupants, irrespective of household size.

Another factor to be taken into consideration when looking at the size of Early Medieval Irish homesteads is the strong possibility that the labor for settlement construction was drawn from the extended kin relations of the occupants. In the Middle Ages, Irish polities were composed of lineages. The basic Irish Early Medieval corporate kin unit was the *derbfine*, consisting of the male descendants of a common great-grandfather (Charles-Edwards 1972:15–17, 1993; Mac Niocaill 1972:49–50; Patterson 1994).[4] This was the precursor of the Medieval period *sliocht*, and so, like the *sliocht*, the *derbfine* may have possessed territorial integrity. If EMP homesteads represented the habitations of minimal ramages or lineages within the *sliocht* or *derbfine*, then it would seem likely that members of the wider kin unit could have been called upon to assist in homestead construction in the Early Middle Ages in a manner equivalent to a *meitheal* (cooperative work party) of the recent past. If client networks and kin networks were potential labor pools for the construction of Early Medieval homesteads, then the effect of household size as a determinant of homestead size would be greatly lessened.

Early Irish homesteads may be classed by two dimensions that bear upon size: the overall diameter of the site and the volume of material contained in the enclosing walls. Both indices reflect the number of concentric enclosing walls a site may possess (up to three), while the latter dimension of size gives an indication of how substantial the walls are.

Except where a site has been heavily plowed or bulldozed, its diameter, that is, the maximum diameter of its outermost enclosing wall, can be measured. Determining the volume of material in the enclosing walls for all site classes is, however, more problematic. Making estimations of wall volume is difficult to achieve in the case of ráth-type homesteads due to the attrition of the earthen banks and the filling in of the ditches over time. However, cashels are well-suited to this type of analysis. With the exception of sites where substantial stone-robbing from the walls has occurred, it is still possible to achieve an estimate of the original volume of stone in them. Cashels are built in areas with little soil cover, so even though the walls may have collapsed, the stones are still there to be seen above ground level.

MEAN SITE EXTERNAL DIAMETER

Only the diameters of sites with concentric enclosing walls, the raths and cashels, are discussed here. The mean diameter of these settlements was calculated by averaging two maximum diameters measured from the sites. Maximum diameters were measured to the external bases of the outermost wall for cashels, or to the outer edge of the outermost enclosing ditch or bank in the case of rath sites. Crews in the field were instructed to measure two diameters, the (magnetic) north-south diameter and (magnetic) east-west diameter for every site. Sometimes a diameter on one bearing would be incomplete due to site disturbance, so another bearing was selected that intersected the middle of the site and ran to two intact sections of wall or ditch.

Figure 5.23 shows the distribution of mean external diameters for both raths and cashels of the settlement sample. In a chiefdom society in which social status is translated into settlement size, one would expect the common populace to reside in the smaller homesteads and these in turn to be the most numerous among all sites. The distribution of site diameters appears at first to be roughly normal with a long tail at the upper end.

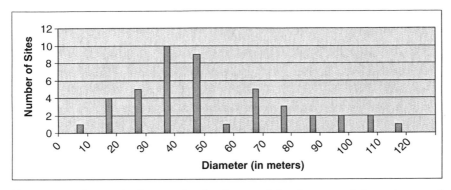

Figure 5.23. Bar graph showing the distribution of the diameters of the enclosures of surveyed raths and cashels.

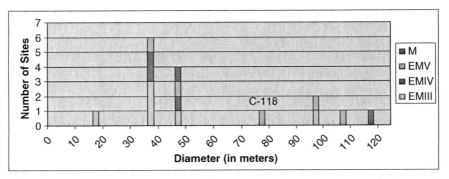

Figure 5.24. Bar graph showing the distribution of the mean external diameters of seriated cashel sites.

However, the normalcy of this distribution is partially an artifact of settlement preservation and the project's sampling strategy. The larger sites are more frequently preserved than the smaller sites since they are more substantial, and the extensive survey sought out sites that were recorded upon Ordnance Survey maps, and these belonged to the larger size classes.

Two peaks are evident in the distribution of the settlement sample diameters from the Burren. The principal frequency peak is between 30–40 meters in diameter and then there is a slight second peak at 60–70 meters.

Past 70 meters, the slope continues its descent to level out, more or less, with a smattering of sites between 80 and 120 meters in size.

We are at a comparative advantage working with cashels over raths in that the cashel sample can be further partitioned by relative age. This can only be done, of course, with the smaller subset of cashel sites for which sections of wall masonry were recorded. The graph (Figure 5.24) shows the pattern in the diameters of the cashels for all periods to remain essentially stable over a span of 500–600 years. Caherconnell C-66 was a section

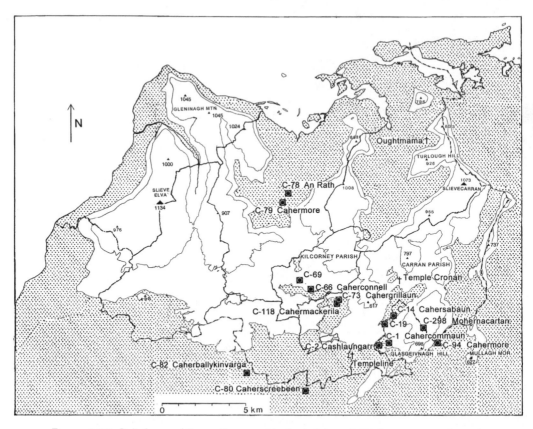

Figure 5.25. Relief map of Barron Barony with the 400-ft. and 600-ft. contours indicated; land lying below 400 ft. is stippled. Some of the larger cashel settlements that figure in the seriation study are shown against the territories of the reconstructed primary parishes.

capital of the tenth century as it is the largest cashel within Kilcorney parish and it is centrally located within this territory (Figure 5.25).

The sole cashel of the sample that is between 70 and 80 m in mean diameter, C-118 Cahermackerrila, is one of the larger cashels within Carran parish. Its location is not even close to the geographical center of this territory, as one would expect if it were a section capital (Figure 5.25). Carran parish can be equated with a secular territory named Toonagh in the sixteenth-century Tripartite Deed. In the twelfth century, the putative date of the cashel, it is possible that this territory had been split between two sections, with a second political center located in Castletown townland, possibly at the cashel C-14 Cahersabaun.[5] The nearby large cashel C-19 in Tullycommon townland may also have continued to have been inhabited, though by the seriation scheme it was founded in the prior century.

Cashels constructed as section capitals, therefore, have a demonstrable diameter range of 40–80 m. Though the current sample size is too small and imperfect to resolve the issue, a question worth pursuing with future

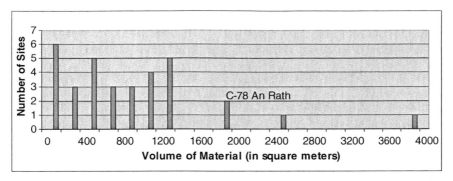

Figure 5.26. Bar graph showing the distribution of surveyed rath and cashel sites by the volume of material in their enclosure walls.

research is whether enclosure wall size increased with time within the aristocratic settlement classes from the tenth to twelfth centuries.

WALL VOLUME

The volume of building material that a site contains in its walls probably reflects more closely the amount of labor that originally went into its construction than does the areal extent of the site. The volume of stone contained in cashel walls was calculated utilizing the formula $\pi(^r\text{ext}^2 - ^r\text{int}^2)H$ (kindly supplied by Michael Geselowitz) where ^rext = the site's mean radius to the wall's exterior face, ^rint = the site's mean radius to the wall's interior face, and H = wall height. In most cases the height of the best-preserved wall section was used for H. The maximum surviving wall height was assumed to apply to the entire circumference of the wall when it was intact. In a few instances the wall was found to be ruined all the way around. When this was the case, the rubble mound was assumed to be uniform and the height and width of the rubble spread were used in the calculations. Though a rubble mound is not rectangular in cross-section, the likely error was not considered to be appreciable.

The first graph (Figure 5.26) shows the distribution of the volumes of material in the enclosure walls of all medieval settlements, raths and cashels, in cubic meters. There are at least four discernible peaks in the frequency scale: between 0–200 cu. m, 400–600 cu. m, 1100–1300 cu. m, and then the sites above 1800 cu. m. The two sites that incorporate the greatest amount of material are, in reverse order, C-82, Caherballykinvarga, and C-1, Cahercommaun.[6] The largest rath is C-78 *An Rath*, at 1925 cu. m. This rath could also be a former chiefdom capital site given its location in Ballyallaban townland .6 km north of C-79 Cahermore within

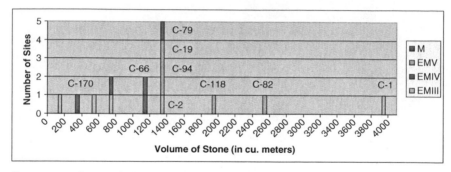

Figure 5.27. Bar graph showing the distribution of the seriated cashel settlements by wall volume.

the chieftain's territory of the Medieval period O'Lochlainn chiefdom (Figure 5.25).

Figure 5.27 displays the distribution of wall volumes for the dated settlements. Though the sample size is smaller, the pattern in the distribution of sites mirrors that seen in the total sample. However, there are some interesting departures from the distribution of cashel diameters. The potential Early Medieval period IV lineage leader's homestead C-170 appears to be close to the commoners' residences in size, but this is an artifact of grouping of sites by 200 cubic meter increments for it has over three times the volume of material in its walls as the largest site of the smallest class. Most surprising is the fact that three cashels presumed on the basis of their diameters and associated satellite cashels to have been chiefdom capital sites, C-19, C-79, and C-94, are only slightly larger than section capitals of the EMP III and EMP IV periods, and cluster with them when the data are grouped in 200 cubic meter increments. C-19 and C-79 had been extensively robbed of stone in the past and so their slight statistics may be excused on that basis. C-94, however, has only a single small satellite site and is relatively well preserved, so it may indeed have been merely a section capital.

Shifts are apparent over time in these data in the scalar relationships between contemporary settlements. The difference between the volume of material incorporated into the walls of the largest EMP III site, Cahercommaun (C-1), and the smaller contemporary settlements is truly impressive. While Cahercommaun has three times the mass of its satellite C-2, Cashlaungarr, it has over seven times the volume of material in its walls of the lineage leader's homestead, C-34. This degree of segregation by mass is not apparent in the later periods. Though the area covered by the Early Medieval period IV site C-19 is nearly identical to the area covered by Cahercommaun, C-19 has less than half of the latter site's mass. Though C-19 has been more extensively robbed of stone than Cahercommaun, it has only one outer enclosure wall and a thinner central enclosure wall. Therefore, it would still be a substantially less massive site even if it were intact.

INTERPRETATION

Though better results could be obtained with a larger sample of cashels, the evidence pertaining to the area and mass of the Burren's raths and cashels is consistent in demonstrating at a minimum that these homesteads segregate into four size classes. If these site-size classes are more than an artifact of the analysis, I believe that they may be assigned to the following tiers in the social hierarchy of Thomond's chiefdoms:

Commoners: the enclosure walls of raths and cashels that could be ascribed with confidence to commoners range in diameter from 15 – 23 meters. However, the examination of wall volume opened up the possibility that two cashels with diameters in the 35–36 m range, C-105 and C-188, may also have been commoners' residences due to the slightness of their enclosure walls. On the basis of their enclosure dimensions and wall archi-tecture, C-105 and C-188 may predate the eighth century. If this proves to be the case, then there are at present no other contemporary settlements to compare them to by which their rank position may be ascertained.

Within several enclosures, C-67 in Caherconnell townland in Kilcorney parish and C-377 in Tullycommon townland, the foundations' definite round huts were noticeable. The hut in C-67 was 7.7 m in diameter; that in C-377 was 5.2 m. The remains of huts without enclosures have been observed near several cashels of the section capital class, for example, in the vicinity of C-93, Caherblonick, and C-80, Caherscreebeen. In these latter two examples, the surveyors noted both rectangular and round house foundations. It is tempting to see these huts and humble enclosures as the houses of servile dependents of the aristocrats situated in the large cashels. However, until several of these small sites can be excavated, this must remain a hypothesis.

Lineage Leaders: Raths and cashels in the 30–39 m diameter range were the most numerous class of homestead, and this site-size class shows the greatest degree of stability through time. Their identification as residences of lineage leaders is premised on the proximity of several examples, C-34 and C-43, to commoners' residences – the amalgam of settlement con-stituting a lineage cluster (Gibson 2008b). Lineage leaders' homesteads of EMP III seem to have lacked the attached yards of the commoners'

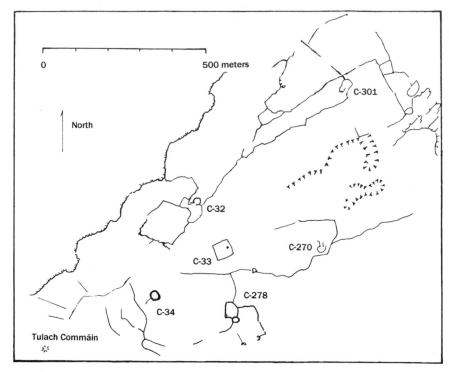

Figure 5.28. A lineage cluster in the vicinity of Tulach Commáin, Tullycommon, Co. Clare.

residences, though the ring of settlement and field walls surrounding C-34 could be construed as a large yard (Figure 5.28). C-170, potentially dating to EMP IV, possesses one. The residences of lineage leaders were also found to be situated in proximity to freestanding rectangular enclosures (e.g., C-33 in Figure 5.28).

Section Leaders: These leaders of *túatha* occupied intermediate-sized homesteads – sites possessing inner enclosures in the 40–50 meter diameter range in the EM III and IV periods, and, beginning with the EM V period, a second enclosing wall and/or substantial attached enclosures as well. Section capitals possibly increased in size during EMP V in the twelfth century.

There is a high degree of stability in the selection of specific locales for the location of section capitals. At a single location in the Burren one often finds sites of this class apparently succeeding one another through time (though not on the exact same spot). For instance, the central location of both C-69 and C-66 Caherconnell within Kilcorney parish indicates that, at differing periods, these were the seats of sections occupying this territory. The eleventh-century section capital C-73 Cahergrillaun is succeeded in the twelfth century by the substantially larger site C-118 Cahermackerrila. These two sites are within 200 meters of each other on a prominence overlooking a valley. This local preference for shifting a settlement's location rather than demolishing and building anew on the same spot has persisted to modern times. Nineteenth-century cottages located in the center of land holdings have been abandoned by local farmers in favor of locations nearer to the roads and towns.

Large Early Medieval centers of exceptional mass and spatial extent were undoubtedly the capitals of composite chiefdoms – *mór thúatha*. Hence it is obvious that they should be called chiefdom capitals. Cahercommaun (C-1), Caherballykinvarga (C-82), and Cahermore (C-79) may be ascribed to this class without hesitation due to their superior size and demonstrable central location within a sizable territory. C-19 and C-94 Cahermore are potentially chiefdom capitals, though in light of its modest mass and lack of satellite cashels and nucleated settlement, C-94 is more likely a section capital despite its three enclosing walls. Aside from their great size, the survey data indicate that chiefdom capitals are often located in proximity to subsidiary cashels and to scattered small enclosures and huts. Chiefdom capitals are also linked to sizable rectangular enclosures and other facilities related to livestock management, giving an indication of their central role in a political economy dominated by cattle.

The textual evidence that bears upon this subject, taken together with what is known about the social divisions within Early Medieval Irish chiefdoms implies that the working parties engaged in the construction of an aristocratic capital were composed of slaves, resident families of alien origin called *fuidir*, servile (*daer*) clients, and nonservile (*saer*) clients. The imprint of these gangs is evident in the vertical joints in the masonry of the walls of the Burren's larger cashel sites, such as Cahercommaun, noted by Westropp (1896b:154–155) and Hencken (1938:5). Evidently, the work teams were allotted different sections of an enclosure wall to build independently of one another and the wall sections were joined by simple abutment. Judging from the relatively greater care with which the aristocratic homesteads were built, and the correspondences in style between cashels, and between the cashels and churches, these gangs were under the direction of a master builder. The imprint of skilled craftsmen is especially evident in structures of the Medieval period, when mortared construction makes its appearance on some of the Burren's sites.

In general, composite chiefdom capitals distinguish themselves from the average rath or cashel by their large size, covering an area at least twice as extensive as the more humble aristocratic sites. The volume of materials incorporated into their walls is also far greater than the volume of stone or earth in the walls of the nonaristocratic homesteads. Capital sites and their facilities, including extensive field systems, represent the products of a substantial amount of labor. This analysis has shown that the composite chiefdom capital sites depart from the other classes of sites in both subtle and overt stylistic attributes of construction, such as the uniformity of their stonework and the presence of *chevaux-de-frise*.

That Cahercommaun was even more massive than Caherballykinvarga shows that, like Ballykinvarga, the polity that it represented was a composite chiefdom, not simply a *túath*. Its location in a territory adjacent to that of the Corcu MoDruad chieftain's district surrounding Caherballykinvarga is evidence that it was the capital of a composite chiefdom carved out of the Corcu MoDruad composite chiefdom. Though one cannot be absolutely certain, the *túatha* associated with it were in what became later *Cenél Fermaic* to the south, Glennamanagh to the immediate north, and Glenarraga to the northwest. Within these districts lay the better agricultural lands of Corcu MoDruad. The Corcu MoDruad managed to persist, however, within their original chiefly district and in the *túatha* in the west.

CHAPTER SIX

Of Settlements and Boundaries: Reconstructing the Chiefdom of Tulach Commáin

Seriating the Burren's medieval settlements is a necessary first step toward being able to view the historical progression of political systems within this region. Like Michaelangelo taking away all that was not David from his block of marble, I am enabled to remove settlements not of EMP III date, hopefully leaving Cahercommaun's associated social system behind. However, isolating contemporary settlements is one thing, but reconstructing a chiefdom out of a settlement system also entails discovering the position of past boundaries. In the first part of this chapter, the methodologies for the discovery of the boundaries of Cahercommaun's chiefdom and the results that they produced will be discussed. The product of these efforts is a reconstituted polity of the eighth/ninth centuries, dubbed here *Tulach Commáin* (The [burial] Mound of *Commán*), after the original Gaelic name of the townland within which Cahercommaun is located, Tullycommon. Both the settlement and a prehistoric mound within the townland bear the name of Commán, a now-forgotten but probably once locally revered individual. The form of the name Tulach Commáin was inspired by the name of a neighboring chiefdom *Tulach Uí Dedaid*, and so it seemed appropriate. Some evidence from the Middle Ages indicates that the polity may have been called *Túath an Mhachaire*, but it should be borne in mind that Irish chiefdoms were known by a multiplicity of names.

COMMÁN'S DEMESNE: RECONSTRUCTING THE CORE AREA OF *TULACH COMMÁIN*

Cahercommaun is located near the boundary between Tullycommon and Teeskagh townlands. Under the field strategy of the Cahercommaun Project, the modern fields in both of these townlands were assigned numbers, and systematic field survey then began in the northwestern section of each townland and proceeded to the south and east. Within two seasons it proved possible to completely survey Teeskagh townland, but Tullycommon townland was so large that at the end of the first season, crews were sent to survey the fields in this townland surrounding Cahercommaun to ensure that they were not missed, since it was clear that there was insufficient time within the season to complete the entire townland. Even after three complete field seasons some sections of Tullycommon remained unsurveyed.

Within the fields surrounding Cahercommaun, survey crews encountered so many sites and ancient field boundary walls that the project's initial methodology of systematically walking every field in a regimented sweep was quickly abandoned. As one crew chief stated, his crew would simply cross over a field boundary wall and immediately set up the compass and start mapping as sites and features were encountered straight away. One outcome of the mapping was to reveal that the elevated plateaus within Teaskagh and Tullycommon townlands were covered with an intricate spider's web of ruined field boundary walls, or, to make the analogy more precise, a tangled mat of a sizable number of spiders' webs of different dates.

It was clear that disentangling this Gordion Knot of ancient field boundary walls would present a great challenge once field operations had ceased. At the outset it was hoped that relationships between field boundary wall systems where they intersected would provide the key to assigning them to different periods, so another strategy was imported from the American Southwest that had been used in the study of patterns of growth within pueblos. It was requested of survey crews that they note where intersecting walls were either bonded, indicating contemporaneity, or abutted, indicating chronological succession. It was quickly discovered that this strategy only worked with standing walls. One could not determine how sections of wall were originally conjoined in the case of ruined or semi-ruined walls. At best, one could only note instances where one wall was superimposed upon another, and this was helpful chiefly in distinguishing the Neolithic and Bronze Age walls from medieval and modern walls. A multivariate statistical technique was ultimately applied to the field boundary wall data to achieve the objective of disentangling tumble wall systems of different dates from each other.

THE SUCCESSION OF STYLES OF STONE FIELD BOUNDARY WALL SYSTEMS

The noticeable variation in the manner of stone arrangement within the standing stone field boundary walls of the Burren, and the preservation of ruined and partially standing remnants of stone field boundary walls within more modern fields in many areas, gave rise to the idea that an analysis of the style of their construction could yield a relative chronology of boundary wall types. These boundary wall types, when found in association with prehistoric settlements, could then assist in determining the relative ages of the sites.

A study undertaken of ancient stone field boundary walls within the Burren by Emma Plunkett Dillon (1985) established the existence of three distinctive prehistoric field boundary wall types: mound walls, slab walls, and tumble walls. She assigned these types to broad cultural historical periods based on their relative states of preservation, the relative heights of the underlying bedrock pedestals and preserved soil that the walls shielded from erosion, and site associations. Mound walls were thought to date from the Early Bronze Age (1985:167–168), succeeded by slab walls dating perhaps to the Later Bronze Age/Early Iron Age, followed by tumble walls, which she loosely ascribed to the "ring-fort" builders of the Early Medieval and Medieval periods (1985:94, 174, 182, 191, 195, 197). Excavations of walls and associated settlements in two Burren localities carried out by Carleton Jones and the author have confirmed the dating of mound walls to the Neolithic – Early Bronze Age (Gibson 2004; Jones 1998).

Slab wall field boundary systems were also encountered by the survey. They were associated with small sites with low, cashel-like circular enclosure walls. The fact that slab walls were all encountered in a ruined state and the fact of their association with sites that appeared to be ancestral to the cashels of the EMP suggest that boundary walls of this type predate Cahercommaun.

Tumble walls were built in the following fashion: orthostatic slabs were erected at intervals, propped up by smaller orthostats placed at their sides. The framework created by the orthostats was filled in with smaller slabs and stones wedged vertically against each other to the height of the orthostats (see Figure 6.1). This was the most common type of field boundary wall encountered by the survey. Not only is this the wall type that currently defines the Burren's fields, but they were found to be connected to EMP sites as well, including Cahercommaun, signifying that they have been constructed for over 1,000 years. Tumble walls seemed variable enough, however, that it was thought that it might be possible to isolate walls of different eras through a systematic analysis of the dimensions of their components. To explore this possibility, the field crews of the Cahercommaun Project were instructed to systematically record the scalar attributes of the

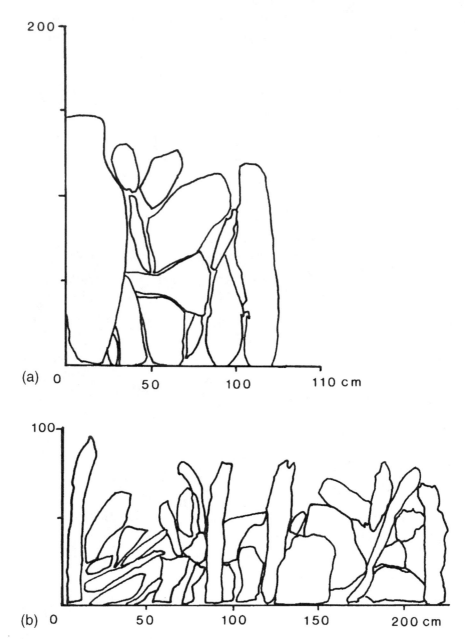

Figure 6.1. Tumble wall varieties from the Glasgeivnagh Plateau: (a) tumble wall T1 with large orthostats of the Cahercommaun demesne field system; (b) tumble wall T2 with smaller stones associated with the putative later Medieval settlement C-291.

extant architecture of the stone field boundary walls, and to both draw and photograph elevations of both ruined and standing walls of all types, including those currently in use.

The walls were broken down into three potentially significant struc-tural components: orthostats, the stones of the bottom course, and all

other filler stones. The means of the two dimensions of these three categories of structural stones that could be measured from an elevation
view were submitted to principal components analysis, along with the
mean distance between orthostats, yielding a total of seven variables (see
Table 6.1).

Two principal components emerged that correspond to two distinctive field wall boundary varieties within the tumble wall class. One type,
called here T1, possessed orthostatic slabs c. 90–140 cm high with a
mean thickness of 23 cm and a width often in excess of 40 cm. The filler
stones tended toward a mean length of 37 cm and a mean thickness of
15 cm (Figure 6.1a). The comparatively large size of the stones reflects
the efforts of a labor pool consisting of clients and other dependents of
the Cahercommaun chieftain that was tapped to quarry the stones and
erect the field boundary system. The orthostats of the second variety of
tumble wall, T2, were shorter, thinner, and spaced at shorter intervals
(Figure 6.1b). The filler stones were also slightly smaller on average (see
Table 6.1).

Walls of the second tumble wall field boundary variety were found
to be associated in one area with a settlement far less imposing than
Cahercommaun, the site C-291. C-291 is situated 470 meters to the east
of Cahercommaun atop the same plateau. C-291 is subrectangular in layout with a low enclosure wall of a single stone's thickness. The stones
of this wall were roughly stacked or wedged vertically in tumble wall
fashion. Foundations of buildings were clearly visible within this enclosure, exhibiting both round and subrectangular ground plans, the latter
predominating (see Figure 6.2). On the basis of the shape of the site, the
predominantly subrectangular plan of the huts, and the fact that the tumble
walls associated with this site are arrayed within fields demarcated by walls
of the other tumble wall variety, it was concluded that the field boundary
walls associated with C-291 were later in date that those associated with
Cahercommaun. The subrectangular buildings point toward a date following the tenth century.

The question may well be raised whether it is possible to tie down the
date of the second variety of tumble wall more precisely than post-tenth
century. Two other sites similar to C-291 were noted in the course of the
survey and one, C-190, was recorded (Figure 6.3). Like C-291, C-190 is
situated in an upland setting. C-291 also resembles C-190 in having a subrectangular enclosure wall, and it is almost exactly the same size (mean
external diameter of C-291: 34 m; of C-190: 31 m). C-190 does, however,
differ from C-291 in having a more substantial enclosure wall of coursed

Table 6.1. Summary Statistics from Factor Analysis of Plateau Wall Data

		EMP walls	Medieval walls
Length of largest orthostat:			
(N = 44)		(N = 19)	(N = 25)
	Range	80–150 cm	65–103 cm
	Mean	113 cm	78 cm
	Sd	20 cm	12 cm
Mean orthostat length:			
(N = 44)			
	Range	75–133 cm	55–85 cm
	Mean	100 cm	70 cm
	Sd	14 cm	9 cm
Mean orthostat thickness:			
(N = 44)			
	Range	12–42 cm	11–31 cm
	Mean	23 cm	16 cm
	Sd	8 cm	4 cm
Mean length of stones of the bottom course:			
(N = 44)			
	Range	25–61 cm	17–40 cm
	Mean	37 cm	31 cm
	Sd	9 cm	5 cm
Mean thickness of stones of the bottom course:			
(N = 44)			
	Range	10–23 cm	8–19 cm
	Mean	15 cm	13 cm
	Sd	3 cm	2 cm
Mean length of other stones:			
(N = 37)		(N = 16)	(N = 21)
	Range	27–59 cm	18–49 cm
	Mean	36 cm	30 cm
	Sd	8 cm	7 cm
Mean distance between orthostats:			
(N = 34)		(N = 15)	(N = 19)
	Range	34–178 cm	18–145 cm
	Mean	90 cm	58 cm
	Sd	40 cm	31 cm

construction 1 m thick. Though only a small section of intact architecture of the enclosure wall of C-190 was recorded (see Figure 6.3), the fact that a number of the blocks exceed 70 cm in length, have a mean thickness of 28.8 cm, and have their ends squared off would seem to place this site among the sites of the Medieval period. The smaller class of tumble wall would be then of this period as well.

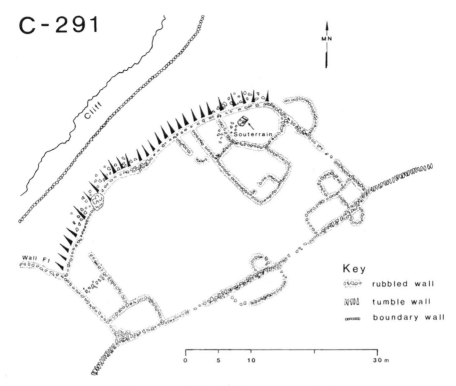

Figure 6.2. C-291, Tullycommon townland.

EARLY MEDIEVAL FIELD BOUNDARY WALL SYSTEMS: THE INFIELD

A hallmark of the field boundary wall systems of the Early Medieval period is their apparent irregularity. On the plateau one encounters coaxial systems from the Neolithic and Bronze Age with long, straight walls that partitioned the land surface into ribbon-like strips (Gibson 2004). Postmedieval systems partitioned the landscape into large blocks. In stark contrast, the fields of the Early Medieval period are highly irregular in shape, and at first glance, land partition does not seem to have been high on the agenda of the walls' builders (Figure 6.4). This is not to say, however, that organizing principles were altogether lacking.

Appended immediately to the dwellings of commoners were enclosures with a "D" shape. C-188, a site of the lineage leader class, has an enclosure that is rectangular, but this may be due to the fact that it was created within a preexisting Bronze Age or Neolithic field system and reused sections of partially standing walls. This is undoubtedly the *macha* or milking yard, which according to Lucas was closely linked to the owner's

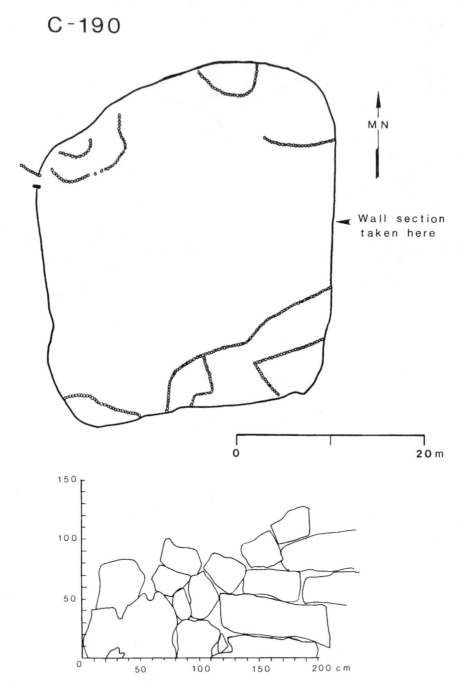

Figure 6.3. Top: plan of C-190, Tullycommon townland. Bottom: section of enclosure wall showing coursed construction.

habitation enclosure (1989:31). Cattle would have been driven to this in the morning and evening for milking. Appended to Cahercommaun is a very large rectangular enclosure created by walls W-7, 52, and W-4 (Figure 6.5). The special character of W-7 as an outer enclosure or

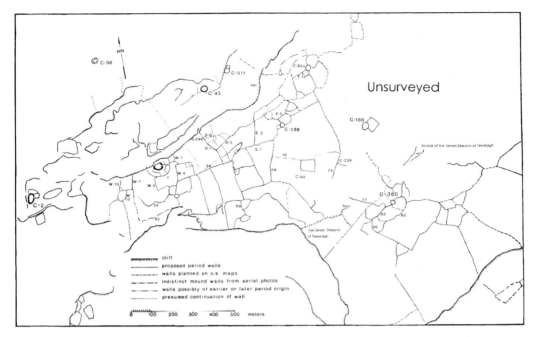

Figure 6.4. The Early Medieval III–IV field systems of the Glasgeivnagh Plateau. Pattern recognition analysis of the enclosure walls of C-43 and C-360 suggests that these settlements may belong to a period subsequent to the occupation of Cahercommaun.

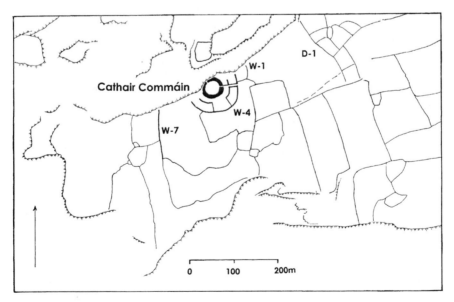

Figure 6.5. Field boundary walls and enclosures in the immediate vicinity of Cahercommaun.

bawn wall is signaled by the fact that it is of coursed drywall construction, not a wall of the tumble variety. This enclosure may have been the *airlise* (that which is in front of the *les* [earthern enclosure]), though for Clare it should be called the *aircathair*. It was stated in the law text *Críth*

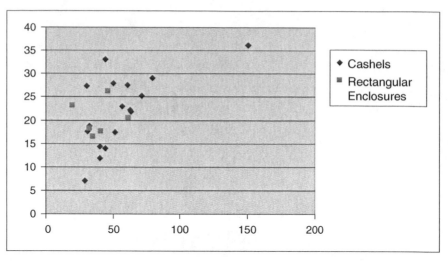

Figure 6.6. Scatter plot comparison of the means of length and thickness of slabs found within 2 x 1 meter sample sections of the external wall faces of cashels and rectangular enclosures 0–100 m.

Gablach that this enclosure extended the length of a spear cast from the *les* (F. Kelly 2000:368). Caisleán Gearr has a sizable kidney-shaped enclosure appended to it (Westropp 1915:270).

Close by EMP sites of just about every class, and often linked to them by short sections of wall, are rectangular enclosures. Rectangular enclosures consist of an area enclosed by four walls built most often of horizontally laid limestone slabs. In masonry technique the walls of these enclosures closely resemble the outer enclosure walls of the cashels, and the distribution of the means of the length and thickness of the slabs used in their construction overlaps that of the cashels (Figure 6.6). However, at least in the neighborhood of Cahercommaun, there is evidence that they may have been constructed originally in slab wall or tumble wall fashion. Such is the case with the rectangular enclosure attached immediately to Cahercommaun by wall W-1 and the rectangular enclosure C-64. Inside this enclosure, parallel to its walls of coursed construction, are the remains of walls composed of large upright limestone slabs (Figure 6.7).

Rectangular enclosures are ubiquitous both spatially and temporally, for not only are they found in association with cashels but they have been observed lying adjacent to recent structures as well. A particularly fine example with enormously high walls constituted a part of the complex of a nineteenth-century manor house in New Quay where the Burren fronts Galway Bay, and another was found while mapping the grounds of O'Dea's castle, a fifteenth-century tower-house to the south of the

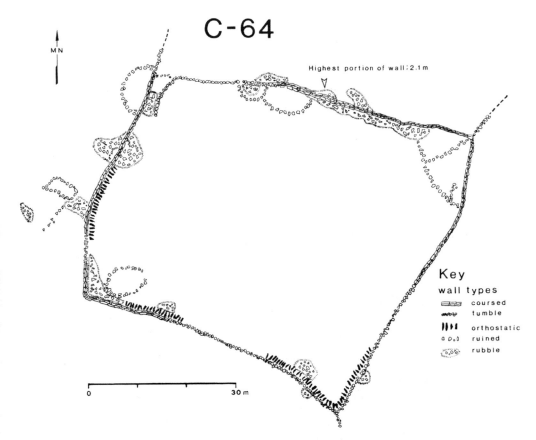

Figure 6.7. Plan of the rectangular enclosure C-64, Teeskagh townland, Co. Clare.

Burren (Gibson 2000, Fig. 12–5). The Cahercommaun Project encountered a rectangular enclosure just behind the twentieth-century farmhouse of Mr. Seán O'Lochlainn in Carron, but it is likely to have been originally constructed by the inhabitants of the small cashel C-162 just behind this house. Several rectangular enclosures were encountered that were unconnected to domestic buildings, such as C-64 and C-33, Knockaun Fort.

In the Early Middle Ages these unconnected rectangular enclosures may have been used communally as calving and milking yards by the inhabitants of the homesteads of commoners that surrounded them. However, given the remains of the earlier period wall inside C-64 and the wedge tomb inside C-33, the question arises whether these two facilities had prehistoric antecedents that might have had an entirely different purpose. Surveys carried out by the Cahercommaun Project demonstrated that both sites were linked to field boundary wall systems of the mound type, and excavation in the neighborhood of C-64 turned up profuse habitation remains that go back to the Early Bronze Age, if not earlier (Gibson 2004). Recent archaeological work in southeastern England has produced support for an interpretation that rectangular structures functioned in mortuary rituals (Bradley 2007:47–48, 56–57; Pryor 1987, 2001: chap. 4). The presence of a large wedge tomb inside C-33 and wedge tombs in proximity to C-64 suggests this function as a fruitful line of enquiry for the Early Bronze Age of the Burren.

Early Medieval rectangular enclosures may have been a different variety of milking and/or calving yard. Whereas in the historic sources *machaí* were directly linked with the habitation enclosure, the *indes* milking enclosure seems to have been located at a distance from the living site (Lucas 1989:32). There is a rectangular enclosure, C-50, close to C-2 so it would seem to be associated with it, but the two are separated by a steep ravine. This is also true in the case of an enclosure built against a butte directly opposite Cahercommaun to the north, but perhaps this enclosure was associated with C-43, Cahereenmoyle to the northeast (Figures 6.4, 6.5). Lucas infers from the sources that *indes* enclosures were sizable, holding a number of cattle at a time, which would have been the case with the examples mapped by the Cahercommaun Project (ibid.).

Several facts concerning the variation that these structures display in their morphology and associations are worthy of note. The rectangular enclosure connected to C-79, Cahermore, Ballyallaban townland, proposed here to be of Medieval period date, is so close to the cashel as to interrupt the outer enclosure wall, and so may have been constructed simultaneously with the site (see Figure 5.3). Westropp reports that it had a breadth of 36 m and walls six feet (185 cm) thick (1901a:291). However, Westropp planned a contrasting rectangular enclosure called "Moher" at Poulgorm (1911:358, Fig. 3).[1] From the plan, it seems that both it and the nearby cashel rest upon an older field system, a characteristic noted for the enclosure C-23 near C-19 as well. Westropp makes a weak argument that Moher is late in date due to the fact that the enclosure has angled corners in contrast to two presumed early rectangular enclosures, Knockaun Fort (C-33) and the enclosure situated opposite to Caisleán Gearr, C-50. In contrast to Moher, both of these enclosures exhibit rounded corners (ibid.:358). If Westropp's surmise is correct, change in this attribute of the morphology of rectangular enclosures is congruent with the seriation scheme for cashel sites proposed here. Moher is smaller than the enclosures found during the survey, exhibiting a mean diameter of 22 m.

THE OUTFIELD

The field boundary wall systems of the Early Medieval period were constructed following a simple blueprint: erect a three-sided corral within a swath of open land, and then run two to four stone field boundary walls from this structure to link it with (a) another corral, (b) a defining feature of the landscape (cliff, rivulet), or (c) another wall (Figure 6.5). In this manner, the landscape was subdivided into fields of irregular shape and size. Three-sided corrals will henceforth be referred to as triangular enclosures or corrals even though in reality they assume a myriad of shapes, and are not even always three-sided.

All told, this system of walls and corrals served to divide the entire plateau into sizable field sections with enclosures as focal points. On account of the dearth of soil in this area and the fact that the field boundary walls fail to follow natural contours, it is unlikely that they functioned to protect or mark off agricultural land. More likely they served to allocate grazing areas and provided foci for livestock collection in a system of livestock management.

It is likely that some field boundary walls did indeed function to separate the land holdings of different groups. This is implied in the law text *Bretha Comaithchesa* (The Judgments of the Neighborhood), which describes types of fences built to prevent animal trespass (F. Kelly 1988:142–143, 2000:372–378). The map of the surveyed portion of Glasgeivnagh Plateau (Figure 6.4) shows the dwellings of the chieftain, subaristocrats, lineage leaders, and commoners clustered tightly together. The dwellings of the subaristocrats are separated from Cahercommaun by cliffs and ravines but commoners' dwellings share the same plateau space. Since the walls emanating from C-288 stop at wall D-1, this was apparently a partition wall. Other partition walls to the south of D-1 can also be traced where wall 68 emanating from C-288 ends. The stream running from the spring to the Seven Streams of Teeskagh waterfall or the relatively straight wall to the south of it may have marked the southern limit of the chieftain's territory on the plateau. This is not altogether certain as on the basis of the style of the stonework of its enclosure wall the settlement C-360 would seem to postdate Cahercommaun, and so that portion of the plateau may also have constituted a portion of the chieftain's holdings.

From the law texts it is known that chieftains possessed a parcel of land attached to their office called *lucht tighe* or *mruig ríg*, with which they could do as they saw fit (Charles-Edwards 1993:111, 160; Gibson 2008; F. Kelly 2000:403; McErlean 1983). The portion of the plateau that was the

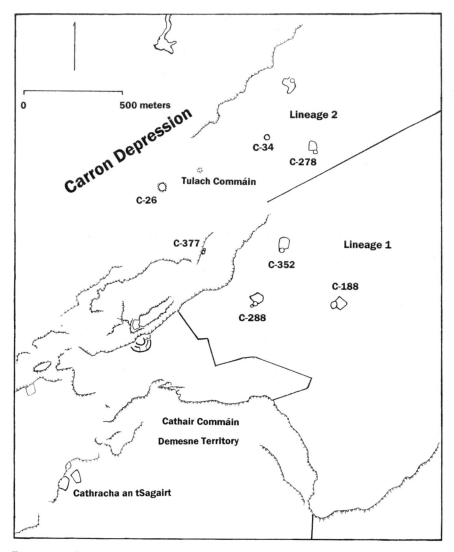

Figure 6.8. Proposed social demarcations of the landscape surrounding Cahercommaun (Ir. *Cathair Commáin*) showing a principal division of the land between the aristocratic inhabitants of Cahercommaun and commoner lineages (Gibson 2008b, Fig. 8).

exclusive property of the inhabitants of Cahercommaun seems rather modest considering their chiefly rank. However, it is likely that this demesne territory continued south onto the lower plateau within Teeskagh townland. The demesne field boundary system of Cahercommaun straddles the present townland territorial divisions, indicating that the townland territorial divisions of the plateau were not coeval with the occupation of the site (Gibson 2008b; see Figure 6.8). The survey verified that the boundary wall between Tullycommon and Teeskagh townlands parallels a portion of the remains of a principal spinal wall that joins W-4 at right angles and then runs east. The surviving small fragmentary stretches of this spinal wall were seen to be displaced c. 1 meter to the south of the townland boundary wall in Teeskagh townland, and had been converted into dung collection bins at intervals. The branch walls coming off of the spinal wall were observed to pass *under* the modern townland boundary wall as they crossed north into Tullycommon Townland. Whereas the name Teeskagh (*Taoscach*) is simply a descriptive toponym meaning "gushing" (referring to the waterfalls), the townland name Tullycommon (*Tulach Commáin* [the Mound of Commán]) refers to the burial site of a revered individual, presumably the same Commán who lent his name to the cashel. Thus, it seems logical that the place-name Tullycommon takes temporal precedence over Teeskagh.

The lower southern portion of Teeskagh townland was found to be devoid of Early Medieval settlement. Significantly, however, there is a series of three enclosures (C-48a, b, & c) located on the same plateau just to the west of this area within Clooncoose townland (Figure 6.8). One of the enclosures is named Carrachantaggart, which is an Anglicization of *Cathracha an tSagairt* (Dwelling Places of the Priest.) One of the enclosures may have indeed had a sacral function, though possibly not in the service of Christ, as it is built against a cliff at the mouth of a large cave, and so may reflect pagan beliefs. The other enclosures appear to have been corrals – versions of the rectangular enclosures of the uplands with more irregular ground plans. Both Teeskagh and Clooncoose, then, probably represent the major portion of the chieftain's demesne territory that was dedicated exclusively to livestock grazing.

The pastoral character of Cahercommaun's demesne field system is exemplified by the quality of the land that the field boundary walls traverse. Today, the land of the plateau is considered by local farmers to be suitable for rough grazing only. That the chiefly family appropriated such land for their own use appears as an archaeological confirmation of the predominance of pastoral values in early historical Irish society. Cattle are at the top of the system of values among states and chiefdoms with a pastoral character. Cattle are necessary for symbolic and political transactions, ranging from bridewealth to tribute. Wealth in cattle is the base requirement for the aspiring aristocrat, and as Early Medieval Irish tracts such as *Críth Gablach* demonstrate, this was certainly true for Ireland. Thus, it is no surprise that Cahercommaun should be the focus of an extensive apparatus for the management of livestock. The demesne field system of Cahercommaun as such should be viewed as a fossilized manifestation of the political economy of the chiefdom.

SECTION LEADERS, LINEAGE LEADERS, AND COMMONERS

Cahercommaun is surrounded quite closely by a ring of univallate cashels; however, only two of them are large enough to be considered to have been section capitals: C-2 Caisleán Gearr and, further afield, C-298 Mohernacartan, though given the slight state of its remains and remote location, it is more than likely that the latter site was rather a lineage leader's homestead (see later discussion under wall volume). In the Late Middle Ages section capitals usually occupied a central location within their own territory (Gibson 2000). One can only speculate, but there are several possible explanations for why Caisleán Gearr is so close to Cahercommaun. First, it should be noted that all capital cashels are seen to be linked directly to what I term here satellite cashels. C-79 is a case in point. Though semi-ruined, it can be seen to be linked directly to an adjacent cashel of the lineage-leader class, and another cashel is not far off in the distance. A cashel and a rath lie in close proximity to C-19, and Caherballykinvarga is also linked to a satellite cashel (Figure 3.12). In fact, the proximity of a satellite cashel can be said to be part of the physical definition of a chiefdom capital site.

The reasons for the existence of satellite cashels are probably to be found in the dynamics of chiefly ramages. In the sixteenth-century chiefdom of Gragans several tower-houses of the O'Lochlainn family within the district controlled directly by the chieftain were owned by sons of the chieftain. Chiefly polygynous families produced numerous sons, and apparently some were important enough to deserve their own residences while their father still reigned, and land for these could be spared only from the chieftain's own district. It is also conceivable that secondary cashels could have functioned as domiciles for co-wives or as extra cattle enclosures. Finally, the defensive siting of Cahercommaun as a reflection of warlike conditions could be acknowledged as a factor. It might have been considered prudent for a leader of a section to have his capital close to the chieftain's capital to preserve the chiefdom's leadership intact in the face of an attack.

The Cahercommaun Project's survey revealed patterns in the distribution of residences of lineage leaders and commoners from which conclusions can be drawn about the social constitution of these groups and their control over land. The cashel of the lineage-leader class that most closely resembles Cahercommaun in all attributes is C-34, located on the upper western flanks of the Glasgeivnagh plateau at a distance of 1.3 km to the northwest of Cahercommaun (see Gibson 2008b:Fig. 9). This cashel was found to be encircled by a field boundary wall system linking together three to four commoner homesteads. The field system also embraced a free-standing rectangular enclosure, C-33 Knockaun Fort, which in turn contained a wedge tomb (Figure 5.28).

The clustering of settlement does not seem fortuitous, and it represents what has been termed by archaeologists working in the Maya sphere a "lineage cluster," a concentration of dwellings occupied by members of the same lineage (Kintz 1983a, 1983b). A lineage cluster is perfectly congruent with what the law texts say about the lands of a *derbfine* lineage being controlled in common by the group, though being parceled out among the various families making up the lineage (Charles-Edwards 1993:64, 417, 419). Charles-Edwards infers from the discussion of trespass in *Bretha Comaithchesa* that members of the *derbfine* constituted a group called the *comingaire* that herded its cattle jointly (1993:421). The presence of a communal rectangular enclosure, central to the lineage cluster, would seem to have been a corollary of this arrangement. Thus, C-33 Knockaun Fort lies at the center of one lineage cluster, and C-64 near Cahercommaun marks another (Figure 6.4).

These field data for the organization of commoner communities lends support to the supposition that in the eighth/ninth centuries AD, Irish lineages owned land communally (Gibson 2008b). Under communal land ownership, a community can restrict access to land and also dictate how it is to be used (Colin 1998). This accords with statements from the law texts that the *derbfine* lineage held in common a parcel of land called the *fintiu*. Graves or pillar stones dedicated to ancestors would mark the boundaries of this block. Members would fence off their individual holdings within this block, but were barred from alienating their holdings from the *derbfine* by sale or gift (Charles-Edwards 1976, 1993:64, 417–418, 419). It would seem that under the bellicose conditions of the Early Middle Ages, lineage members lived in *clachan*-like proximity to each other and used the lands father afield for grazing. The communal mode of land ownership that prevailed among commoners was in contrast to the existence of a mode of private property among the chieftains and other nobility.

LOCATING THE EXTERNAL BOUNDARIES OF *TULACH COMMÁIN*

The Cahercommaun Project's intensive survey did not progress far enough after four field seasons to be able to yield the data required to reconstruct the boundaries of the Tulach Commáin chiefdom through analysis of patterns of settlement and field boundary wall distribution. It did not even prove possible to completely survey the initial three townlands that were selected for intensive survey. An investigation of the history of the boundaries of the Burren's various territorial units seemed to be another route that might have the potential of revealing the boundaries of the Burren's Early Medieval chiefdoms. In England and on the continent parish boundaries had been shown to have been established upon the boundaries of Early Medieval polities (Applebaum 1954; Berry 1987).

The churches of the diocese of Kilfenora, the diocese that contains both Corcomroe and Burren baronies, are listed for the first time in a papal taxation list of 1302–1306 (Sweetman and Handcock 1886:289–299; Westropp 1900). This list may be compared with a text of the late fourteenth century, called *Suim Cíosa Uí Briain* (O'Brien's Rental), that lists land denominations of different classes within unnamed larger territorial units within the Burren and Corcomroe chiefdoms of northern Co. Clare. These larger territorial units were probably secular territories that would have been subdivided into parishes. The late sixteenth-century *Books of Survey and Distribution* (BSD) constituted Ireland's first systematic census. It also lists all smaller land denominations by parish.

These data revealed that at some point after the fourteenth century, Carran parish within Burren Barony had lost a number of land parcels (including what are now the townlands of Sheshymore and Deerpark) in a block to Noughaval parish (Gibson 1990:112–115). Once these lands are restored to Carran parish, the Carran/Noughaval parish boundary is seen to directly intersect the Inchiquin/Corcomroe barony boundary. The boundary between Corcomroe and Inchiquin baronies is also the boundary between Kilfenora and Killinaboy parishes, and the continuation of the Carran/Noughaval boundary south as a boundary separating Kilfenora and Killinaboy parishes suggests extraterritorial connection between Carran and Kilfenora parishes on either side of the Inchiquin/Burren Barony boundary.

There are good reasons for concluding that the boundary between Inchiquin and Burren baronies postdates the parish boundaries – that is, it came into being following the late twelfth century, when the parishes of the dioceses of Kilfenora came into being (Ní Ghabhláin 2006). The odd detour that the boundary makes at C-94 Cahermore exemplifies the archaeological/geographical evidence for the late date of this boundary (Figure 4.3; Figure 5.23). Following field boundary walls, the barony boundary crosses over the plateau past Mohernacartan (C-298) and descends the northwestern-facing slopes of the plateau.[2] Then it crosses the Carron turlough, until it intersects the Castletown River. The barony boundary then turns to the southwest to meander along the bottom of the Carron depression. It follows the Castletown River until intercepting Cahersabaun (C-14), passing to the east of this cashel and the tower-house at Castletown. The barony boundary then reverts to the southwest again to bring C-18 and C-19 within the boundaries of Inchiquin Barony. After this, it zigs and zags around the rath C-36, Caisleán Gearr (C-2), and the enclosures of Carrachantaggart (C-48), including all but the latter in Inchiquin Barony. Then the boundary wraps around Clooncoose and Ballyline townlands, reverting to its former course eastward.

C-94 is a bivallate cashel and, by its size, ranks as a chiefdom capital. The stonework of its inner enclosure wall dates it to the twelfth century. It can be demonstrated conclusively that chiefdom capitals of the Medieval and Late Medieval periods always occupied a central location within their chiefdoms (Gibson 1995, 2000). Therefore, the barony boundary and the baronies themselves must have come into being following the twelfth century. The fact that the boundary between Burren and Inchiquin baronies closely skirts an O'Lochlainn tower-house in Castletown townland suggests that the boundary is post-sixteenth century.

When the barony boundary between Killinaboy parish in Inchiquin Barony and Carran parish in Burren Barony is removed, it is apparent that Cahercommaun is then positioned roughly at the center of the resulting joint territory (Figure 6.9). This result may be viewed as satisfactory from the standpoint of the principle of capital centrality, but there is further geographical evidence that suggests that the territory of this polity may have had somewhat different configurations. Co. Clare's parishes cannot be older than the twelfth century, whereas Cahercommaun dates to the eighth/ninth centuries. The Burren's churches may have been founded at an earlier point in time, and their distribution may hold clues for the location of earlier polity boundaries as it was the practice from pre-Christian times to locate sacred sites at the boundaries of polities (Mytum 1982; Ó Riain 1972; Sheehan 1982).

To the north, the boundary of Carran parish passed between Gortclare Mountain and Slievecarran (Ir. *Sliab Carn*). The only passage to the north here was through the narrow pass at Deelin (Figure 6.9). This was the site of several bloody encounters in the fourteenth-century saga *Caithréim Thoirdhealbhaigh* (e.g., O'Grady 1929 27:21–23, 89), a fact that demonstrates that Deelin possessed the attributes of a social boundary in these times. The presence of a boundary here in antiquity is further suggested by the name of a townland to the south, Crughwill. This place is named *Críchmhaill* in CT.

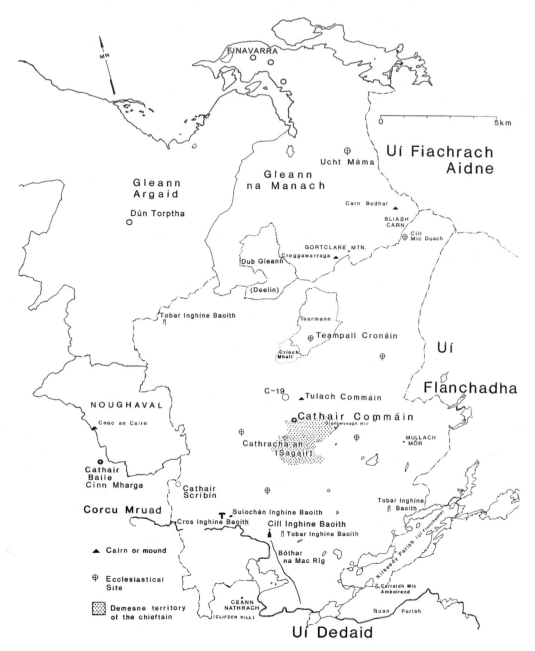

Figure 6.9. Reconstruction of the territory of the eighth/ninth century chiefdom *Tulach Commáin*. Open circles are settlements of either the rath or cashel variety. The extent of the chieftain's demesne territory is based upon available survey data and in all likelihood was probably substantially larger.

My guess is that the original name was *Críoch Mhail*, which could be either the "Boundary of Máel," or the "Boundary of the Servant" (Figure 6.9).[3]

The valley to the north of this boundary is called *Gleann na Manach* (Valley of the Monks), due to the presence in this valley of the monastery at *Ucht Máma* and later Corcomroe Abbey. The valley was a single secular territorial entity that survived down to the sixteenth century when it was identified as such in the Tripartite Deed of 1585, even though it had been subdivided into two parishes in the thirteenth century. In back of the monastic site of *Ucht Máma* is *Tobar Cholmáin* (Colmán's Well), a well dedicated to St. Colmán Mór MacDuach. In Keelhilla townland in the northernmost recess of Carran parish is a church dedicated to the saint and another holy well, *Tobar MacDuach*. Close by is a roadway *Bóthar na Mias* (Road of the Dishes) associated with a legend referring to a chieftain named Guaire who was MacDuach's cousin and principal patron. Colmán MacDuach was the tutelary saint of the Uí Fiachrach Aidhe and Guaire was a chieftain of the same group. It seems therefore likely that prior to its coming into O'Lochlainn possession, Gleann na Manach and the northern tip of Carran parish were held by a section of the Uí Fiachrach Aidhe.

From the standpoint of archaeology, considering the distribution of EMP III settlement, the proposed northern boundary of this proposed chiefdom would seem to be rational. Past Crughwill townland to the north, there do not seem to be any potential section capitals until one reaches the peninsula of Finavarra, where three large rath-type settlements are situated (Figure 6.9). This gap is consistent with the existence of a social boundary here. Otherwise, such a settlement gap is unexpected in an area of otherwise very fertile land. The distribution of intermediate-sized sites in the south of the Tulach Commáin chiefdom would seem to be more uniform.

The western boundary of Carran parish is composed of mountain ridges, while the eastern boundary of Killinaboy parish within Inchiquin Barony takes in the bare limestone pavement around *Mullach Mór*, a district formerly called *Danganmackya* (Mac Kya's Fortress). Further south, the boundary links together four large lakes and then follows the course of the Fergus to Lough Inchiquin and *Ceann Nathrach* (Clifden Hill). The only part of this boundary that does not follow pronounced geographical barriers is the stretch passing west and north from Clifden Hill to *Cathair Scríbín* (C-80 Caherscreebeen).

Proceeding north from *Cathair Scríbín*, affixing the eastern boundary of Tulach Commáin becomes a little trickier. Though there is evidence of a connection between Noughaval and Carran parishes, all indications point to Noughaval having been created de novo in the twelfth century from a portion detached from a territory that is now Kilfenora parish. North of Noughaval is Kilcorney parish, and there is slight but nonetheless compelling evidence that this parish was formerly a district of Tulach Commáin.

Though small, Kilcorney parish is as old as the rest of the Burren's parishes, figuring in the 1302–1306 papal taxation list, and it possesses on architectural grounds a relatively old (twelfth-century) parish church. The church is dedicated to an individual named *Corr*, whose name does not appear in the *CGSH*. However, Corr is a rare name that appears only twice in the *CGH*, both times in mythological sections of genealogies of chiefdoms of the Éoganachta, and within the Éoganacht Uí Meic-leir as the father of Baíthíni, another variation on the name Báeth. Corr, then, may have been an ancestor god of the Éoganachta, and there is evidence that the chieftains of Tulach Commáin claimed Éoganachta affinities (Bhreathnach 1999:85).

In the northern reaches of Kilkorney parish in Glenslead townland, there is a holy well dedicated to Saint Ingen Báeth (Báeth's Daughter). On the evidence of a substantial monastic site bearing her name, *Cill Inghine Baoith* (Killinaboy), three holy wells dedicated to her, and a high stone cross bearing her name (*Cros Inghine Baoith*), she was the principal tutelary saint of the Tulach Commáin chiefdom. Since the distribution of the monastery, two holy wells, and the cross parallel the course of the boundary of Tulach Commáin in the southwest, south, and southeast, it can be assumed that the third holy well in Kilcorney parish establishes the chiefdom's northwestern boundary as the western boundary of this parish. It is therefore likely that this parish and co-terminous secular section territory were carved out of the dominion of Tulach Commáin several centuries subsequent to the abandonment of Cahercommaun.

The reader may be struck by the apparent small size of the chiefdom of Tulach Commáin. Tulach Commáin was probably not much greater in extent than 14 km from north to south, and 11 km from east to west.[4] The area contained within its boundaries was approximately 150 sq. km. However, from a comparative perspective the size of this polity is not surprising. This polity is much larger than the South Pacific polities of Tikopia Island and the Trobriands described by Firth and Malinowski, and only 60 percent of the size of the Halelea District of Kaua'i studied by Earle (1978), though possibly a smaller proportion of the land area of this district was directly involved in food production than was the case for Tulach Commáin. On the Aran Islands Carleton Jones has noted the striking correlation between townland territories and the distribution of Early Medieval cashels – that is, each townland possesses a cashel (2004:170). The townlands are smaller than Tulach Commáin and contain less arable soil, or soil of any kind for that matter, so these divisions may represent sections of one or more composite chiefdoms.

Returning to the subject of the geographical character of the reconstituted polity of Tulach Commáin, several facets of this chiefdom stand out to the observer. Tulach Commáin straddles two fairly distinct physiological zones: the Burren uplands with its glacial valleys and barren hills and plateaus, and the lower-lying lands with deep soils in the vicinity of the villages of Corofin and Killinaboy. The presumed earliest capital of this chiefdom, Cahercommaun, is located in one of the most rugged areas within the highland region. One may safely assume that it was not the economic potential of the Glasgeivnagh Plateau that impelled the choice of this area for the location of the chiefdom's capital site. More likely, the decision to have the capital in this spot was inspired primarily by political and military considerations.

From a defensive standpoint, the only soft spot in the boundary of Tulach Commáin was the valley between Killinaboy and Kilfenora. The Corcu MoDruad capital site of Caherballykinvarga lay a scant two kilometers past this boundary to the west, demonstrating in convincing fashion that Tulach Commáin had been carved out of territories formerly under its control. The founders of Cahercommaun placed their capital at a distance from the western boundary, demonstrating the existence of what were almost certainly hostile relations with the Corcu MoDruad. Most likely, the strongest consideration was to place the capital where it would be least vulnerable to attack from potential enemies, and where communication with the section leaders within a polity could be maximized. The net gains from a centralized seat of rule to the chiefdom would lie in the minimization of administrative costs due to the central location of the capital site, and in speedy responses to external attacks due to the ease of internal communication (Gibson 2000). As Cahercommaun lay in the dead center of its polity, it is apparent that the leaders of Tulach Commáin expected attack from any direction.

As Irish aristocrats of the Early Middle Ages largely subsisted on livestock production and contributions of food and labor from clients, it did not make much of a difference from a catchment standpoint where the capital site was located. One can graze cattle or receive contributions in almost any locale in Clare. A tendency existed in the Early Middle Ages to locate capitals *preferentially* in agriculturally marginal locales. Cahercommaun and Caherballykinvarga are both positioned on land with thin or absent soil cover, and crannogs are distanced entirely from land.

From a symbolic perspective, Cahercommaun was located in an area with preexisting mythical associations, making it a favorable place for the capital of a sacral *rí*. As previously mentioned, to the south below Cahercommaun is a spring with a large cave behind it. The mythical smith

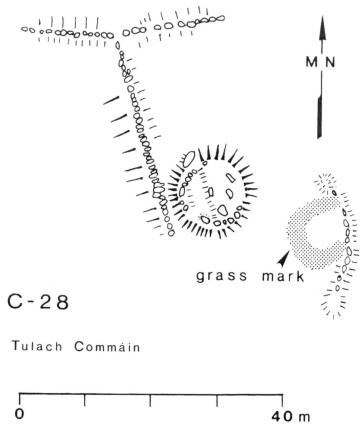

C-28

Tulach Commáin

0   40 m

Figure 6.10. Plan of C-28 Tulach Commáin.

Lon is associated with this cave and the enclosures near the spring that
bear the name *Cathracha an tSagairt* (Dwellings of the Priest) emphasize its
sacral quality. Caves and springs in general were portals to the otherworld
in Celtic belief, and so this place could have been a cultic site.

The cairn of inauguration for the Cahercommaun chiefdom would have
been most likely *Tulach Commáin* (Commán's Mound). Westropp was certain
that this mound was the "Carn" located atop the "green ridge" next to the
"Giant's Grave" (C-27), a diamond-shaped cairn, and 200 m to the northeast of the rath C-26 (Westropp 1905:219–220). When I visited this site in
1984, it appeared as a small cashel, a circular heap of soil and stones. Next
to it was a linear mound with protruding stones with a grass mark leading
off of it that seemed to betray the outline of some structure (Figure 6.10).
My impression of the site substantially matched Westropp's:

> On the summit of a green ridge ... is a low, defaced mound of earth and stones.
> It is 35 feet across, and has on the summit a well-marked ring of stones round a
> circular hollow 15 feet in diameter. (Ibid.:219)

Tulach Commáin was regarded as a supernaturally potent spot as late as the nineteenth century, for Westropp was told by an informant in 1895 that "it had more fairies than all of the other forts of the hill" (ibid.:220). This mound is clearly visible from Cahercommaun across the ravine to the northeast.

Pinpointing the third element of the capital set for this chiefdom, the principal church, is more problematic – not the least because one is uncertain when Christianity would have penetrated northern Co. Clare. Thanks to recent archaeological work, we have a better understanding of the timing of the appearance of Christian communities in western Munster. Recent excavations have been carried out at two small monasteries in Co. Kerry: Reask at the extreme west of the Dingle Peninsula and Illaunloughan Island further to the south between Valencia Island and the Iveragh Peninsula. The excavator of Reask dated the Christian cemetery at the site to the fifth-seventh centuries AD, and the construction of the monastery to between the seventh and eighth centuries (Fanning 1981:158). The foundation of the monastic community at Illaunloughan has been dated to the mid-seventh century (Marshall and Walsh 2005).

Historical sources strongly associate the Aran Islands in Galway Bay with the Burren. Mortar samples drawn from the walls of stone churches on Inis Mór and Inis Oírr that have been subjected to radiocarbon analysis date to no earlier than the eleventh century (Berger 1995). However, the excavations of Reask and Illaunloughan have demonstrated that the erection of stone buildings was often a secondary development at religious sites, the stone oratory at Illaunloughlan having been built in the eighth century (Marshall and Walsh 2005). Sinéad Ní Ghabhláin's excavation of occupation levels at Mainistir Chiaráin on Inis Mór has yielded radiocarbon dates to the seventh century, though it cannot be determined whether the occupation layer is related to the ecclesiastical foundation (Ní Ghabhláin, pers. comm. 1998). The presence of cross-inscribed pillars at the site is evidence in favor of a seventh-century date for this church's foundation (Ní Ghabhláin, pers. comm.). On architectural grounds none of the extant stone churches of the Burren are earlier than the twelfth century, though there is speculation that several have been rebuilt from the remains of earlier buildings (Ní Ghabhláin 1985, 2006; O'Keeffe 2003). Given the seventh-century dates for the foundation of monastic communities elsewhere in western Munster and Connaught, it seems plausible that similar institutions could have existed in northern Co. Clare by the end of EMP III.

Two religious centers may have received patronage from the chieftain at Cahercommaun. Of the religious centers that immediately surround

Cahercommaun, the site of Templecronan, *Teampall Chrónáin* (St. Cronán's Temple [church]), is the most elaborate (Figure 3.6). There are two gable-shrines at the site, the presumed resting spots of the translated bones of saints, and Sinéad Ní Ghabhláin has taken this as an indication that Teampall Chrónáin was a focus of pilgrimage (1995a:202). The church is surrounded by double concentric enclosure walls, and the presence of surviving numerous house foundations and enclosures in a field to the north of the church indicates that this ecclesiastical center was monastic in nature. A high cross that was formerly on the premises fortifies this impression. Teampall Chrónáin is situated within a townland called Termon. The Irish word *termonn* refers to the lands belonging to an ecclesiastical establishment extending beyond the grounds at the core. Termon townland extends north up into the hills behind Teampall Chrónáin, reaching to the projected northern boundary of Tulach Commáin. This territory might encompass the grazing lands belonging to the monastery.

Paralleling in the south Teampall Chrónáin's location in the far north of Tulach Commáin is the church and certain monastery of *Cill Inghine Baoith*. It is located upon a ridge overlooking the Fergus and the Medieval period route leading west to Kilfenora *Bóthar na Mac Rí* (Road of the Chieftain's Sons, Figure 6.9). Its former monastic status is strongly indicated by the stump of a round tower on its grounds. As discussed previously, one may readily ascertain that the identity of St. Ingen Báeth and the chiefdom of Tulach Commáin were intertwined by the number and distribution of sacred monuments, most prominently holy wells dedicated to her and the fact that these are not spatially restricted to the immediate environs of Killinaboy (Figure 6.9). Excavation would be required to determine which of the two monasteries, Teampall Chrónáin or Cill Inghine Baoith, was more prominent in the eighth/ninth centuries. However, their status may be indicated by the life of St. Crónán, which presents Crónán and Briga as brother and sister. It has been noted that the chiefdoms of pagan Ireland had male and female tutelary divinities, such as, for example, Ailill and Medb of the Connachta. Crónán and Briga may represent a translation of this institution into a Christian context.

In addition to Teampall Chrónáin and Cill Inghine Baoith, Cahercommaun is ringed by a further four ecclesiastical foundations: Templepatrick/ Correen Friary in Glenquin, St. Columbkille's Church in Glencolumbkille, Templeline in Ballyline townland to the southwest, and *Cill Mic an Domhain* in the south. The exact foundation dates of these ecclesiastical sites are at present unknown though claims have been advanced in favor of an Early Medieval foundation date for Templeline, despite the twelfth-century style of the extant masonry (Ní Ghabhláin 2006:153–154). Their fairly even spacing from each other and the neat ellipsis that the positions of these sites trace around the demesne territory of Cahercommaun are suggestive of some sort of former relationship with this capital site. These ecclesiastical sites could represent the religious centers of sections or lineages contemporary with the existence of Tulach Commáin. If this supposition were true, it would mean that the supposedly simple chiefdom of Tulach Commáin was structurally analogous to a composite chiefdom in microcosm, containing six or seven sections.

CHAPTER SEVEN

The Rulers of Tulach Commáin

The boundaries and social configurations of Tulach Commáin have been reconstructed utilizing geographical and archaeological data. Since it was a chiefdom of reasonable size and one that appeared relatively late in the Early Middle Ages, one would think that it might prove possible to establish the identity of its ruling ramage within the mass of genealogical and historical data. Achieving this goal is indeed possible, but only when geographical and place-name data are added to the mix. Following the identification of the rulers of Tulach Commáin, the subsequent history of this polity in northern Clare will be traced in this chapter.

GEOGRAPHICAL CLUES TO THE IDENTITY OF TULACH COMMÁIN'S CHIEFTAINS

In the previous chapter, the topographically irrational diversion taken by the boundary between Inchiquin and Burren baronies was discussed (Figures 4.3; 5.23). In the area where the boundary turns to the north, the barony boundary ascends a cliff and cuts the Glasgeivnagh plateau in half, whereas one would expect it to continue following the cliff face until reaching Clooncoose townland. Another peculiarity of the diversion is the fact that not only does it take so many Early Medieval settlements as its reference points, but it also appears to have been positioned purposely to include the heartland of Tulach Commáin, including three presumptive capital sites – C-94 Cahermore, Cahercommaun, and C-19 – within the limits of Inchiquin Barony.

It is obvious that the present border between Inchiquin and Burren baronies was established at a relatively late date. A "feoffment" of 1620 AD (Ainsworth no. 1015) is the earliest text that alludes to two townland parcels, Slievenaglasha and Teeskagh, within the boundary deviation. This text places them within Inchiquin Barony as they are today (Figure 4.1). The putatively fourteenth-century *O'Brien's Rental* (Hardiman no. 14) enumerates lands in Carran parish to the exclusion of those in Inchiquin Barony. It names Ceapacaibh (Cappagh, Cappagh Kennedy), Cnocain (Knockans), and Croibidhi (Creevagh), all of which (with the exception of Cappagh) are townlands that front the present barony boundary. Therefore, the boundary must go back to the period of this document at the very least. A title search of the history of ownership over these parcels within the Tulach Commáin heartland reveals who the likely former proprietors were.

THE PATRIMONY OF THE UÍ CHUINN

According to Thomas Robert Westropp, the site of Cahercommaun, or perhaps rather the land that it sits upon, is first mentioned in a will of 1585 (1901b:430, 1909b:125). Cahercommaun is presently situated within Tullycommon townland, which is listed in the late seventeenth-century *Books of Survey and Distribution*. It is a large townland, the size of 2 quarters, and so it contained many named parcels that are listed in Table 7.1 below. In the late seventeenth century, the townland was in the possession of the Earl of Inchiquin and eleven individuals are listed as tenants.

Slievbegg (Ir. *Sliabh Beag* [Little Mountain]) is most probably the modern townland of Slievenaglasha, or in Irish *Sliabh na Glaise* (The Mountain of the Grey Cow). The mountain or hill also takes the proper name of this legendary cow: Glasgeivnagh (Ir. *Glasgaibhneach* [Grey Iron-work]). The rectangular townland is located within Inchiquin Barony within a right-angle junction of Tullycommon and Teeskagh townlands. An O'Hogan is given as the tenant of Slievbegg by the Books of Survey and Distribution.

Table 7.1. The Portions of Tullycommon, after the *Books of Survey and Distribution* (IMC 1967:520–521)

Gleacrane (prob. modern Glencurran)
Lehhesse
Slievbegg
Lisheeneyeeragh
Dullisheene
Cahir Comaine
Lyshidlyane[a]
Reyboy

[a] It is interesting to note that three of the parcels in this list incorporate the Irish word *lios* as a part of their name. There are a number of unnamed rath sites within the townland, and some of these names probably refer to them.

Richard mac Edmond O'Hogan is listed in the same source as a principal proprietor of "Gleankeen." This is the modern townland of Glenquin in the valley below and to the east of Slievenaglasha. Glenquin and Slievenaglasha are linked in a document of 1620 that records the transfer of possession of these parcels from "Brien mac Connor Mac Brien of Glankyne, Co. Clare, gent., to Edmond O'Hogaine of Mahill, Co. Clare." (Ainsworth no. 1015).

Glenquin is *Gleann Chuinn* (the Glenn of Conn [38]).[1] The place-name incorporates the name of the former leading ramage of the *túath* of the Uí Chuinn, a territory that in all probability became what was in the seventeenth century the parish of Killinaboy. They and their territory were also known as *Clann*, or *Muintir hIffearnáin* after an ancestor [37] preceding Conn [38] in their genealogy (see Appendix). From the fourteenth-century saga *Caithréim Thoirdhealbhaigh* we learn that in the thirteenth century an O'Brien aristocratic residence was located on an island in Lake Inchiquin, called *Inis Uí Chuinn* (Island of the *Uí Chuinn*) (Macnamara 1901:210, 349; O'Grady 1929:63). The name of the island signifies that formerly it was in the possession of the Uí Chuinn, and was possibly their chieftain's residence given its central location within *Cenél Fermaic* and proximity to a significant monastery, *Cill Inghine Baoith*.

Very little is known of this ramage. In the twelfth-century saga *Cogadh Gaedhel re Gallaibh*, Niall Ua Cuind [39] is stated to be one of the three bodyguards, or *cometidi* (Mod. Ir. *coimdire*), of Brian Bóroimhe [6] at the battle of Clontarf in 1014 AD (Todd 1965:167). In the same source he is listed among the fallen (ibid.:209). This fact is corroborated in the *Annals of the Four Masters* in an entry of the same year. The name Niall Uí Chuinn [39] is also to be found in the Uí Chuinn genealogy (see Appendix). The *Annals of the Four Masters* record the demise of five Uí Chuinn in the battle of Moin-Mór in Emly along with nine of the Uí Dedaid in 1151 AD. It is further recorded in the same source that their chieftain, Diarmad Uí Chuinn, was slain by the Cineal Aedha of Echtge in 1170 AD. The *Four Masters* report the demise of Edaoin Ní Ua Cuinn, the wife of the Munster paramount chieftain in 1188. The last annalistic entry for them states that Conchobur Ua Cuinn [40] was slain by a Gaelic-Norman raiding party led by Conchobur Ruad Uí Briain [15] in 1197 AD.[2] Conchubur [40] is also the last name in the Clann hIffernáin genealogy in the *Book of Munster* (see Appendix).

The Uí Chuinn are given only passing mention in the fourteenth-century saga *Caithréim Thoirdhealbhaigh* (O'Grady 1929 26:19). Mathghamain Uí Briain [13] had his chief residence at Inis Uí Chuinn, so clearly by this time

the Uí Chuinn had been usurped from their chieftainship over their territory by the O'Briens. The historical evidence indicates that the Uí Chuinn
lost the chieftainship over their territory to the Uí Briain (O'Briens) sometime between 1197 and c. 1300 AD. The place-name and archaeological
evidence places them at Inchiquin Lake and in Glenquin, indicating that
their territory was probably coextensive with Killinaboy parish. The following two texts prove, moreover, that they did not vanish from the area.

AINSWORTH NO. 996

16 June 1615

"Be it knownen to all men by this presents that I Darby Nestor of Sessymore
in the County of Clare freeholder doe hearby appoint and ordayne my
wellbeloued Conor O Flannagan of the Crosse in the said County gentleman to redeeme my proportionable part of my enheirtance of Teskagh at
ths next fest of St. John the Babtist for which it lieth in mortgage by Donell
Mc Owen I Quyne of Rowshane in the saied county yeoman ... at what
tyme ... in ... May next ... I the saied Derby Nestor, Donell Mc Conoghor
O Qoyne, Conogher Oass brother to the same, or our heyres males law-
fully begotten ... shall ... redeeme my saied part ... of Teskagh ... etc."

AINSWORTH NO. 1064

1 May 1644

"Acknowledgement by Connor Clanchy of having given to Connor O'Brien
of Leameneh, esq., his "full interest & title" in Roghanbeg, Roghanemore,
Teascagh, and Cragganridge, and all other lands "descended unto mee by
way of purchase, or otherwise from the sept of the O'Quins, & specaill from
Loghlen O Quin and Donogh O Quin & from their father ..." O"Brien
paying the mortgage on the lands," being four cows and four horses."

These texts show that the Uí Chuinn persisted in some of their lands
in Inchiquin Barony up to the early seventeenth century, *four hundred years*
after losing political control of their territory! The appearance of the word
"sept" in the 1064 text implies, moreover, that they were still incorporated
as an aristocratic ramage at a time not too distant from the mid-seventeenth
century. Of the three parcels of land that can be identified from these
texts, Sheeshymore, Teeskagh, and Roughan (to call them by their modern names), the first two lie along the Burren/Inchiquin border. Roughan

is likely to be the Roughaun townland on the Fergus west of Killinaboy. Sheeshymore lies within Burren Barony. Teeskagh is one of the three townlands within the boundary diversion near the site of Cahercommaun (Fig. 4.1). The evaluation of Teeskagh in the *Books of Survey and Distribution* lists the townland as consisting entirely of stony pasture intermixed with shrub (*IMC* 1967:520), a description that could apply to the townland today. It would seem from this evidence that by the seventeenth century, the Uí Chuinn had only a toehold in marginal areas of their former territory, which they were in the process of losing.

THE UÍ CHUINN AND CATHAIR COMMÁIN

The documentary evidence shows that up to the Tudor period, the Uí Chuinn still maintained a toehold in that part of the plateau within Inchiquin Barony, principally in Teeskagh and Slievenaglasha townlands, where Cahercommaun was situated. The seventeenth-century land deeds, place-name evidence, and annals all demonstrate that they were the most likely former owners of the site of Cahercommaun. It remains now to explore the body of documentary evidence bearing upon these people and the early history of the area to see if further support for this position exists.

To start with the genealogical evidence, the genealogy of Clann hIffernáin shows that the name Uí Chuinn was of late origin. The eponymous ancestor [38] was, according to their genealogy in the Book of Lecan and the Book of Ballymote, the father of the Niall [39] who died at Clontarf in 1014 AD. The ancestor Iffernán [37] occurs five generations back on the line from Conn [38] according to the twelfth-century Rawlinson B 502 genealogy, or about eighty years earlier (O'Brien 1976:245). This figure was calculated using an estimated mean regnal generation length arrived at by dividing the time interval between the two Clann hIffernáin chieftains with known dates of death, Niall and Conchobor, by the number of chieftains on the pedigree occurring between these = 16.6 years. Assuming Conn died in the early eleventh century, this places Iffernán in the early tenth. Using the same estimate of the standard length of a reign would establish the origin of this ramage at around 800 AD.[3]

That estimate works well for placing Clann hIffernáin at Cahercommaun. The site dates to the latter part of the eighth/early ninth century, and its defensive location makes it appear as an initial settlement in new swordland. There is even a tie-in from the Annals of Innisfallen that records the death of Bishop Colmán mac Comáin on one of the Aran Islands in

751 AD. The Irish name behind Cahercommaun is *Cathair Commáin*, or Commán's Residence, just as Tullycommon is *Tulach Commáin*, (the) Mound of Commán. There is a Colmán [36] in the Clann hIffernáin genealogy, and a St. Colmán mac Commáin occurs in the *CGSH*.[4] Colmán mac Comáin, otherwise known as MoCholmóc, was a man famous in his time as a scholar and key figure in the *Céli Dé* (Client of God) ascetic movement within the Irish church (Bhreathnach 1999:87–88). His presence in the Aran Islands demonstrates a link between Tulach Commáin in the Burren and the polities of the Aran Islands, and the likelihood that Tulach Commáin was either Éoganacht Árann, or a leading chiefdom within a composite chiefdom of this name. This figure also provides a link of identity between the Uí Chuinn and the Uí Chormaic.

THE IDENTITY AND ORIGINS OF TULACH COMMÁIN

The Corcu MoDruad were under military pressure from the ancestors of the Dál Cais, the Déis Tuaiscirt (and presumably from the earliest avatar of this ramage, the Déis Becc), as well as from the Uí Fidgeinti from at least the early eighth century AD onward. An entry in the *Annals of Innisfallen* and *Annals of Ulster* records the demise of Célechair mac Commáin in the battle of Corcmodruadh in either 704 or 705 AD. Célechair mac Commáin was of the Eóganacht Uí Chormaic ramage. The Uí Chormaic were in turn one of three principal ramages composing the Uí Fidgeinti. The genealogy of the Uí Cormaic lineage gives out after Célechair's successor, Cethernach (O'Brien 1976:152 A 17). According to Frost, the Uí Chormaic were the former inhabitants of Uí Caisín and the owners of Magh Adhair before being driven out by the Uí Caisín of the Dál Cais sometime after 1100 AD (1978:113). They settled thereafter in what is now Islands Barony on what was formerly a territory of the Corcu Baiscind. After the poet ÓhUidhrin, a branch of the Uí hAichir (O'Hehir), the ruling family of the Uí Chormaic in the Early Middle ages, ruled Uí Flanchadha, the territory directly to the east of Tulach Commáin (O'Donovan 1862:125). These facts would seem to indicate pressure on the Corcu MoDruad from the Uí Chormaic as they themselves were pressed from the east by the expanding Déis Tuaiscirt and their descendants, but it is difficult to gauge the timing and extent of their displacement.

Several facts support the hypothesis of a short-lived Éoganacht chiefdom centered at Cahercommaun. To start with, there is mention of an Éoganacht Árann in a list of Éoganacht chiefdoms (O'Brien 1976:147 b

29; Byrne 2001:178). Árann is the genitive form of Ára, the Irish name of the Aran Islands situated in Galway Bay north of the Burren. The chiefdom may have incorporated part of the Burren in addition to the islands in the same manner that the islands were a part of chiefdoms on the mainland in the later historical periods. The glosses of a text that enumerates tributes due to the paramount chieftain of cashel, *Ceart ríg Caisil ó críchaib* (The Right of the Chieftain of Cashel from the Boundaries) places the Éoganacht Árann in the eastern half of the Burren (Bhreathnach 1999:85). Secondly, there is notice of the death of Colmán mac Commáin in Ára (Aran Islands) in 751 AD. Following this line of reasoning, Colmán was a long-lived son of Commáin who persisted in the Aran Islands after the demise of his brother Célechair forty-six years before his own death. In line with Bhreathnach's interpretation of the historic data, Célechair's defeat was concurrent with the founding of Tulach Commáin by a ramage of the Uí Chormaic in the early eighth century, rather than signaling a frustration of Uí Fidgeinti designs upon North Clare. Subsequently, the Uí Chormaic lineage persisted at the site following their defeat and became transformed into Clann hIffernáin. Finally, one could point to the physical resemblance between Cahercommaun and the tri-vallate cashel Cahercalla in Uí Caisín and imagine that a branch of the Éoganacht Uí Chormaic had set up an imitation of their former capital at Cahercommaun. This hypothesis is complicated somewhat by arguments recently advanced by Eoin Grogan of the North Munster Project that only the inner enclosure at Cahercalla is Early Medieval, the two outer walls having been erected possibly in the Late Bronze Age, to judge from associations with *fulachta fiadh* (Grogan 2005 I:32, 43, 83, 126, II:130).

In 744 AD, the Annals of Ulster record the devastation of the Corcu MoDruad by the Déisi. This could have been the event that portended the demise of the Cenél Báeth ramage of the Corcu MoDruad. The *Annals of Ulster* and the *Annals of Tighernach* record a battle between the Corcu MoDruad, Corcu Baiscinn, and Uí Fiachrach Aidhne in 763 AD. (It does not say who was allied with whom.) The omission of mention of the Déisi newcomers in this battle is interesting, for if Cahercommaun was inhabited at this time, Tulach Commáin would have been geographically interposed between the Corcu MoDruad and these two other groups.

SUMMARY

To recapitulate, several indices point to the establishment of the chiefdom of Tulach Commáin in the early eighth century AD. These indices are the dates of key battles, the radiocarbon dates from the site of Cahercommaun (though these cannot be said to represent the *span* of occupation at the site), and the lengths of the genealogies of Clann hIffernáin, which extend back in time only as far as to reach this target period. There is some evidence for the existence of an Éoganacht chiefdom, perhaps led by a branch of the Uí Chormaic, in northern Clare during the eighth century AD.

THE THREE-WALLED SETTLEMENT

Mention has been made of the physical resemblance between Cahercommaun in the Burren and the site of Cahercalla near Magh Adhair in Uí Caisín. Cahercalla's proximity to the ceremonial center of Magh Adhair, in the Middle Ages the inauguration place of the Uí Briain chieftains and kings, and its central location within Uí Caisín indicate that it possessed special significance. It may have been a former capital site of the Uí Chormaic. The resemblance between Cahercommaun and Cahercalla lies in the three concentric stone walls that both settlements possess and in the fact that the two sites are roughly comparable in their overall size: Cahercommaun is 92 m in overall diameter while Cahercalla is c. 104 m. However one cannot overlook the likelihood that the ultimate source of inspiration for both sites may have been the remains of Mooghaun hill-fort, constructed during the Late Bronze Age (Grogan 2005). Mooghaun was constructed as the ritual center of a Late Bronze Age/Early Iron Age composite chiefdom in southern Co. Clare that I have here called the Tradraige, and it had probably endured as the inauguration place of the leaders of the Early Medieval descendant polity, the Corcu Baiscind. When the invading Uí Fidgeinti defeated the Corcu Baiscind in the early eighth century AD, the chieftain of the ramage that was to become the Uí Chormaic possibly erected a cashel within a preexisting bivallate hill-fort as his capital. The inauguration mound at Magh Adhair was erected or modified for use as a sacred focus for the newcomers to make a break from their defeated rival's inauguration place of Mooghaun.

The tri-vallate enclosed settlement is somewhat rare in northern Clare (see Figure 7.1). However, three were surveyed by the Cahercommaun project: C-1, or Cahercommaun itself; C-3, a triple-banked rath 75 m in diameter bisected by the boundary between Crughwill and Ballyconry townlands in Carran parish; and C-94, a triple-walled cashel named Cahermore (*Cathair Mór*) in Lackareagh townland in Inchiquin Barony. This latter site is 113 m in overall diameter. Though these two latter sites approach or exceed Cahercommaun in diameter, neither is as substantial

Figure 7.1. Distribution of sites with three enclosure walls in the survey region. Note that these sites cluster in the former heartland of the chiefdom of *Tulach Commáin* (see Fig. 6.10).

as Cahercommaun. The outermost wall of Cahermore is merely a low, loosely stacked string of rocks and boulders one stone in thickness. The inner enclosure of Cahercommaun is 42 m in diameter with walls over 7 m thick, while the inner enclosure wall of Cahermore is 34 m in diameter and 3.5 m thick. As all three of these tri-vallate sites are reasonably close to one another, they possibly represent a material manifestation of the Tulach Commáin chiefdom. The fact that these sites possess three concentric stone walls like Cahercalla appears as a potential indication of the geographical origin of Tullach Commáin's founders.

To push this conjecture a bit further onto thin evidence, if the three-walled settlement traces the extent of the Uí Fidgeinti wave that broke over Clare in the eighth century, the site of Dún Aonghasa on Inis Mór may mark the furthest reach of this wave. As stated above, Tullach Commáin and the Aran Islands may have been bound together as a composite chiefdom. Excavation has revealed that like Cahercalla, Dún Aonghasa was a Late Bronze Age hill-fort modified by the expansion of the interior enclosure into a cashel, probably during the Early Middle Ages (Cotter 1996a, 1996b). Early Medieval habitation evidence was scant, but that does not preclude the site having functioned as a place of inauguration/sacred focus of the Aran Islands polity.

THE TROUBLED EARLY HISTORY OF
THE CORCU MODRUAD

The difficulties of deciphering the early affiliations of Tulach Commáin from the ethnohistorical sources are compounded by the problem of untangling the puzzle of leadership in the chiefdom of the neighboring Corcu MoDruad. Not only are the names of chieftains of the Corcu MoDruad cited in the annals not in agreement with existing genealogies, but the genealogies themselves are not internally consistent.

To begin with the annals first, the two earliest entries pertaining to Corcu MoDruad record the names of chieftains whose names are absent from the surviving Corcu MoDruad genealogies: Flann Féorna [53] (d. 737 AFM; 739 ACl) and Torpad [54] (d. 769 AI). In Chapter 3, it was noted that Flann Féorna was a chieftain in many of the Cíarraige lineages, and in the *Annals of Innisfallen*, Flann Féorna, rí Cíarraige Lúachra, dies in 741, surely not a coincidence. Torpaid is a name that also frequently appears in Cíarraige genealogies, and also in genealogies of the neighbors of the Corcu MoDruad such as the Uí Fiachrach Aidhne in what is now Co. Galway. Moreover, there is place-name evidence for Torpaid's existence in North Clare as there is a Dún Torptha in Drumcreehy parish in the Burren (though this a relatively small rath site; see Figure 3.15). These annal entries, taken together with the testimony of the "West Munster Synod" discussed earlier in Chapter 3, suggest a dominion by the Cíarraige

Luachra over the Corcu MoDruad in the eighth century and the imposition of a lineage of the Cíarraige upon them.

The first *rí* of the Corcu MoDruad genealogies to appear in the annals is Flaithbertach mac Dub-Ruip [50], who died in 873 AD (*AI*). The annals record the deaths of three sons of Flaithbertaich, starting with Bruatiud in 899 AD and ending with Cett [55] in 919. These two possessed the chieftainship of Corcu MoDruad in sequence. After Cett, deciphering the political constitution of the Corcu MoDruad becomes difficult. The Book of Leinster genealogy of the Corcu MoDruad ends with Bruatiud and the later genealogies in Rawlinson B 502 omit him, creating a lacuna. As the following chapter will spell out, the lacuna was apparently due to another spate of interference in the affairs of Corcu MoDruad, this time stemming from the aggressive actions of the chieftains of the Uí Tairdelbaig of In Déis Tuaiscirt who were to become shortly thereafter the Dál Cais.

CHAPTER EIGHT

The World of Brian Bóroimhe

The ninth–twelfth centuries AD in Co. Clare are of interest in that the earlier part of this period witnessed the origins of one of the most storied chiefdom confederacies in Ireland, the confederacy of the Dál Cais. Whereas the specific circumstances of the origins of the earlier Connachta and Éoganachta confederacies are lost to the mists of time, the rise of the Dál Cais can be traced almost from the beginning in the annals. Thus it is possible to disentangle fact from fancy in the genealogies of the Dál Cais, and the process of chiefdom confederacy formation becomes clear.

As a result of the accomplishments of the tenth-century Uí Thairdelbaig leaders of the Dál Cais confederacy, most prominently Brian Bóroimhe (Anglicized Brian Boru), first Co. Clare and then all of Munster became subordinated to them. In the early twelfth century this conquered area coalesced into a primitive state under the leadership of Muirchertach Ua Briain [12] (Gibson 1995). The expansion of first the Dál Cais confederacy and then the primitive state of the Uí Briain naturally had political consequences for the formerly independent chiefdoms of Co. Clare, including the chiefdom of Corcu MoDruad in northwestern Clare. Indeed, the structural changes to Corcu MoDruad, including boundary changes and shifts in the position of capital sites, cannot be understood without reference to these larger-scale long-term processes. It is for this reason that an examination of the sources for the early history of Clare is necessary.

SOURCES FOR THE EARLY HISTORY OF THOMOND

As before, the principal sources of information for the tenth and eleventh centuries are the annals kept by the more important religious houses in Ireland, and the great body of genealogical material that has come down to us in a number of compilations of the Medieval period. These copious yet prosaic records are supplemented by a saga that charts the career of the illustrious leader who emerged from the Dál Cais of Tipperary and Clare to seize nearly all of Ireland, Brian Bóroimhe [6]. No narrative matches *Cogadh Gaedhel re Gallaibh* (The War of the Irish against the Foreigners) for detail in portraying events in Co. Clare during the tenth century AD.

Brian mac Cennétig, otherwise known (in modern Irish) as Brian Bóroimhe [6] (d. 1014 AD), was the dominant figure of Clare of the late tenth and early eleventh centuries. He was no mere regional chieftain. His importance extended to the provincial and supraprovincial levels as well. The career and life of this hero can be traced in the annals and, more extensively, in the colorful saga *Cogadh Gaedhel re Gallaibh*, written anonymously in the twelfth century (Todd 1965).

Since Brian was a chieftain of island-wide importance, *Cogadh Gaedhel re Gallaibh* is very much a national saga. It was modeled on the life of Alfred the Great of England and was in turn the influential model for the other great saga to depict tumultuous political events in medieval Clare, *Caithréim Thoirdhealbhaigh* (Ó Corráin 1972:120). CGrG devotes most of the narrative to conveying the particulars of Brian's career at the national level and only parenthetically are events, peoples, and places in Co. Clare described. Nevertheless, enough information relevant to Clare can be gleaned from this text to establish the basic political configurations of Clare and Munster at this time. Much more attention will be given to the information in the annals and genealogies in the following discussion.

MUNSTER IN THE TENTH–TWELFTH CENTURIES

What is now the modern county of Clare was in the two centuries after 1000 AD the largest part of the province of *Tuadmumu* (North Munster, Anglicized Thomond), a territorial section of a threefold division of the province of Munster. The other two divisions were Deas Mhumu (Desmond), which took in the modern counties of Cork and Kerry, and Iar Mhumu (East Munster) or Ormonde, which took in present-day Waterford, Limerick, and Tipperary. This medieval threefold division of Munster ensued upon the pyrrhic victory of Brian Boru at the battle of Clontarf in 1014. Prior to Clontarf, only a twofold division of Mumu into northern and southern halves, divided by the Sliabh Luachra, was known.

In the period 970–1197 AD Tuadmumu was dominated by the chiefdoms of the Dál Cais. The Dál Cais were originally a branch of the Déisi called the Déis Tuaiscirt, who in the eighth century were situated in eastern Limerick (Ó Corráin 1972:7). During or prior to the tenth century they had changed their name to the Dál Cais in conformity with an origin myth and genealogy that they had created to link them with the then politically dominant Éoganacht chiefdoms that prevailed in Munster. They took their name from Cass, a descendant of Lugaid Mend, who was in turn descended from Cormac Cass – a supposed brother of Éogan Mór, the ancestor of the Éoganachta (O'Brien 1976:206–207; O'Rahilly 1999:184).

THE POLITICAL STRUCTURE OF TENTH-CENTURY MUNSTER

The origin of the idea of a paramount chieftain of Munster can be dated back to sometime around 700 AD, or somewhat before, when a number of disparate Munster chiefdoms forged themselves into a confederacy with fictive genealogical ties. As a confederacy the Éoganachta were not terribly cohesive. Ó Corráin states that they were split into two mutually hostile groups, the eastern and western Éoganachta (1972:1). Byrne further makes much of the fact that often the "office" of rí Mumhain (paramount chieftain of Munster) went unfilled, or that the individual stated to have filled it in the annals or chieftain lists seems to have engaged in no discernible activities worthy of the title (Byrne 2001:203–204). The perceived weakness of the Éoganachta confederacy and of the office of provincial chieftain broaches a greater problem whose resolution lies in the definitional sphere. Can a confederacy be said to possess the qualities of a polity when it exhibits little demonstrable political cohesion or stability?

The answer, I believe, is affirmative when one defines the problem in terms of the quality and intensity of interaction between constituent political units. Political cohesion can be seen to vary in intensity with respect to two poles of political constitution (see Davies 1993). On one hand, there are those political systems predicated upon symmetrical relationships of subordination and superordination between individuals. In political systems of this nature, latitude for independent political behavior is restricted, and in complex examples, deviance from permissible norms of political action is circumscribed by force. At or near this pole of integration are the centralized chiefdoms and states most frequently encountered in the anthropological literature. The more stratified chiefdoms of Polynesia, such as those of eighteenth-century Tonga, come to mind, as do the archaic states of the Middle East and Mesoamerica. These polities are similar in that a body of officials existed that was directly responsible to the paramount leader, and in that the administrators of subterritories of the polity were either appointees of the paramount leader or, if not, derived their authority from the paramount leader and were directly responsible to him.

At the other end of the spectrum are voluntary relationships of political cooperation for the mutual benefit of the participants. In practice, these relationships range in intensity from narrowly defined conditional alliances such as economic treaties or defense pacts to long-term and multifaceted relationships of confederation such as the military-economic confederation of the Hansa States during the Middle Ages. There are several well-known examples of confederate systems of political organization existing among societies of varying social complexity. The segmentary alliance system of the Nuer described by Evans-Pritchard (1940) is probably at one extreme in terms of the loose and conditional nature of the links between the components and levels in the system. This system apparently only functioned in military undertakings and had no other political or social significance. At a higher level of social integration, the seventeenth–eighteenth-century confederation of the Iroquois, though also of military import, was more sustained than the Nuer segmentary system, and the leaders also exercised authority beyond the military sphere. Some of the confederacies of the societies of pastoral nomads of southern Iran, such as the Qashqa'i, are of more recent vintage and are comparable to the confederacies of medieval Ireland in the existence of a central leader with jural authority and powers of taxation (Beck 1986). More to the point, the Qashqa'i confederacy can be said to be a true *chiefdom* confederacy. Within this confederacy there were three levels of leadership, and the lineages of the Khans (chieftains) and Ilkhanis (paramount chieftains) constituted an aristocracy (Beck 1986:193–195, 233; Gibson 2011).

The confederacies and alliances of pre-Norman Munster differed slightly from that of the Iroquois in the degree to which leadership was institutionalized. The office of *rí Mumhain* was a recognized institution, though largely bereft of the institutional trappings of kingship, and there was a provincial ceremonial center at *Caisel* (Cashel), established by the Éoganachta confederation. Cashel had probably been a ceremonial center from the fifth century onward for the ancestors of the eastern Éoganachta, but had not attained the status as a symbolic center of provincial power until several centuries thereafter (Mac Niocaill 1972:5–8). There is no evidence that the *rí Mumhain* actually resided or held court at Cashel. It is more than likely that Cashel functioned as a symbol of supreme provincial power in much the same way that Tara, Rathcrochan, and Emain Macha did in their respective provinces.

THE PARAMOUNTCY OF MUNSTER

As stated earlier, the Éoganachta confederation was never strongly cohesive, and the office of provincial paramount chieftain was ceremonial in nature. It existed as an acknowledgement of the pact that existed between the member chiefdoms of the confederacy. When the paramountcy was occupied in force, it promulgated the position of the strongest chieftain of the most powerful *mór thúath* within the interaction sphere of the *cóiced* of Munster. The possession of this office ratified the chieftain's ability to defeat militarily any other leader of a composite chiefdom. The ascension to office was usually the culmination of a series of military campaigns against the strongest would-be challengers. Apparently, however, there were also protracted periods of comparative political/military equality among chiefdoms when the confederacy had little binding force and the office, when occupied at all, was filled by the leaders of the chiefdom that held the site on a nominal basis, the Éoganacht Caisil.

The Dál Cais ascended to the provincial paramountcy during a period of Eóganacht decline and political tumult instanced by attacks on Munster by the Uí Néill of Leinster (Ó Corráin 1972:114–117). The rise of the Dál Cais had been relatively rapid. The first mention of them under the name Dál Cais occurs in the *Annals of Innisfallen* in an entry of 934 AD. Prior to this entry, the chiefdom of the sons of Cennétig [3], the Uí Thairdelbaig, is given a mention in the *Vita Tripartita*, which dates to around 900 AD (Ó Corráin 1972:114). According to Frost, in the Early Middle Ages the territory of Uí Thairdelbaig was probably coextensive with the parishes of Killaloe, O'Briensbridge, and Kiltenanlea (1978:157). This territory is indicated in Figure 9.2. This configuration of the territory possibly dates to the Medieval period, when the fortunes of the Uí Thairdelbaig had diminished from their Early Medieval IV high water mark. Frost states that Briain mac Cennétig [1] was eighth in descent from Tairdelbach [1], the founding ancestor of Uí Thairdelbaig (ibid.).

Ó Corráin cites evidence that under Cennétig mac Lorcáin [3], the Uí Thairdelbaig had established themselves over the Dál Cais by the 930s (1972:114).[1] One of his sons, Mathgamain mac Cennétig [5], established his claim to the paramountcy of Munster in 964 AD with an attack on the Éoganacht Caisil, the owners of the provincial capital. This thrust him into a series of battles against the Norse of Limerick (Ir. *Luimneach*), the Éoganacht Rathlind, and the Éoganacht Aine, over all of which he prevailed. In 976 AD he was captured and killed by his arch-enemy Máel

Muad, *rí* of the Éoganacht Rathlind. His younger brother Brian [6] then became *rí* over the Dál Cais.

Brian then embarked upon a long career that ended with his death at the battle of Clontarf in 1014 AD, by which time he had become the most powerful chieftain in Ireland. *Cogadh Gaedhel re Gallaibh* documents that his career as chieftain began, as one would expect, at the local level with attacks on the neighboring Uí Fidgeinti and their Norse allies of the Shannon Estuary.[2] In 978 Brian widened his military campaigns to take in his chief rivals in Munster (ibid.:103–107). By 984 AD Brian was effectively the master of Leth Mogha (ibid.:109). He spent the next two years quashing revolts and consolidating his grip on the province (Ó Corráin 1972:122). The military campaigns that he undertook after his conquest of Munster up to the time of his death were at the national level of political interaction.

THOMOND OF BRIAN BÓROIMHE AND HIS DESCENDANTS: THE EVOLUTION OF CHIEFDOM TO STATE

Cogadh Gaedhel re Gallaibh asserts that in the ninth century, prior to the campaigns of Brian Bóroimhe, the Corcu Baiscind, Corcu MoDruad, and Tradraige bore the brunt of the fighting against the marauding Norsemen (Todd 1965:9, 27–28). The Corcu Baiscind, under the leadership of the Uí Domhnaill, achieved victory over two Norse chieftains on Inis Mór at the mouth of the Fergus River (103). Tradraige is stated to have been completely overrun by Norsemen at this time (61).

Sometime after his ascension to the paramountcy of Munster, Brian [6] established his capital at Cenn Coradh on a hill on the west bank of the Shannon River.[3] This location was obviously chosen for strategic reasons – it is the only place where the Shannon narrows sufficiently to be spanned by a bridge. Hence it was the gateway into Thomond from the east (145). Cenn Coradh also sat at a place where river traffic coming up the Shannon could be intercepted before entering the vast reaches of Lough Derg. The saga and contemporary entries in the annals make it clear that Lough Derg was the embarkation point for attacks on Connacht and the Midlands, including wealthy monasteries such as Inis Celtra and Clonmacnoise (21, 39, 109; *AI*: 983 AD; Gwynn and Gleeson 1962:95).

Near his capital, probably on or near the site of a previously existing monastic establishment, Brian erected the church of Cill da Lua (Angl.: Killaloe; Todd 1965:139). Though he sponsored other public works at

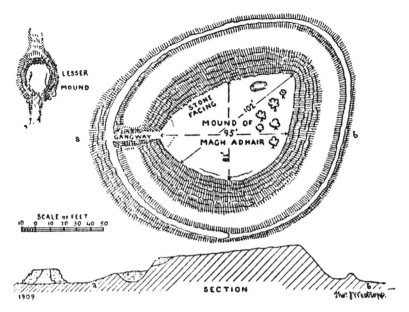

Figure 8.1. Plan and section of the mounds at Magh Adhair (Westropp 1907–1908b:382, Fig. 4).

nearby religious sites in Thomond (e.g., Tuam-Gréine, Inis Celtra), this was obviously his principal church. Cill da Lua was located in proximity to his capital, and it became the seat of the chief bishop of Munster following his death (Gwynn and Gleeson 1962:105–108). Prior to this the principal church of the Dál Cais was almost certainly Tuam-Gréine, as Rebachán mac Mothlai was both rí of the Dál Cais and abbot of this monastery when he died in 934 (*AI*: 934 AD; Fig. 8.1).

The inauguration site of the paramount chieftains of the Dál Cais was on Adhair's Plain (Irish *Magh Adhair*). According to Frost, initially the whole territory that was later to become Uí Caisín was called Magh Adhair (1978:35). Later, the name became restricted to the inauguration site only. This site was to remain the venue for the inauguration of the Dál Cais paramount chieftains, and later of the O'Brien kings of Thomond up through the Middle Ages (FitzPatrick 2004:59).

The site at present is located in Toonagh townland in the parish of Clooney, Bunratty Upper, on the east side of the Hell River, a small tributary of the Rine. The antiquarian T. J. Westropp described the particulars of the site in the nineteenth century (see Figure 8.1):

> North of the bridge, over this rivulet we find a sort of amphitheater, fenced by crags, and enclosed by a low bank, marked here and there by blocks of stone. In the area of this space rises a large flat topped mound, girt with a fosse and bank. The tumulus measures from 85 to 100 feet on top, and is over 20 feet

high. The top has only a few sloe bushes, and a worn slab of limestone, level with the ground on the north side. A sloping way, with steep sides, leads across the fosse westward to the level of the field. A second but much smaller mound, or rather cairn, of earth and large stones, about 10 feet high and 17 feet on the top, rises 30 feet from the brink of the stream. North of the great mound, and within the leveled enclosure, is a boulder of purple conglomerate, embedding pebbles of rose quartz and purple porphyry; it is about 4 feet long by three feet high, and has, in its upper surface a small oval basin apparently hollowed by grinding. Across the stream, 141 feet to the west ... stands a rough slab of limestone, 6 ft. 3 in. high, from 3 ft. to 2 ft. 6 in. wide, and 10 in. thick, forming a pillar in the line of the two mounds and the sloping foot-way; between it and the stream is a shattered block like the base of a second pillar. (Westropp 1896a:55–56)

The excavations conducted on Tara Hill and at Knowth in County Meath have substantiated the fact that the Irish Celts utilized passage grave cemeteries of the Late Neolithic for their own rites (Eogan 1968, 1974, 1977; Ó Ríordáin 1955). The mounds at Magh Adhair may also prove to have been originally constructed during the Neolithic or Bronze Age periods (FitzPatrick 2004:55). A perusal of the first edition Ordnance Survey map of this area reveals other mounds in the immediate vicinity of the two mentioned by Westropp.[4]

Originally a large sacred tree or *bile* existed at Magh Adhair, under which the Dálcassian *ríg* were inaugurated. It was cut down by Máel Sechnaill II, *ard rí* (paramount chieftain) of the Uí Néill while on a raid of Munster in 982 AD (Ó Corráin 1972:121).[5] Strangely, Magh Adhair had lapsed into almost complete obscurity by the nineteenth century.

As stated in the previous chapter, just one half mile to the southwest of the inauguration mound of Magh Adhair in Cahercalla townland is an enormous cashel site (Figure 8.2). Its inner enclosure is stated to be 100 feet (30.5 m) in diameter, with walls 17 feet thick. After Westropp's measurements and plan, Cahercalla measures 316′ x 336′ in total diameter (96 x 102.5 m) (1896a:56, Plate II). According to Eoin Grogan, the middle and external walls are prehistoric (2005 I:32, 83). However, it is likely from the placement of the inner enclosure that the intention was to incorporate the preexisting walls to effect a tri-vallate plan, thus elevating the site to a status of special character – marking its occupant as someone of the *nemed* or "holy" class. This presumption is grounded in the obvious sacral qualities attributed to the number three and its multiples by the Irish intelligentsia in the Early Middle Ages, and the description of chieftains and the grounds of their residences as *nemed*.[6] Given its proximity to Magh Adhair, and what has been outlined above concerning the properties of the

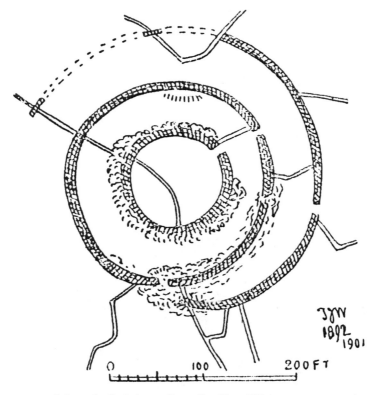

Figure 8.2. Cahercalla Cashel near Quin, Co. Clare (Westropp 1907–1908b:381).

capital set, it is difficult not to view both sites as two parts of a capital set, an inauguration mound and a chieftain's homestead.

Whose capital set lies in the vicinity of Magh Adhair is an open question. The first candidate is the progenitor chiefdom of the Dál Cais, the Déis Tuaiscirt, who pressed into eastern Clare in the early eighth century from western Limerick (Ó Corráin 1972:7, 114). It is difficult to get a geographical fix on the earliest distribution of the chiefdoms of the Déis Tuaiscirt in Thomond due to the disruptive impact of the Vikings in the tenth century. According to a reconstruction of their genealogy, the two principal clusters of chiefdoms that composed the Dál Cais – the Uí Caisín and Uí Bloid – were the earliest segments of the Déis Tuaiscirt (Ó Corráin 1973:Table 1; Ryan 1943: Genealogical Table). In the Early Middle Ages, the Uí Caisín were in the west and incorporated Magh Adhair within their boundaries while the Uí Bloid were in the east nearest to the presumed point of entry of the Déis Tuaiscirt into Clare across the Shannon.

At first the paramount chieftainship over the Déis Tuaiscirt rested in the Uí Oengusso branch of the Uí Blait (Uí Bloid). There were three principal ramages of Uí Oengusso: Uí Cernaig, Uí Eichtígern, and Uí Róngaile. The

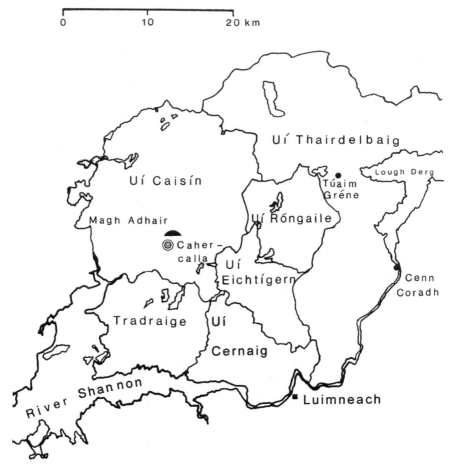

Figure 8.3. Reconstruction of the composite chiefdom of the Dál Cais in the ninth–tenth centuries AD (after O'Donovan and Joyce in White 1893; Frost 1978; Ryan 1943).

first two chiefdoms monopolized chieftainship of the Déis Tuaiscirt from the late seventh to early ninth centuries AD (Ryan 1943:195). The territories of Uí Cernaig and Uí Eichtigern were located in the south-central portion of the Déis Tuaiscirt composite chiefdom. This would seem to make good geographical sense from what we now understand of the principles governing early Irish capital location (see Figure 8.3) (Gibson 1995). The capital territories are near the center of the chiefdom, but since the chiefdom is bordered on the south by water (the Shannon River), providing some protection from attack in this direction, the capital territories are in the south rather than at the true geographical center as we would predict if the chiefdom were landlocked and surrounded by external enemies.

However, it is not clear why the Dál Cais inauguration site would have been located in Uí Caisín to the east of Uí Oengusso. One can only speculate that either Uí Oengusso was formerly where Uí Caisín came to be

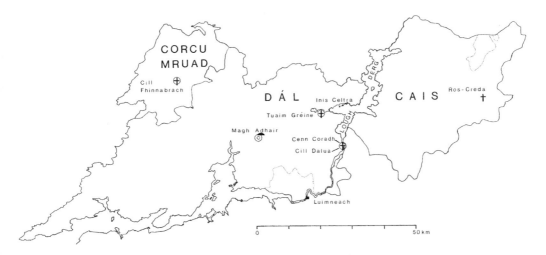

Figure 8.4. Map of the dioceses of Kilfenora (*Cill Fhinnabrach*) and Killaloe (*Cill Dalua*) showing the principal sites in each. Brian Bóroimhe's chiefdom would have taken in the territory of the diocese of Limerick to the south as well.

located, or that Uí Caisín provided the first paramount chieftains of the Déis Tuaiscirt. Another strong possibility is that the Déis Tuaiscirt had simply taken over the inauguration site of the formerly dominant chiefdom in eastern Clare that they displaced. After Frost, the former owners of Magh Adhair were the Uí Chormaic, a chiefdom professedly of the Eóganachta, but, as proposed above, they were an offshoot of the Uí Fidgeinti. The Uí Chormaic were led in the Early Middle Ages by the Uí hAichir ramage. After the *Annals of the Four Masters*, the Uí hAichir managed to persist in Magh Adhair up until the twelfth century though they were dominated by the Mac Con Mara, the descendants of the Uí Caisín. Thereafter they were driven to the west. So it is possible that Cahercalla was the abode of the Uí Chormaic chieftain, and that Magh Adhair was originally their inauguration site. Following this line of conjecture, Cahercommaun and potentially Dún Aonghasa display their Uí Fidgeinti affinities in their multiple ramparts.

Does the geographical location of the chieftains' capitals discussed above conform to the principles that have been derived from historical analysis governing the location and structure of Irish capitals? The answer is a resounding yes. A perspective on this may be gained by viewing the position of Cenn Coradh, Brian's capital, against the configuration of the diocese of Killaloe (see Figure 8.4).

The creation of the diocese of Killaloe was an outcome of the Synod of Rathbreasail (or *Fiadh-mic-Oengusa*) held in 1111 AD. Prior to this synod informality characterized the organization of the Irish church – there were no archbishops or fixed diocesan boundaries (Gwynn and Gleeson 1962:120). Two dioceses, Killaloe and Limerick, were created out of the bulk of the Dalcassian territory accumulated from the conquests of Brian and his descendants. With respect to location, Brian's capital at Cenn Coradh adheres to the principle of capital centrality when it is observed that territory to the east and south, within the later boundaries of the dioceses of Killaloe and Limerick, lay under his rule.

THE ORIGINS OF THE STATE IN MUNSTER UNDER THE UÍ BRIAIN

Early states vary only slightly from complex chiefdoms in organizational details and so it is a tricky matter to make a determination as to exactly when a complex chiefdom has evolved into a state. This is especially true when the data at hand are Irish medieval ethnohistorical texts – in this case the annals and a saga. The language of the annals is terse and sometimes ambiguous. *Cogadh Gaedhel re Gallaibh* is propagandistic and was composed over a century after the events it describes had transpired. However, apart from its organizational attributes, the state possesses geographical characteristics and these can be deduced even from ambiguous data. This analysis will therefore place greater weight on geographical data in the determination as to when a state had come into being in Munster.

The earliest form of state, which Elman Service has called the "primitive state," has a short list of characteristics by which it can be recognized (Service 1975). The head of the state is termed the "king." Not only does the king occupy a separate stratum within the state above the rest of the aristocracy, but his family constitutes a separate caste. No longer is the king looked upon as a superior kinsman to the rest of the aristocracy as would be the case in a chiefdom. The king has life and death power over his subjects, and executions of enemies and rebels is often ritual in form (Sagan 1985). Kingdoms are administered by the king through a "primitive bureaucracy" of counselors and the administrators of provinces. The king has the power to both allocate administrative positions to inferiors and take them away. Therefore, the tenure of secondary positions of authority within the primitive state rests entirely upon a personal relationship with the king. The administrators function as overseers of local chieftains who are left in place so that the former constitute a layer of administration superimposed upon a preexisting multitiered hierarchy of chiefdoms. The apparatus of the state was supported by a system of taxation rather than ad hoc levying of tribute.

The power of the king rests in part upon the sacred character of early kingship, but more concretely upon the king's authority over a full-time body of professional warriors with permanent leadership. Since the king and his family constitute a superior caste, and since he derives authority from force of arms rather than shared kinship with a ramage, the king is free to leave the territory of his chiefdom in order to locate his administrative headquarters in a place where administrative efficiency is maximized.

Brian mac Cennétig had carried out far-reaching military conquests, and as we have seen, had replaced indigenous ramages with lineages of his own kinsmen even in Thomond's remote chiefdoms. There is slight evidence from the sources that the Dalcassian polity under Brian was on its way to becoming a state. True to his nickname *bóroimhe* ("cattle-tribute"; Old Irish *bóraime*), he imposed tribute payments upon defeated chiefdoms, but this fact in itself betrays the existence of a nonstate system. The imposition of tribute attests that he had left defeated leaders in place, and the fact that even his own saga relates that he had difficulties exacting tribute shows that it was no system of taxation. Within the *Annals of Innisfallen* is an entry for 985 AD that hints that Brian may have employed professional fighters: "*Crech lasna Désse co amsu Briain co rucsat .ccc. bó ...,*" which Seán Mac Airt has translated as "The Déisi raided Brian's mercenaries and took three hundred cows ..." (Mac Airt 1988:167). The word *amus* can mean "mercenary" but it can also mean "servant" or "attendant" – that is, the passage may refer to persons employed to watch over Brian's cows. Translating *amus* this way better accounts for Brian's violent reaction to the deed.

Within *Cogadh Gaedhel re Gallaibh*, one can find a complete description of a state-level administrative apparatus said to have existed in Brian's time:

> Do ordaih, imorro, rigu ocus taisechu, maeru ocus reachtairedu, in cach tir ocus in cach thuaith iarun, ocus da thogaib in cís rigda.

> He ordained, moreover, kings and chieftains, stewards and bailiffs, in every land and every chiefdom after that, and he levied the royal tax ...

> Ri for cach tir uathib, ocus toeseach for cach tuaith iarsin, ocus abb for cach cill, ocus, ocus maeir for cach mbali, ocus suartleach cach tigi ... (Todd 1965:48–49)

> A king from them for each land, and a chieftain over every chiefdom, and an abbot over every church, and a steward over every district, and a mercenary in each house.... (ibid.)

The "he" of these passages is, however, not Brian mac Cennétig but a Viking leader, and the text is from the twelfth century when state-level organization would have been familiar to the author. Seen from the perspective of the text, this administrative structure and taxation were curses visited by the Vikings upon the Irish, and were eventually swept away by Brian. "He enslaved and reduced to bondage their stewards and their bailiffs" (Todd 1965:138–139). Further on, Brian is said to have had stewards (*maer*), one of which was a Viking. "It was on this occasion was slain Osli, son of Dubhcenn, son of Imar, a man of rank of Brian, and one of his great stewards (*mórmaer*) . . ." (ibid.:146–147). And within his army at the battle of Clontarf in 1014 AD, he is said to have had chieftains and great stewards (ibid.:168–169). One of these great stewards, Mael Sechnaill mac Domnaill, was not an appointee nor a subject chieftain but a powerful paramount chieftain who was leading an army of his own people. According to the annals, he was a competitor who made a pact with Brian similar to Hitler's pact with Stalin to divide Ireland between them. Clearly, *Cogadh Gaedhel re Gallaibh* cannot be trusted to provide a true account of Brian's administration. Perhaps most telling is the fact that Brian's late capital at Cenn Coradh was situated within his own chiefdom of Uí Tairdelbaig. He was not willing to break with his indigenous base of power.

The evidence for the formation of a state in Munster is less equivocal in the twelfth century. Whereas Brian had created a capital within his traditional power-base in Uí Tairdelbaig, Muirchertach Ua Briain had moved his capital to the Viking-founded town of Luimneach (Limerick), and that town became the center of the church in Munster as well as its political center. At the first synod he convened in 1101 AD, the Synod of Cashel, he handed Cashel, the old Éoganacht sacred center, over to the church. Later, at the Synod of Rathbreasail, Cashel was made the seat of the archbishop of *Leth Mumhain* and endowed with the lands of the by now hapless Éoganacht Caisil. Since Cashel had been in all likelihood a sacred pagan center in the manner of Mooghaun and Tara, its new role as the center of the church in Munster was entirely in keeping with its former character.

These acts signify that Muirchertach Ua Briain possessed power to a degree substantially above that of his great-grandfather Brian. He was powerful enough to physically remove himself from his supporters within the Uí Tairdelbaig chiefdom. Moreover, he was powerful enough to eliminate a subordinate chiefdom wholesale and reallocate its lands, rather than subordinating or removing its leaders. These acts demonstrate that Muirchetach had become the leader of a state, in other words, a king.

Philip Dwyer advanced the argument that the configurations of the diocese of Killaloe may have been influenced by the boundaries of the Dál Cais polity that encompassed it (1878:8). To support this assertion he quoted the assessment made by O'Donovan concerning the extent of the Dál Cais polity and the lands they dominated at the height of their expansion:

> The principality of Thomond, generally called the county of the Dalcassians, comprised the entire of the present county of Clare, the parishes of Inniscaltra and Clonrush, in the county of Galway, the entire Ely O'Carroll, the baronies of Ikerrin, Upper and Lower Ormond, and somewhat more than the western half of the barony of Clanwilliam, in the county of Tipperary. The baronies of Owneybeg, Coonaght, and Clan-william, and the eastern halves of the baronies of Smallco'y and Coshlea in the county of Limerick. (O'Donovan in Dwyer 1878:8)

The shifting of the center of political and religious power in Munster south to Luimneach (Limerick) during the reign of Muirchertach [12] explains the chunks of territory that this diocese removed out of Killaloe diocese north of the Shannon. These territories, Uí Ainmire and Uí Cearnaigh, lay just across the Shannon from this town, and the thought was probably to enlarge the demesne lands of the cathedral there. Killaloe had been superseded in importance by Limerick and so was made to sacrifice territory to Limerick's diocese. The distended configurations of the territory of Killaloe diocese in the region around Roscrea is a product of the addition of a part of the territory of *Eile Uí Cherbail* (Ely O'Carroll) to Killaloe by Muirchertach [12] (Gwynn and Gleeson 1962:120–127). This is yet another act of dispossession that shows Muirchertach to have been a king.

As *Cogadh Gaedhel re Gallaibh* is a twelfth-century text, quite possibly even created under Muirchertach Ua Briain's patronage, it delivers insights into the administrative structure of Muichertach's state. Muirchertach as king ruled through regional administrators (*mórmaer*) to which local chieftains (*toísigh*) reported. The term mórmaer first appears in a Scottish source dated to 918 AD and is of Scottish, possibly Pictish origin (Grant 2000:65). In Alexander Grant's analysis of the growth in power of the Scottish monarchy, mórmaer had been the autonomous chieftains over composite chiefdoms ("multiple estates") whose status had been downgraded with the growth in power of the central monarch. The word *maer* does not appear in the *Annals of Innisfallen* until 1095, its cognate and predecessor *rechtaire* appearing as late as 1031 AD in the same source. The rechtaire formerly functioned in the Early Middle Ages as an adjunct or major-domo of a chieftain, one who collected the payments of clients or meted out punishment to those who had incurred the displeasure of the chieftain. It seems, then, that this status term was borrowed from the earlier Scottish state and was used in Munster over a century later when Muirchertach's power had grown sufficiently great to justify it.

In twelfth-century Ireland *toísigh* were formerly referred to as *ríg* (pl. of *rí*) in the Early Medieval law texts, and were the chieftains of simple chiefdoms. The switch to *toísech* is a direct outgrowth of the loss of autonomy of these leaders under the emergent Ua Briain state. A parallel development occurred in Scotland, where the *toísech* became the *thayn*, the king's administrator of a local district (Grant 2000:53). *Cogadh Gaedhel re Gallaibh* makes direct reference not only to professional fighters (*súaitrech*), but also to their manner of support – being consigned to the chief's subjects' households.

How was the state of Muirchetach Ua Briain financed? Again, *Cogadh Gaedhel re Gallaibh's* description of Viking taxation is probably a projection of tax collection under Muirchertach. The tax that supported the layers of state administration and the military undertakings of Muichertach Uí Briain was in all likelihood called *cís*. In the Early Middle Ages, *cís* was tribute paid by a subordinate chieftain to a paramount chieftain. It was probably levied in a similar manner by Muirchertach since in all early states, including the Roman Empire, tax was collected from the immediately lower administrative node by the higher node and so on down the line. By Late Medieval times *cís* had developed to become an ad hoc exaction by chieftains from commoners, and so a tax pure and simple.

THE CORCU MODRUAD IN BRIAN'S TIME

As previously stated, there is little overlap between the chieftains of the Corcu MoDruad listed in the genealogies and those mentioned in the annals, though this is not a problem restricted to the Corcu MoDruad. Those Corcu MoDruad genealogies found in the different collections are seen to be relatively shallow once gods and heroes have been omitted (see Appendix). The *Book of Leinster* contains a pair of disconnected genealogies. The shorter of the two begins with Rechtabra, a name of an eighth-century Corcu Baiscind chieftain and also a chieftain that occurs in genealogies of the Cíarraige. The genealogy ends three chieftains later with Bruatiud mac Flaithbertaich who is said by the *Annals of the Four Masters* to have died in 899 AD. Two other sons of Flaithbertach show up in the annals; the last, Cett [55], is said by the *Annals of Innisfallen* to have died in 919 AD.

In 925 AD, the *Annals of the Four Masters* state that Anrudán mac Máel-Gorm [7] assumed the chieftainship of Corcu MoDruad. Anrudán mac Máel-Gorm is in the genealogy of the Uí Tairdelbaig ramage of the Dál Cais (O'Brien 1976:153 a 10). It is clear, then, that Anrudán was imposed upon the Corcu MoDruad from without by the Uí Tairdelbaig. Ó Corráin states that Cennétig mac Lorcáin [3] had established himself as *rí* of the Uí Tairdelbaig possibly by 934. Since the ascension of Anrudán over the Corcu MoDruad preceded this achievement by nine years, perhaps Cennétig's predecessor Lorcán [2] was responsible for engineering the rise of the Uí Tairdelbaig to achieve preeminence over the Dál Cais. A much later poem in the Book of Munster, the saga of Lorcán, displays the enmity of the Uí Tairdelbaig toward not only the Corcu MoDruad, but towards the Uí Chormaic Tradraige as well:

Ruidhleas Dál gCais cédaibh armach
dá thuaith dég Tuadhmhumh an-tuaidh
intan nach leó Caisiol cubhaidh
ní mhaithid do Mhumhain mhuaidh
Corca Baiscinn, Corca Modhruadh
comhall Ard nGabhla[7] go ngráin
Uí Chormaic Tradraighe tréinghlic
Uí Aimrid tuath Liumnigh láin.
Freehold of the Dál Cais hundredfold armed
two chiefdoms on account of Thomond from the north
when not with Cashel harmonious
it is not good to Munster from it
Corca Baiscinn, Corca Modhruadh
fulfill hated Ard Gabhla
Uí Chormaic of Tradraige strongly cunning
Uí Aimrid coveted by túath Liumnigh.
(Ó Donnchadha 1940:116)

What happened to the leadership over the Corcu MoDruad following the death of Anrudán in 936 is not clear. He left behind an heir named Congal whose death date of 987 in the *Annals of the Four Masters* falls after that of the next named chieftain of the Corcu MoDruad, Máel Sechnaill. Máel Sechnaill is said to have had two progenitors, Sairennán [51] and Argddae [52], but this is unlikely to have been true. A genealogy of the Corcu MoDruad in the Book of Lecan, probably dating to the twelfth century, lists the descendants of Argddae for two generations and Máel Sechnaill is not mentioned (Ó Corráin 1975:26). Who then was this chieftain?

The key to the resolution of this problem is an entry in the *Annals of Innisfallen* for 983 AD:

[983] A large fleet [was brought] by Brian mac Cennétig into the territory of the Connachta, and a portion of his force was slain there, i.e. Máel Sechnaill mac Croscrach, and Finn mac Dubchrón, and Lochlainn mac Máel Sechnaill *rígdomna* of Corcu Mruad.

Lochlainn [57] is described as *rígdomna*, "materials of a king." *Rígdomna* was the institutional equivalent of *tánaiste* in Irish society. The passage signifies that Lochlainn was the heir-designate to the chieftainship of Corcu MoDruad, implying that Máel Sechnaill was still chieftain at this point in time. The Máel Sechnaill mac Croscrach [8] who also died on Brian's expedition was a first cousin of Brian (though, by the classificatory Irish system of kin nomenclature, he would have been termed a brother, see the Uí Tairdelbaich genealogy, Appendix). The Uí Tairdelbaig genealogy also indicates that Máel Sechnaill mac Croscrach had a younger brother named Flann [9]. This name crops up in a Corcu MoDruad genealogy from the Book of Leinster as the father of Conchobor [58], the successor to Máel Sechnaill. From this evidence, it is all but certain that Brian had imposed a cousin of his on the Corcu MoDruad, and upon the deaths of Máel Sechnaill and his son and anointed successor Lochlainn [57] on a military expedition, probably either Flann [56] or Flann's son Conchobor [58] succeeded to the office of chieftain. The name Cathal [60] appears later on in the Corcu MoDruad genealogy, and this was also a common name in the coeval section of the Uí Tairdelbaig pedigree (see Appendix).

There are several plausible explanations for why the names Sairennán and Argddae appear before the name of Máel Sechnaill in the Corcu MoDruad chieftain lists of the twelfth century. Both Sairennán [51] and Argddae [52] are rare names that could mark the reassertion of rule by the ramage of the Corcu MoDruad that had been displaced by the Uí Tairdelbaig. The name Argddae points towards affinities with the Cíarraige-derived Uí Fidgeinti as Argddae (in the form of Mac-Arddae) was one of their principal ancestor-deities to judge from his role as overseer of the "West Munster Synod." This is a Cíarraige text and he appears in it as their paramount chieftain. The prominence of this chieftain or god among the Corcu MoDruad is attested in the place-name *Gleann Argaid*, a valley facing Galway Bay where the seats and demesne lands of the O'Lochlainn chieftains of the Burren, the later leaders of a successor chiefdom of the Corcu MoDruad, were situated. In the fourteenth-century topographical poem of Giolla-na-Naomh Ó hUidhrín, the Corcu MoDruad under the Ua Conchobhair are referred to as *Tríocha chéd Fear nArda* (the Thirty Hundred [Territory] of the Men of Arda).

In the same vein, Sairennán and Argddae could have been local Corcu MoDruad deities that were appended to Máel Sechnaill mac Croscrach in the genealogy as ancestors. The intention on the part of the twelfth-century compilers was to legitimize the descendants of Máel Sechnaill by hiding his true origins, instead presenting him as an indigenous Corcu MoDruad chieftain who was descended by an unbroken line of succession from the chiefdom's supposed founding deity-ancestors.

Conchobor mac Máel Sechnaill [58] was apparently a vigorous chieftain, for the annals have him leading three attacks on Connacht in 993, 996, and 1003 AD. He was killed in the last attack along with a son of Lochlainn [61]. Perhaps it was this chieftain who instigated the demise of the Uí Chuinn. As it now seems that the Uí Chuinn were neither Corcu MoDruad nor Dál Cais in origin, Conchobor might have felt little compunction in attacking them. In any case, as Conchobor was closely related to the dominant ramage of the Dál Cais and the Uí Chuinn ranked only as recent confederates, he probably would have been granted greater freedom of action. Two of Conchobor's sons followed him in the chieftainship of Corcu MoDruad [59, 60], but both of these had been slain by 1015 AD.

After 1015 AD, the leadership of Corcu MoDruad seems to have reverted to the senior lineage, to the descendants of Lochlainn [57], and to have remained with this lineage throughout the rest of the eleventh century. Only chieftains with the Uí Lochlainn patronymic are mentioned in the annals for the Corcu MoDruad during this period. Beginning in the late eleventh century the Uí Conchobur branch of the Corcu MoDruad apparently regained the chieftainship under Conchobor mac Máel Sechnaill [62], and this line seems to have predominated throughout the twelfth century, though not exclusively, as upon his death in 1149 AD the *Annals of the Four Masters* designate Máel Sechnaill Uí Lochlainn [63] *rí* of the two Corcomroes and Corcu Baiscind (FM). This entry establishes a terminus post quem for the split in the Corcu MoDruad chiefdom.

SUMMARY AND CONCLUSIONS

This analysis of the early ethnohistorical sources for northern Clare has established the pattern of disruption to the Corcu MoDruad chiefdom. Commencing in the early eighth century AD, Corcu MoDruad was under siege, and periodically under the hegemony of chiefdoms to the south of it. Byrne has stated that the Cíarraige of Kerry and the Corcu Baiscind of southern Clare may have been part of a maritime federation that controlled the waterways in the west of Munster, a hypothesis suggested by an interchange of kings in their genealogies (1973:170). The intrusion of names of Corcu Baiscind or Cíarraige origins in the genealogies of the Corcu MoDruad, Cenel Báeth, and Clann hIffernáin certainly suggest that the push came from the south in the eighth century. Cenél Báeth was either a chiefdom or a section of Corcu MoDruad ruled by an alien people carved out of territory of the Corcu MoDruad by aristocratic lineages from the southern chiefdoms.

The founders of Tulach Commáin, be they Cíarraige, Corcu Baiscind, or Uí Chormaic were, on the balance of available information, not Déisi. The only information that supports Déisi origins for Tulach Commáin is the notice of the devastation of Corcu MoDruad by the Déisi in 744 AD in the *Annals of Ulster* and the *Annals of Tigernach*. However, the first substantial intrusion by the descendants of these people, the Dál Cais, into the politics of northwestern Clare seems to have been in the early tenth century in the person of Anrudán mac Máel-Gorm [7]. His imposition upon the Corcu MoDruad is tangible evidence that the Uí Tairdelbaig under Lorcán was not only the preeminent chiefdom of the Dál Cais, but of Clare as well. Brian mac Cennétig merely continued this pattern of regnal interference in the affairs of Corcu MoDruad that was begun by his predecessor.

On the evidence of the tenth-century Psaltar of Cashel, the three ramages that constituted the chiefdom of Cenél Fermaic to the south of Tulach Commáin, Cenél Báeth, Clann hIffernáin, and the Uí Dedaid, claimed an affinity with the Dál Cais (Appendix). However, earlier genealogies and other lines of evidence indicate that these ramages were most likely of disparate origins. The progenitor Báeth of Cenél Báeth appears in the reconstituted origin myth of Clare's Iron Age chiefdoms as a brother of Rúad, and the *Life of Mac Creich* links him with the Corcu MoDruad.

An alternate genealogy links the Uí Dedaid with the Éoganachta. In the twelfth-century tract *Ríg Érenn* (The Chieftains of Ireland). Dedad mac Sin is one of the *cóicedag* (chieftains of a fifth), referring to the five mythical provinces of Ireland (O'Brien 1976:120 (135 b 27). The idea of a provincial paramount chieftain is both mythical and late, but of import in this text is the descent of Dedad from Sin, a late cognate of the name Senach, the progenitor god of Clare's gods (chap. 3). Dedad then augments the number of claimed descendants of this god to three, and his linkage to the origin myth of Clare's tutelary deities amounts to evidence of a past claim of unity between the Uí Dedaid, the Corcu MoDruad and Corcu Baiscind. Dedad would have been seen as a brother of Rúad, the tutelary deity of the Corcu MoDruad. The presence in Cenél Fermaic of the Uí Dedaid along with Cenél Báeth strengthens the impression that Cenél Fermaic was an original member chiefdom of the Corcu MoDruad composite chiefdom.

In the tenth century the ramages of Cenél Fermaic, including the Clann hIffernáin refugees from Tulach Commáin, had bound themselves with the Dál Cais through claimed common descent from the Dál Cais ancestor Oengus. The union of this chiefdom with the Dál Cais promoted this entity from a composite chiefdom to a chiefdom confederacy, as Cenél Fermaic was not geographically contiguous with this composite chiefdom.[8]

THE COMPOSITE CHIEFDOM AND THE GENESIS OF THE CHIEFDOM CONFEDERACY

In early Irish society, genealogies functioned as the constitutions of individual composite chiefdoms and chiefdom confederacies. They laid out the relations of one section or chiefdom to another within these entities and documented the relative social ranking of the polities according to seniority (promulgated in the presumed birth-order of the founders) and, presumably, according to the supposed historical origins of the peoples involved. As we have seen with the Corcu Baiscind and Corcu MoDruad, the genealogies also promulgated the relationship of one composite chiefdom to another, and the relationship that a simple or composite chiefdom might have with a politically ascendant confederacy. Generally speaking, the genealogies are usually structured so that first the political structure and affiliations of the most inclusive group are laid out followed by the genealogies of related individual *túatha*, which in turn subsume the genealogies of specific aristocratic sections of the leading ramage.

Genealogies were written to describe the contemporary political circumstances of an Irish chiefdom. Since the political constitution of Irish chiefdoms changed frequently as a consequence of their military successes and failures, genealogies were also subject to frequent alteration. Fortunately, the genealogies of durable chiefdoms were written down frequently enough so that it is possible to pinpoint the timing and direction of political changes. In the case of the Corcu MoDruad genealogy, the internal evidence indicates at least three separate periods of compilation.

The considerable variation between the eighth and twelfth century Corcu MoDruad genealogies is a product of repeated defeats and subsequent changes stemming from the outside to its chiefly lineages from at least the early eighth century onward. This finding, taken together with the study of the geographical and place-name evidence demonstrates that the composite chiefdom of Corcu MoDruad was an amalgam of lineages of differing ancestry. It appears that the process of section formation in the eighth–tenth centuries was probably identical with what could be perceived of this process in Tudor times. Simply put, the chieftain, whether he be born within the chiefdom or new to it via conquest, produces male offspring who are invested with territories or portions of territories of former sections.

The Corcu MoDruad genealogy also allows greater insight into the formation of the Dál Cais confederacy in the tenth century. Developments in the political center of Thomond were unlikely to completely blot out antecedent political systems at the periphery, and so it is possible to apprehend details of the creation of the Dál Cais confederacy from changes in Corcu MoDruad. What the Corcu MoDruad genealogies and relevant entries in the annals reveal is that the origin of Dál Cais was predicated upon the emergence of the Uí Tairdelbaig *túath* as a political power in the early tenth century under Lorcán [2], the grandfather of Brian Bóroimhe [6]. This chieftain imposed Anrudán mac Máel-Gorm [7] (or his father) upon the Corcu MoDruad.

The process of the formation of Irish chiefdom confederacies proceeds with the conquests of an ambitious and militarily successful *túath*. An ambitious chieftain probably forged (or forced) alliances among neighboring, possibly related ramages of *túatha* and then carried out military campaigns against close-by unrelated chiefdoms. He ensured the cooperation of the defeated foreign chiefdoms by imposing kinsmen from his ruling ramage onto the defeated territories. Despite the interruption instanced by the Norsemen in the late ninth and tenth centuries, a string of four successful chieftains of the Uí Tairdelbaig – Lorcán [2], Cennétig [3], Mathgamain [5], and Brian [6] – managed to establish the chiefdom confederacy of the Dál Cais and subject all of Munster to their rule within the space of seventy-five years. However, the histories of the Corcu Baiscind and Corcu MoDruad demonstrate that this technique of political domination of chiefdoms at the periphery of the province by the Dál Cais chiefdom confederacy produced only transitory results. Even though Brian mac Cennétig [6] may have imposed his cousins on the Corcu MoDruad in the tenth century, or Muirchertach Mór Ua Briain [12] his son on the Corcu Baiscind in the twelfth century, no apparent effort was made to follow up these impositions with any kind of overarching administrative apparatus or arrangements to ensure cooperation or allegiance with Uí Tairdelbaig past the death of the conquering *rí*, with the result that within a generation or two, peripheral chiefdoms reverted to their former conditions of political autonomy and belligerence toward the ramages of the ancestral founders of their leading septs.

CORCU BAISCIND AND CORCU MODRUAD IN THE
ELEVENTH AND TWELFTH CENTURIES

In an earlier section, it has been demonstrated that Late Medieval barony and parish boundaries are extremely informative with respect to the former disposition of the territories of Early Medieval chiefdoms, and also provide clues as to the identity of the aristocratic lineages that dominated them. At the point that they are established, ecclesiastical territories effectively freeze in time the outlines of the territories of contemporary social groups. Diocesan territories offer similar insights as to the outlines of early political entities of comparable scale. Moreover, because the dioceses were established at an early date, the chiefdom territories that they encompass are of greater antiquity than those represented by the boundaries of Late Medieval baronies.

A glance at Figure 8.4 shows that while the territory of the Corcu Baiscind was included in the diocese of Killaloe, the two baronies of Corcomroe and Burren were combined into the single diocese of Kilfenora (*Cill Fhinnabrach*). *Cogadh Gaedhel re Gallaibh* mentions victories of the Corcu Baiscind over the Norsemen in the early and late tenth century, so we may assume that they were still independent at this time (Todd 1965:29, 103). Their last victory followed shortly upon Brian's ascension to the position of *rí* of the Dál Cais in 976 AD. As the map indicates, however, by the time of the Synod of Rathbreasail in 1111 AD, they had become completely subjugated by the Dál Cais. *Ríghe* (chieftainship) over the Corcu Baiscind passed to Mathgamain [5], a son of Muirchertach Mór Ua Briain [12], who was to give his name to the later ruling ramage of the territory, the *Mac Mathghamhna* (Mac Mahons).

The annals are somewhat more clear on the position of the Corcu MoDruad vis-à-vis the Dál Cais. Under 983 AD, the *Annals of Inisfallen* tell us that Lochlainn mac Máel Sechnaill, the heir apparent or *rígdomna* to the chieftainship of Corcu MoDruad, was slain while accompanying Brian mac Cennétig [6] upon a raid on Connacht. In 993, we learn from the same annals that Máel Sechnaill's other son Conchobur, by now *rí* of Corcu MoDruad, led a successful attack on the Connachta Uí Briúin on his own. This feat was repeated in 996. However, in 1003, Conchobur was himself slain in battle against the Uí Briúin.

Subsequent to the death of Conchobur, several entries inform us of the demise of two of his sons in 1015, and the demise of the son of Lochlainn in Ára, apparently while fighting the Conmaicne Mara of Connacht for possession of the islands. In 1027 another Conchobuir mac Maíl Sechnaill is slain while accompanying Donchadh mac Briain on a hosting to Osraige. By the eleventh century the chieftainship of Corcu MoDruad had passed to the line of Lochlainn, and the deaths of two of his descendants are given under 1037 and 1045. In 1054 AD, Corcu MoDruad was raided by three sons of Donchadh mac Briain [2]. In 1055, Corcu MoDruad was the setting of a battle between two claimants to the paramountcy of Thomond: Toirdelbach [3], who would become *ard rí* in 1063, and his brother Murchad. In 1094, the Corcu MoDruad were soundly defeated by the Síl Muiredaig while allied with an army of West Connacht. In 1113 AD Máel Sechnaill Uí Conchobuir died in Luimneach, Muirchertach Mór Ua Briain's capital.

It is difficult to conclude from the genealogy of the Corcu MoDruad and the annal entries when Corcu MoDruad split (or was partitioned) into two chiefdoms. The entries show the Corcu MoDruad to be allied with Brian mac Cennétig [6] but also to be acting autonomously during the late tenth and eleventh centuries. The entry for 1055 shows that Corcu MoDruad was a refuge area and a potential ally during Dál Cais succession struggles. That they were possibly on the losing end of that particular alliance of 1055 is brought out by the fact that their principal church, Cill Fhinnabrach, was burnt down during the campaign. Nevertheless, the diocesan boundaries show the Corcu MoDruad to have preserved some unity down to the synod of Rathbreasail in 1111. The diocese of Cill Fhinnabrach (Kilfenora) was not, however, created during this session; rather, the territory was excluded from Cill Dalua. It was not given official recognition as a diocese until 1152 AD (Gwynn and Gleeson 1962:130–131).

CHAPTER NINE

The World of *Caithréim Thoirdhealbhaigh*

... a great affliction befell the country then, the loss of Cathal Crobderg mac Toirrdelbaig Moir Uí Conchobair, *Rí* Connacht; a *rí* most feared and dreaded on every hand in Ireland; the *rí* who carried out the most plunderings and burnings against Galls (foreigners) and Gaels who opposed him; the *rí* who was the fiercest and harshest towards his enemies who ever lived; the *rí* who most blinded, killed, and mutilated rebellious and disaffected subjects; the *rí* who best established peace and tranquility of all the *rígaib Érenn*. The *rí* who built most monasteries and houses for religious communities; the *rí* who most comforted clerks and poor men with food and fire on the floor of his own habitation; the *rí* whom of all the *rígaib Érenn* God made most perfect in every good quality; the *rí* on whom God most bestowed fruit and increase in crops; the *rí* who was most chaste of all the *rígaib Érenn*; the *rí* who kept himself to one consort and practiced continence before God from her death till his own; the *rí* whose wealth was partaken by laymen and clerics, infirm men, women and helpless folk ... (ACon 1224 AD)

As perhaps no other text can, the historical saga *Caithréim Thoirdhealbhaigh* (*The Battle Triumphs of Turlough*) imparts in great detail the social structure, institutions, and dynamics of Irish chiefdoms of the Middle Ages. *Caithréim Thoirdhealbhaigh* was composed in Thomond in the mid-fourteenth century by Seán mac Ruaidhrí Mac Craith, a poet of the O'Briens. Up to the twelfth century, Irish sagas were terse in language and sparing in detail. *Caithréim Thoirdhealbhaigh* is written in the alliterative, effusive, and bombastic style of the Early Modern Irish period. It describes events in detail, giving fairly extensive descriptive renderings of the personages and factions involved in the political struggles within the Uí Briain primitive state. While earlier Irish sagas often culminated in great battles and only alluded parenthetically to other military undertakings, *Caithréim Thoirdhealbhaigh* describes many minor raids and ambuscades in addition to the principal battles. So detailed and vivid is this account that it can be called without exaggeration an autobiography of an Irish primitive state.

Emulating the earlier Munster saga *Cogadh Gaedhel re Gallaibh*, the author of *Caithréim Thoirdhealbhaigh* attempts to cast his epic broadly as a conflict between noble Irish kings and villainous foreign invaders – in this case the Anglo-Normans who first set foot on Irish soil in 1169 AD. However, if this was his intention, Mac Craith's saga falls short, for the story is in sum an account of the struggle of two rival Thomond confederacies for the kingship of Thomond over the space of two generations. *Caithréim Thoirdhealbhaigh* begins with a short, rambling historical synopsis of events in Thomond contemporary with the advent of the Anglo-Normans in Ireland. This sets the stage for the opening of the feud between the then *rí* of Thomond, Brian Rua Uí Briain [20], and the usurper Tordhealbhach Uí Briain [22], Brian's nephew. According to the saga, the expulsion of Brian Rua from the kingship of Thomond created an opportunity for the advent of Thomas de Clare as the would-be Earl of Thomond in 1277. De Clare had received a royal grant of Thomond from Edward I and was looking for an opportune time to assert himself there. He entered Thomond in support of the claim of Brian Rua to the kingship of Thomond. Tordhealbhach [22] triumphed first over Brian Rua's son Donnchad [23], and then over Thomas de Clare himself in 1287 to become the king of Thomond (Nic Ghiollamhaith 1981, 1995; Westropp 1903:141).

After Tordhealbhach's death in 1306, his faction *Clann Toirdhealbhaich* was challenged again to establish itself in the kingship by a resurgent de Clare family under the leadership of Thomas's successor and son Richard.[1] Clann Thoirdhealbhach was led at this stage of the conflict first by Tordhealbhach's son Donnchad Uí Briain [24], who was assassinated in 1311, and then by the brothers Muirchertach [25] and Diarmait [26]. *Caithréim Thoirdhealbhaigh* ends with the death of Richard de Clare at the battle of Dysert O'Dea in 1318 and Muirchertach's consequent attainment of kingship over Thomond.

This chapter will mine the rich deposits of social and political information contained in the narrative of *Caithréim Thoirdhealbhaigh*, covering the Medieval period of Thomond (thirteenth–fourteenth centuries AD). The objective of this analysis will be to reveal the social structure and political institutions of the kingdom's chiefdoms during this period. At this juncture of Thomond's history with the weakening of the office of king as a consequence of segmentary warfare between O'Brien branches, and attempted colonization by the English, the chiefdoms within the O'Brien state were experiencing a resurgence of autonomy and influence (Nic Ghiollamhaith 1995). The text of *Caithréim Thoirdhealbhaigh* will be scanned to identify contemporary chiefdom capital sites, and these will be located within the chiefdom territories as best as these can be reconstructed. Evidence from *Caithréim Thoirdhealbhaigh* will be brought together to determine exactly what constituted a political capital in the Irish Middle Ages. In the following chapter Thomond's Tudor period political systems will be compared to the polities described in *Caithréim Thoirdhealbhaigh* to see if they exhibit similar patterns of social and geographical organization.

THE POLITICAL TOPOGRAPHY OF CLARE
1268–1318 AD

A number of ramages of differing historical origins were to be found within the boundaries of the primitive state of Thomond in the thirteenth century (see Figure 9.1). Quite a number were ancestral cadet branches of the O'Brien ruling ramage, which had settled on conquered territories during and following the ascent of Brian Bóroimhe [6] to the paramountcy of Munster in the tenth century. Included among these were the Mac Mahons (*Mac Mathghamhna*) of *Corcabhaiscinn* (Middle Irish rendering of Old Irish *Corcu Baiscind*), the O'Briens of *Uí Breacáin* (Angl.: Ibrickan) and *Ára* (the Aran Islands), and the O'Briens of *Túath Uí Glae* in northern *Corcamruad* (Middle Irish rendering of *Corcu MoDruad*). One can read from the geographical pattern of the lands acquired by O'Brien septs that weak ramages in the peripheral chiefdoms of the kingdom had been supplanted by cadet branches royal family. This is evident in the possession by Mahon O'Brien of the residence at *Inis Uí Chuinn*. Inis Uí Chuinn is described as an island residence in the saga (1929:63), and the remains of this residence still exist on the island (Macnamara 1901). The name of the residence (Island of the O'Quins) indicates that formerly Inis Uí Chuinn had belonged to them and was probably their principal residence. The O'Quins get only a passing mention in *Caithréim Thoirdhealbhaigh* and had probably ceased to be chieftains within their portion of *Cenél Fermaic* in the previous century (see Chapter 7).

Other chiefdoms were dominated by the descendants of other ramages of the former Dál Cais composite chiefdom. Mirroring the rivalry between the two branches of the O'Brien royal family, the old Dál Cais composite chiefdom had become divided into two antagonistic segments: a western segment composed of Uí Caisín, and in the east, Uí mBloid, which included a number of chiefdoms including the Uí Briain's chiefdom of origin, Uí Toirdhealbhaigh, but excluded a section of it called *Eichtghe* (Figure 9.1). Eichtghe served as a refuge area for both sides of the conflict. There was even rivalry and division within individual chiefdoms. At the start of the conflict in the late thirteenth century the Uí Ghrada dominated Uí Caisín. However, they were eventually superseded by the MacNamaras (*Mac Conmara*) (Nic

Figure 9.1. The thirteenth-century political divisions of Thomond.

Ghiollamhaith 1995). As previously mentioned, the Corcu MoDruad had also split into two chiefdoms, Corcamruadh and Boireann.

THE IRISH COMPOSITE CHIEFDOM
AND DUAL ORGANIZATION

Nic Ghiolamhaith paints the factionalism and the fissioning of Thomond's polities as a result of the disruption caused to Ireland's political evolution by the intrusion of the Anglo-Normans (1995). In her view, prior to the advent of the Anglo-Normans, Ireland's political systems were coalescing into a small number of sizable polities led by a handful of powerful kings. In her view, the Anglo-Normans truncated this tendency toward political centralization through the seizure of blocks of land, which left Gaelic leaders geographically isolated (ibid.). However, she overlooks the fact that the fissioning of composite chiefdoms into rival segments was a common occurrence with deep historical roots. The Dál Cais had emerged in the tenth century out of a segment of the western Déisi or Déis Becc called the Déis Tuaiscirt, whose opposite were the Déis Deiscirt (Ó Corráin 1972:8; Ryan 1943:192). In the early ninth century, there were two segments within Dál Cais in competition for the post of paramount chieftain: the Uí Tairdelbaig and the Uí Oengusso (Ó Corráin 1972:114). Perhaps in an earlier period when the Dál Cais were the Déis Tuaiscirt, their predecessors as rivals for this office were the Uí Eichtigern and Uí Cernaig. As we have seen, by the early fourteenth century, the Dál Cais subsequently became divided into two large rival sections, Clann Chuiléin and the Uí mBloid. The Cíarraige had split prior to the eighth century AD into the Cíarraige Lúachra to the west, the Uí Fidgeinti in the east, and perhaps the Ciarraige Cuirche to the south.

These examples establish the splitting of Irish composite chiefdoms into rival halves (or even thirds) as a norm of political life during the Middle Ages. Dual organization within Irish composite chiefdoms should then be viewed not as a unique historical occurrence of the post-Norman period, but as a natural and predictable outgrowth of status rivalry between the aristocratic ramages of a composite chiefdom's constituent chiefdoms (Goldman 1955). Status rivalry posed a constant centrifugal force within the context of the composite structure of Irish *mór thúatha*. However, as Irish chiefdoms existed in an environment of constant military threats from external enemies, there must have been pressure running counter to the centrifugal force of fission to maintain the alliance structure of the composite chiefdom so that it remained at a size sufficient to repel military challenges from other composite chiefdoms. Therefore, Irish chiefdoms split internally into autonomous segments that competed for political primacy within the polity while maintaining their unity against rival chiefdoms of similar size and social constitution. Irish chiefdoms were then confederate systems at the composite level. The difference in political organization between a composite chiefdom and a chiefdom confederacy lay simply in the fact that in a composite chiefdom, the alliance was maintained in the face of pressure to fission between ramages that were presumably related. Weaker chiefdoms of alien origin were brought into a confederacy with a composite chiefdom when the latter was expanding militarily.

In a way, the processes of polity building among the Irish bear strong resemblances to the processes of complementary opposition and military expansion described by Evans-Pritchard and Robert Kelly for the Nuer, though the Nuer possessed segmentary organization, not chiefdoms. It is entirely possible that similarities in political behavior between the Irish and the Nuer – the organization of society into large social segments and the fashioning of new segmentary and ethnic identities followed by segmentary opposition and military conquest – are due to their common agropastoral subsistence base (Evans-Pritchard 1940; R. Kelly 1985).

Returning to Nic Ghiollamhaith's thesis, assigning to intrusive Anglo-Norman ramages blame for disrupting a purported trend toward Irish political centralization requires some special pleading. The events of *Caithréim Thoirdhealbhaigh* play themselves out a century following the Anglo-Norman invasion of Ireland, by which time the Anglo-Normans had lived in Ireland for generations and had evolved to become the Anglo-Irish. Rather than constituting a united ethnic block that was unflinchingly antagonistic toward the Irish, the principal Anglo-Irish lords had by the mid-thirteenth century turned to fighting each other over control of the best arable land (Duffy 1997:125–126). It is clear from the involvement of the Anglo-Irish Butler, de Burgh, and Fitzgerald lords in the rivalry between the two O'Brien segments that these aristocrats had in fact become the functional equivalent of the Irish kings of the immediate pre-Norman period. One must therefore look beyond invasion and ethnicity for the reasons for the consistently decentralized Irish medieval political landscape. It is more likely that the Irish facility for the creation of elaborate alliance systems worked against political centralization.

THE OPPOSED CONFEDERACIES OF THE UA BRIAIN CIVIL WAR

Beyond the sphere of the core Dál Caiss composite chiefdom were chiefdoms of non–Dalcassian origin whose ramages in several instances had in the past been displaced by these. To this category belong the O'Hechirs (later O'Hehir, Ir. *Uí hAichir*) of Uí Cormaic who are thought to have been the former inhabitants of Uí Caissín, the MacMahons (*Mac Mathgambna*) of Corcabhaiscinn, and the O'Deas (*Uí Dedaid*) of Cenél Fearmaic. The O'Lochlainns and O'Conors (*Uí Conchobhair*) of the Burren and Corcamruad were politically autonomous with respect to the O'Briens though they were bound to them by military alliances.

The annals and *Caithréim Thoirdhealbhaigh* are in agreement that with the exception of the MacMahons, all of the above chiefdoms were allied with Clann Toirdhealbhaich. The northwestern ramages faced off against Mathgamain O'Briain [21], *tánaiste* of Thomond, the largest single landowner in the west of Thomond and a chief figure in the Clann Briain Ruaid faction. Their opposition to him is understandable as several of the lands that he possessed had been removed from districts that had been under the rule of the western ramages. The MacMahons of Corcabhaiscinn also owed allegiance to Clann Briain Ruaid and the de Clares. Looking away

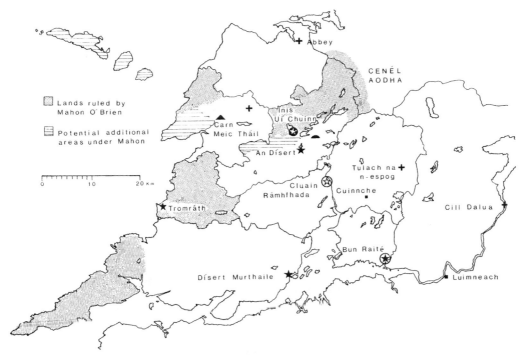

Figure 9.2. The chiefdom capitals of Thomond cited in *Caithréim Thoirdhealbhiagh* and the landholding of Mathgamain Uí Briain.

from the participation of Mathgamain Ó Briain, the conflict takes on a strong west-north vs. east-south cast. This is made more obvious by reference to the pattern of external alliances – Clann Toirdhealbhaich with the aristocrats of Connacht to the north and Clann Briain Ruaid with the lords of Desmond to the south.

The saga tells us that Donnchad Cairbreach mac Domnaill Mór [16] established the O'Brien royal capital at *Cluain Rámhfhada* (Clonroad), "... in the very heart of his own near dependents and of his domain ..." (O'Grady 1929 26:2). The map of Thomond (Figure 9.2) bears out this fact. Not only is Cluain Rámhfhada in the geographical center of Thomond on the Fergus River, but it also lies at the point of intersection of three territories as well, Cenél Fearmaic, Uí Chormaic, and Uí Caisín. Cluain Rámhfhada was established in the years following Donnchad's accession in 1202 AD (possibly around 1210; Nicholls 1972:154). The realm ruled by Donnchad was considerably smaller than the kingdom of his immediate ancestors, necessitating the reestablishment of his capital so as to be at the center of his shrunken polity. From the description in the text we may infer that it was a *ráth*-type settlement; a homestead surrounded by concentric earthen banks and ditches (2).

According to Mac Craith, in 1277 Henry III of England bestowed a license upon Thomas de Clare that allowed him "to come into Ireland and seize all that he could win from the Gael" (6). In 1276 de Clare had actually received title to lands in Thomond from Edward I that were originally held by Robert de Muscegros (granted 1248–1252) from Henry III (Duffy 1997:144). De Muscegros had been burned out of his possessions by Conchobor Uí Briain [18] and his son Tadhg Caoluisce [19] (Westropp 1903:195). Thomas de Clare arrived at a time when Brian Rua mac Conchobhair Uí Briain [20], after reigning nine years as king of Thomond, had been challenged by a coalition of dissenters led by a nephew Tordhealbhach mac Taidgh Chaoluisce (Angl. Turlough [22]), and had been expelled from the kingdom. In circumstances similar to those that first brought the Anglo-Normans to Ireland, de Clare came to Thomond on the invitation from the beleaguered Brian Rua who desired to be restored as king of Thomond (Westropp 1903:141).[2]

De Clare installed himself as the paramount ruler of Thomond, expelling "the ancient dwellers on the soil of Tradraige," and he erected his capital at Bun Raité (a name that describes its location at the mouth of the Raité River), the site of an earlier castle built by de Muscegros (Frost 1978:185; O'Grady 1929:8). In so doing, de Clare appropriated lands in Thomond of the highest quality from an agrarian standpoint, as the soil in Tradraige was rich and the weather relatively dry (see Figures 2.4 and 2.5).

Kingship over the Irish in Thomond was given over to Brian Rua and Mathgamain mac Briain mac Domnaill Chonnachtach [21] became the equivalent of *tánaiste* to de Clare. *Tánaiste* means literally "second" and has the implied meaning of heir-designate (Mac Niocaill 1968). In practice, this was a title and office offered to the competitor in a succession struggle as a consolation prize, probably as a stratagem for staving off further violence (Charles-Edwards 1993:110; Jaski 2000:28–30; Ó Corráin 1971). This explanation fits this case since Mathgamain never did become *rí*. Supporting de Clare and *Clann Briain Ruaidh* were the Uí mBloid and some of the Cenél Fearmaic. Arrayed against this coterie was a league of chiefdoms under the leadership of Turlough [22] and his kinsmen, known as *Clann Toirdhealbhaigh*. The principal force among these allies was the MacNamaras, otherwise known as *Clann Chuiléin*. The MacNamaras were near-equals with the O'Briens in power (Nic Ghiollamhaith 1995). In the second rank within the confederacy were the O'Deas of Cenél Fearmaic and Uí Chormaic. The O'Lochlainns and O'Conors of the far north apparently played both sides of the equation and were beset at times and imposed upon by both factions in the conflict.

The political order of Thomond presented by *Caithréim Thoirdhealbhaigh* deserves some explication. At this point in time one can speak of politics at the national level and provincial level. *Caithréim Thoirdhealbhaigh* identifies the Anglo-Norman Butlers (originally *de Buitleir*) and the Mac William Burkes (originally *de Burgh*) as the reigning powers at the national level. The former were Earls of Ormond and Ossory (Mid. Ir.: *iarla* (sic) *Urmuman agus Osraighe*), the latter Earls of Ulster (*iarla Uladh*). The Gaelic *rí* of Desmond, Domhnall Ruadh Mac Carthaigh, is mentioned early on in the saga, but apparently he had little power or influence in Thomond (1929 27:15). The greater scope of the power of the Anglo-Norman Earls is indicated in an incident in the saga when after having his rival Donough mac Brian Rua [23] killed, Turlough O'Brien [22] dropped the siege of Bunratty Castle upon orders from the Earl of Ulster (31). On occasion, the leaders of both O'Brien branches sought the favorable intervention of the Butler Earl (86), and several times the Butlers sought to arbitrate or impose a peace on Thomond (121). Apart from this, the Butlers had no direct say in the affairs in Thomond.

On the provincial level, the conflict over the kingship of Thomond between Clann Toirdhealbaigh and the de Clares is a principal theme of *Caithréim Thoirdhealbhaigh*. The extent of the political influence of the de Clare baron shifted with the military fortunes of his alliances. However, it may be said that during the time that Thomas de Clare, and, after a break, his son Richard occupied the castle at Bunratty, their position as paramount ruler was viewed as legitimate by both O'Brien factions, or as legitimate as that of any Irish chieftain in a comparable position. The legitimacy of de Clare rule derived from two sources, one internal and one external to their domain. In Thomond, the de Clares offered protection and the shelter of an alliance to the Uí mBloid who were under threat of encroachment or expulsion by Clann Chuiléin, and to Clann Briain Ruaid who had been expelled by Clann Toirdelbaich. The de Clares demonstrated their legitimacy as barons on several occasions when they managed to effect temporary partitions of Thomond between the two warring O'Brien factions (18, 20, 70).

Though attacked and raided on several occasions, Thomas de Clare held on to his position even after Toirdhealbhach's triumph over Clann Briain Ruaid in 1284. That de Clare survived the demise of his alliance was due to support from Anglo-Irish aristocrats such as the Earl of Ulster and the Justiciar of Ireland (Westropp 1903:177). That the de Clares held title to Thomond in the first place and were able to stage a comeback after experiencing severe military reversals was due to their relationship with the English crown. Thomas de Clare, having served as governor of

London and as secretary to Henry III, was a confidant of the king, and his brother was married to the king's daughter, Joan (Westropp 1903:141). Upon Thomas's death in 1287 in a battle with Turlough in Tradraige, his elder son Gilbert became a ward of Joan. The support of the crown further enabled Richard de Clare to return to Bunratty in 1310 to resume the claim of his family to their estate and lordship in Thomond (ibid.:180).

The position of Mathgamain (Mahon) mac Briain mac Domnaill Chonnachtach [21] deserves some attention. A passage in *Caithréim Thoirdhealbhaigh* lists the territories over which he exercised dominion. The text implies that Mahon held these lands in trust from his superior lord, Richard de Clare:

Acht énní chena: nír miad is nír maise le Muirchertach O mBriain [25] gan Mathgamain O mBriain [21] do chreidem dó féin amail do chreid dá athair agus dá dherbráthair .i. do Toirdelbach [22] agus do Donnchad [24], agus ba chrád croide ‖ leis a beithsiun i longportaib a athar .i. i nisad uasal innse úi Chuinn; agus ba hannsa leis Irrus agus na dúinte agus úi Brecáin, agus blagh do Chorcmodruaid iartharaig, agus lethtricha céd uachtarach, agus úi Flannchada agus cénel Aodha iartarach i gcionn a chéile, gan techt eturru ó'n léim aniar go cill mic Duach, do beith fái a hucht in Chláraig. (1929 I:134; II:118)

One thing alone there was: It was neither an honor nor a thing of beauty to Murtough O'Brien [25] that Mahon O'Brien [21] had not given his allegiance to him, just as he had given allegiance to his father and to his brother by birth; that is, to Turlough [22] and Donnchad [24]. And his (Mahon's) presence in his father's fort, the noble residence of *Inis Uí Chuinn*, wrang his heart. And it was hard for him to bear that Irrus and the dunes and Uí Breacáin, and a fragment of western Corcamruadh, and half of the tricha céd uachtarach (Cenél Fearmaic), and Uí Flannchada and western Cénel Aodha, assembled together without a break between them from (Cuchullin's) Leap eastwards to Cill Mac Duach, being under him (Mahon) in behalf of de Clare.][3]

Mahon's principal residence was at *Inis Uí Chuinn*, an island settlement on the lake of that name in Killinaboy parish of Cenél Fearmaic (see Figure 9.2). I assume that he was the lord in this parish and in Kilkeedy parish to the west as well (*Uí Flannchada*). O'Brien castles were to be built in these places in later centuries. It is also possible that he administered Rath parish in Cenél Fearmaic, as these lands were owned entirely by the O'Briens in the sixteenth century. Cenél Aodha is what was formerly called Uí Fiachrach Aidne in what is now the county of Galway. The western fragment of Corcamruadh I presume to be Túath Uí Glae, an area of older O'Brien settlement to the west of the Burren.[4]

The lands under Mahon's sway were then enormous in extent. A poem in *Caithréim Thoirdhealbhaigh* puts Mahon's holdings at a third of

Thomond (O'Grady 1929 27:156). Mahon was the grandson of Domhnall Connachtach Uí Briain [17], the sixth of nine known sons of Domhnall Mór Uí Briain [14], a king of Thomond who died in 1194 AD (see O'Brien pedigree, Appendix). The office of king had been held by four older brothers of Domhnall Connachtach, so how was it that his grandson Mahon had come by so much land? The answer is not provided by the saga but is instead to be found in an entry in the *Annals of Innisfallen* for 1308 where it is stated that Mahon possessed the office of *tánaiste*.

The lands of Mahon are distributed along the northern and western fringes of the polity of Thomond. Inis Uí Chuinn was to become the seat of the Barons of Inchiquin in the sixteenth century, but it is obvious that this position had been established in everything but name as far back as the thirteenth century. The position of Mahon's landholdings and location of his seat at a considerable geographical remove from the O'Brien seat at Cluain Rámhfhada is a magnification of the expected pattern of landholding for the *tánaiste* within an Irish composite chiefdom (see Chapter 10). It is in keeping with the tension that would have existed between former competitors for the office of king. The solution to this tension was to enfeoff the former rival with ample lands, but lands at the maximum spatial remove from the king and his capital at the center of the kingdom.

THE ORGANIZATION OF THE O'BRIEN STATE
IN THE THIRTEENTH CENTURY

Within the primitive state of Thomond, the tier of the smaller chiefdoms, or *túatha*, constituted the local level of administration. In the Medieval period sources, one encounters another term for referring to a district: *tríocha céd* (thirty hundred), a term referring to a levy made upon the resident population either in fighting men, cattle, or both (J. Hogan 1929; Patterson 1994:93). The polity described by this term constituted an intermediate level of administration within the primitive state of Thomond between the *túath* and the king (Nugent 2000:57). Patterson is probably correct in arguing both for the equivalency of this territorial unit with the Old Irish *mór thúath*, and in noting that *triocha céd* are only encountered as subordinate polities within larger entities (1994:93, 173). In the *Annals of Innisfallen*, both Uí Caisín and Uí mBloid are termed *trícha cét*.

Varying levels of control exercised by the king over subordinate polities is also signaled by references in Irish Medieval ethnohistorical sources to *túatha* within a primitive state as *saer* and *daer*. The polities that are designated as such in *Lebor na Cert*, a tribute list of the Munster kings, indicates that the distinction that the law texts made in the eighth century between dependent (*daer*) and independent (*saer*) clients had by the twelfth century been extended to describe the status of chiefdoms vis á vis the king. The application of these terms to subordinate chiefdoms is altogether appropriate since it is obvious from the isomorphy in terminology and economic exchanges that the leaders of subordinate ramages were conceived to be the clients of the king. Mac Craith states within *Caithéim Thoirdhealbhaigh* that after dispossessing Mathgamain Uí Briain [21] and banishing him from Thomond, Muirchertach Uí Briain [25].

do suid féin in ninnse í Chuinn, agus do chóirig a rechtaireda ar a saortuathaib ina timchell. (O'Grady 1929 I:136).

He sat himself down in Inis Uí Chuinn, and arrayed his *rechtairí* (bailiffs) over his *saertúathib* around him.[5]

Saertúatha were chiefdoms that still enjoyed political autonomy, though not independence, and had to pay rent to their overlord through his *rechtairí* (bailiffs). The fourteenth-century text *O'Brien's Rental* names a bailiff over the O'Lochlainns, the maximal ramage that ruled the Boireann (Burren) chiefdom of the O'Lochlainns. The O'Lochlainns managed to retain some measure of political autonomy from the O'Briens throughout the Middle Ages. *Daertúatha* were nonautonomous territories directly under an overlord of the dominant ramage. The *saertúatha* immediately around Murtough at Inís Uí Chuinn were Corcamruadh, Boireann, and the O'Deas and O'Griffys of Cenél Fearmaic.

Local leaders were termed collectively *uaisle* (nobles) or sometimes singly *triath* (chief). Below these were *toísigh* (first, foremost, the leaders of individual *túatha* that in battle became fighting squadrons (27:72–73). It seems that at least some *toísigh* were also to be counted among the *uaisle* (see 27:37, 41, 54, 80). Underneath these nobility and seminobility were the *oireachtaí*. An *oireacht* in older usage was a periodic assembly of the freemen of a *túath*. In Medieval period times, it took on a more general meaning to indicate the inhabitants of a *tríocha céd* or *túath* either at peace or assembled for a military hosting (see Nicholls 1972:23).

Ties of kinship by virtue of common descent, marriage, or fosterage remained an important ingredient in structuring political alliances between the aristocrats of Irish chiefdoms:

Donough, on this well-intentioned errand bound, resorted to O'Brien's camp and in the presence of the whole assemblage disclosed his articles of reparation. Comprehensively also with accurate memory, Donough Mac Conmara set forth his consanguinity with each and every *cinedh* (sept) of his hearers; thus they were

without pretext to bear a discontented mind towards the *árd-flaith* (high aristocrat). (1929 27:37)

... Clancullen (headed by Sída mac Neill mac Conmara above, and incited by
attachment of kinship with Taidg Chaoluisge's son Turlough [22]), rose against
him and were joined by the O'Deas, among whom Turlough had been fostered
and had imbibed his ethics. (6)

These forms of relationship are not only typical of chiefdoms, but found
described in detail in the legal texts of the Early Medieval period. Their
prominence in *Caithréim Thoirdhealbhaigh* shows that following the creation
of the state in Munster in the twelfth century, and even in the face of invasion by Anglo-Normans, Irish chiefdom social structure had passed intact
into the Medieval period (see Patterson 1994).

OF FORESTS AND FORTRESSES: THE POLITICAL
GEOGRAPHY OF THOMOND

Though *Caithréim Thoirdhealbhaigh* weaves a complicated web of political
intrigues, raids, and battles, it presents a clear overall picture of the political resources of Thomond's topography. Especially important to the dis-
putants were large tracts of forest land within Thomond. Apparently, each
tríocha céd maintained a reserve of underdeveloped back-country that provided a refuge in a political crisis. For Clann Chuiléin this was Eichtghe –
the foothills of the same-named Aughty Mountains to the northeast of Uí
Caisín. In Cenél Fearmaic the wet tracts at the base of Slieve Callan called
Bréntír were resorted to in crisis. Irrus was a place of similar last resort in
Corcabhaiscinn (25, 81).

Under pressure, the chiefdoms moved their entire stock and population to these areas (O'Grady 1929 27:7). It would seem from passages in
Caithréim Thoirdhealbhaigh that these refuge areas could support a chiefdom's
population and cattle over the winter months (75) until spring, when those
in refuge could act on one of three options. An attack could be made on the
belligerents in a gambit to seize back the lost lands (7, 22). If this strategy
seemed likely to fail, then either the changed political circumstances would
be acceded to by an act of submission (76), or the flight would be protracted
by leaving the territory altogether for a protecting lord in a neighboring
polity (15). Thus the people of Clan-Turlough (*Clann Toirdhealbhaigh*) sought
at times the protection and sponsorship of the Burkes of Connacht and the
Mac Carthys of Desmond. Clan Briain Ruaid (*Clann Briain Ruaidh*), for its
part, sought temporary refuge in Irrus (81) and the support of the O'Neills
of Ulster and support from the invading Scots under Edward Bruce (83).

THE CAPITAL SET

Unfortunately *Caithréim Thoirdhealbhaigh* is not clear on the identification and location of the capitals of composite chiefdoms. Those that are identifiable seem to foreshadow the locational pattern of the Tudor period capitals (indeed, several are the same; see Chapter 10). Three considerations seem to have been operative in capital location. In those *tríocha céd* bordering on the Shannon or Atlantic the capital was positioned on the coast. This type of location reflects the understanding that waterborne attacks were relatively rare. In landlocked chiefdoms, the capital was near the geographical center, a placement that would minimize the chance of an attack by outside forces reaching the capital, and maximize the coordination by the center of a response to the attack (Gibson 2000). Though the data are comparatively weak, there may have also been a tendency to locate the capital of a *tríocha céd* nearer to Cluain Rámhfhada, the capital of the kingdom. Only Dísert Murthaile exhibits this tendency strongly, and it is not altogether certain that this was the principal Corcabhaiscinn capital. This tendency is clearer for Late Medieval chiefdoms (see Chapter 10, and Gibson 2000).

The *túath* and *tríocha cét* capitals can be identified by recurring diagnostic elements that I refer to as the capital set. The capital set consists of features that, taken together, presumably fulfilled the requirements for the maintenance of the political institutions of an Irish chiefdom. In Thomond these are three in number. They are (1) the principal residence of the ruling primary lineage, or *derbfine*, of the aristocratic ramage; (2) a church presumably patronized by this family; and (3) an inauguration and chiefdom assembly site, which for several of the chiefdoms of Thomond was a mound dedicated to a renowned past ancestor.

The eighth-century law tract *Coibnes Uisci Thairidne* supplies proof that the capital set had an existence back in the earliest historical era (and presumably beyond), and was an overt native concept:

§ Ataat .iii. tíre la Fénin tar nach assa[e] do-airc[h]est(h)ar uisce: nemed cille no clúin, no (a) maigen f[e]irt.

There are in Irish law three lands across which it is improper that water be conducted: the sanctuary of a church or of a chiefly residence or the precinct of a grave mound. (Binchy 1955:70–71)

This combination of diagnostic elements can be verified in *Caithréim Thoirdhealbhaigh* in the case of the ruling O'Briens. As has been stated above, Cluain Rámhfhada was their capital since early in the thirteenth century.

Ennis Abbey was erected in 1240 by Donnchad Cairbreach O'Brien [16] within a kilometer of the capital, and their inauguration site was Magh Adhair near Cuinnche (Quinn). Inauguration sites were the symbolic\ritual centers of Irish chiefdoms – embodiments of the persistence of the pre-Christian religion into the Christian era, and of the ancestor cult behind Irish chieftainship. Given the symbolic importance of these places, the sacral character of the spot, and the fact that neither leaders nor functionaries lived at the site, one would expect that inauguration sites would be the most conservative element of this set, and so would be expected to remain fixed in position. The principal residence and ecclesiastical establishment can be expected to change in position more frequently, as political and social factors influencing locational behavior have a stronger bearing on these. Indeed, Magh Adhair had been in use for centuries by the Dál Cais as an inauguration site for their paramount chieftains before the events of *Caithréim Thoirdhealbhaigh*.

Several more examples of capital sets in Thomond can be adduced. In Uí Caisín, Tulach na nEspog (Hill of the Apostles) was both the principal church, probable inauguration site, and political capital of the MacNamaras (see Figure 9.2). It was auspiciously located upon a hill or *tulach*. Though the prose passages of the *Caithréim Thoirdhealbhaigh* allude only parenthetically to Tulach as the political capital of Clann Chuiléin (27:12), two laments within the text identify Tulach explicitly as the capital (O'Grady 1929 27:142):

> Were but one of the two fallen, in all our countries it had been a thing of woe; this event 'is the quern' of *Tulach*, [home] of the noble two [i.e. this misfortune crushes *Tulach* as a quern the corn].

In the sixteenth century, the principal residences of the eastern *and* western MacNamara chiefdoms were situated in proximity to this site. A tower-house existed on the hill at Tulla (*Tulach*) up to the nineteenth century (Westropp 1899:363).

In Cenél Fearmaic one also encounters this recurring set of diagnosts. *An Dísert Tola* is a famous church and monastery dedicated to St. Tola *Cráibdech*. This was located in the center of Cenél Fearmaic within lands later controlled by the O'Deas. It was most likely both the O'Dea principal residence and church.[6] In the sixteenth century the principal O'Dea tower-house was located within a short walking distance of the church and former monastery at Dísert Tola. Dysert O'Dea was the locus of the final battle in *Caithréim Thoirdhealbhaigh* in which Richard de Clare and his son were defeated by the O'Deas of Cenél Fearmaic and

O'Conors of Corcomroe. Four kilometers to the northeast of Dysert O'Dea is the townland Tullyodea, named after the hill it incorporates within its boundaries, Tully O'Dea (*Tulach Uí Dheaghaidh*). Though this hill is not named in the saga as the inauguration site of the O'Deas, it is certainly signalized as an auspicious place in *Caithréim Thoirdhealbhaigh*. In 1312 AD, a key battle is stated to have been fought on its sides between the forces of Muirchertach mac Thoirdhealbhaigh Mór Uí Briain [25] and the forces of Clann Briain Ruaid (27:57–59).[7] Later in the narrative it is referred to as an assembly point for Muirchertach's army (27:72). Aside from being named for the O'Deas, what indicates that this hill was the O'Dea inauguration site more than anything else is the fact that in the texts of the Tudor period the chiefdom took its name from the site (see previous discussion).

Mountains and prominences are stereotypical locales for military assemblages, camps, and battles in the saga. This is due, no doubt, to their religiously auspicious character in the pagan Celtic world. Mounds are the abodes of the *síde* – the often malevolent supernatural beings feared by many of the Irish to this day. Mountains were held to be the abode of certain gods both in ancient saga and later Christian belief (e.g., Croagh Patrick, Co. Mayo), and as such were frequently the focus of religious rites, a famous example being the pilgrimages associated with the festival of Lugnasad in many areas (see Mac Néill 1962). With the coming of Christianity, there was a movement to Christianize these places, as for example with the rock of Cashel, or the Hill of the Apostles in Uí Caisín.

In the topographical literature of the Middle Ages, and in place-name lore, the obviously man-made prominences of the Neolithic and Bronze Age periods were frequently said to be the burial sites of mythological heroes. In the Early Iron Age temples devoted to the worship of tutelary deities were erected on prominences (e.g., Rath of the Synods on Tara Hill; Dún Ailinne, Co. Kildare; Emain Macha, Co. Armagh). This practice is directly attested in a well-known passage from a story contained in the *Fragmentary Annals of Ireland* under the year 605. The story concerns the *rí* Áed Alláin. He had fallen mortally ill, and he summoned the cleric Muru Othna to deduce the cause of his illness, since the same saint had promised him a long life:

"I shall relate," said the *rí*, "that which I think likely to have offended the Lord. I attempted," said he, "to gather the men of Ireland to this mountain to the east, that is, to Carrlóeg, to build it up, and to construct a huge house on it, and I wished that the fire of the house might be seen every evening in Britain and Argyle; and I know that was great arrogance."

"That was evil," said the cleric. . . ." (Radner 1978:7)

A mound with clearer ties to chiefly ancestors and inauguration was Carn Mhic-Táil in the townland of Ballydeely in Corcamruadh. The cairn is presently a heap of stones 300 feet in diameter and 25 feet high, located on the south bank of the Deereen River in the very center of Corcamruadh (Figure 3.14). Mac-Táil was an ancestor-god in the genealogies of both the Corcu MoDruad and the Corcu Baiscinn, and so was venerated as a joint ancestor of both the O'Conors of Corcamruadh and the O'Lochlainns of Boireann in the Middle Ages. Carn Mhic-Táil is mentioned in the Corcu MoDruad genealogy in the Book of Lecan and Book of Ballymote (O'Brien 1976:392). Its significance as a place of assembly for the Corcu MoDruad appears in a passage of the *Life of St. Mac Creiche*: "The four of them proceeded until they came to Carn Meic Tail, where Tuath Mumu and Corcumruad met them ..." (Plummer 1925:64; see also FitzPatrick 2004:90; Frost 1978:95, 192).

By now it should be apparent that a capital for an Irish polity was the sum of its parts – those parts being the principal church, the capital homestead of the *rí*, and the ancestral nucleus of the chiefdom, the inauguration site. These elements were all bound together by symbolic and historical associations to the ramage of the *rí*. They collectively promulgated and reinforced the belief system that justified the elevated status of the chieftain and his family. At its base, in common with early chieftainship worldwide, the office of chieftain was sacred. The law texts make very clear that the quality of *naofacht*, or holiness, attached itself both to the person of the chief and to his residence (MacNeill 1923:273).

This holiness accrued to the chief, at least in the earlier periods, through his descent from deific ancestors, and through the inauguration ceremony, or *feis*. This word literally means the sexual consummation of marriage, and has been shown to derive from the ceremonial marriage performed at the inauguration site between the chieftain and tutelary goddess of the chiefdom (Byrne 2001:16–17). Attendant upon the establishment of Christianity in Ireland was a desire on the part of churchmen to enhance their prestige and to solidify the position of the church by involving themselves in the inauguration of chieftains. However, the first direct evidence for the participation of clerics in inauguration does not appear until the twelfth century (FitzPartick 2004:174). As has been stated previously, the former presumed inauguration site of Cashel was transferred to the church in this century, and Cormac's chapel was constructed upon the summit in 1134 by the Éoganacht *rí* Cormac Mac Carthaigh. It was subsequently claimed that the Mac Carthaigh kings were inaugurated in the chapel (FitzPatrick 2004:178). It is possible that at the time of the events described in *Caithréim Thoirdhealbhaigh*, some of the local inauguration sites had lost their function as a venue for chiefly inauguration to the church, but it is very clear from the prominence of these places in the saga that such sites still possessed to a strong degree their importance as the spiritual/symbolic centers and political foci of the polities of Thomond.

Irish chieftains were tied to the Irish church as principal patrons and through ties of blood. The patronage aspect of chieftainship was expressed in almost every praise-poem and lament to come down from the Middle Ages, where the importance of the chief as both the protector and patron to church establishments and clerics was stressed (see the lament at the beginning of this section). The important monastic establishments in Clare, such as the abbeys of Quin (*Cuinnche*), Corcomroe, and Ennis were established with grants of land by the O'Brien kings. It was they who footed the costs of construction of the church buildings – probably the only buildings of stone in Thomond built by the Irish until the fourteenth century. They were clearly public works meant to impress the populace with the munificence of the O'Brien kings. The church that was most strongly associated with chieftains at any level in the political hierarchy almost invariably was or became the chief church at the commensurate level in the religious hierarchy, and was administered by a person of equivalent rank to the chief, sometimes to the point of being one and the same person.

Given the nonurban character of Irish society, it should come as no surprise that the three elements of the capital set were not completely centralized so as to be found always in direct association. There was a tendency to move the capital homestead much more frequently than either the central ecclesiastical establishment and/or the inauguration site due to the volatile nature of secular Irish politics. The churches and monasteries had their own lands and ecclesiastical lineages, termed *airchinnigh*, not to mention substantial capital investments in stone buildings and other civic works such as monumental crosses, so there would have been a reluctance to relocate the religious capital once it was established.

However, it is likewise evident that, given these constraints, these three elements of the capital set tended to congregate broadly within a central region of a chiefdom, to use a much overused term a "core area," with great regularity. Thus, as the borders of the individual *túatha* remained fairly steady between the thirteenth and sixteenth centuries, the chiefdom capitals tended to recur in the same "capital areas" as well, and the inauguration sites and principal churches retained their significance down to the dissolution of the Irish church in 1537.

RECOGNIZING THE GEOGRAPHICAL IMPRINT OF STATE ORGANIZATION IN MEDIEVAL THOMOND

Alexander Grant was able to discern the effects of the expansion of the power of the medieval Scottish state between the tenth and twelfth centuries in the loss of geographical integrity of the territories controlled by *mormaer* (great stewards). These provinces shrank and assumed irregular shapes as land was confiscated by the crown and converted into royal thanages under direct control of appointees of the king (Grant 2000). The situation in Thomond seems on the surface to bear a resemblance to the progress of state expansion in Scotland, as the Early Medieval composite chiefdoms of Corcu MoDruad, Corcu Baiscind, and Dál Cais were broken up, yielding smaller territories that lacked the circular shape of their progenitors.

Does this geographical trend reflect state formation in Thomond? The answer is no and yes. The chief agent of the demise of the Early Medieval composite chiefdoms was probably the expanding O'Brien royal family rather than the state per se. As Donnchadh Ó Corráin pointed out, it was in the nature of Irish chiefly lineages to segment given the norm of polygynous marriages, and in the case of the O'Briens the segmentation was especially vigorous. So rather than reflecting the expansion of a state bureaucracy of stewards managing royal estates, the O'Brien estate used its power to enfeoff cadet branches of its family. One might argue, however, that this is how Irish chiefdoms have always operated. The difference is that under prior conditions the cadet lineages would have undergone a name change and would have eventually asserted their autonomy from the main O'Brien ramage. The geographical result would have been that the pattern of pie-shaped territories would have eventually reemerged, as territories with this shape would have been the most defensible against external enemies (Gibson 2000). As the following chapter will show, this did happen in the case of the O'Lochlainn chiefdom of Boireann in the far north. However, the maintenance of state power by the O'Briens ensured that their political hold on Thomond did not recede, and only the MacMahons of Corcabhaiscinn, descended from Mathgamain (Mahon) Ua Briain [5], dropped the O'Brien surname. Subsequent invasive lineages of the O'Briens maintained the surname and ties to the central O'Brien ramage, as evidenced by the uniting of diverse O'Brien lands in Thomond's periphery under the control of Mahon O'Brien [21], the presumptive tánaiste of the kingdom. The territories of Thomond in the twelfth and thirteenth centuries, then, do betray the expansion of the state, but that expansion took on a form that differed significantly from the example in Scotland.

CHAPTER TEN

The Political Topography of Late Medieval Clare

The ethnohistorical sources that have been reviewed so far, spanning the eighth–fourteenth centuries, provide much social, economic, and mythic information but give few insights into the specifics of the social geography of Irish chiefdoms. It has been necessary to project historical parish and barony boundaries into the past in order to approximate the boundaries of the Early Medieval and Medieval period chiefdoms of Co. Clare. Prior to the imposition of English administration, it was not the practice of the Irish to document landholdings in writing, and written records did not enter into legal disputes. This situation began to change in the fourteenth century with the appearance of two taxation lists, termed rentals, listing land divisions within the *saertúatha* of Thomond. The purpose of these records was to list the parcels that were let out by the O'Brien king and MacNamara chieftain for livestock grazing in return for payments (Hardiman 1828; Nugent 2000).

Aggressive campaigns against the autonomous Irish lords undertaken by Henry VIII and his daughter Elizabeth I culminated in Thomond in the swearing of fealty to the crown by the O'Briens and their conversion to Protestantism. In return, they were confirmed in their lands and received English titles. Thomond's lesser nobility likewise submitted and entered into treaties with the English in return for title to their lands. For the first time, districts within chiefdoms are named in these documents. Following the introduction of English administration, the English courts took on the settling of land disputes and Irish landholders began to put their agreements concerning land into writing. These documents permit an understanding to be gained of the stability of territorial boundaries and of the processes of land transfer.

CO. CLARE IN THE LATE MEDIEVAL PERIOD

The twilight of Irish political autonomy commenced with the advent of the English Tudors, beginning with Henry VIII, and the end came with the campaigns of William of Orange in 1689–1691. During this period what is now Co. Clare consisted of a patchwork of estates held by members of the O'Brien and MacNamara aristocratic ramages and remnants of formerly autonomous chiefdoms. Thomond was under the leadership of the O'Brien king, who in 1542 accepted English sovereignty and assumed the title of Earl (Frost 1978:236). As a part of the process of the political appropriation of the Irish polities by the English crown, the O'Brien and MacNamara estates and remaining chiefdoms were translated into baronies, and the Irish titles of the Clare aristocrats were dropped in favor of English aristocratic titles, though not without considerable dissent.

The Irish estates that endured during this period strongly expressed the character of the earlier chiefdoms out of which they were fashioned. The barony boundaries that were established by English officers in the latter half of the sixteenth century followed the configurations of former chiefdoms rather than the outlines of individual estates. As we have already seen, the more peripheral of the Tudor period baronies of Thomond, specifically that of Burren in northern Co. Clare, retained the original character and structure of chiefdoms albeit in a considerably emasculated state with regard to freedom of independent action. It is in the records for these peripheral chiefdoms that we would most likely discern the internal territorial organization of Late Medieval Irish chiefdoms. The Tudor polities of Clare will be reconstituted by combining the geographical and social information that survives in the copious sources of the sixteenth and seventeenth centuries.

INTRODUCTION TO THE SOURCES

The most complete records pertaining to the social situation of Gaelic Clare naturally originate, as stated previously, during the period of the ultimate disruption and displacement of the Gaelic polities, that is, the period from 1537–1691 spanning the dissolution of the Irish monasteries by Henry VIII to the end of the Williamite wars. In the Tudor period many transactions between the Irish nobility that related to property, and that had probably heretofore been commuted solely through verbal agreements, were committed to writing. Many of these transactions had been preserved by the O'Brien Barons Inchiquin. The English and Latin texts from this collection were edited by John Ainsworth (1961), and seven of the documents in Irish were later edited and translated by Gearóid Mac Niocaill (1970).

The imposition of English authority in Clare in the mid- to late sixteenth century entailed the introduction of the institutions of English law, and so beginning in the 1570s inquisitions were held to administer the disposition of property upon death. Depredations upon the property of English settlers by the Irish in the course of the 1641 revolt resulted in depositions that listed the losses of English settlers in detail. These are sometimes useful in making identifications of the names and location of parcels of land and in identifying individuals. A number of these have been published by Frost (1978: chap. 15–18, 20).

There are several detailed lists of the castles of Clare dating from the latter portion of the sixteenth century. These lists enumerate a synchronic stratum of capital sites and, in combination with the textual information, provide the basis for the reconstruction of the internal structure of sixteenth-century Gaelic polities. The majority of these castle sites can be located from the place-names associated with ruins on Ordnance Survey maps. The most comprehensive early record of the lands and population of Co. Clare is the product of the surveys and census carried out by the British government in the latter half of the seventeenth century following the Restoration. This corpus is described in detail below.

THE PETTY (DOWN) SURVEY

In 1659, following the Restoration, Sir William Petty was commissioned by the Crown to make a survey of Clare. The purpose of the survey was to facilitate the redistribution of land that had been confiscated from the allies of the Confederation by Cromwell's officers. This land was to be returned in part to the former proprietors following the Act of Settlement of 1653. Each county in Ireland was surveyed. Maps were made showing the shapes and distribution of territories and the land parcels contained in them. In the *Books of Survey and Distribution*, each parcel was listed, and the size, the economic quality of the land, and the names of individuals owning them were given. Many of the maps and volumes were destroyed in an eighteenth-century fire, but copies of the books and the surviving maps have been published by the Irish Manuscripts Commission. The *Books of Survey and Distribution* for Co. Clare is volume IV in this series (Irish Manuscripts Commission 1967).

Figure 10.1. 1685 Down Survey map of County Clare by Sir William Petty, showing disposition of baronies, parishes, and townlands.

In the course of completing the survey, Petty conducted a census of the existing inhabitants, and the names of the old landowners were entered into books of reference. These data became incorporated into the *Book of Forfeitures and Distribution* (Frost 1978:390, 396–397; White 1893:267–268). The census data were later published by Petty in a tract called the *Political Anatomy of Ireland* (White 1893:290).

The surviving 1685(?) Down Survey map of County Clare shows it to have been divided up into nine baronies. On the map these are set off by dashed lines, and the barony names have been rendered phonetically into seventeenth-century English approximations of the original Irish names (see Figure 10.1). These are the baronies of Burren, Corcomroe, Inchiquin, Ibrickan, Moyfarta, Clanderligh, Islands, Bunratty, and Tullagh.

These baronial divisions were first established in 1579 by Sir Nicholas Malley, president of Connacht, under orders from Elizabeth I (White 1893:198). However, the process of barony formation had commenced as early as 1542 at the parliament held in Limerick by Lord Deputy Anthony St. Leger to ratify the submission of Thomond's chieftains to the English crown (ibid.:175–178). The idea behind the formation of baronies was to bring the Irish aristocracy into the web of English rule by converting their

Figure 10.2. Co. Clare – showing the current barony divisions.

Gaelic chieftainships into English titles that entailed obligations of taxation, loyalty, and allegiance to the English monarch. This was achieved through the conversion of the preexisting Gaelic territories into taxable regions with established limits. These baronies have endured down to the present day, their boundaries remaining largely unaltered throughout the passage of 400 years (see Figure 10.2).

The Down map of Clare further displays each barony's parishes. The boundaries of the parishes are indicated with solid lines, and in many instances the parish center is indicated by a church symbol. In all instances, the parish centers are easily identifiable, as the parishes are named after their churches and the ruins and place-names of these are still to be found on maps today. Parishes are in turn subdivided into parcels of land that are today collectively called townlands, the smallest Irish geographical unit. On the Petty map, these are indicated solely as names in phonetic English, placed so as to approximate the geographical position of these entities.

THE RECONSTITUTION OF THE TUDOR POLITIES

A list of castles in Clare is contained in a manuscript of the collection of the library of Trinity College, Dublin (Ainsworth 1961: no. 899; Dwyer

1878:568–572; White 1893:394–397). Ainsworth and White give 1584 AD as the date of this list. However, by this date, at least three of the individuals named in the list would have been dead. The list names "Donel (Donnell) O'Brien" as the chief of Tuagh More Y Conor, and "Teige Mac Morrogh" as the second most important personage in this barony. Sir Donnell O'Brien [27] of Ennistimon died in 1579 AD, and Teig Mac Murrough [28] died in 1577. Donnell was formerly the *rí* of Thomond, the last to bear that title, but was deposed by the Earl of Sussex in 1557. He returned in 1558 and fought together with Teig and Donough Mac Murrough O'Brien [29] against his nephew Conor O'Brien [30], whom the Earl had selected to replace him as *rí*. A treaty was arranged between the warring factions in 1564 by which Donnell relinquished his claims to Thomond in return for the barony of Corcomroe. The list therefore probably stems from the period c. 1564–1570 AD.[1]

In the list, one finds the castles grouped under eight baronies: Tallaghnanaspull, Dangen West, Cloynderlaw, Moyarta, Tuagh More Y Conor, Gregans, Tullagh O'Dea, and Clonrawde. The barony of Ibrickan has been omitted from the list, possibly because by this time it was in complete possession of the Earl of Thomond (see Sir J. Perrott's Tripartite Deed (PTD) in White 1893:380). Unfortunately, the list gives the names of the castles phonetically as an Elizabethan English ear would make them out, so that it is impossible to know the original Irish names of a few of them. For most baronies, the list also gives the name of the owner of each castle and names the chieftain of the barony as well so that it is possible to locate the political center(s).

A complete listing of the lands and notable families of the baronies is given in the 1585 composition, or treaty, drawn up between Sir John Perrott and the leading men of Clare (published in toto in White 1893:377–390). From this and other sources we know the above barony names derive largely from the names of the contemporary and past chief residences of the chieftains of the leading ramages of these baronies. They are as follows: Tallaghnanaspull (PTD: Tullaghynaspyll) is a corruption of *Tullach na nApstoil* (Mound or Hill of the Apostles), the capital of Tullagh, the traditional seat of the MacNamara septs of the east (Frost 1978:56).[2] Dangen West (PTD: Dengynvyggon) takes as its point of reference the tower-house of Dangan Iviggin (Daingean?), the capital of the western MacNamaras in Bunratty built by Cuvea MacNamara in 1380 (White 1893:205; Westropp 1899:351). Likewise, Cloynderlaw (PTD: Clonraude) is the barony of Islands, and takes its name from the O'Brien royal residence of *Cluain Rámhfhada* (Clonroad) situated opposite

Figure 10.3. Map showing the distribution of barony territories within Co. Clare during the Tudor period. "Former barony capitals" are the principal residences of indigenous rulers supplanted by an O'Brien.

the modern town of Ennis on the river Fergus, and Tuagh Mor Y Conor is *Dabbac Mór Uí Conchobair*, the former principal seat of the O'Conors of Corco Mruad (Corcomroe, Old Irish *Corcu MoDruad*). Gregans (PTD: Gragans; Ir. *Greagnais? Creagach?*) signified the principal seat of the O'Lochlainns of the Burren, and as discussed in the previous chapter, *Tullach Uí Dedaid* was the assembly place of the O'Deas of Inchiquin, the former leading ramage of that barony.

THE O'BRIENS, HEREDITARY RULERS OF CLARE

In Figure 10.3, an effort has been made to locate the main seats of each barony and some of the principal residences of the O'Briens, the ramage of the hereditary rulers of Thomond. The map is informative on several accounts. First of all, it illustrates the extent of O'Brien dominance in Clare. Of the nine baronies, five capitals of these were castles belonging to a branch of the O'Briens. Of 161 castles, a total 66 castles, or 41% of the total, were in possession of an O'Brien.[3] On a barony-by-barony basis, the following figures represent the percentage of castles of the total number of castles in each barony occupied by a branch of the O'Briens: Clonrawde 74%,

Tullagh O'Dea 50%, Tuagh Mor Y Conor 95%, Dangan 34%, Moyarta 29%, Cloynderlaw 14%, and Tallagh 14%. The list names no O'Brien castles in the Burren.

Of the four autonomous capitals, *Tullach* (Tulla), as stated previously, was the hereditary capital of the ramage of the eastern MacNamara (Irish *Mac Conmara*), the second most powerful confederacy of septs in Clare. They remained the most populous and powerful of the ramages in Tullach Barony and the second most powerful group in Clare overall. Clonrawde and Ibrackan were almost exclusively O'Brien demesne, Ibrackan constituting the patrimony of the heir to the Earl of Thomond in the same way that Wales at present is considered the traditional domain of the successor to the English crown. Corcomroe (PTD: Tuagh Mor Y Conor) was entirely ceded over to Donnell O'Brien [27] in 1564. The former leading inhabitants displaced by this action were the eponymous O'Conors (Frost 1978:93). No castle in the list is stated to be in O'Conor possession. As previously stated (Chapter 9), the O'Deas (*Uí Dedaid*) were formerly the leading ramage of Tullagh O'Dea, and their capital was at Dysert O'Dea. However, the list ascribes only this castle and one other to them.[4]

PROCESSES OF EXPANSION BY THE O'BRIENS

Though at times the O'Brien overlords disempowered weaker non-O'Brien ramages within their sphere of influence by dictate, certain processes also achieved creeping disenfranchisement of the politically weak by the politically powerful. These processes entailed the creation of conditions resulting in the indebtedness of members of politically inferior groups accompanied by the piecemeal transfer of land to the politically superior creditor as collateral for a loan. At least one text dating from the reign of Elizabeth documents the transfer of two parcels of land, Lysduffe and Ballyedearnane, held by Seán (John) mac Lochlainn O'Dea over to a sept of the O'Briens headed by Tadhg (Teig) mac Murrough O'Brien [28] in return for rights to certain rents, money, and protection (Ainsworth 1961: no. 888). In the text below, the transfer of land from the lineage of Seán O'Dea to the lineage of Tadhg O'Brien is reciprocated by the provision of money to Seán ("one moyetie of the sayd Rents," "the sayd mortgadge") and by a pledge by Tadhg to Seán of assistance in the pursuit of legal claims ("the sayd Teyg shall aid the sayd John in all his lawfull causes . . .").

AINSWORTH NO. 888

20 June 1566

Agreement between Teig O'Brien and John O'Dea

"In the name of God amen, this ys the condytion of Teig mc. Murrough O Brian & John mc. Laughlin O Dea for the cheyf Rents of O dea upon the Barrony of Kinalash(?) ... the sayd Teyg to spende wyne & recov[er] the same agaynste any man by Her Maties. lawes or otherwy[se] ... the one moyetie of the sayd rents so recovered ... unto the use of the sayd John O Dae & his heyres & the other [to the use of the said] Teyg [& his heyres] ... and the sayd John dothe gyve the halfe quarter of Lysduffe from him selfe & his sept to the said Teyg & his sept for ever ... yf the inherytors or founders do redeame the same, the sayd mortgadge to be delyvered unto the sayd John, & the sayd John to gyve the sayd Teyg half a quarter of his lande in leywe ... & the sayd John hath gyven all his right tytell & interest of the halfe quarter of Ballyedearnane to the sayd Teyg & his heyres for ever, & thearwthall the sayd Teyg shall aid the sayd John in all his lawfull causes & ... wch soever of the sayd parties shall breake these covenants his portion of the sayd bargayne shalbe forfeyted unto the other ... & thesse be the wytnesses ... Shane O Shaughnes & John Lynch & John Moyle Mc. Gyllisaght Murtaghe og O Duvlanna & Dermott og O Nealan & Cnoghor O Hear & Mortogh McDermot McCnoghor & Edmonde Roe O Hear & Thomas O..ngsay ..." (Ainsworth 1961:273).

In Irish Tudor texts one frequently encounters the transfer of land for "protection" or *slánuigheacht*. This is simply a continuation of the practices of clientship from the era of the eighth-century law texts (Nicholls 1972: 41–42; see also Gibson 1982:60–66; Mac Niocaill 1972:60–66; Ó Corráin 1972:43–44). In return for a payment to the lord, the lord undertook to represent the client in all affairs and to personally prosecute trespasses against the client. This was completely analogous to the practice in the earlier era by which an aristocratic patron conferred his honor-price upon his client.

Two other practices ensured the diminution of the holdings of subchiefs and their ramages. The most numerous Tudor period economic texts are documents that have to do with the pledging of land. The word for pledge (Old Irish *gíall*, Modern and Middle Ir. *gill, giull, or geall*) is the same word that in the oldest Irish texts signified the offer of oneself or a near relative to an opposite party (often hostile) as a physical guarantee of an agreement (Jaski 2000:91; McLeod 1992; Patterson 1994:329). In similar fashion, *gíalla*, in the sense of "hostages," were demanded by a militarily superior chieftain from a subordinate or vanquished polity as a guarantee of future good (or at least neutral) conduct.

The pledging of land involved the surrender of use-rights to another party in return for a payment, usually in kind. Land would be returned to the original owner upon redemption of this pledge (Nicholls 1972:65–67). However, the one mortgaging his land could always continue to receive additional advancements upon his pledge to the point where it was impossible to redeem the amount and gain the return of the land. Thus the pledge became the first step in a process by which land was alienated from weaker ramages by wealthier ones, and the text above is a case in point.

The second way in which land accrued to an O'Brien lord or to the Earl was through inaction or lack of resolve on the part of subordinate chiefdoms or ramages. By custom, ramage lands which lay in waste reverted in ownership to the paramount chieftain (Nicholls 1976). There was also a custom that came into play when subordinate aristocratic lineages failed to resolve or provide for succession. When this happened, the rights and privileges of leadership were conferred upon the superior chieftain (Frost 1978:20). A declaration of submission on the part of a *sliocht* or section of the O'Lochlainns of the Burren dating from 1591 illustrates this practice.[5]

And this is the agreement, namely, that we ourselves, the posterity of Malachy of Ballyvaughan and of Benroe, and their people and country, are and shall be bound, and their heirs after us, to Conor O'Brien, and his heirs after him. And that it shall not be in the power of any of us or of our descendants, to cause a sod of the country or any of the castles to be mortgaged or sold, except with the consent of said Conor, or his heirs after him, And that Conor or his heirs after him shall be heirs to the Sliocht Mealachlin (Frost 1978:20).

Irish chiefly succession was often contentious, and so failure to provide for succession by a subordinate aristocracy was probably defined by the need for new holdings on the part of the superior lord. In Inchiquin, the O'Dea capital at Dysert continued to be occupied by the O'Dea chieftain following the establishment of an O'Brien Baron Inchiquin in 1542. This state of affairs demonstrates that the usurpation of the prerogatives of subordinate aristocracy by the O'Briens can be said to precede the collapse of the political integrity of the subordinate ramage.[6]

One might think that perhaps the O'Lochlainns (*Uí Lochlainn*) of the Burren and the Mac Mahons (*Mac Mathghamhna*) of Moyarta and Cloynderlaw would enjoy greater autonomy due to their more isolated geographical positions with respect to the O'Brien centers of power. This was at least partially true. However, several texts document the erosion of O'Lochlainn power and land.

The first text (Hardiman 1828: no. 10) is a rambling account from the 1580s presenting justification for the confiscation of the *baile* of Ballyvaughan (*Baile Uí Beachain*; see Fig. 10.2) by a branch of the O'Briens from an O'Lochlainn section, among other matters. Within the framework of the medieval Irish system of land assessment, the *baile* was the most important designation for a holding. More specifically, it was the demesne land connected to the seat of an aristocratic ramage, in this case one possibly closely connected to the O'Lochlainn chieftain, as Ballyvaughan lay within the O'Lochlainn's traditional mensal territory (Duffy 1981:8; Gibson 2000, 2008b; McErlean 1983:330; Ní Loingsigh 1994). That Laois was the O'Lochlainn section head of Baile Uí Beachain is signified in the document by his appellation *cean Laois* (chief Laois). It is clear from the text that Laois is deceased, and so the matter concerns his son and successor. The initial pretext for the confiscation of this *baile* is that in the past some individual of Laois Uí Lochlainn's household stole a cow from an aristocrat of the O'Conors of Corcomroe and brought it back to the section capital at Baile Uí Beachain.[7] Moreover, the text establishes compensation for the killing of the wife of Mathgamna *ballaigh* O'Brien and their servants pursuant of some raid or ambush.

TRANSLATION OF AN EXCERPT FROM HARDIMAN TEXT NO. 10

This is the first cause of Murchad O'Brien's possession of the lands of *Baile i Beachain*, viz. The son of the Madra Dun (Dog of the Fort) stole a cow from Fergus mac Conchubhair meic Maoilseachlainn, and brought her to *Baile i Beachain* unto Laois, and for this act he forfeited that *baile*, in satisfaction for that cow, and also fourteen cows *fágbáil* were imposed upon him, and through these said possession accrued. These are the persons onto whom he [Laois] gave these cows, viz. 20 *sgilling* (shillings) unto Tadhg mac Feidhleme Uí Conchubhair, a mark (*marg*) onto Taodhg mac Taidg meic Conchubhair, a mark unto Taodhg Og mac Taidg Uí Dalaid, and ½ a mark unto Moir Ini Domnallain. Seven cows were to be taken from said Laois in payment of that ½ mark, and it was due only a year, and he was even to pay that ½ mark at the expiration of a year unto Moir. The witnesses that these seven cows were paid in satisfaction of that ½ mark viz. *Cland* Eogain Uí Conraigh and Seán Mac Caisia and *muintir* Duda. The testament of Laois Uí Lochlainn at his death, concerning Baile i Bheachain was that Baile i Bheachain was not subject to any debts, not so much as one *phinginn* (penny), at the time of his death. The witnesses to said testament are these, viz. the abbott O'Bruaidigh, and Seán O'Tigarna, and Muirise O'Mionain, and Toirdealbac dub Sagart (priest). These are the alienations of Mathghamhna ballaigh onto *Cland* Muiris Uí Briain viz. Murchadh O'Briain was to go to baile i beachain, and to permit him [i.e., Murchadh] to enter and dress food there, and take possession of the *baile* from Toirdhealbhach, and to keep same to himself, and that they should have neither right, title nor covenant to said *baile*, except what they acquired by these entries, against the will of the inhabitants of the same. Further four in-calf cows belonging to Mathghamhna were killed by *muintir* Taidg Uí Briain in baile i beachain, the night that Diarmaid O'Briain came there. In addition, an ounce of gold and 13 marks taken from O'Lochlainn in redemption for the killing of the wife of Mathgamna *ballaigh* and their servants, and the value of 15 marks of cattle to be taken from him, by virtue of the covenant entered into between Donncha O'Briain and O'Lochlainn respecting Baile i Beachain (Hardiman 1828: 30–31).[8]

The text contains apparent contradictions which go some distance toward explaining the political circumstances of northern Clare in the sixteenth century. The text states that the O'Lochlainn section leader paid a fine in compensation for receiving stolen property from one of his people. The fine was to be paid not to the victim but to another O'Conor, Tadhg mac Fedhlim, and his son. From this circumstance, we may assume that the latter O'Conor was acting as the superior chieftain to the first; accepting the fine payment on his client's behalf.[9] It seems unusual enough that the lord of the transgressor should lose his patrimony over the theft of a cow – especially as the document records the payment of a sizable fine to the lord of the victim. However, an odd fact emerges in that the land apparently remained in Laois' possession throughout his lifetime, his will stating that there were no outstanding debts upon Baile Uí Beachain upon his death. Moreover, the text specifically states that possession had to be taken anew of the land by the O'Briens.[10]

The explanation of these contradictions lies in a not-so-subtle legal sleight of hand on the part of the O'Briens. As has been previously stated, Donnell O'Brien [27] assumed the chieftainship of Corcomroe in 1564. Apparently, the original offence against the O'Conors was also interpreted as an offence to the contemporary Earl of Thomond as their paramount, or, more likely, the suzerainty of the O'Brien chieftain of Ennistimon[11] over the O'Conors was backdated to include the offence as a pretext for the confiscation. The following actions are described in the text: the O'Brien paramount of Ennistymon, Toirdhealbhach (Turlough) Uí Briain, first had to go to Baile Uí Beachain in order to pave the way for Murchad Uí Briain (the fourth Baron Inchiquin [32]?), to enter the *baile* and perform a ritual signaling his installment there as overlord to Mathghamhna ballaigh (spotted) O'Brien. Probably there was a practical necessity to this order of events, as the text states "they should have neither right, title, nor covenant to said *baile*, except what they acquired by these entries, against the will of the inhabitants."[12] The text then lays out the compensation paid by the O'Lochlainn chieftain for the killing of Mathghamhna's wife and servants. That the settlement was reached between the earl and the O'Lochlainn chieftain underscores the O'Lochlainn resistance to the takeover.

The rest of the document details injuries done to the property of the new proprietor of Baile Uí Beachain by a brother of the earl and an attempt of the O'Briain *ceann* at Leamenagh to seize the land under English sponsorship. What the examination of this legal document has revealed is probably a forcible seizure of land on the death of a section chief or *cenn* by aspirants of the ruling family on a legal pretext. It is further indicated that aristocrats from the intermediary echelons of authority of the leading family could be sponsors for such takeovers. These individuals would be attempting to create patrimonies for the cadet branches of their lineages in areas ruled by weaker alien chieftains. The competition for such holdings by aristocratic members of the same ramage probably denotes an interest in, and competition over, new areas of revenue.

Further evidence of O'Lochlainn decline in the face of O'Brien expansion is found in Tudor documents that signal the loss of political autonomy. The earliest text is a grant, dated 1575, made by the English crown, of the office of seneschal over the baronies of Corcomroe and Burren to the aforementioned Turlough O'Brien, knight of Ennistimon (White 1893:390–391).[13] The sense of the text is that he was to become the chief legal officer of these territories, though it is clear that, in effect, lordship is being conferred upon him. This grant was renewed with respect to Turlough's son Daniel by King James I in 1621 (ibid.:391–392).

Other sources make it clear, however, that the grant was in all probability preceded by a covenant, described above, between Conor O'Brien [30], the third Earl of Thomond (d. 1580), and the leaders of the O'Lochlainn section that had authority over Baile Uí Beachain, whereby the latter pledged their obedient submission to the rule of the earl. This pact is alluded to not only in the text discussed previously concerning Baile Uí Beachain, but also in a renewal of the covenant made in either 1590 or 1591 between Donogh [31], the then Earl of Thomond, and Irial and Donogh O'Lochlainn.[14]

The engine that propelled the expansion of the O'Briens and MacNamaras was the paired practices of aristocratic polygyny and partible inheritance. Kenneth Nicholls is principally responsible for recognizing the process whereby the lineages of the paramount ramage (or conical clan) expanded at a rapid rate and squeezed out the lineages of subordinate ramages. He also furnished an explanation for this process (Nicholls 1972:10–12, 57–79, 1976). The old Celtic practice of marriage consisted of coming to an agreement with the potential bride's father (including payment of bride-wealth), fetching the woman, the holding of a feast, and sleeping with her. This practice was little modified with the advent of Christianity, and Irish chieftains of the Medieval period frequently had up to ten wives. Not only were all the sons produced by these wives potential heirs to the chieftainship, but illegitimate sons could also easily claim, and were often granted, a share of the patrimony as well. So, for instance, Turlough *an fhíona* O'Donnell, the paramount chieftain of Tirconnell, produced eighteen sons by ten different wives, and had fifty-nine grandsons (Nicholls 1972:11).

On top of this, like the Normans, the Irish followed the custom of partible inheritance, whereby a head of a household tried to enfranchise as many of the male heirs as possible, though it was not always possible or practicable. Given that the overriding concern of a paramount chieftain would be to preserve the holdings of the paramountcy intact for the successor to that office, an optimal strategy was to carve entitlements for his other male offspring out from the holdings of political subordinates. Evidently, the problem of entitlement creation was most acute in the case of politically powerful rival claimants to the paramountcy, who correspondingly exacted the greatest rewards in return for their claims. The instance has already been alluded to in which suzerainty over Corcomroe was granted by the Earl Conor O'Brien [30] in 1564 to Donnell O'Brien [27] to quell his violent efforts to realize his claims to the paramountcy of Thomond (Nicholls 1972:157–158).

THE SPATIAL CONFIGURATIONS OF TUDOR CLARE

The matter of the position of the O'Briens being resolved, it is now appropriate to view the distribution of baronies and their political centers from a purely spatial perspective. Another look at Figure 10.3 reveals some important patterns in this respect. Considering the aboriginal barony capitals to the exclusion of the later centers of O'Brien aristocratic lineages, it is clear that in the case of those baronies that border on bodies of water such as the Atlantic Ocean or Shannon Estuary or River, the capital tends to be located on or near the coast or riverbank toward the center of the territory.[15] The two exceptions to this rule are the O'Lochlainn capital at Gragans, which is nevertheless somewhat removed in location from the borders with neighboring baronies to the south, and the Macnamara capital at Tullagh (modern Tulla). Tullagh, as shall be shown later, owes its geographical position to historical circumstances and is indeed the exception that proves the rule.

The only barony in a truly landlocked position is Inchiquin. The original capital of this barony, Dysert O'Dea, is located fairly close to the geographic center of Inchiquin. The true center of power of the barony, Inchiquin Castle, the sixteenth-century seat of the O'Brien Baron Inchiquin, is likewise to be found in the center of the barony removed six kilometers to the north of Dysert. In addition to the contemporary forces that determined the locations of these centers, their sitings were also predicated on historical/political antecedents, and these will be discussed in a later section.

The important O'Brien centers share a commonality in that they lie on major lines of communication.[16] Bunratty is positioned on a tributary of the Shannon, Clonroad on the Fergus, Inchiquin is located near a major inland route of communication paralleling approximately the course of the Fergus, and Ennistimon is positioned at the confluence of two rivers, the Cullenagh and Inagh. Furthermore, the O'Brien capitals were placed so as to administer lands often distributed in several baronies. Hence the junctions and borders between territories were favored for capital placement. For example, Clonroad lies on the border between Islands and Bunratty baronies, and Leamaneh Castle is positioned at the intersection of three barony boundaries, and is indeed peripheral to all three.

The contrast between the two patterns of barony capital location, one exhibiting centrality and border avoidance, and the other showing site placement so as to facilitate communication between centers, probably relates to sets of concerns held by those who established these centers, and to the historical factors that predetermined the barony divisions. The original capitals were, of course, established by the original maximal ramages that dominated the territories that were later to be circumscribed as baronies. Often, as in the case of the O'Lochlainns of the Burren and the O'Conors of Corcomroe and the O'Deas of Tullagh O'Dea, their historical origins were distinct from those of the politically superordinate O'Briens.

Since intrapolity violence is intrinsic to chiefdoms (and to societies with a pastoralist orientation as well), the security of the polity center must have been a consideration foremost on the minds of those involved in establishing its location (Earle 1997:120; Gibson 2000). As we shall see later, the highly mobile character of Irish warfare must have been an important contributing factor.

The owners of the O'Brien centers were genealogically related and therefore possibly not as fearful of an attack from one of their distant agnates as they would be of one coming from an alien ramage. The location of their seats would seem to indicate that cooperation and intercommunication between them were considerations of primary importance in affixing their location. There may have also been a desire to monopolize the material and other exchanges that occurred between the nonrelated maximal ramages of adjacent baronies. This locational aspect of dominating ramages has been hinted at by Gearóid Mac Niocaill, who noted that in the earliest historical period, the then dominant Éoganacht polities of Munster were positioned so as to form barriers between the presumably hostile non-Éoganacht polities (1972:34). That the prevention of hostile military alliances and the monopolization of communication was necessary for the preservation of political ascendancy over nonrelated peoples seems a safe conclusion to draw from these data.

The centrality of barony capitals was probably predicated upon administrative concerns. Irish chieftains often had to mobilize people quickly to counter a raid or attack, and this would be facilitated by locating the principal chiefly residence in the center of the chiefdom (Gibson 2000). Under the expectations of central place theory modified to accommodate a marketless economy, the political capital of a complex chiefdom would be positioned at the geographical center of its territory in order to average out the costs of goods transportation between subsidiary centers and the capital, thereby facilitating economic exactions (Steponaitis 1978). The behavior of Irish capital sites of the Middle Ages seems to belie that explanation. The two positions that have been observed – in the geographical center of the chiefdom or at the center but adjacent to a large river or the sea – suggests that the primary desire on the part of the builders was to place as much distance as possible between the capital and external threats coming overland.

In her examination of the location of Late Medieval castles of Gaelic chieftains in Co. Donegal, Máire Ní Loingsigh also took notice of the defensive character of the siting of many of these strongholds. However, as an explanation for the frequent siting of castles on the coast or adjacent to bodies of water in Donegal, she advanced the hypothesis of the strong economic importance of the control of fishing and waterborne commerce to the fortunes of local chieftains (1994:148). Her hypothesis is undercut, however, by a lack not only of direct documentation of this commerce for the Late Medieval period but also by her admission of a deficit of large watercraft on the part of the Irish by which this commerce could be pursued or controlled (1994:150). Though she also brings up the vulnerability of a coastal location to an amphibious assault, she notes further on that the Irish used boats for military purposes chiefly on lakes (1994:151). Defensive considerations would then seem to have been the primary factor in influencing the location of a chiefdom capital.

TUDOR PERIOD SOCIAL SPATIAL CONFIGURATIONS AT THE BARONY LEVEL

The Tudor period documentation from Co. Clare that touches upon Gaelic social relations is complete enough to support an examination of the distribution of lands and settlements within an individual barony in order to reveal social principles by which these were organized. Naturally, a barony in which social relations have been distorted as little as possible through O'Brien impositions is preferred so that we may grasp how Irish chiefdoms were organized during this period. Burren Barony retained some measure of political autonomy throughout the Middle Ages and is thus an ideal candidate for scrutiny.

The seventeenth-century parish boundaries of the Burren were reconstructed by combining the information in the Petty/Down Survey Map with the listing of townlands by parish in the *Book of Forfeitures and Distribution* (Frost 1978:399–426). This procedure entailed the assumption that the townland boundaries have not changed significantly since the seventeenth century. The resultant map clearly demonstrates the general validity of this assumption (see Figure 10.4), as the configurations of the reconstructed parishes strongly resemble the shapes of the Petty map parishes (Fig. 10.1).

Next, those castles (or to refer to them by the proper historical/archaeological term, tower-houses) that could be identified from the late sixteenth-century Trinity Ms. list (Dwyer 1878:568–571; White 1893:394–397) were located upon the map. This was not an altogether easy task, as distorted Elizabethan phonetic equivalents are given of the original Irish names, which must then be matched with the nineteenth-century Anglicized place-names on the Ordinance Survey maps. The concordance is given in

Figure 10.4. The Tudor period parishes of Burren Barony. Deerpark townland is just to the northeast of Leamaneh Castle, and its boundaries are indicated by stippling.

Table 10.1. For the other baronies, the castle list also identifies the chief of the barony, and then lists the "gentleman" owner of each castle. The names of the chief and gentlemen are not given for the Burren, but from other sources (e.g., the Tripartite Deed) it is known that Gragans was the principal seat of the O'Lochlainn chieftain.[17]

When the Late Medieval parish boundaries of the Burren are superimposed upon a contour map, it is clear that many of the parish boundaries follow points of geographical demarcation (see Figure 10.5). The most common of these are the pervasive hills and mountains that exceed 300 m in elevation, and which stretch in a band from west to east across the center of the barony. It is also clear from the contour map that the parishes are centered upon pockets and sections of low-lying arable soil. Though the stony hills give the Burren a barren appearance, the soil in the valleys and depressions is of the highest grade as far as tillage is concerned (see Figure 10.6). In the coastal parishes and in areas close to the barony boundary, the maximum elevation of arable soil is about 90 m (300 ft.). In the higher inland regions, the boundary between arable soil and exposed

Table 10.1. Concordance Tudor Castle Names for the Burren

Name from list	19th-century place-name	Parish	Original Irish name
Caherclogan	Cahercloggaun	Kilmoon	Cathair Clochán
Lysegleeson	Lissylisheen	Noughaval	Lios Uí Ghlisín
Cahirenally/ Cahiricnacty	Cahermacnaghten	Rathbourney	Cathair Mhic Neachtain
Ballymonoghan	Ballymahony	Noughaval	Baile Uí Mathghamhna
Meghanos	Muckinishnoe(?)	Drumcreehy	Muc Inis Nua
Glensteed	Glenslead	Kilcorney	Gleann Slaod
Gregans	Gragans	Rathbourney	Greagnais or Creagach
Glaninagh	Gleninagh	Gleninagh	Gleann Eidhneach
Ballyvaughan	Ballyvaughan	Drumcreehy	Baile Uí Beachain
Shanmokeas	Shaumuckinish	Drumcreehy	Sean Muic Inis
Nacknasse	Muckinishoe	Drumcreehy	Muc Inis Nua
Kynvarra	Kinvara	Co. Galway	Ceann na Mara[a]
Turlough	Turlough	Oughtmama	Turlach
Glancollymkilly	Glencolumbkille	Carran	Gleann Colmcille
Neassalee/ Nacapaghee	Cappagh	Carran	Caisleán na Ceapaí
Ballyheaghane	Ballyhehan	Abbey	Baile Uí hÉacháin
Castleton	Castletown	Carran	Baile na Caisleán
Creaghwell	Crughwill	Carran	Críoch Maol
Rughaine	Roughan	Kilfenora Corcomroe Br.	*Ruachan*[b]

Note: *Burren* Barony castle sites not on the list: Ballyganner (Baile Uí Dhanair) and Ballymurphy (Baile Uí Murchadha), Noughaval Par.; Cappagh Castle (Caisleán na Ceapach) and Fahee (Faiche), Carran par.; Faunrooska, Rathbourney par. (Frost 1978:33), Faunarooska, Killonaghan Par. (Frost 1978:30), Newtown Castle, Drumcreehy par., and a castle depicted on the Down Survey map in Abbey parish that could be in Ballyvelaghan townland, or it could also be the O'Heyne castle in Corranroo.

[a] This tower-house place-name is somewhat surprising as it implies that an O'Lochlainn sept had a residence near this town, which lies about 5 kilometers to the east of the Clare-Galway border at Corranroo Bay. One can only imagine that either this is a mistake, or an interpolation of the name of some other O'Lochlainn seat within the barony (perhaps Finavarra?).

[b] This townland is Ballyroughan in the *Books of Survey and Distribution*, and in a will of 1717 (Ainsworth no. 1504:522; 1967:188).

bedrock is between 140–150 m (450–500 ft.). The simplified contour map, Figure 10.5, shows just the 400 ft. and 600 ft. contours. The areas with arable soil are therefore somewhat smaller or larger in extent than the territories circumscribed by the 400 ft. contour, depending upon whether the specific place within the Burren is at a lower or higher altitude, respectively. This is clear when the soil suitability map, Figure 10.6, which shows actual soil areas, is compared with the contour map.

The placement of the tower-houses likewise reveals some interesting spatial regularities. Usually in Tudor period Irish texts, the word gentlemen designates the heads of aristocratic lineages (*clanna* or *sleachta*, what I

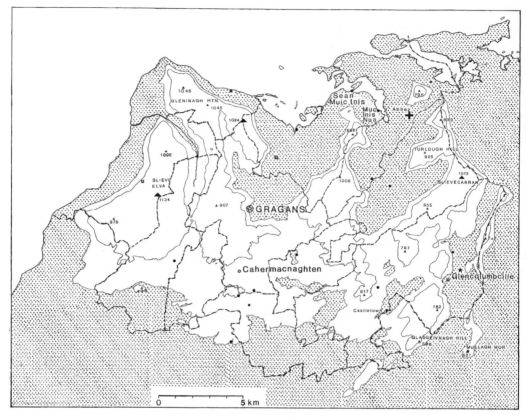

Figure 10.5. Simplified relief map of the Late Medieval chiefdom of Gragans. Only the 400- and 600-foot contours are shown and the land below 400 ft. is stippled. See Fig. 10.4 for an explanation of symbols.

have been calling a section). Dwyer's redaction of the castle list gives the gentleman associated with each castle except for the castles of the Burren, where the owner is simply given as "O'Loughlen" for each. If each Burren castle named in the above list stands for an individual aristocratic lineage or section, then *sliocht* holdings could not have been exactly co-terminous with the parishes. As far as can be determined, no castles are named in the Trinity list for Killonaghan and Killeany parishes, while in Carran, Noughaval, and Drumcreehy parishes there are up to three named castles. Only Kilcorney, Gleninagh, and Oughtmama parishes seem to exhibit a pattern of one section, one parish.

The pattern of distribution of the *sliocht* capitals with respect to the chiefdom capital, and of all other parishes with respect to the central parish of Rathbourney, displays and underscores the political centrality of the capital at Gragans. With the exception of Carran parish all parishes have at least a portion of a border contiguous with Rathbourney parish, though

Soil Suitability Classes

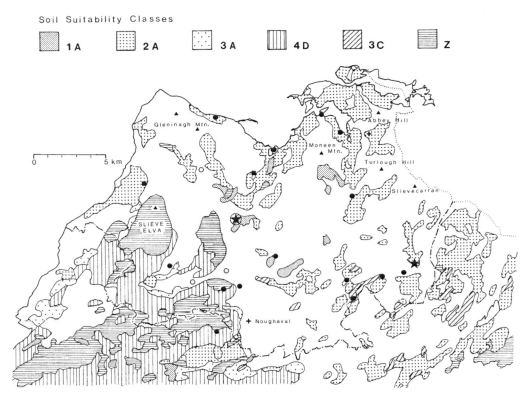

Figure 10.6. Soil suitability map of the Burren, Co. Clare. The soils are ranked as to their suitability for tillage on a scale from 1 to 5 and as grassland for grazing on a scale of A to E (1 and A = Very Good, 3 and C = Moderate, 5 and E = Very Poor). Soil class Z is bogland and unshaded areas are of class 5Ew "Very shallow soil, liable to drought" (from Finch 1971).

direct communication with Gragans via the individual sections of shared boundary was in many instances impossible.

The location of many of the section capitals seems to bear out the spatial predictions of the central-place model for chiefdoms put forward by Vincas Steponaitis (1978). His argument was consistent with the tenets of the original central-place model of Von Thünen, that in a situation in which an economy of kind exists and the political economy is patterned upon tribute payments flowing to a central place, it is expected that subsidiary settlements will tend to be positioned nearer to that portion of their territory that lies adjacent to the central place. A position closer to the capital reduces the costs of bulk transport between subsidiary centers and the central place.

Though not very revealing as to specifics, unambiguous references to the goods-provisioning of capital sites by subsidiary centers crop up in ethnohistorical sources from throughout the Middle Ages. In Early Medieval law texts like *Críth Gablach*, the relationship between inferior leaders and a superior leader was most often cast in clientship terms, which carried the inference that the subordinate leaders would make clientship payments to their patron. In the early eighth-century *Audacht Morainn* (The Testament of Morann), there is the line

Cíallfhlaith, ar-clich side crícha sceo túatha, to-lécet a séotu agus a téchte ndó.

The intelligent ruler defends borders and chiefdoms, they yield their *séotu* and possessions to him. (F. Kelly 1976:19)

In this instance, what is actually paid to the paramount chieftain is not directly stated, though the word *séotu*, which Fergus Kelly has translated as "valuables," can have the literal meaning of "heifers." In the fourteenth-century saga *Caithréim Thoirdhealbhaigh*, reference is made several times to "rent," "tribute," and "dues" owed by subordinate lords to a king (O'Grady 1929:3, 5). One may safely assume that such payments were probably patterned after the flows of goods between section leaders and a chieftain. Patrick Duffy posits the existence of economic relationships of this sort between the local "headmen or 'gentlemen' of the septs" and the chieftains of the MacMahons in Late Medieveal Airghialla (2001:133).

Assuming that section capitals still provisioned composite chiefdom capitals into the Late Middle Ages, the fact that livestock can move themselves or be used to transport goods would minimize goods transport costs. While not denying that goods transport costs to the chiefdom capital were a factor in deciding where to position a section capital, a consideration that would have been equally strong, if not stronger, is the coordination of a response to military aggression from outside the composite chiefdom. Roads connecting section capitals with the chiefdom capital were conduits of information regarding incursions by raiders. A chieftain would be better able to coordinate a military response if the secondary nodes in the network were located closer to the capital in the center (Gibson 2000). The data from the Gragans chiefdom lend support to this hypothesis, as those sections that are closest to the land boundary with another polity are closer to the capital than are the capitals of those sections that face the sea (Figure 10.4).

Where the parish section capitals are seen to be located at a greater distance from the chiefdom capital, as in the case of Caherclogan in Kilmoon and Castletown in Carran, it must be remembered that in the Burren the shortest distance between two points is rarely a straight line. Most of the tower-houses lie adjacent or near to present-day routes of communication – routes that connect the fertile pockets at the heart of

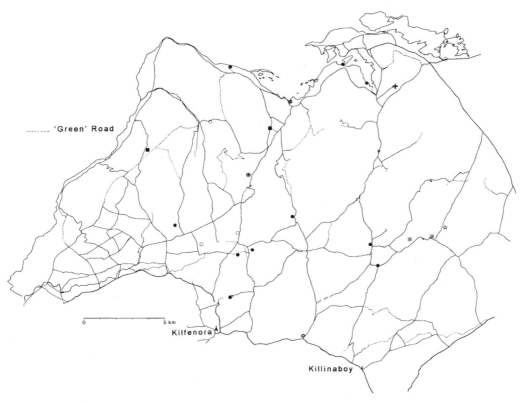

Figure 10.7. The present-day road system of the Burren. The roads in this region were not paved until the 1950s. A "green" road is an unpaved track thought to be of some antiquity. It is clear from the map that some of these green roads provided a more direct route to the O'Lochlainn chiefdom capital at Gragans from some of the subsidiary castles.

most parishes with the center at Gragans via passes over the mountain ranges (see Figure 10.7). In several cases, the former drive of the tower-house can still be traced up to a modern road, which demonstrates that these routes are of some antiquity. The route from Castletown to the chiefdom capital of Gragans passes over a range of hills through a fertile valley in the south of Kilcorney parish before it deviates to the northwest past Glenslead Castle to Gragans. Caherclogan is likewise located nearest to the direct route skirting Slieve Elva to Gragans.

PARISH BOUNDARIES AND ARISTOCRATIC LINEAGES

The exceptions to the rules and hypotheses that have been generated so far governing capital location and social boundaries are of importance in revealing further social patterns, and assist in the reconstruction of the processes of historical change. In the valley at the far eastern edge of Burren Barony is the tower-house of Glencolumbcille (indicated in Figures 10.4–10.7 by a large star). According to Frost, Ross or Rossa O'Lochlainn is identified with this castle in the 1580 tract he cites (Frost 1978:28). Rossa O'Lochlainn "Rosse O'Lochlin") was a signatory of Perrott's 1585 Tripartite Deed (White 1893:390). However, in the same text it is stated that Glencolumcille castle (Glancollidkylle) was in the possession of Owney O'Loghlin, the then-chieftain (ibid.:388).[18] In the prologue to the deed where the signatories are identified, Rosse O'Laughline of Glancollumkyle is identified as tanist to (the) O'Laughline (White 1893:377).

In the Middle Ages the office of *tánaiste* was usually occupied by a close relative of the chieftain: a brother, son, or first cousin. He was the second most powerful individual in the chiefdom and enjoyed considerable autonomy of action, often initiating military expeditions without the participation of the paramount chieftain. As discussed briefly in the last chapter, often the office was used to accommodate the political aspirations of a powerful rival for chiefly office, probably with the intent of heading off or curbing the violence and chaos that repeatedly accompanied Irish chiefly succession.

Rossa may have been a son of Owney and his attendance at the parliament called by Perrott in 1585 is an indication of his importance. However, though he put in a bid, he did not succeed Owney to the chieftainship at his death in 1590. The chieftainship was assumed eventually by Melaghlin, a son of Owney (see a text of 1603 [Ainsworth no. 957] and an inquisition of 1623 [Frost 1978:308]).[19] Thereafter, the descendants of Rossa may have retained property in this area, as evidenced by two deeds of 1590 and 1591 that document a conflict between five sons of Rossa over the castle and lands of Turlough in Oughtmama (Ainsworth 1961: nos. 907 & 914).[20]

As in the case of Mathgamain O'Brien discussed in the last chapter, powerful rivals for office of king within Thomond were given large holdings at a distance far removed from the kingdom's center as a way of mitigating potential conflict.[21] The case of Rossa O'Lochlainn shows that this was true at the level of a composite chiefdom as well. It is important to remember that relations could be very strained between members of chiefly lineages, even between individuals as closely related as father and son. The frequent lack of respect for close consanguineous ties may have been abetted by the fact that aristocratic children were not raised in the households of their natural parents but were sent off to the households of allied aristocrats to be fostered.

Other instances where multiple tower-houses are found in a single parish are explained by the practice of enfeoffment from above: the granting of land in subordinate territories by a chieftain to his offspring. Muc Inis Nua in Drumcreehy parish is listed as a possession of the O'Lochlainn chiefly family in an inquisition taken upon the death of Owney (Ir. *Uaithne*) Og O' Lochlainn in 1625 (Frost 1978:307). This castle had been granted to Turlogh, another son of Uaithne, for the *Annals of the Four Masters* state:

> AD 1584. Toirrdhealbhach mac Uaithne mic Maoileachlainn, was, in the beginning of the month of March in this year taken prisoner on Muicinis by Toirdhealbhach mac Domhnaill Uí Bhriain and put to death at Ennis by Captain Brabazon at the ensuing summer sessions.

Lissylisheen castle is located close to Ballymahoney castle in Noughaval parish. An inquisition states that in 1585 it was occupied by Gillananeave O'Davoren, who is given the designation "gentleman" (Frost 1978:267).[22] The O'Davorens (Ir. *Uí Duib da Boirenn*) were a family of famous jurists and scholars, the hereditary brehons of Burren Barony, and ran the renowned school out of Cahermacnaghten (Ir. *Cathair Mhic Neachtain*) located up the road about 1.5 km to the northwest from Lissylisheen (Figs. 10.4 & 10.5).[23] A partition of 1675 details the extensive holdings of the O'Davoren *sliocht* at Cahermacnaghten, which covered the portion of Rathbourney parish to the west, north, and south of Gragans, and a section in the southwestern section of Kilcorney parish (Frost 1978:18–19). Today, the O'Davorens are the wealthiest of the Burren's farmers with the most extensive land-holdings. Their farms are still in the region they occupied in the sixteenth century, though they are now spread over half, if not more, of Kilcorney parish. Indeed, one could say that they personify the persistence of the vestiges of the chiefdom social order in the Burren into the present era.

The hereditary jurists and scholars of Irish society occupied a social position comparable to the barony chieftains. As has been indicated previously, they often had large holdings that were exempt from tribute. Moreover, as literati and specialists in land transactions, they adapted most rapidly to, and were in a position to manipulate, the legal institutions introduced by the English. Thus in the sixteenth and seventeenth centuries the MacClancys, the hereditary brehons of Thomond, had accumulated large estates amounting to the greater part of the parish of Killilagh in Corcomroe Barony. Boetius MacClancy renounced Catholicism and became the first sheriff in the newly constituted County of Clare (Frost 1978:96). Likewise, a branch of the O'Dalys, who were renowned poets, were granted the rich lands of Finavarra (*Fiodh na beara*) in the north of Burren Barony by the Earl of Thomond in 1590 (Hardiman 1828: no. 38). Thus, under English administration, these families of intelligentsia enjoyed wealth and a great deal of social autonomy. Within the context of the Irish chiefdoms, they were able to aspire to aristocratic social position though they were not of the ruling ramage. Indeed, it was only within the ranks of the clergy and literati that *sleachta* alien to the dominant ramage of a chiefdom could achieve and maintain aristocratic position (see Ó Corráin 1973).

THE LANDS AND TERRITORIES OF THE ARISTOCRATIC LINEAGES: GAELIC LAND ASSESSMENT

Thus far the commentary has been concerned with explaining the geographical patterning of the *sleachta* capitals; what of the distribution of the holdings of these lineages of the aristocratic ramage? That most informative text, the 1585 Tripartite Deed of Sir John Perrott (PTD) again provides incisive insight in this respect. In this document, the subterritories within the individual baronies are *not* enumerated by parish names, but are sometimes referred to by names of the *sleachta* that were the primary landholders (see Table 10.2). Unfortunately, they are rendered in a manner phonetic to the sound system of Elizabethan English, but enough can be made out to grasp their significance, and in some instances to match them to individual lineages.

Understanding Table 10.2 necessitates some knowledge of the Medieval period Irish system of land organization and valuation. In the Middle Ages in Clare the following Gaelic land units were recognized: the *baile*, which was frequently translated into "townland" or "town" in English texts; the *cedhramrum* (modern Irish *ceathrú*), which is Anglicized in place-names as "carrow" or given the literal translation of "quarter;" the *seiseach* meaning literally "sixth;" and *seisreach* (plowland). It is easy to be led to thinking of the Gaelic land assessment system of Co. Clare as a rational system of nested units given the existence of terminology such as "quarter" and "sixth," which suggest subdivisions of a larger entity. And, following this train of deduction, one is quickly led to surmise that the *baile* would have been that maximal entity. Scholarly discussions of the various Gaelic land assessment systems of Ireland have mostly hewn to this course (J. Hogan 1929:175–179; McErlean 1983; Ní Ghabhláin 1996:50–51; Ní Loingsigh 1994).

One is quickly waylaid from this line of thinking, however, when confronted with the fact that in texts such as the Tripartite Deed the smaller units are not consistently invoked as subunits of the larger denominations, and the name of the land unit does not seem to correspond to its expected valuation. Hence, in the Tripartite Deed, the valuation of *Baile na Greagnais*

Table 10.2. Named *Sliocht* Holdings from PTD for Graganes Barony in 1585
(White 1893:380–581)

Territory name	Probable original name	Number of quarters;	parts
Toofflanneth	Túath Flaithniadh	25	
Toonagh[a]	?	37	1/3
Moynterargagh	Muintir Argaid	12	1/2
Glannomannagh	Gleann na Manach	21	2/3
Gloight-Donough-O'Loghline	Sliocht Donchadh Ua Lochlainn	8	
Gloight-Jerroll	Sliocht Oiriall	9	1/3
'Towne of the Gragannes'	Baile na Greagnais	2	2/3
Muckenish	Muc Inis	2/3	
Carricogane	Carraig Locháin?	1	1/3
Aghnis	Ath Inis	1	1/3

[a] The Irish word behind "Toonagh" is difficult to arrive at. White offers *Tambnach* (meaning a grassy upland) as the original name, though this would not seem to work due to the contrast in initial vowel sounds. A better phonetic fit is the Irish *túath* and this should be followed by a genitive form of a name. Ó hÓgáin proposes *Túath Eannuigh* (The Chiefdom of Einne) following upon his surmise that this district formerly contained the parishes of Killmoon and Killeany (*Cill Einne*) (1938:115). Historical evidence in favor of this proposition is however lacking. *Túath an Mhachaire* (The Chiefdom of the Plain) is a territory that is said to lie in Burren Barony according to a document in Irish laying out the settlement of a dispute over lands in northern Corcomroe and Inchiquin dated August 13, 1600 (Mac Niocaill 1970 III:54–55). However, there is hardly any level land within Carran parish. Toonagh occurs as a place-name in several other localities in Co. Clare, including one to the south of Carran parish in Dysert parish.

breaks down into two and 2/3 quarters, not four quarters as one would expect under the present paradigm. The Tripartite Deed offers evidence of only one named unit of land, the *cedhramrum* (quarter). Parcels smaller than a quarter or territories that had areas that worked out in excess of an even number of quarters were rendered in terms of thirds or a half of a quarter.

That the word *baile* appears as an element in the names of territories rather than as a unit of area in the Tripartite Deed is a clue to the way this territory was conceptualized by the Irish of Co. Clare. Baile na Greagnais became the two modern townlands of Gragans North and Gragans South, which surround the sixteenth-century seat of the O'Lochlainn chieftain at the Gragans tower house (Figures 10.8, 10.9). It is evident that this smaller tract was singled out for inclusion in the treaty, which lists mostly section territories, because it was the demesne territory of the O'Lochlainn chieftain.

In the Burren, this relationship between aristocratic seats and *bailte* (pl. of *baile*) seems obvious enough. Of the twenty townlands of Burren Barony that have names with "bally" as a prefix, or "town" as a suffix, nine contain or are immediately adjacent to a tower-house or tower-house site.

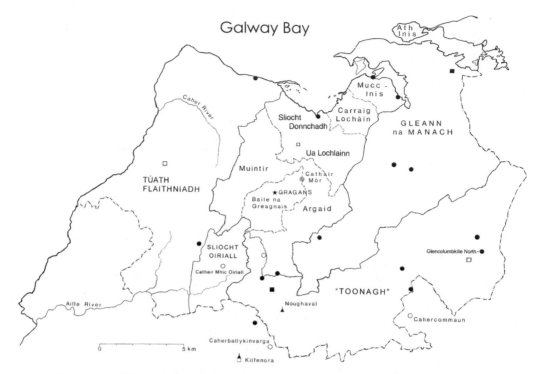

Figure 10.8. The probable secular territories of the sixteenth-century Gragans chiefdom that are listed in the Tripartite Deed. Contemporary churches, Late Medieval tower-houses and cashels are shown, as well as a likely Medieval period residence of the O'Lochlainn chieftain at Cathair Mór. See Figure 10.4 for a key to the symbols.

Perhaps more telling from a chronological perspective, a further six "bally" townlands contain cashel sites. The larger cashels were occupied by individuals of aristocratic rank. There are two cashel sites, Ballydanaher and Ballayallaban, that enclose the remains of Late Medieval period structures. The cashel wall of Ballydanaher encloses a tower-house. The gatehouse of *Cathair Mór* (C-79) in Ballyallaban townland has been recently excavated (Figure 5.2). This has been shown to have been a late (seventeenth-century?) insertion into a preexisting cashel dating back at least to the fourteenth century (Fitzpatrick 2001).

From these data, it seems clear that the chief significance of the *baile* term was social, and only secondarily was it conceived by the Irish of Thomond as a unit of valuation (Gibson 2008b). The *baile* was a district that served as the mensal land of an aristocratic settlement. This finding is not surprising, as a similar geographical link of demesne territory to aristocratic center also obtains in Early Medieval Wales and England (Jones 1976) and Late Medieval Donegal (Ní Loingsigh 1994). There would have been a multitude of causes accounting for the variation in the size of this parcel. A *baile* might have been established in the distant past, and then was

Figure 10.9. Gragans tower-house, the seat of the O'Lochlainn chieftains, photographed in 1990 (photo: Blair Gibson).

subsequently subdivided. The *baile* could also be expected to vary in size in relation to the social rank of the family that occupied it, or could change in size as the social rank of the lineage possessing it changed. Finally, the geographical situation of the *baile* could have had a determinative effect on its size and valuation. All of these factors would explain not only its variable valuation, but also the inconsistent employment of this designation in texts bearing upon land.

THE SECULAR TERRITORIES OF THE O'LOCHLAINN CHIEFDOM

Locating the territories that were listed in the Tripartite Deed for the chiefdom of Gragans is by no means an easy task. Linking the names on the list with surviving place-names yields a few relatively easy identifications. From the list of valuations it is apparent that four of the territories are large, two are small, and the remaining four are parcels. Of the last category, the parcel *Muccinis* most certainly can be associated with two townlands bearing this name: Muckinish East and West in Drumcreehy parish. These townlands contain two tower-houses of the same name that were held by sons of the O'Lochlainn chieftain (Figure 10.8). It is tempting to see *Carraig Locháin* as a demesne territory of one of the two tower-houses in Muccinis, deriving its name from *Lochán Liath* (Grey Pool), which is located nearby in the same parish.

The amount of land listed with Muc Inis is identical to the amount of land attributed to Carraig Lochán, and they find their match in number and size with the townlands associated with the tower-houses Sean Muc Inis and Muc Inis Nua in Drumcreehy parish, showing that just the coastal strip and mountain immediately behind it constituted the land held by sons of the O'Lochlainn chieftain in his name (Fig. 10.8). Aghinish is Aughinish Island/Peninsula to the north of Finavarra peninsula. It seems, then, that all of the small entries at the end refer to the piecemeal holdings of the *sliocht* of the O'Lochlainn chieftain, and so verifies the extent of their original territory before it was subdivided.

The demesne territories of the O'Lochlainn chieftain and his sons are clustered within a uniform physiographic entity, *Gleann Argddae*, a valley that opens up onto Galway Bay to the north (Fig. 10.6). As mentioned previously, Argddae was an ancestor-deity of the Cíarraige and, to judge from the proliferation of place-names alluding to him in the Burren, later of the Corcu MoDruad as well. A section of this territory bears the name *Muintir Argaid* (The Family of Argddae). This territory is co-terminous with the parish of Rathbourney (Ní Ghabhláin 1996:56). A number of lines of evidence indicate that the parishes of Rathbourney in the Burren's center and Drumcreehy to the north along the coast were subdivisions of a preexisting territory (Gibson 2000:251). The parish of *Gleann Eidhneach* and the PTD territory *Sliocht Oiriall* were most likely subdivisions of *Túath Flaithniadh*; the latter territory was probably separated from Túath Flaithniadh by the descendants of an O'Lochlainn chieftain named Oirial. One Irial O'Lochlainn is stated by the *Annals of the Four Masters* to have died in 1396 AD, though there were other subsequent O'Lochlainn chieftains who also bore this name (see previous discussion). The establishment of Sliocht Oiriall can therefore be dated to the fourteenth century at the earliest, and there is independent textual evidence that supports a date in this century (discussed later).

This line of inference leads us to the hypothesis that in the list from PTD, the term *sliocht* designates a territory allotted to a former chieftain's descendants. Both Sliocht Oiriall and Sliocht Donnchadh O'Lochlainn are of equivalent size and equidistant from the capital. Oirial and Donnchadh are the names of former O'Lochlainn chieftains, the latter name borne by two O'Lochlainn chieftains of the fourteenth century. It could be that the territory Sliocht Oiriall had been taken from Túath Flaithniadh, but it is also a possibility that this was the demesne territory of the chieftains of this *túath*.

Not only did the chieftain of the O'Lochlainns and his sons possess land within Muintir Argaid, but the chiefdom's judges, the O'Davorens, did as well. Thomas McErlean has noted a pattern whereby demesne land (*lucht tighe*) was attached to aristocratic offices, including those of the indigenous intelligentsia (McErlean 1983). It would seem that prior to the sixteenth century, the section territory of the leading ramage of the O'Lochlainns had been repeatedly subdivided between the proximate descendants of the chieftain and the ramage of the chief judge. Gleann Eidhneach is stated to have been wholly owned by the Bishop of Kilfenora in the seventeenth-century *Books of Survey and Distribution* (IMC 1967), indicating that lands of other sections could also be dedicated to the support of the intelligentsia as well. Further O'Davoren holdings in Noughaval and Kilcorney parishes, such as the O'Davoren law school at Cathair Mhic Neachtain (Cahermacnaghten) in Noughaval parish, bear out this point (Figure 10.4).

Of the larger territories, Glannomannagh in Table 10.2 is transparently *Gleann na Manach* (Valley of the Monks), which is currently a place-name that can be found on the modern Ordnance Survey maps within Abbey parish. Abbey parish takes its name from Corcomroe Abbey, established by the O'Brien king in the early thirteenth century. The boundaries of Abbey parish take in less than half of a larger glacial valley, and this must be the eponymous Gleann na Manach. That Abbey parish was cut out of larger territory is substantiated in the Tripartite Deed when it states that 10 quarters and 2/3 (part) belong to the Queen "... as in right of the Abbay of Corcomroe ..." (White 1893:380). It is also indicated by the location of the O'Lochlainn tower-house, which practically straddles the Abbey/Oughtmama parish boundary (Figure 10.4).

GRAGANS' OTHER TERRITORIES

Less confidence can be attached to posited locations of the remaining territories of the PTD. In 1938, Seán Ó hÓgáin published his deductions concerning the locations and extent of the Gragans chiefdom's Tudor period territories. Though his book has a bibliography and is run through with seemingly relevant excerpts of medieval texts, he is mute as to the precise items of evidence and methodology whereby he reached his conclusions. One suspects from his choices and citations that interpretations

Table 10.3. Constitution of Secular Territories within Gragans Chiefdom after Ó hÓgáin 1938

Territories from the TD	Quarters/parts		Medieval parishes	Valuation from the BSD	Difference in valuations
Toofflanneth	25		Killonaghan & Gleninagh	11.62	−13.38
Toonagh	37	1/3	Killeany, Killmoon, Kilcorney, Noughaval, S. part of Rathbourney[a]	c. 45	+7.67
Moynterargagh	12	1/2	Most of Rathbourney and Drumcreehy	c. 22	+9.5
Glannomannagh	21	2/3	Abbey & Oughtmama	19.65	−2.01
Gloight-Donough-O'Loghline & Gloight-Jerroll	16	1/3	Carran	24.01	+7.68

Mean of differences: 8.05

[a] Ó hÓgáin's map is not drawn with enough precision to clearly indicate the land parcels from the parish of Rathbourney that he thinks were included in *Túath Eannuigh*. In order to make an estimate, I included the denominations of *Crogh-South, Lismatheige, Lisnalogherne, Lisduane, Grassene, Lisselissey, Kragavakoge* and *Kahirevoolly* from the *Books of Survey and Distribution*. These parcels are found grouped together in the *Books*, and matches of the names of three denominations with modern townland names in the south of the parish, the location of a third on the surviving Down map in the south of Rathbourney, ownership by members of the "O'Daverin" (O'Davoren) ramage, and place-name evidence locates these parcels in the south of the parish.

of place-name evidence and the distributions of Late Medieval landholdings and tower-houses played a key role. His conclusions are presented in tabular form above (Table 10.3).

His reconstructions of the territories of Gragans chiefdom acknowledges the former existence of primary parishes in connection with Toofflanneth and Glannomannagh – territories that had been subdivided when the parish system was established. However, Carran parish is represented as having been subdivided into two secular territories and it is implied that a number of parishes and a sizable parcel within Rathbourney parish were collected together in Toonagh. From Ó hÓgáin's scheme, it is difficult to determine how the secular and parochial systems evolved, and there emerges a substantial mismatch between the valuations of the secular territories as given in the PTD and valuations written down a century later in the *Books of Survey and Distribution*.

There is in general a close agreement between the land valuations presented by the PTD and BSD for the Burren, with those of the latter source being uniformly slightly higher (Table 10.4). This appraisal is not reflected in Ó hÓgáin's scheme where there is wide variance, both low and high, between the extents of his units and the valuations in the two sources.

Table 10.4. Proposed Concordances of the Territories of the Tripartite Deed with Medieval Parishes

Toofflanneth	25		Kilmoon, Killlonaghan, & Gleninagh	24.25	−.75
Toonagh	37	1/3	Carran & Noughaval	36.34	−.99
Moynterargagh	12	1/2	Rathbourney minus Baile na Gregnais[a]	12.77	.27
Glannomannagh	21	2/3	Abbey, Oughtmama & Kilcorney	27.32	5.66
Gloight-Donough-O'Loghline	8		Drumcreehy minus Carraig Lochláin and Mucc Inis	8.14	.14
Gloight-Jerroll	9	1/3	Killeany	9.31	0
				Mean of differences:	1.3

[a] What I am taking to be the Baile of Gragans are the three *seisreach* parcels listed under it valued at 2 quarters, minus two detached parcels that are listed with it: *Oghtgalene* and *Kragavakoge*, which on the basis of their similarity to the modern townland names Aghaglinny and Cregavockoge, were located at a distance from the chiefdom's core.

In Table 10.4 and Figure 10.8, I present a realignment of the secular territories with the medieval parishes, one that marks a departure with an arrangement that I have promulgated in two prior publications (2000, 2008b). This scheme represents the best fit between the valuations presented in the Tripartite Deed and the *Books of Survey and Distribution* for the Late Medieval parishes, place-name evidence, and historical groupings of parishes into rectories (Ní Ghabhláin 1995a:264–268).

It is to be appreciated that the mean of the differences between the valuations for the territories between PTD and BSD are far more modest under this match-up. The only real outlier is Glannomannagh, and this may be due to the inclusion of Kilcorney parish, which was valued at 7.67 quarters in the BSD (Ní Ghabhláin 1995a:290). Kilcorney was included with Abbey and Oughtmama parishes in Glannomannagh because together they constituted (with Killeany parish) the Rectory of Kilcorney (Ní Ghabhláin 1995a:268). The combinations of parishes contained within rectories may have medieval antecedents. It is also a credible possibility that when it was created, Kilcorney Parish had been carved out of the territorial antecedents of Toonagh and Moynteraragh in the same manner as Sliocht Oiriall. The central location of two large cashels in the center of Kilcorney, including Caherconnell, which has yielded a radiocarbon date in the tenth century, indicates some antiquity for the territory. Ní Ghabhláin dates the church in Kilcorney to the thirteenth century on architectural grounds (1995a:164; Figure 10.10).

The division of the valley between Abbey and Oughtmama parishes can be fairly closely dated. Corcomroe Abbey was founded either in 1194

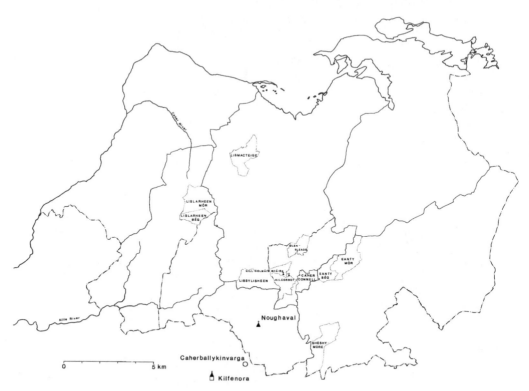

Figure 10.10. Reconstruction of the Medieval period primary parishes of the Burren. Kilcorney parish (save Poulbaun townland) is outlined by single dashed lines, and several potential original routes of the northwestern border of Carran parish, one running south of Caherconnell townland, the other north, are indicated. Carran, Kilcorney, and Gleann na Manach may also have constituted a single territory.

or 1200 AD by Conchobor Rua Ua Briain *rí* of Thomond (Frost 1978:22; Gwynn and Gleeson 1962:131). Hence, this parish was an O'Brien holding, as exemplified by its use as a stopover place, hospital, burial ground and army camp by O'Brien armies in *Caithréim Thoirdhealbhaigh* (O'Grady 1929). After the dissolution of the monasteries by order of Henry VII in 1537, title to the lands of the Abbey reverted to the Earl of Thomond.

However, not all the lands within the boundaries of Abbey parish were actually of this parish. The *Books of Survey and Distribution* makes it clear that the bottom lands in the valley and the coastal strip consisting of Ballyvelaghan, Carrowilliam, Cartron, Munnia, and Rossalia townlands belonged to Abbey parish (*IMC* 1967:443–445).[24] Oddly, however, a portion of the mountainous townland at the southern end of this parish, Kilmoylan or Kilmulran (modern Kilweelran), and all the townlands that make up Finavarra, and Aughinish Island were accredited to Oughtmama parish (*IMC* 1967:443, 445–446).[25] Obviously, the O'Brien king only appropriated the good bottom land of Gleann na Manach to create Abbey parish, much like the operation of a cookie cutter, leaving geographically separated scraps at its fringes.

CONCLUSIONS CONCERNING THE TERRITORIES IN THE TRIPARTITE DEED

It seems clear from the foregoing analysis that the territories of the Burren that are enumerated in Perrott's Tripartite Deed reflect a primary focus on the contemporary holdings of the chiefly lineage and its recent off-shoots. The holdings in this category are those from Sliocht Donchadh Ua Lochlainn on down in Table 10.2. On the other hand, the larger territories do not really reflect sixteenth-century land divisions or land ownership patterns to judge from sixteenth-century documentary evidence and the distribution of tower-houses (Gibson 1990: 99–102). These larger territories must therefore represent territories that preceded the creation of the medieval parishes. As data adduced below will demonstrate, these large territories go back to the thirteenth century at the latest, and are remnants of preexisting Early Medieval territories.

RECONSTRUCTING PRIMARY PARISHES

This evidence pertaining to land ownership that has been surveyed points to the prior existence of large secular districts that had been apportioned to branches of the O'Lochlainn ramage and then subjected to subdivision and reapportionment. Not only had the land been reallocated among O'Lochlainn aristocrats, but it is likely that Late Medieval parishes were the product of the subdivision of larger parishes. I will follow the example of Ní Ghabhláin in calling these presumed larger ecclesiastical districts "primary parishes" (1995a, 1996). All of the Burren's parishes of the sixteenth century are present in a papal taxation list of 1302–1306, so if the Late Medieval parishes are the product of subdivision, the partitioning of the primary parishes must predate the fourteenth century (Westropp 1900:114–115). If this was the case, the primary parishes were of short duration, as the parish system itself was devised at the Synod of Rathbreasail in 1111 AD. Ní Ghabhláin has put forth the hypothesis that primary and secondary parishes were created simultaneously in the twelfth century and that they represent secular administrative levels within the *túath* (1996:49)

A document that potentially sheds some light on the boundaries of the parishes in the fourteenth century, as well as offering some clues to the con-figurations of the secular districts prior to this century, is a well-known yet somewhat enigmatic text called "O'Brien's Rental" (Ir. *Suim Cíosa Uí Briain*) (Hardiman 1828: no. 14). The translator Hardiman dates this text "with some certainty" to the middle of the fourteenth century, attributing it to the reign of Muircheartach Uí Briain (1828:39). However, Hardiman does not cite any evidence supporting his determination. T. J. Westropp places the date more narrowly at "about 1380 or 1390" (1899:348). His date(s) are apparently based on two lines of evidence. The morphologically similar *Suim Tigernagh Meic na Mara* (literally "Sum of the Rule of Macnamara") gives Conmeda mac Meic Con meic Lochlainn mac Conmhedha Mór, who reigned at this time, as the author's patron (Hardiman 1828:43; Westropp 1899:350). Secondly, these rentals make no mention of tower-houses, though several "cahers" (*cathracha* [settlements]) are mentioned (Westropp 1899:350).[26] Westropp goes on to proffer evidence that the first stone tower-houses were not constructed until 1380, and not in any number until the period 1410–1430 AD (ibid.:352).

As circumspect as this evidence may be, on internal evidence "O'Brien's Rental" certainly predates the Tudor period. Lands known to have been taken over by O'Brien ramages during the Tudor period are not mentioned in the text. Indeed, the purpose of the text seems to be to fix rents on land owned by them in areas not under the direct political control of one of their lineages; namely, lands in Corcu Baiscinn, Corcu Mruad, and Boireann (Nugent 2000). This latter name is the Irish word meaning "rocky land," which later became Anglicized to Burren. The name in the text of this area is *Cargi a Ledhoiren* (Rock of the Rocky Half?), which clearly implies that the Late Medieval capital at Gragans had not yet been established at this point.

Though the rental makes no reference to territorial subdivisions within the Burren, the names of the parcels of land are grouped in clusters so as to imply the existence of such. This is demonstrated in Table 10.5, where these parcels are listed in the order in which they are presented, and the modern parish location is given for those that can be identified with modern townlands.

The rental presents a bewildering range of land value names: half-*baile*, *cedrama* (quarter), *seiseach* (plowland), and their usage varies by district. Since Corcomroe and Burren show variation in terminology, and as they had become separate chiefdoms by the fourteenth century, it would seem that these valuation systems go back no further than the Middle Ages. As noted above, in the Burren the *baile* figures as a portion of the place-name but not as a unit of land value, and only two parcels with *baile* as an element of the name are valued at four plowlands. This finding supports

Table 10.5. Land Units in the Burren from O'Brien's Rental

No. Original name	Modern name	Valuation (seiseach)	Modern parish location
Section 1			
1. Baile G. Martan	Ballykilmartin	4	Killeany
2. Cathrach Medain	Cahermaan	2	Killeany
3. Baile Danar	Ballyganner	4	Noughaval
4. Cathrach Polla	Caherpolla	1	Noughaval
5. Leasa Morain	Lismorahaun	1	Kilmoon
6. Lis na Liathanach	Lisheeneagh	2	Kilmoon
7. Raithneach	Rannagh	2	Carran
8. Ceapacaibh	Cappagh(s)	1	Carran
9. Cnocain	Knockans	2	Carran
10. Urluinne	Turish?	1	Carran?[a]
11. Seisreadh O'nDonaill	Sheshodonnell	1	Carran
12. Croibidhi	Creevagh	1	Carran
13. Muidhi Domnaill	Mogouhy	1	Carran
14. Matar Briain	?	1	?
15. Seisreadh Mór	Sheshymore	1	Noughaval
16. Fanadh Gealghain	Fanygalvan	1	Carran
17. Cathrach Mec I Gril	Cahergrillaun[b]	1	Carran
18. Tulglaise	?	1	?
19. Mingeach	Meggah	1	Carran
20. Aenrig Beg	Eanty Beg	1	Kilcorney
21. Baile I Ustadh	?	1	?
Section 2			
1. Baile I Mathgamhna	Ballymahony	4	Noughaval
2. Baile I Murcha	Ballymurphy	1	Noughaval
3. Caltrach	?	1	?
4. Gleanna Slaod	Glenslead	2	Kilcorney
5. Baile I Tuathail	?	2	?
6. Formail	Formoyle	2	Killonaghan
7. Cathra[ii]	?	1	?
8. Liss na hAlba	?	1	?
9. Seisi ni Muireda	Murroogh?	1	Gleninagh
10. Fanad Fodhman	?	2	?
11. Doirnib	Derreen(s)	3	Killonaghan
12. Liss Flaithri	?	3	?
13. Baile I Maeil-Ceir	?	2	?
14. Lessa Guagain	Lisgoogan	1	Rathbourney
15. Baile I Comultain	?	1	?
16. Baile I Catail	Ballycahill	1	Drumcreehy
17. Daingin	Dangan	3	Drumcreehy
18. Cnocan Tighe	?	3	?
19. Coill Breac	*Killbrack*[c]	1	Rathbourney
20. Liss na Luacharnaidi	Lisnalogherne	1	Rathbourney
21. Ruda	?	1	?
22. Baile I Gedail	?	1	?
23. Fidhnaig	Feenagh	1 1/2	Rathbourney
24. Daingin	Dangan	1 1/2	Drumcreehy?

(continued)

Table 10.5. *(continued)*

No. Original name	Modern name	Valuation (seiseach)	Modern parish location
25. Baile I Beachain	Ballyvaughan	1	Drumcreehy[d]

Section 3. Properties of the Camluas Steward[d]

Original name	Modern name	Land unit type	Parish location
Baile Uí Conraoí	Ballyconry	cedrama	Carran
Lis mBerchain		½ seiseach	
Cathair Lapain		seiseach	
Cathair Mec Oilille Sella	Cahermackerrila	seiseach	Carran

[a] This *seiseach* was recorded during Stafford's survey of 1636–1637 and during the Petty survey (Ainsworth 1961: no. 1464, 1967:444). A chancery of Sir Lucius O'Brien would put it in proximity to Fanygalvan (Ainsworth 1961: no. 1474).

[b] This could be a townland adjacent to the Caher (*Cathair*) River.

[c] Identified as part of Cahermacnaghten in the *Books of Survey and Distribution* (1967:465).

[d] *Cathrach Mec Oilille-sella* may be Cahermackerrila in Carran parish, which would then make *Cathrach Meic I Gril* Cahergrillaun. However, it is important to note that there is another Cahermackerrila townland in Killeany parish.

the conclusion that the principal significance of the *baile* term is that it indicates the territory immediately surrounding a residence. The *baile* element was probably retained in the name of a parcel after a dwelling was abandoned and the parcel subdivided. This may explain why some parcels with *baile* as an element of the name are valued at fewer than four *seiseach*.

The lands out of which the O'Briens received rents were overwhelmingly composed of land that is now stony or broken terrain or rocky uplands lying above the 500 ft. gradient. Charging rent on these parcels would be the equivalent of collecting a grazing fee since that is the activity for which these lands are best suited. The parcels are widely scattered throughout the Burren, many being located in boundary areas. This would imply that the O'Lochlainns surrendered these pieces of property as a part of some agreement – perhaps tributes were exacted as a fee on a portion of grazing land in this period. This text then casts another perspective on the location of the O'Lochlainn tower-houses in areas of lower-lying, arable land. These are the lands that would have remained in their direct, exclusive ownership.

O'Brien's rental also presents some support for the seriation scheme in Chapter 5. The pattern recognition examination of the Burren's cashels indicated that C-118, Cahermackerrila, dated to the Medieval period. The site can be identified with one of the properties listed in the third section belonging to the Camluas family. The Camluas were appointed by the O'Brien king as stewards over the Burren chiefdom, and were evidently set up with lands in Carran parish. Their other property, Ballyconry, was good valley bottom land and there is local memory of a medieval structure as once having existed within this townland.

If the sequence of the enumeration of the parcels is accepted as reflecting extant territorial subdivisions, as I believe it should, then these older territories had boundaries at some variance from the Burren parishes of the sixteenth century (see Figure 10.10). The disposition of the land units between the two principal sections of the rental reflects a general division between the south and west, and the north and east. Significantly, the starting point for both sections is in the center-south in what were in the sixteenth and seventeenth centuries the parishes of Killeany and Noughaval. The importance of this area is its proximity to what was then the common religious center of Corcomroe and Burren Baronies, the diocesan seat of Kilfenora (*Cill Fhinnabrach*, Modern Ir. *Cill Fhionnúrach*).

Prior to the eleventh century Corcomroe and the Burren constituted a single chiefdom, Corcu MoDruad, and Kilfenora was the religious center. The primacy of Kilfenora is obvious from the facts that in Early Medieval times its church was the seat of a bishop (hence it was a cathedral), and that its diocese takes in both Corcomroe and Burren baronies. Kilfenora diocese was recognized by Cardinal Paparo in 1152 AD, and a bishop of this diocese was first mentioned swearing an oath of fealty to Henry II at Cashel in 1171–1172 (Gwynn and Gleeson 1962:131).[27] It remained the religious capital when Corcu MoDruad split into the chiefdoms of Boireann and Corcu Mruad. The original Irish name behind Noughaval could be either *Nua Gabháil*, meaning the "New Acquisition," or *Nua Congbháil* (Westropp: *Nua Congbabhaile;* Robinson: *Nuachabháil*), which means "New Holding," or "New Settlement," but which also had the more specific meaning of an ecclesiastical settlement (Robinson 1977; Westropp 1900:133). All of these terms have the same sense in conveying the laying hold of new land, or the creation of an area of settlement. The church at Noughaval, or rather the chancel arch and windows, are thought to be of the twelfth century (Leask 1955:83; Westropp 1900:133). The small size and semicircular shape of this parish, taken together with the name, imply that it was cut out of some larger territorial entity. Logic would seem to dictate that a partition was made of the territory of Kilfenora itself, and the O'Lochlainns set up the church of Noughaval shortly after the partition on the portion of the territory of Kilfenora that remained in their possession. This would explain the relatively small size of this parish compared to the others.

After finishing with Kilmoon, the rental lists properties in Carran parish moving from northeast to southwest. Most of these can be identified with modern townlands, and the sequence makes it clear that Carran parish was at one time larger than it was in the sixteenth century. Noughaval was likewise enlarged with land from the southwestern end of Carran, as the presence of Sheshymore in midst of the Carran lands indicates (Figure 10.10). The irregularly rectangular block of land that this shift entailed was to come almost completely into O'Brien possession as part of the demesne of Leamaneh Castle. Indeed, part of the apparent divot on the eastern side of Sheshymore is Deerpark townland (shown in Figure 10.4), obviously the former hunting preserve of the O'Brien inhabitants of the castle.[28]

The parcels of land that can be attributed to Noughaval are scattered throughout the rental, though the association is strongest with parcels in Carran parish. We may draw two conclusions from this pattern: (1) that Carran and Noughaval parishes were portions of a greater territorial entity, that is "Toonagh," and (2) as in the sixteenth century, the lands of Noughaval and Carran were not controlled by any one section but instead were apportioned between several sections. Though by no means certain, Kilcorney parish may have been a third territory comprising "Toonagh."

The dichotomous grouping of the townlands of Killeany and Kilmoon parishes in the rental supports the facts of the papal taxation list in showing that these two parishes were separate territorial entities in the fourteenth century. In Figure 10.10 I have added the townlands of Lislarheen Mór and Beag to the Killmoon/Killeany unit primarily for reasons of geographical integrity. The *Books of Survey and Distribution* attributes a quarter of Lislarhee townland to Killeany parish (*IMC* 1967:472). These are rocky and boggy uplands in the northeastern section of Kilmoon, and perhaps the inhabitants of several parishes enjoyed common rights to the peat there.

The second section commences with Noughaval parish. Glenslead within Kilcorney parish follows in isolation (Figure 10.10). It is curious that parcels that are today located in Kilcorney and Noughaval parishes are scattered throughout the rental, a fact that may reflect that the parcels within these parishes were owned by different sections just as they were several hundred years later.

The next properties that can be identified in the text are in Killonaghan and Gleninagh parishes. These parcels are interdigitated in the rental without apparent regard to these two parishes, underscoring the fact that they were once a single territory. This would make geographical sense since this area constitutes a narrow continuous stretch of coastline dominated by the bog-covered slopes of Slieve Elva.

Lands in Rathbourney and Drumcreevy are also interdigitated in the rental, supporting the hypothesis of a preexisting primary parish. Additional support for this premise comes from the *Books of Survey and Distribution*, which states that a quarter of Lislarhee townland belonged to Drumcreevy parish (*IMC* 1967:472). The Lislarsheen townlands would have been very remote from Drumcreevy parish in the sixteenth century (see Figure 3.8). The *BSD* also ascribes one-third quarter of Lismatheige (Lismacteige) to Drumcreevy (ibid.). This townland is situated in the northwestern extension of the valley to the northwest of Gragans, within Rathbourney parish (Figure 10.10). Other Drumcreehy townlands cited in the *BSD* that found themselves stranded in Rathbourney parish in the seventeenth century are Lisduane, Grassene, Lisselissey, and Kahireivoolly (*IMC* 1967:473). Only Lisselissey can be identified with confidence with the modern townland of Lissylisheen and, as stated previously, this was in the extreme <u>south</u> of Rathbourney parish, giving conclusive proof to the supposition that Rathbourney was cut out of Drumcreehy (Figure 10.10).[29]

The map of the Burren that results from this exercise is identical in most respects to the map of secular territories extracted from the late sixteenth-century PTD. (Figure 10.10, compare to Fig. 10.8). There is a large central territory, presumably the political center, surrounded on three sides by the other primary parishes, all of which share a common border with the central parish. All of the parishes encompass areas of low-lying land (glacial valleys, coastal strips) with potentially arable soils. These fertile lowlands are ringed by rocky mountains and hills, where the borders were established. Reflecting the geographical conservatism of the sacred elements of the capital set, the religious center of this chiefdom at Noughaval is at the periphery rather than in the central territory.

The difference between the pre-fourteenth-century primary parishes and the sixteenth–seventeenth-century parishes is the change in scale. The parishes went from large, physiographically well-defined territorial units to smaller units that were less well circumscribed by geographical barriers. The early units that have been reconstructed here bear a striking physical resemblance to the *ahupua'a* districts of the Hawaiian chiefdom of Kaua'i described by Timothy Earle, and are roughly the same size (1978:25–36). The Hawaiian *ahupua'a* were defined by stream-cut valleys with high ridges at the sides, which radiated from the central volcano of Kaua'i to the sea. These primary parishes were also without a doubt secular chiefdoms, or *túatha*, just as the *ahupua'a* were at one time independent chiefdoms. They were larger in scale than the Late Medieval parishes because the political system to which they were once constituent parts, the composite chiefdom of the Corcu MoDruad and the chiefdom of Tulach Commáin in the case of Túath an Machaire, were larger polities than the Late Medieval chiefdoms of Corcu Mruad and Gragans. As the chiefdoms became reduced in scale, so did their internal sections.

SUMMARY

Plotting the data culled from texts from the fourteenth–seventeenth centuries AD against the information on boundaries and place-names contained in the nineteenth-century Ordnance Survey maps enabled a near-complete realization of the location of Late Medieval boundaries and capitals in northern Clare. From the information contained in the deeds pertaining to political settlements and transactions in land, it even proved possible to reconstruct the extent of the holdings of the individual aristocratic lineages that existed in Burren Barony in Tudor times.

The next step is to distill the principles of Irish medieval political organization from the maps that have been created from the historical information. These principles can be presented as a spatial model (see Figure 10.11). In its broad configurations, it is analogous to a wheel with a large central hub. At the center was the territory of the chiefly lineage containing the chiefdom capital. The territories of the chiefdom's principal aristocrats, including that of the *tánaiste,* surrounded the chieftain's district. These aristocrats stood at the head of multilineage units, which I have termed sections. Each section district was found to share a common boundary with the central chieftain's district, and the section capitals were positioned so as to minimize communication distances between them and the central capital. It is not coincidental that routes of the Burren's present road system run past each major sixteenth-century residence toward the center.

The pattern of the location of the aristocratic section capitals is similar to the pattern of location of the barony capitals. In landlocked parishes the section capital will tend to be located at the center of the territory. In coastal parishes the capital will be on the coast, often on a sea promontory. This locational pattern of Irish section capitals may have considerable chronological depth as large promontory forts are a frequently-encountered site type in the Irish archaeological landscape of the Late Iron Age.

Each capital site within a section territory or *túath* was located within a demesne territory that in the Medieval period and later was called a

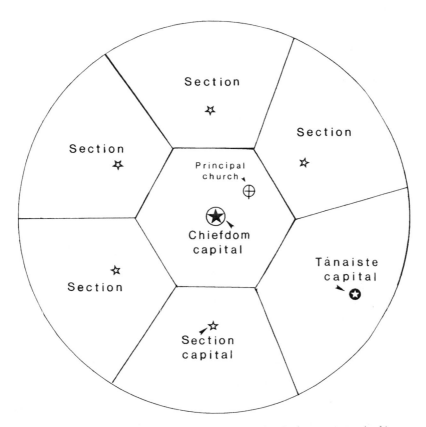

Figure 10.11. Model of the territorial structure of an Irish composite chiefdom.

baile. The institution of the demesne territory can be traced to the Old Irish period in the concept of *mruig ríg* (kings' land) (Kelly 2000:403), land specifically attached to the office of chieftain. As we have already seen, a demesne territory could be established in association with the eighth/ninth-century chieftain's residence of Cahercommaun (Chapter 6). The Old Irish sources refer only to land attached to the office of chieftain, but Fergus Kelly believes that other offices were also coupled with tracts of land (ibid. 403–404). Sources from the Late Medieval period reveal a plethora of land valuation units. As McErlean has noted, this variation is attributable to differences between regional traditions (1983). From the perspective of this study it seems that only one unit of land assessment was in use at any one time. Deviation in the extent or quality of a parcel against the standard was expressed in multiples or fractions of this unit.

Even in the sixteenth century, the landholdings of the aristocratic lineages tended to be concentrated within the parish of the section capital. Areas where this rule was seen to be violated were places of instability in the boundaries, amounting to locations where there was a lack of an obvious geographical barrier. The southwestern boundary of Noughaval with Kilfenora, and the southern boundaries of Kilcorney parish are two such "soft" boundaries where historical adjustments were frequent. As we have seen, the outcomes of such boundary adjustments favored the politically dominant social groups.

The distribution of the ownership of the land itself reflected the asymmetrical political relationships between the lineages making up a composite chiefdom, as well as the asymmetrical relationships between composite chiefdoms. The engine of change was the polygyny of chieftains. Aristocratic polygyny led to a profusion of political aspirants who, when conjoined with the social institutions of partible inheritance and the relatively open system of regnal succession, exerted continuous pressure on weaker lineages lower on the scale of power to yield territory and political autonomy.

The outcome of the social process is noticeable on two levels in the Burren. On the one hand, ownership rights to a portion of winter grazing lands were surrendered to the O'Briens as the chief vehicle for the generation of tribute in rent. The rent was collected by officers of the paramount chieftain, called *moir* (singular *maor*), most often translated as "steward." The administration of a steward is *maersecht* in O'Brien's Rental, and the text makes it clear that they were enfoeffed with lands within the chiefdom they administered (Hardiman 1828:38–39; see also note 33).

Gradually, the O'Briens appropriated land in the valleys outright, as evidenced by the appropriation of the land in Gleann na Manach for the foundation of Corcomroe Abbey in c. 1200 AD, and the stripping of O'Lochlainn *sleachta* of lands in Carran and Ballyvaughan in the sixteenth and seventeenth centuries. These lands passed to O'Brien lineages and the O'Lochlainns found themselves increasingly marginalized within the bounds of their own chiefdom.

On the other hand, the chiefly line of the O'Lochlainns produced sons who came into lands at the expense of older lineages. Hence the parish of Carran was carved in half to accommodate the *tánaiste*, and a chunk was taken out of Drumcreevey parish to support another son. This was one process that produced the phenomenon of multiple aristocratic residences in a single parish – a factor bound to confuse the archaeologist not aware of the operation of such processes in similar contexts. Ultimately, expansion of the O'Brien aristocratic lineages led to the dismemberment and dissolution of politically and socially subordinate groups.

CHAPTER ELEVEN

An Overview of the Social and Political Systems of Thomond

At this point it is appropriate to ask what has been learned about chiefdoms as political systems from this diachronic survey of Thomond's chiefdoms spanning 1,400 years. The well-documented Irish chiefdoms contribute examples of social structure and social dynamics pertaining to this level of sociocultural integration that complement existing historical case studies drawn from Polynesia, North and South America, and Africa. The comparison of chiefdoms from different corners of the globe allows conclusions to be drawn about those features that are common to all chiefdoms, and those that pertain solely to chiefdoms of a specific place and time. The following discussion will draw inferences about two principal dimensions of chiefdoms: the organization and dynamics of the social structure and the potentiality of change to their political systems.

CHIEFDOM STRUCTURE: HETEROGENEITY

Irish chiefdoms display a number of salient characteristics that modify our present understanding of the structure of chiefdoms from the anthropological literature. Standard definitions of the chiefdoms stress the kinship principal as the glue that holds the constituent lineages of chiefdoms together. In a simple chiefdom, such as those described by Raymond Firth on Tikopia Island in Polynesia, membership in the polity is defined on the basis of common descent from a founding ancestor (Firth 1963:chap. IX). This principle of the organization of society on Tikopia has been found to apply to all Polynesian societies.

However, for Ireland the model of chiefdom structure that is more apt is Jean Buxton's description of the chiefdoms of the Mandari cattle pastoralists of the Sudan (Buxton 1963). Buxton found the Mandari to be socially heterogeneous, their chiefdoms consisting of agglomerations of the lineages of a politically dominant landowning ramage and nonrelated politically inferior lineages. These latter lineages originated either from an older landowning social stock that had been superseded by the dominant newcomers, or were lineages founded by alien peoples seeking new grazing lands (Buxton 1963:26–66). Therefore, the lineages within the Mandari can be seen to have been arrayed among three social tiers.

Turning to the Irish, the principle of heterogeneity is well-illustrated by the Corcabhaiscinn chiefdom after the twelfth century AD. At the social pinnacle of the chiefdom were the lineages of the descendants of Mathgamain Uí Briain [13], who imposed himself upon the chiefdom in the twelfth century. Just below the Uí Mathghamhna in rank, and still persevering in portions of Corcabhaiscinn left to them by the Mac Mathghamhna, were the lineages of the former chiefly ramage, the Uí Domnaill. They would have shared this secondary level of prominence within the chiefdom polity with the lineages of the hereditary literati.

Occupying the third social tier within a medieval Irish chiefdom were lineages whose names come down to us only as place-names for pieces of land or habitation sites. That such a third tier existed is supported by the earliest census of the seventeenth century where the names of the commoner populace appear for the first time. It is not known what proportion of the population of an Irish chiefdom this social class constituted. It is probable that their lineages were genealogically shallow, as their ability to expand their landholdings was constrained from above by the ever-expanding politically dominant groups. The cascade effect created by aristocratic polygyny created a constant force of downward pressure, causing displacement of those occupying the two subordinate tiers (Ó Corráin 1972:41–42).

COMPOSITE CHIEFDOMS AND CHIEFDOM CONFEDERACIES

A second finding from the analysis of the historic documents of Thomond concerns the political constitution of Irish chiefdoms. As stated above, the individual *túatha* were heterogeneous in their internal social constitution. However, the composite chiefdoms, the *mór thúatha*, were equally heterogeneous. The composite chiefdoms were apparently composed of *túatha* of disparate historical origins that had become incorporated within the composite chiefdom by a mixture of force and entreaty.

The saga *Caithbréim Toirdhealbhaigh* brings out this facet of early Irish political organization better than any other text. In the saga, two sections of the leading ramage of the Dál Cais fight it out for the office of paramount chieftain of Thomond aided by allies from both within and without the old Dál Cais chiefdom confederacy. Dál Cais itself was split down the middle, with most of Cenél Fermaic and Uí Caisín lining up against the Uí mBloid. The glue that held the alliances together was a combination of traditional loyalties, the perception on the part of the leading aristocracy of potential political gains, and antagonisms generated by the encroachments of an opposite party.

Uí mBloid itself was a confederacy of small, genealogically related polities apparently lacking strong central leadership. One of its constituent chiefdoms, Uí Toirdhealbhaigh, was formerly the ancestral polity of the Uí Briain (O'Briens), the leading chiefdom of the Dál Cais in the tenth–eleventh centuries, and it was still dominated by Brian Bóroimhe's ramage, the Ua Cennétig (O'Kennedys). The Uí mBloid were resisting the expansion of the MacNamaras of Clann Chuiléin and, indeed, lost considerable lands to them following the demise of Clann Briain Ruaid and the de Clares (Nugent 2000).

The thirteenth- and fourteenth-century boundaries of chiefdoms formerly of the Dál Cais give an impression of the probable tenth-century structure of the Dál Cais composite chiefdom that lay at the core of the confederacy (Figure 8.3). It, too, was probably composed of a number of *túatha*, somewhat larger in size than the corresponding *túatha* of the fourteenth century, linked together into a roughly circular cluster. The Dál Cais chiefdoms were split into two major competing factions at even this early period, the Uí Óengusso and Uí Thairdelbaig (Ó Corráin 1972:114; Ryan 1943:195–199). The Uí Oengusso were the leading faction of Dál Cais until the tenth century. The Uí Cernaig, Uí Eichtígern, and Uí Róngaile were the ramages that the Uí Oengusso comprised (Ó Corráin 1973: table I). Figure 8.3 shows that the territory of this faction occupied a geographical position at the center of the Dál Cais composite chiefdom. Thus, the geographical relationship of the Uí Óengusso to the spatial structure of the composite chiefdom of the Dál Cais mirrors the position of Rathbourney parish, the parish containing the O'Lochlainn chiefdom capital site of Gragans, within the eponymous sixteenth-century O'Lochlainn chiefdom of the Burren.

Probably as a result of successful military campaigns, chiefdoms beyond the core of the original Dál Cais composite chiefdom, such as Cenél Fearmaic and Uí Chormaic, were added onto it, expanding the assemblage of polities into a full-blown chiefdom confederacy. The process of confederacy formation entailed concocting or elaborating a genealogy propounding the common descent of the leading ramages of the member chiefdoms, such as found in the Psalter of Cashel (O'Brien 1976:235). This genealogy then functioned as the constitution of the confederacy, laying out the degree and kind of relationship of one chiefdom to another. It must be stressed, though, that due to the deliberate distortions introduced into the genealogies it is difficult to say on the basis of the textual information alone where a composite chiefdom leaves off and a chiefdom confederacy begins. Geographical contiguity is the principle that is availed of here to distinguish between composite chiefdoms and chiefdom confederacies – the composite chiefdom is composed of allied chiefdoms that were geographically contiguous and the member chiefdoms of chiefdom confederacies were not. But in reality, the Dál Cais composite chiefdom was most likely a confederacy at its very conception, and so the distinction between a composite chiefdom and chiefdom confederacy should be viewed as a heuristic device rather than as an absolute reality.

The chiefdoms making up medieval Irish chiefdom confederacies probably held together as long as it was to their mutual advantage to do so. Indeed, if David Sproule's thesis holds up, their raison d'être was the pursuit of military objectives against similarly constituted polities. In the case of the Dál Cais, the initial objectives were the cutting up of the Corcu Baiscind and the Corcu MoDruad chiefdoms at the regional level, and then the dismantling of the Éoganacht confederacy at the provincial level. These chiefdom confederacies were not egalitarian – one chiefdom within the confederacy provided the political leadership. At first, the paramountcy of the Dál Cais was held by the Uí Oengusso, the original owners of the Dál Cais inauguration site at Magh Adhair. As the Uí Oengusso were pushed back by the Norsemen in the tenth century, leadership passed to the Uí Thairdelbaig under Cennétig mac Lorcáin [3] and his descendants, including Brian Bóroimhe.

THE SOCIAL DYMAMICS OF IRISH CHIEFDOMS: CYCLING

A number of recent studies of the Native American chiefdom political systems of the prehistoric Midwest and Southeast, the protohistorical southeastern United States, and the Eastern seaboard have delineated several outstanding characteristics of these systems (Anderson 1994; Blitz 1993; Gallivan 2003; Knight and Steponaitis 1998; Milner 1998; Pauketat 2004, 2009; Scarry 1996; Smith 2000). The prominent chiefdoms that existed during the period of European exploration of the continent (sixteenth–eighteenth centuries), such as Coosa, Cofitachequi, and Ocute, exercised influence over a wide geographical area, were separated from other contemporary chiefdoms by wide thinly populated swaths, and seem to have been prone both to rapid florescence and irreversible collapse. One may find grounds for the collapse of protohistorical American chiefdoms in the destabilizing effects of European exploration and colonization such as disease and political violence, though contact with European explorers and colonists have also been offered as a stimulus for the emergence of the Powhattan chiefdom of the Chesapeake Bay region (Gallivan 2003). However, one cannot turn to these factors to explain either the origins or collapse of earlier complex societies at Moundville or Cahokia.

Taking the long view, David Anderson has seen the florescence and collapse of American chiefdoms since the Woodland period as constituting an autochthonous pattern that he has termed "cycling" (Anderson 1994, 1996a & b). Looking beyond the Midwest and Southeast, the cycling pattern may be seen to fit the cultural history of the Southwest as well. Well before the entry of the Spanish, complex centers arose in localities such as Paquimé in the Sonoran desert of Mexico and at Chaco Canyon in New Mexico. Both centers arose in comparative isolation from other complex societies, enjoyed several centuries of prosperity, and then went into irreversible decline leading to total abandonment.

Though the cycling pattern seems well grounded in the prehistoric and protohistorical chiefdoms of North America, cycling does not seem to be a concept that is applicable to the fortunes of medieval Irish chiefdoms. In spite of the constantly churning political violence between aristocratic factions and the waxing and waning fortunes of individual ramages, Irish chiefdoms as corporate territorial entities were astoundingly stable. The history of the chiefdom of the Corcu MoDruad is a case in point. This composite chiefdom was apparently already in existence at the dawn of written records at c. 150 AD. It experienced a loss of territory in the eighth century AD, and the reduced chiefdom had fissioned into two chiefdoms by the thirteenth century. Nonetheless, the last surviving descendant chiefdom, the O'Lochlainn chiefdom of Gragans, did not completely lose autonomy until the mid-seventeenth century.[1] Therefore, as a corporate entity, this chiefdom lasted a minimum of 1,500 years!

One may argue that due to their geographical isolation in the far north of County Clare, the Corcu MoDruad would have been an understandable exception to the cycling pattern. However, in the south of Clare, the Dál Cais composite chiefdom first appears in the mid-seventh century, had expanded to become a chiefdom confederacy in the tenth century, and had also fissioned prior to the thirteenth century into rival confederacies. The Dál Cais chiefdom confederacy then had a run of approximately 600 years. By contrast, Cahokia, one of the most enduring of the Mississippian complex chiefdoms did not last even half that long (Milner 1998:176). The complex chiefdom at Moundville also rose and fell within the space of 300 years (Anderson 1994:145–149).

How then does one account for the apparent durability of Irish chiefdoms in contrast to their American counterparts? Explanations for the collapse of North American chiefdoms have stressed the overexploitation of resources and permanent environmental damage, such as deforestation inflicted on the surrounding landscape by large sedentary populations (Anderson 1994; Lopinot and Woods 1993; Milner 1998). Several authors have indicated the inherent fragility of the subsistence–prestige goods complex (Blitz 1993:17; Welch 1991:194). Sustained droughts and floods have also been cited as important contributing factors. Finally, John Blitz has concluded from a survey of historical and archaeological data that Woodlands era chiefdoms were never strongly centralized to begin with and therefore they disintegrated readily when confronted with destabilizing conditions (1993). Populations simply walked away from collapsing chiefdoms, moving to more favorable locales.

Why the greater durability of Irish chiefdoms? First, one might think that the subsistence economy of the Irish could have been more resistant to extreme environmental swings. Sustained droughts never occur and the offshore ocean current shields Ireland from snow and frost. Prehistoric humans did visit environmental destruction on regions such as the Burren through deforestation, but this had occurred during the Late Neolithic/ Early Bronze Age and the degraded environment had stabilized since then. The annals do make it clear, however, that Irish cattle herds were vulnerable to cattle plagues that swept the island with devastating effects, and it is likely that these had a destabilizing effect on political systems. However, the wholesale collapse of complex chiefdoms does not seem to have issued from these plagues.

Probably the chief factor that inhibited cycling in medieval Ireland was the demographic structure of the island. Simply put, in contrast to native North America, apart from mountain areas and bogs, extensive unpopulated or underpopulated areas did not exist in medieval Ireland. The Irish medieval landscape was completely filled in with chiefdoms so that populations could not easily desert a chiefdom experiencing economic or military reversals. Indeed, the Irish laws make it clear that people seeking shelter within the boundaries of a friendly chiefdom had to assume a social status barely above that of a slave and were at the host chieftain's beck and call (F. Kelly 1988:34). During the political turbulence in Thomond of the thirteenth century described in *Caithreim Thoirdhealbhaigh*, populations under sustained attack did flee periodically to Eichtghe, a wooded area in the northeastern corner of the province, but this was just a temporary refuge.

The practices of Irish chieftains in war also perpetuated the continuance of a defeated chiefdom's boundaries and identity. Rather than annex a conquered chiefdom's territory, they were content merely to either place a defeated ramage under obligations of tribute, or replace their aristocrats with a lineage from their own ramage. From the evidence of the genealogies it is clear that ramages imposed from without retained the former name and traditions of their new realm, as they were content to alter only short sections of the genealogy of the former ruling ramage. After the passage of only a single generation, descendants of the interlopers would defend the autonomy of their inherited chiefdom as vigorously as had the ramage that they had displaced. Thus, despite high levels of political violence, Irish chiefdoms typically endured for centuries with only sporadic changes in identity or boundaries.

THE SOCIAL DYNAMICS OF IRISH CHIEFDOMS: STATUS RIVALRY, WARFARE, AND ALLIANCE FORMATION

Irving Goldman viewed status rivalry as the engine that drove the social evolution of chiefdoms in Polynesia. "The growth of the political community represents the fulfillment of chiefly ambitions and of Polynesian status ideals. In this respect it is a progressive structural modification and a focal point of cultural development" (1970:542).

Goldman was impressed by the copious evidence of competition over status rankings between aristocrats within Polynesian societies in a variety of social venues. Students of Polynesia coming after Goldman were not swayed by his emphasis on human agency, and the prevailing focus of explanations of Polynesian social evolution shifted to human ecology, demographic increase, and concomitant warfare (Kirch 1984:11). Robert Carniero's theory of social circumscription was especially influential in compelling anthropologists to accept the key role played by warfare between adjacent communities over resources in stimulating political centralization, and today anthropologists have come to view chiefdoms as inherently warlike social entities (Carniero 1970, 1981; Earle 1997:108).

These conflict models explaining the emergence, expansion, and structural transformation of chiefdoms are well-grounded in ethnological and ethnohistorical data. Chieftains, whether they are in Polynesia or medieval Ireland, come across as avaricious, boastful, arrogant, ambitious, and ruthless aggrandizing agents who will stoop to anything to undermine or kill rivals, even if they are close blood kinsmen. The Irish annals are an unceasing litany of battles and raids conducted against adversaries, and battles and cattle raids figure prominently in the heroic literature of the Irish Middle Ages as well. What tends to be slighted by scholars of chiefdoms, annalists, and saga writers alike is the equally critical role that alliance-making played in chiefdom politics and evolution.

Compared to the hundreds of records of battles and raids contained in the Irish annals and sagas, accounts of the creation of alliances are fewer, though not rare. The so-called "West Munster Synod," already mentioned above in Chapter 3, recounts the formation of a historical confederacy of composite chiefdoms in western Munster, putatively in the late sixth century, under the leadership of the Cíarraige. Though the dramatis personae of the account are probably wholly mythical, the story is probably faithful both to the circumstances and process by which such alliances came about in the Early Middle Ages. A number of composite chiefdoms under military pressure from powerful adversaries came together under the leadership of the strongest composite chiefdom among them. Notably, in this instance, the alliance is brought about without recourse to military coercion by the leading chiefdom. It also seems plausible that churchmen may have acted as go-betweens and guarantors of such pacts, given their religious status and higher degree of social mobility (Byrne 2001:217).

The alliance of the West Munster chiefdoms is referred to as *bráthirse* (brotherhood) and in other sources the alliances are referred to as *caratrad* (friendship). From the sources we learn that such covenants between chiefdoms were sealed and guaranteed in Ireland, as they were in most pre-industrial societies, with an exchange of high-ranking personnel between the two parties to the pact. So the tenth-century chieftain Ceallachán mac Buadachain is said to have wished to enter into an alliance with the Deisi, "and take hostages and pledges of Domnaill mac Fhaelain. There was concluded a matrimonial alliance and made friendship with him (*cleamnas ocus caradrad fris*) and Gormflaith, the daughter of Buadachan, was given to him" (Bugge 1905:71). Brian Mac Cénnetig was no stranger to the process of alliance-making. An entry in the *Annals of Innisfallen* for 984 states that "a great naval expedition by the sons of Aralt to Port Láirge, and they and the son of Cennétig exchanged hostages there as a guarantee of both together providing a hosting to attack Áth Cliath." In this case, the alliance is with the Vikings of Limerick to carry out a joint attack of Dublin, which was also under the control of Vikings.

An alliance of another kind, in the form of a nonaggression pact, is also attested in the literature. The *Annals of Innisfallen* state that in 997 AD:

> Brian mac Cennetich, with the chieftains of Mumu, and Máel Senchnaill mac Domnaill, chieftain of Temrach, went to Port Da Chainéoc, and they divided Ireland between them into two, viz. Leth Cuinn (Conn's half) to Máel Sechnaill and Leth Moga (Slave's Half) to Briain; and the hostages of the Laigin and of the foreigners which Máel Sechnaill had, were given to Brian. (Mac Airt 1988:173)[2]

In this instance, the two most powerful paramount chieftains of Ireland, who had long been military adversaries, make a pact to halt hostilies and confirm each other in the halves of Ireland that they had managed to dominate by force of arms – Máel Sechnaill to the northern half and Brian to the south. A similar pact is described in *Caithréim Thoirdhealbhaigh* in 1313 AD between the exhausted adversaries Murtough mac Turlough Mor, the leader of Clann Turlough, and Donough mac Donall mac Brian Rua, the leader of Clann Briain Ruaid, whereby they divided Thomond between them (O'Grady 1929:70).

As these examples illustrate, alliances were often expedient and insincere to boot. However, the existence of chiefdom confederacies, whereby chiefdoms "cooked" genealogies and created false origin myths to propound a common origin argues that some alliances assumed a more permanent character. As these confederacies assumed a more permanent, corporate character, chieftains who were not of a leading ramage were denied access to higher office by the commonly agreed genealogy. Still, as the careers of Ceallachán mac Buadachan and Brian mac Cennétig illustrate, exclusion was by no means permanent or total, and the right political circumstances could make an opening for a chieftain of a previously excluded ramage.

Alliances and military aggression were the principal tools by which Irish chieftains sought to elevate their status. The sagas concur that a chieftain could not be successful in war without being an effective architect of alliances. Paramount chieftains of chiefdom confederacies continuously sought to enlarge their spheres of influence by enlisting greater numbers of composite chiefdoms in alliances so as to carry out conquests of the leaders of other confederacies in order to dominate ever larger subdivisions of the island. These efforts often came to naught as the alliance networks that the paramount chieftains erected precluded the absorption of lower-level units and hence produced roadblocks to the institutionalization of power. This fact is manifested in the consensual procedures that existed for choosing successors to chiefly office.

THE SOCIAL DYNAMICS OF IRISH CHIEFDOMS: SUCCESSION TO OFFICE

An evergreen topic of interest to Irish historians is the mechanisms by which medieval Irish chieftains succeeded one another. Every prominent Irish historian has weighed in on the subject since Eoin Mac Neill's paper "The Irish law of dynastic succession" was published in 1919 (1981:chap. VIII). Most treatments of the subject have striven to understand the significance of terms that occur in the ethnohistorical sources that describe statuses related to chieftainship, such as *rígdomna* (the makings of a chieftain) or *tánaiste* (second [to a chieftain]), or qualities attributed to successful claimants of chiefly office such as *febas* (excellence), seniority in the family, or the status of the birth mother of the prospective heir (Charles-Edwards 1971, 1993; J. Hogan 1932; Jaski 2000; Mac Niocaill 1968; Ó Corráin 1971; Ó Cróinín 1995:70). These approaches have been for the most part text-driven and emic, examining succession as it is treated in the Early Medieval law texts or as it is represented in annalistic entries. As such, these sources present succession in somewhat idealistic terms as how it should unfold commensurate with the value systems of the medieval scholarly authors.

A fresh, and one might say more reality-bound approach was taken by Donnchadh Ó Corráin, who examined actual patterns of succession within Early Medieval period Leinster chiefdoms as they have come down to us in the genealogies and annals. He reached the conclusion that putative rules and personal qualities mattered less than a claimant's ability to organize a faction of aristocrats to back up his claim with force. Ó Corráin's view is reflected most spendidly in the twelfth-century saga *Caithréim Cellachán Caisil*. The saga's protagonist, Cellachán mac Buadachain, is stated to be the illegitimate son of the chieftain of the Éoganacht Caisil. Ó Corráin states that Cellachán's ramage had been out of contention for the position of paramount chieftain of Munster for over 200 years (1972:113). According to the saga, this office had been rotated by agreement between the most senior leaders of the Éoganacht and Dál Cais chiefdom confederacies. In order to assert her son's claim to the chieftainship over more powerful candidates, Cellachán's mother

"... was herself collecting arms and clothes, and treasures, and retaining companies of foot-soldiers and gentle household troops. And this is the number of those who were fed (?) by and fully bound to her, viz. 500 armed men.

The day on which Cellachán came to Cashel after he had obtained this host, was the day on which there was a great host of the two provinces of Munster at Glenamain of Cashel electing a chieftain." Cellachán's mother advised him:

"... when the nobles of Munster were sitting down, he should come with his people in the best of arms and dress, and ask hostages and pledges of them and tell Cennedig (a rival claimant) to remember justice." (Bugge 1905:59–60).

This passage exposes the most important dimension of an accurate understanding of the operation of succession of Irish chieftains: *togha rígh* (electing a chieftain). Of the Irish historians who have engaged the subject over the past century, it is Eoin Mac Neill alone who pays elections more than cursory attention:

> The right to elect apparently belonged to the whole body of freemen. A general meeting was called. The greater nobles held a conference apart, and when they came to a conclusion they made known their choice to the popular assembly, which no doubt was guided by them in its decision. (Mac Neill 1981 [1921]:121)

Mac Neill reveals the reason that the topic of succession by election has been slighted by generations of Irish historians, himself included, when he goes on to deem this aspect of the process "the weakest feature of Irish polity" (ibid:122). In his view, the absence of strict rules of succession was "a prominent cause of the gravest political disorders" (ibid.). Indeed, Mac Neill determined that a preponderance of the violence recorded in the annals was the result of internal factional disputes, not warfare between hostile polities (ibid.:123).

Mac Neill reasoned that the reason for the existence of such open-ended and democratic provisions for the selection of future leaders to a composite chiefdom, confederacy, or alliance was to select the most able war leaders. Cattle raiding was a vital aspect of political leadership to the medieval Irish (ibid.:122), as followers depended on rewards in livestock, and livestock replenishment through raiding was the approved recovery technique in the face of losses incurred through a raid or cattle plague. Mac Neill's explanation finds resonance in other areas of the world where agropastoral subsistence economies predominate. The oral history of the interlacustrine kingdom of Ankole in modern Uganda describes institutionalized succession wars following the death of kings as his sons assembled their factions and engaged each other in conflict (Oberg 1978:157).

Apart from the role played by the prominence of the chieftain as war leader, one should also consider another, possibly even more plausible, reason for the existence of this mode of succession – the fact that *mór thúatha* are polities that are de facto alliance networks. Carole Crumley advanced the concept of heterarchy to model the Celtic political systems of proto-historical Gaul (1979; Marquardt and Crumley 1987). She realized that power in the Gaulish polities arose not from a single centralized dynasty, but from the confluence of multiple political centers. Political power in Munster was likewise diffused among the larger and smaller chiefdoms making up a composite chiefdom, chiefdom confederacy, or alliance. For the political system to work, individual chieftains had to cede some measure of their power to the political center; however, they still retained a great measure of power and autonomy – evidenced by the fact that they controlled the selection of the paramount chieftain. In the saga *Caithréim Thoirdhealbhaigh*, Cumea MacNamara appears repeatedly as the principal officiate at O'Brien inaugurations. Not only was their loyalty key to the survival and success of Clann Thoirdhealbhaigh, but it has been plausibly claimed that the MacNamaras exceeded the O'Brien royal family in power (Nic Ghiollamhaith 1995). Since the larger polities of the Early Medieval period were alliance networks, not monarchies with supernumerary royal families, democratic election was the only possible method of choosing a paramount leader. That this procedure continued in use into the thirteenth and early fourteenth centuries in *Tuadmumu* (Thomond) was in all probability a direct manifestation of the political weakness of the O'Briens (Nic Ghiollamhaith 1981, 1995).

Bart Jaski makes the valid point that the procedure used to choose the paramount leader of a *mór thúath* may not have been the same that was used to select a chieftain of a simple *túath* (2000:31). It is true that it is mostly descriptions of the elections of paramount chieftains and leaders of alliances that appear in the sagas, and these postdate the tenth century. However, in an article on the worth of the glosses to the Early Medieval law tracts, Katharine Simms reveals a valuable discussion on succession within a simple chiefdom contained in the Old Irish text *Di Astud Cirt ocus Dligid* (1998). The Old Irish text stipulates a preference that kinsmen succeed other kinsmen to office, and describes a three-day conclave of local nobility at the house of the hospitaler, or *bó-aire*, to choose the next chieftain. The method of selecting a successor to a chieftain by election seems, then, to have deep roots. That it did not work faultlessly, even at the local level, is demonstrated by the geographical evidence of the bifurcation of Medieval period *túatha* districts in the chiefdom of

Gragans in the Burren between what are assumed to be related branches of the ruling lineage.

Finally, it must be borne in mind that chiefdoms that had been subsumed within a composite chiefdom may not have been able to reach decisions concerning leadership with complete autonomy. It is clear from sources from the Late Middle Ages that paramount chieftains sometimes intervened in the process to promote the candidates of their choice (Simms 1998:39).

IRISH CHIEFDOM TO IRISH STATE

Brian Bóroimhe [6] occupies an exceptional position in Irish history as the only chieftain who is considered to have come close to asserting himself as the sole king of Ireland. Brian's ascent was propelled as much by his facility for alliance formation as it was by his successes on the battlefield – that is to say, that he was more a shrewd Irish chieftain than a conquering autocrat. Brian's control of the chiefdoms he had subjugated was probably nominal at best. There is simply no evidence that he followed up any of his conquests with attempts at regulated exactions or administration. Defeated chieftains were left in control of their provinces after submitting to Brian. We must therefore conclude that Brian was attempting to achieve a kind of symbolic preeminence at the head of a great alliance, to define himself as the true *ard rí* of all Ireland much like a boxer attains a world championship after successive victories, a title that he must thereafter defend to retain.

Ireland is large enough that Brian mac Cennétig could have created a primitive state along the lines of Saxon Wessex or Kent without having achieved the goal of an island-wide conquest. That being said, the focus of discussion here is whether *any* early historic Irish polity could be said to have assumed the characteristics of a state. For the most part, I have couched the analysis of the political systems of Thomond in the descriptive terminology of complex chiefdoms, as the vast majority of polities during most time periods prior to the eighteenth century can be said to express strongly the well-known qualities of chiefdoms. Chiefdoms, though bereft of much of their original territory and autonomy, persisted within the primitive state of the O'Briens that emerged in the twelfth century. Now that the historical development of the polities of Thomond has been described in some detail, it is time to reflect upon whether there were any significant departures from the general conception of how chiefdoms are organized.

In his book *The European Past*, Robert Dodgshon has put forward Early Medieval Ireland as an example of early state development. The central theme of his section on the emergence of the feudal state in Europe is the territorialization of chiefdom polities – the transformation whereby groups that had defined themselves on the basis of relations between people became defined by relations to land (1987:135–139) or, as he put it, "communities of kin were replaced by communities of place" (163). This transformation accompanied greater hierarchization and concomitant differentiation of functions at the top of society, and an appropriation of some of the functions of lower administrative units by the political center in order to make them less complete and therefore more dependent upon the central power (132–135). The characteristic outcome of this scenario in the context of European feudal states was the notion of all land being vested in a king, and the gaining by him of the exclusive authority to grant licenses to subordinates to collect fees and taxes.

No one, I believe, would quibble with Dodgshon's characterization of the organizational changes accompanying the emergence of the feudal state in Europe. However, the stress laid on the territorialization of the community is problematic from the outset. Dodgshon himself admits that "tribal societies too, were bounded, divided off one from another by boundaries, natural or otherwise" (164). Anyone familiar with case studies of chiefdoms is aware that complex chiefdoms are invariably distinguished by boundaries that set them apart from other chiefdoms, and that also set off administrative districts inside them (see Earle 1978; Sahlins 1958:196). Clearly, then, one cannot speak of any sort of geographical transformation of spatial ordering when chiefdoms become states.

Dodgshon chose Ireland as a case study for the emergence of the early state in Europe. He correctly realized that the nonurban nature of Irish society presents us with "a different trajectory of development" (152). His case for Ireland devolves upon the perceived change from a ritualistic and symbolic kingship to the integration of small chiefdoms into complex provincial chiefdoms under a single ruler. This process commenced with a chieftain that in the earliest of times embodied all of the functions of kingship in himself, those of "chief priest, war-leader, law-giver and controller of tribal exchange" (153). Over time, it is supposed, the *rí* devolved a number of these functions onto specialists and a primitive administrative bureaucracy was born. During the centuries of the first millennium AD, the great chiefdom confederacies emerged with multiple administrative tiers and consequent complex systems of ranking between chieftains at different levels. Thus, a real hierarchy of power had emerged by the eighth century AD, supplanting a loose, and largely symbolic, system of titles and offices (152–153).

There are a number of problems with this appraisal of Irish social evolution in the first millennium. An Irish primitive bureaucracy can be traced with confidence to the earliest of the historical sources. As far as one can tell, Irish chieftains were always accompanied by *briugaid* (hospitallers), *rechtairi* (bailiffs), *filid* (druid/poets), and *brithemoin* (judges). One suspects that one would have to go back a very long way in European prehistory to find a chieftain who embodied everything in one person. Even the speakers of Proto-Indo-European may have possessed differentiated leadership roles 7,000 years ago (Anthony 2007:160). Dodgshon's principal claim that early, or primary, states appeared in Ireland during the Middle Ages can be sustained, but not, however, his contention that they had emerged by the eighth century AD, and not for the reasons he gives.

Distinguishing complex chiefdoms from primitive states is a difficult task, as the differences between the two levels of sociocultural integration hinge upon subtle changes in the structural organization of society and economic production, and an increase in scale. In a review article with Michael Geselowitz (1988), I have argued for four distinguishing characteristics of primitive states. The first characteristic that distinguishes primitive states from complex chiefdoms is the strengthening of the office of kingship, principally by converting subchiefs into local administrators for the crown or superseding them with appointed administrators (Gibson and Geselowitz 1988:26). The legitimacy of subchieftains in Irish complex chiefdoms accrued from their leading position in the aristocratic ramage of a local *túath*. Their rights to rule and to property originated in their local ramage and had nothing to do with their relationship to an overchieftain. A transformation whereby the office of king was strengthened naturally followed upon the act of stripping subchieftains of this source of legitimacy. In the new order, the right to rule became an exclusive prerogative of the king to grant or delegate. Chieftains at the local level became dependent upon the king for their office and holdings and achieved legitimacy through their relationship to him.

The second distinguishing mark of states is that the primitive bureaucracy emerges as a permanent and significant factor of royal administration (ibid.). Complex chiefdoms possessed simple bureaucracies. In the last chapter it was shown that Irish ramages were paired with lineages of jurists even at the local level, and within a chiefdom *brithemoin* possessed considerable land and power. With the emergence of the primitive state, the bureaucracy increased in size and probably moved beyond the confines of hereditary lineages. In Ireland, this change was probably most pronounced in the office of *maor*, or steward. The analysis of O'Brien's Rental and the evidence in *Caithréim Thoirdhealbhaigh* showed that by the fourteenth century, the O'Brien paramount chieftain could impose his stewards upon local *saerthúatha* to collect his rents. There is no evidence to suggest that stewardship was a hereditary office.

Thirdly, with the emergence of the primitive state, economic production became bureaucratized as the political economy expanded to embrace production at the local level (see Johnson and Earle 1987:246, 270). The king intervenes at the basic level of food and craft production by appointing managers to set production quotas and allocate resources among the producers. This cannot be said to be an exclusive trait of primitive states, as the chieftains of the complex chiefdoms of Hawaii appointed local economic managers with powers of absolute control over resource allocation and crop production in the time preceding the emergence of the Hawaiian state (Earle 1978:16–18).

According to the brehon laws, Irish chieftains amassed wealth through an all-embracing system of clientship. Subaristocrats and the well-off common populace were classed as free clients (*saer céilí*) and were obligated by their attachment to a chiefdom to accept gifts and capital in the form of cattle from the chief, and to make annual contributions of calves and produce to the chiefly lineage. Lower status *daer céilí*, on the other hand, were forced by necessity to accept the burden of a more onerous contract of clientship that was of longer duration and involved greater economic demands.

Though all-embracing, this system of capital accumulation was indirect, as each client and client aristocrat was left to manage his own economic affairs. The chieftain was only concerned with getting his stipulated contribution at the prescribed time of payment. O'Brien's Rental shows a dramatically different mode of staple finance having come into being by the fourteenth century. If the interpretation of this text is correct, personal contracts, though probably persisting on the local level, had been translated into rent assessed on grazing land levied by the paramount chieftain and collected by his stewards. This development represents a bypassing of the local chieftain in matter of goods mobilization by the household of the king. In this new system, the king acquired title to land in subordinate chiefdoms, made assessments of its productive value, and fixed proportionate rents to be collected by a functionary that had been enfeoffed within the local territory. In the context of a subsistence economy dominated by livestock production, this mode of staple finance represents a significantly greater degree of direct economic control by the paramount leader and a sure indication of statehood.

Fourth, state development was accompanied by the maintenance of permanent standing bodies of fighting men. Medieval Ireland saw the advent of the galloglass – a professional mercenary in the pay of the chieftain. However, the body of the Irish fighting force still consisted of local levies. The constant fighting and raiding ensured that the local leaders and populace were well-drilled in the martial arts. The agropastoral kingdom of Nkore (Ankole) of the interlacustrine region of Uganda provides a better illustration of the effect of the emergence of a state upon military conduct in an agropastoral setting. Beginning in the mid-eighteenth century, trained warriors of a certain age were billeted by the *omugabe* (king) in strategically placed camps under an appointed chief to enable either a rapid response to a raid from a neighboring kingdom, or troops to be assembled into a military offensive (Oberg 1978:131; Karugire 1971:54, 112, 187, 200–207). Thus, in Nkore the creation of a permanent fighting force went hand-in-hand with the development of local administration by appointed bureaucrats, both attributes of state organization.

Returning to Dodgshon's thesis of the territorialization of the populace as an aspect of European state formation, the data discussed so far offer a clear test case. In many ways the Irish data are paradoxical. As Dodgshon would predict, Irish society did become increasingly territorialized throughout the latter part of the first millennium and the initial centuries of the second. This fact is promulgated by the complex system of land assessment that had come into being by the twelfth century AD, which involved units such as the *baile* and *cedhramrum*. However, the saga *Caithréim Thoirdhealbhaigh* and the documentary evidence from the Tudor period discussed previously show clearly that the elementary structure of Irish chiefdoms, expressed in the institutions of *ríghe* (chiefship) and *tánaiste* and in the existence of aristocratic sections, their territories and capitals, persisted in Ireland on the local level until the ultimate demise of the Gaelic polities in the seventeenth century. Substantive changes in the nature and structure of Irish political life did occur, however, at the *upper* levels of the regional hierarchy, and these changes are reflected in territorial organization.

Looking back at the structure of the Dál Cais polity under Brian Bóroimhe [6], Brian was the principal chieftain over a vast territory by Irish standards. However, insofar as he maintained his chief residence at Cenn Coradh in Uí Thairdelbaig, and apparently made no effort to establish any administrative apparatus over the chiefdoms he defeated, he was clearly a chieftain in the old model of Irish chieftains, albeit a very successful one. His continued attachment to the territory of his ramage, the Uí Thairdelbaig, demonstrates that he was the strongest chieftain of the leading *túath* of the Dál Cais chiefdom confederacy. Though he was clearly the paramount chieftain of Munster, he did not remove himself from his ramage and territory to take up residence at the Éoganacht provincial capital at Caisel.

The Dál Cais capital remained at Cenn Coradh under Brian's son and successor Donnchad (d. 1064) [10], and grandson Toirdelbach [11] (d. 1086, Gwynn and Gleeson 1962:95–105), though they made Limerick a subsidiary capital (Ó Corráin 1972:142). However, the reign of Brian's great-grandson, Muirchertach Mór Uí Briain [12] (reigned 1086–1119) bore witness to changes in the geography of Irish politics that may truly be said to signal the appearance of the state in Ireland. In 1101 AD Muirchertach gave Caisel to the church and ten years later made it the seat of the first Archbishop of Munster (Gwynn and Gleeson 1962:110). This act ended Caisel's role as the symbolic center of secular power in Munster. More importantly, it was an act that demonstrated in concrete terms the quality and extent of Muirchertach's power in Munster. Establishing a metropolitan capital at Caisel involved the expropriation of a considerable territory to support it. The granting of land for the support of an ecclesiastical capital was a habitual practice of Irish chieftains. Munificence is at the core of the acquisition of prestige by leaders in big man and chiefdom societies alike. However, in Thomond, up to the time of Brian, ecclesiastical establishments were created and invested *within* the area of the composite chiefdom, and most frequently in or near the territory of the leading *túath*. Muirchertach was, however, sufficiently powerful to strip lands from alien chiefdoms and create religious capitals outside of his chiefdom and composite chiefdom of origin.

Of greater significance is the fact that during his reign Muirchertach made the city of Limerick his principal capital by making it his chief residence, possibly after Cenn Coradh was destroyed in a joint raid by Domnall Mac Lochlainn of Cenél Éogain and Ruardrí Uí Conchobair of Connacht (Gwynn and Gleeson 1962:123–124; Ó Corráin 1972:143). This act showed that Muirchertach no longer considered it necessary to locate his capital within the lands of his traditional ramage, the Uí Thairdelbaig. This was due on the one hand to his considerable power and influence – his rule extended over all Munster, and he dominated Connacht and Leinster (Ó Corráin 1972:142–146). By all appearances, Muirchertach had ceased to be of the Uí Thairdelbaig, though no doubt he was aware of his origins and ties to this group. Rather, he and his immediate predecessor Toirdelbach were the initial leaders of a new dynasty, the Uí Briain, the "Descendants of Brian."

Ó Corráin has inveighed against seeing the state in the polity of Muirchertach Uí Briain:

> In many ways, Muirchertach was a great king: ultimately, he was a failure. The dominance he achieved was one of personal sovereignty, which depended on his own great abilities and not on any new form of organisation or institutions. It perished with his illness in 1114 and the supremacy of Munster vanished in the dynastic struggles which racked his immediate successors. (1972:149)

This logic would deny statehood to the polity of Charlemagne, which likewise disintegrated upon his death into smaller states ruled by his sons. Kingdom-building by gifted individuals and subsequent disintegration due to partible inheritance practices or dynastic struggles are intrinsic to the dynamic of the primitive states of the European Early Middle Ages. Rather than constituting a failure, by international standards Muirchertach Uí Briain was a modest success as a leader and innovator. The measure of his success in state creation lies in the fact that following his death there was no reversion to the composite chiefdom pattern that preceded his rule. The Uí Briain did not seek to establish a *túath* named after themselves at the heart of their polity surrounded by confederate chiefdoms. In the face of pressure from the ascendant Uí Conchobair of Connacht, the Uí Briain continued to maintain their capital at Limerick until 1216, when further political setbacks at the hands of the Anglo-Normans forced them to relocate it to Cluain Rámhfhada (Gwynn and Gleeson 1962:194).

Though the extent of the area under Uí Briain political domination contracted following the demise of Muirchertach Mór Uí Briain in 1114 AD, throughout the twelfth–sixteenth centuries the extent of the land-holdings directly subject to members of this ramage increased steadily. This was accomplished by disenfranchising subject chiefly ramages such as the Uí hAichir of Uí Cormaic and Uí Flanchadha, the Uí Domnaill of Corcabhaiscinn, the Uí Concubair of Corcamruad, and the Uí Chuinn of Cenél Fearmaic. Aristocratic ramages that retained political autonomy within their former chiefdoms were squeezed off portions of their lands either through onerous exactions or through outright confiscations on flimsy or contrived pretexts. Prior to the thirteenth century, a centrifugal force counteracted the maintenance of hegemony by the Uí Briain, as individuals from this ramage implanted upon subordinate chiefdoms (e.g., Mathgamain mac Muirchertaich Uí Briain [13] who was implanted in Corcabhaiscinn) eventually gave rise to lineages with separate political identities. In Thomond after the thirteenth century, the process of displacement from above seems to have moved with sufficient speed to more than counteract this tendency. The victory of Clann Thoirdhealbhaigh and Clann Chuiléin (the MacNamaras) in 1318 over their adversaries resulted in the hegemony of these two ramages over most of Thomond.

AGROPASTORALISM AND THE PRIMITIVE IRISH STATE

A number of local ramages survived within the boundaries of their original chiefdoms within the O'Brien state into the high Middle Ages. The O'Brien dynasts also tolerated features and social institutions that had been appropriate to chiefdoms, such as the keeping of genealogies, the adjudication of disputes by independent jurists, and the method of chiefly succession. However, these facts do not discredit the attribution of statehood to the Uí Briain polity of Thomond. Rather, these features should be seen as an expression of a different trajectory of statehood, the trajectory of cultures with an underlying agropastoral subsistence base.

I have argued elsewhere that the trajectory of the evolution of societies with livestock management as the predominant aspect of the subsistence strategy would be expected to diverge from the course of social development of agrarian societies (Gibson 1988; 1995). In broad outline, similar levels of social complexity can be found under either economic regime. However, the respective trajectories of social evolution differ in the organizational and institutional features generated by the differing demands and potentialities of the subsistence strategies of agropastoral and agrarian societies.

All throughout their history, the subsistence economy of the Irish remained agropastoral in orientation – an economy of limited vegetable and grain production dominated by the raising of livestock, principally cattle (see Gibson 1988; F. Kelly 2000; Lucas 1989; Nicholls 1972:114–119; Ó Corráin 1972:48–58, 2005; Proudfoot 1961). The cattle of the Irish are prominently featured in the great epics, law texts, early descriptions of the island by foreigners (Giraldus Cambrensis 1982:34–35, 101–102), and in the sagas of the Middle Ages. Direct evidence of their importance to subsistence is afforded by the enormous quantities of animal bones found on well-preserved sites such as Lagore crannog in County Westmeath, which was mined for bone in the nineteenth century but still yielded 47,976 lb. of animal bone to Hugh O'Neill Hencken's excavation team in the 1930s. Roughly 80 percent of the bones were of cattle (Hencken 1950:36, 225).

Cahercommaun itself produced over 9,000 lb. of bone, 97 percent of which were of cattle (Stelfox in Hencken 1938:74). These latter two sites were former political capitals and so one may expect dietary differences between the aristocratic and nonaristocratic sections of the population. It is difficult on present evidence to determine the extent of dietary differences between different strata of the population. However, the relative paucity of quern-stones on smaller sites would seem to indicate that livestock production was at least as important as grain cultivation in the domestic economy.

In Thomond, the emphasis placed on livestock production seems to have had a number of demographic and political consequences. Livestock production is less land-intensive than agriculture, and in the context of a rugged landscape, one would expect low population densities. In the most rugged part of Thomond, the Burren, a census dating to either 1659 or 1600 records a population of 859 (Plunkett Dillon 1985:128). Graham has suggested that the census recorded only individuals over 15 years of age, and Plunkett Dillon has put forward a correction factor of 66 percent, bringing the estimated population to 2,500 individuals, the same population as exists in the Burren in the present day (Graham 1970; Plunkett Dillon 1985:128). Burren Barony was probably not much larger in the seventeenth century than it is today, and I estimate that it would have contained 300 sq. km. The two population estimates would then yield a density of between 3.5 and 8.3 persons per sq. km in the Burren, and I do not think it would have been much higher than this in the ninth century AD.

Co. Clare as a whole contains 3,447 sq. km (Finch 1971:1). In 1659 the county had a population of 16,474 (excluding 440 English Protestants, Frost 1978:384), and so the population density was 4.8–4.9 persons per sq. km. This census was taken eight years after the devastation wrecked by the struggle of the Irish Confederation against Cromwell, and so the population was likely to have been reduced as a consequence. Nevertheless, even with substantially higher population numbers, the landscape cannot be said to have been densely inhabited at this time. The low population densities of Thomond, the distribution of this population into scattered homesteads during the eleventh and twelfth centuries AD, and also the lack of critical resources amenable to centralized manipulation explains the fact that Irish polities at the macroregional scale – the composite chiefdoms and confederacies of the Early Medieval and Medieval periods – had a strongly "federal" character.

Irish paramount chieftains relied on indirect means of political manipulation of semiautonomous polities through the threat and display of superior force, through the implantation of close kin on defeated neighboring chiefdoms, and through asymmetrical alliances promulgated by feigned kin relations between themselves and subordinate ramages. In the histories and law texts the relation between subordinate and superior aristocracy was expressed and advertised as an extension of the principle of clientship. The subordinate aristocrat accepted a payment from his superior of sumptuary items, and thereby consigned his honor-price to his superior and became bound to him.

> Now in time of old it was the custom that whoso, being ruler whether of a cantred (*triucha ced*) or of a province (*cúigid*), accepted another chief's gift or wage (*tuarastal*) [for in this manner they are synonyms] did actually by such acceptance submit to the giver as his chief paramount, and in virtue of the same take on himself to do him suit and service, to pay him rent and tribute. Therefore, and or ever they took their seats in order to this conference, northwards across the river O'Brien sent to O'Neil a hundred horses by way of stipend. (O'Grady 1929, 27:3)

Clientship is itself an institution universal to the more stratified of pastoral societies (Gibson 1988). It is a natural reflex of these societies to the insecurity of an economy predicated upon the raising of livestock. Livestock are vulnerable to disease and drought, and this is especially true of cattle, whose water requirements are much higher than those of sheep, goats, or camels (Dahl and Hjort 1976). Lost cattle cannot be quickly replaced, a number of years being necessary to replenish a herd.

Societies whose economies are oriented around cattle have recourse to a number of institutions to compensate for their losses in stock. Cattle raiding on a communal or familial level is one such institution common to all cattle pastoral and agropastoral societies. Pastoral societies probably owe their long history of military success against agricultural societies to the fact that they are in a continuous state of military vigilance due to the high frequency of cattle raiding. Indeed, as Evans-Pritchard's classic study of the Nuer revealed, the raison d'être of suprafamilial social units among the Nuer was to organize and facilitate the conduct of war against social bodies of variable scale.

Aside from raiding, societies of cattle pastoralists utilized elaborate systems of livestock banking, that is, systems whereby surplus cattle were kept by kin and friends geographically remote from the household's herds as a hedge against future needs. Where personal resources failed, pastoralists were either forced to give up the pastoralist lifestyle and go into fishing, as among some Nuer and Turkana, or take up agriculture full-time where this was an option (Ankole). A third option was the practice of binding one's self personally to a wealthy individual in return for either subsistence, or for a loan of cattle. Clientship is an institution exclusive to the more stratified of the livestock-oriented societies. As far as I am aware, the least stratified of the pastoral societies for which this institution is attested are the Mandari of the Sudan, who were organized into simple chiefdoms at the time of the extension of British administration to their area (Buxton 1963).

The law texts make clear that Irish aristocrats of the Early Medieval period could raise their status through the acquisition of clients (*céili*). The texts differentiate between those of high rank who become clients by virtue of standing in subordinate status to a paramount chieftain within a chiefdom (*saer céile*) and those of nonaristocratic status who bound themselves to their lord through the transfer of their honor-price for stock (*daer céile*). Notions of *saer* and *daer* were used in the native sources in contexts other than clientship, such as to describe the relations of chiefdoms to each other or to describe the relative ranking of specialized crafts. It is clear that they are relative terms that indicated statuses of either autonomy or servitude in relation to chieftains.

The extension of the language and exchanges of clientship into the realm of the political relations between polities clearly signals the fact that the Irish aristocrats considered client relations and political relations to be structurally similar, if not altogether isomorphic. The quality of the relations between the constituent chiefdoms of a composite chiefdom or a chiefdom confederacy can be most aptly characterized by the relation of a patron to his client. The patron exerted his influence through his outstanding obligations and through intimidation, but left the client to manage his own affairs. The chief requirements of the patron/paramount chieftain of his subject aristocrats were for expressions of fealty, assistance upon demand, and periodic contributions of goods and cattle. Any notions that paramount chieftains might have entertained toward outright annexation of defeated polities were probably constrained by the difficulty of establishing direct control in the context of a dispersed population of relatively low density with a mobile, slowly reproducing resource base.

The solution to this dilemma at early stages of Irish political development was the parasitization of subordinate aristocracy through the extension of the clientship principle. This was intrinsically a temporary solution, as even ramages under the yolk for several generations were known to have asserted independence when an opportunity to shift alliances presented itself. Kings of the Irish Early Middle Ages, such as Muirchertach Uí Briain [12] and Ruaidhrí Uí Conchobair, seem to have made the transformation to statehood through the intensification of this technique, possibly through the retention of a permanent band of professional warriors and through an expansion of the body of stewards making up the primitive bureaucracy. However they effected greater control, they were enabled to wrest themselves from their ancestral chiefdoms and ramages and set themselves up, however tentatively, as a ruling caste defined by access to power, rather than ties to a territory.

Genealogies and Chieftain Lists

uí TAIRDELBAIG

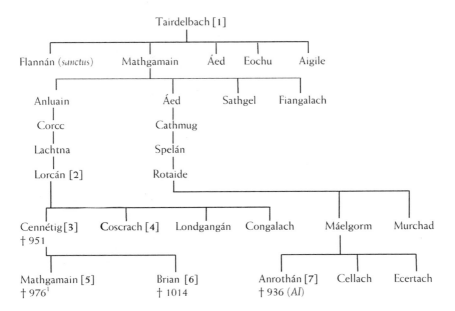

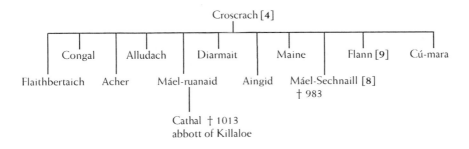

¹ Predeceased by four other sons.

UÍ BRIAIN (AFTER FROST 1978: APPENDIX VI)

Note: Only the more important descendants are given due to space considerations. Paramount chieftains are in bold.

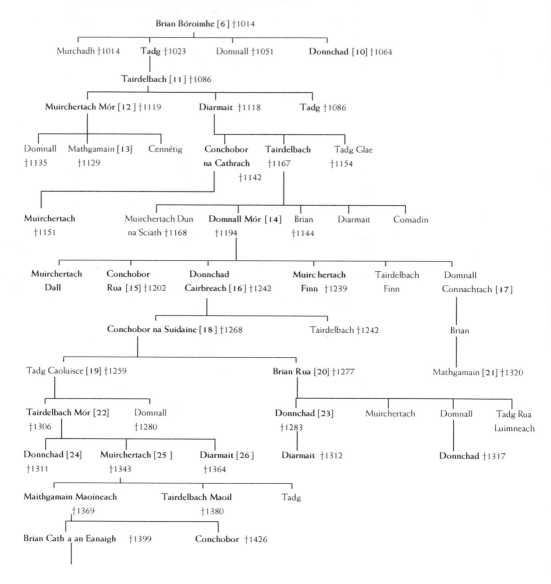

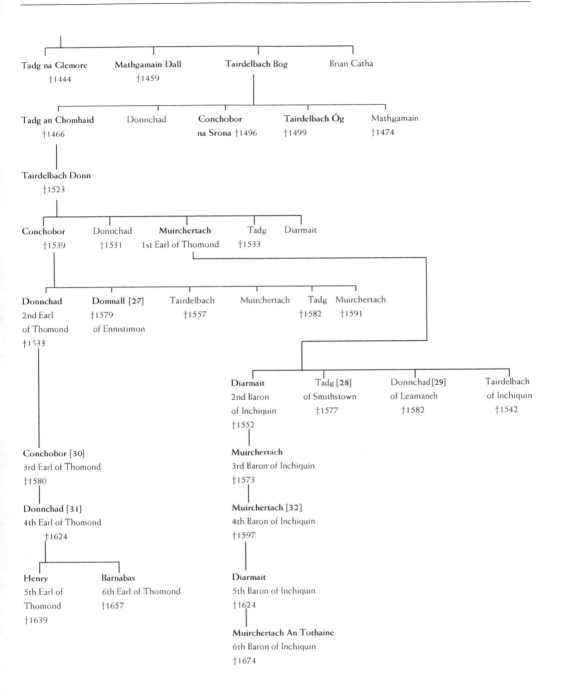

UÍ CHUINN

Note: (Clann hIffernáin – sources: Raw. B 502; Book of Lecan; Book of Ballymote).

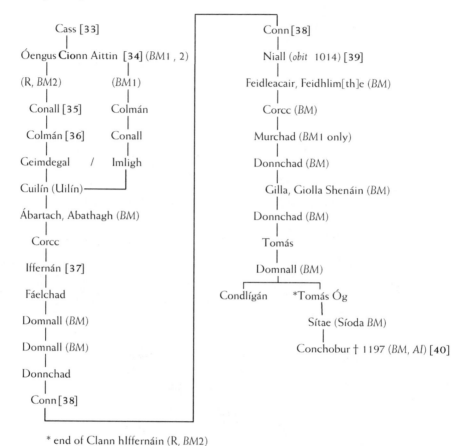

Cass [33]
|
Óengus Cionn Aittin [34] (*BM*1 , 2)
| |
(R, *BM*2)   (*BM*1)
| |
Conall [35]   Colmán
| |
Colmán [36]   Conall
| |
Geimdegal   /   Imligh
|
Cuilín (Uilín)—————┘
|
Ábartach, Abathagh (*BM*)
|
Corcc
|
Iffernán [37]
|
Fáelchad
|
Domnall (*BM*)
|
Domnall (*BM*)
|
Donnchad
|
Conn [38]

Conn [38]
|
Niall (*obit* 1014) [39]
|
Feidleacair, Feidhlim[th]e (*BM*)
|
Corcc (*BM*)
|
Murchad (*BM*1 only)
|
Donnchad (*BM*)
|
Gilla, Giolla Shenáin (*BM*)
|
Donnchad (*BM*)
|
Tomás
|
Domnall (*BM*)
| |
Condlígán   *Tomás Óg
|
Sítae (Síoda *BM*)
|
Conchobur † 1197 (*BM*, *AI*) [40]

* end of Clann hIffernáin (R, *BM*2)

AES IAR FORGUS ("PEOPLE WEST OF THE FERGUS": CENÉL BÁETH, CENÉL FERMAIC)

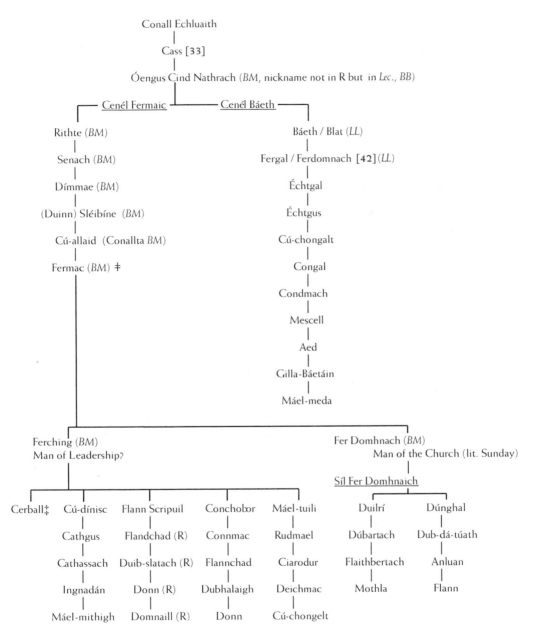

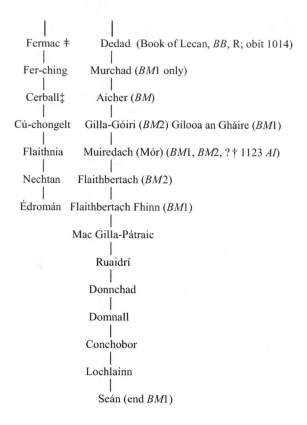

Fermac ‡   Dedad   (Book of Lecan, *BB*, R; obit 1014)

Fer-ching   Murchad (*BM*1 only)

Cerball‡   Aicher (*BM*)

Cú-chongelt   Gilla-Góiri (*BM*2) Gilooa an Gháire (*BM*1)

Flaithnia   Muiredach (Mór) (*BM*1, *BM*2, ? † 1123 *AI*)

Nechtan   Flaithbertach (*BM*2)

Édromán   Flaithbertach Fhinn (*BM*1)

Mac Gilla-Pátraic

Ruaidrí

Donnchad

Domnall

Conchobor

Lochlainn

Seán (end *BM*1)

‡ ‡ = Indicates beginning and end of a repeated sequence.

DATABASE: CHIEFTAINS OF THE CORCU MODRUAD

Section 1. Pseudohistorical

(Yellow Book of Lecan)

Milead Easbáine (sons of whom defeated the Túatha De Dannan)

Ir [43] (*ACl*, pg. 25, 30)

Ebir (of Ulster, see *ACl*, pg. 28)

Artt

Artrí

Sétnae Airrt (*ACl*, pg. 33)

Fiachach Fínscothaig (*ACl*, pg. 33)

Ollam Fótla (of Ulster, *ACl*, pg. 34)

Cairpre Olloman

Labraid Condilg

Bláth

Find

Sírlám (*ACl*, pg. 37)

Airgedmáir (*ACl*, pg. 38)

Fomair

Duib

Sithrigi

Section 2. Mythological

Rawl. B. 502	Book of Leinster
Rudraigi mac Sittride[2]	
Ross	Ross
Fergus	Fergus
Corcc	Corcc Dothi
Echdach	
Déoda[3]	Déoda
Ollomna[4]	Follomnu
Me-druí	Me-drúi
Aislithe	Fedlimid
Áed Gnóe Fir Gaí Lethain[5] *Handsome Aed, man of the broad spear*	
Artt-Corb[6]	
Nectan[7]	Necta
Ochon[8]	Máethon

[2] Clanna Rudhraighe (*BM*), the first three names are also initial ancestors of the Fir Maige of Co. Cork.
[3] "Divine," Dagda otherwise.
[4] "Masterly" Eochaid Ollathair (O'Rah:469).
[5] Áed "fire," with a lightning spear, perhaps a local name for the sun god (O'Rah:58).
[6] Artt-Corb (O'Cathasaigh:44, 46).
[7] Another name for god Nuadu (O'Rah:320).
[8] "Young wolf," perhaps to be equated with Mac Con (O'Rah:78–79).

Section 3.

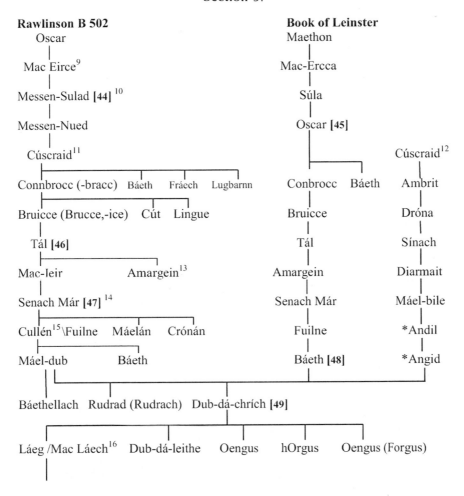

Rawlinson B 502

Oscar

Mac Eirce[9]

Messen-Sulad [44] [10]

Messen-Nued

Cúscraid[11]

Connbrocc (-bracc)   Báeth   Fráech   Lugbarnn

Bruicce (Brucce,-ice)   Cút   Lingue

Tál [46]

Mac-Ieir   Amargein[13]

Senach Már [47] [14]

Cullén[15]\Fuilne   Máelán   Crónán

Máel-dub   Báeth

Báethellach   Rudrad (Rudrach)   Dub-dá-chrích [49]

Láeg /Mac Láech[16]   Dub-dá-leithe   Oengus   hOrgus   Oengus (Forgus)

Book of Leinster

Maethon

Mac-Ercca

Súla

Oscar [45]

Cúscraid[12]

Conbrocc   Báeth   Ambrit

Bruicce   Dróna

Tál   Sínach

Amargein   Diarmait

Senach Már   Máel-bile

Fuilne   *Andil

Báeth [48]   *Angid

---

[9] Ercc may have been a diety. He appears in the Ulster Cycle as a mythic paramount chieftain of Tara, and was later euhemerized as a legendary Bishop and Saint (O'Rah:179).

[10] Old Ir. *Suil* "Sun." *Messen-Sulad* "Fosterling of Sulá." Perhaps another name for the sun god.

[11] Cúscraid Menn was a son Conchobor Mac Nessa in the Ulster Cycle.

[12] Here begins an alternate section from the Book of Leinster.

[13] Name of Conall Cernach's father from the Ulster Cycle.

[14] Muinnter Seanaigh, *BM*.

[15] There is a Senach mac Cuilíne among the Eóganacht Mac-Caille 151 b 43.

[16] Cúchulainn's charioteer.

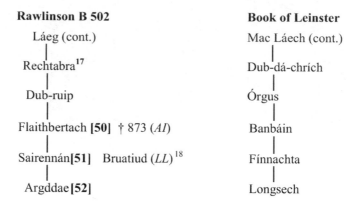

Rawlinson B 502

Láeg (cont.)
|
Rechtabra[17]
|
Dub-ruip
|
Flaithbertach **[50]** † 873 (*AI*)
|
Sairennán**[51]**   Bruatiud (*LL*) [18]
|
Argddae **[52]**

Book of Leinster

Mac Láech (cont.)
|
Dub-dá-chrích
|
Órgus
|
Banbáin
|
Fínnachta
|
Longsech

---

[17] Rí Corcu Baiscinn, † 774 (*AI*). The name appears in Ciarraige geneaologies as well.

[18] Died 899 (FM). The FM further records the death of Flann mac Flaithbertaich, chieftain of Corcu MoDruad, in 902. The *AI*, *AU*, and FM record the ascension and death of the chieftain Cett mac Flaithbertaich [55] in 907, 916/919).

Eighth–Tenth-Century Corcu Modruad Chieftains
Appearing Solely in the Annals

Flann Féorna **[53]** † 737 (FM)

Torpaid **[54]** † 769 (*AI*)

Máel-Gorm
|
Anrudán **[7]**[19] assumed lordship 925 (FM), † 936 (*AI*)
|
Congal † 987 (FM), name not in genealogies

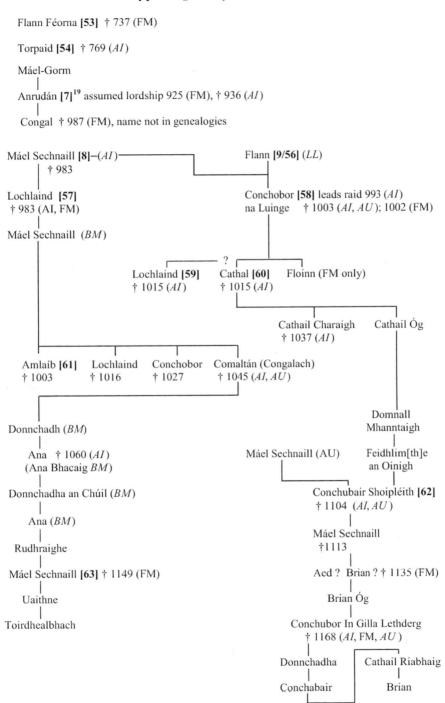

Máel Sechnaill **[8]**–(*AI*) ———————————— Flann **[9/56]** (*LL*)
| † 983

Lochlaind **[57]**   Conchobor **[58]** leads raid 993 (*AI*)
† 983 (AI, FM)   na Luinge   † 1003 (*AI, AU*); 1002 (FM)

Máel Sechnaill (*BM*)

                              ?
Lochlaind **[59]**   Cathal **[60]**   Floinn (FM only)
† 1015 (*AI*)   † 1015 (*AI*)

                                          Cathail Charaigh   Cathail Óg
                                          † 1037 (*AI*)

Amlaíb **[61]**   Lochlaind   Conchobor   Comaltán (Congalach)
† 1003   † 1016   † 1027   † 1045 (*AI, AU*)

                                                              Domnall
                                                              Mhanntaigh
Donnchadh (*BM*)
| Feidhlim[th]e
Ana † 1060 (*AI*)   Máel Sechnaill (AU)   an Oinigh
(Ana Bhacaig *BM*)
| Conchubair Shoipléith **[62]**
Donnchadha an Chúil (*BM*)   † 1104 (*AI, AU*)
|
Ana (*BM*)   Máel Sechnaill
| †1113
Rudhraighe
| Aed ? Brian ? † 1135 (FM)
Máel Sechnaill **[63]** † 1149 (FM)
| Brian Óg
Uaithne
| Conchubor In Gilla Lethderg
Toirdhealbhach   † 1168 (*AI*, FM, *AU*)

                                          Donnchadha   Cathail Riabhaig

                                          Conchabair   Brian

[19] Both Máel-Gorm and Anrudán are in geneaology of the Dál Cais: 153 a 10.

UÍ LOCHLAINN, UÍ CONCHOBAIR CHIEFTAINS FROM *CAITHRÉIM THOIRDHEALBHAIGH* AND OTHER CONTEMPORARY SOURCES

Dermot mac Muirtaigh *florit* 1268 (*ACl*)
   Sean Dublochlainn *florit* 1268 (*ACl*)

Conchobur Carrach O'Lochlainn † 1283 (*AI*)

Conghlach O'Lochlainn *florit* 1283 (*CT*)
                                 Domnall O'Conchobair
                                   florit 1283, 1316 (*CT*)
     Mathgamain O'Lochlainn
     florit 1284 (*ACl*)
                       Aed O'Conchobuir
                       obit 1313 (*AI*)
Donnchad O'Lochlainn *florit* 1313 (*AI*)

Donchadh † 1361 (FM)
                            Fedhlimidh an einigh Daonachdach
                                 † 1365 (*ACl*)
Irial † 1396 (FM)

Notes

Chapter 1. Theoretical Considerations

1. By "predictable," I mean that an institution will bring together individuals with stereotypical roles who act to bring about a recognized objective and hold to specific norms of behavior that serve to regulate interactions between them. I do not mean that the specific outcome, or even the future nature of the roles, objectives, and behavioral norms, is invariant or predetermined.

2. In practice, his application of this concept to sets of data was somewhat ambiguous and arbitrary. It could be taken to apply to subcultures within a state-level society as well as to the state itself (1955:47). Further, his application of the concept to archaeological data was divergent from his use of the concept in ethnographic contexts (see Gibson and Geselowitz 1988:16–17).

3. I have deviated somewhat from the standard term for this measure of scale, which is "administrative levels," as I believe the word "administrative" inaccurately and incompletely conveys the role of leader at any level in a chiefdom. Otherwise my use is analogous.

4. Carneiro, citing the work of Gregory Johnson (1978) and Sarunas Milisauskas (1978), notes that these authors concur that states can be distinguished from chiefdoms based on the number of levels of authority that they exhibit, chiefdoms possessing two levels of authority and states three. This study will show this position to be manifestly untrue, as complex Irish chiefdoms routinely exhibited at least three levels of authority. As Carneiro points out, qualitative criteria are as important as structural criteria in distinguishing levels of sociocultural integration (1981:46). Chiefdoms vary too greatly in structure in different cultural settings to establish any rigid standards for distinguishing them from states on the basis of the number of levels of authority.

5. White symbolizes purity, a quality leaders were supposed to exhibit in their faces and in their appurtenances (e.g., the white rod they held during inauguration ceremonies).

6. Feinman and Neitzel's survey of pre-state societies is the most flagrant example of the blurring of sociocultural distinctions (1984). They critique the importance of redistribution as an aspect of leadership, but their survey includes few societies that would be considered to be chiefdoms (Earle 1987:288). Indeed, their study can be taken as an example of the importance of the concept of the level of sociocultural integration as a way of instilling control in cross-cultural comparisons.

7. A number of scholars have taken the position in recent decades that urbanism had appeared within Gaelic society in the Early Middle Ages in the form of "monastic towns" (Bradley 1998; Doherty 1985; Soderberg 2004). Even if large monasteries qualify as towns, this form of settlement was the exception, not the rule.

Chapter 3. Clare's Chiefdoms at the Dawn of History

1. Beyond the four hundred stones with complete or partial inscriptions, there are numerous fragments.

2. Though the earliest manuscripts of the *CGSH* date to the twelfth century, Ó Riain cites evidence of a date of composition in prior centuries (1985:xvii). Another text, *On the mothers of the saints*, attests Sin as the mother of these saints (722.22), but Ó Riain sees this as a name derived from Sinell (ibid.:220).

3. The reference to a lake is annotated in the margin as *Eas Ruaydh* (Waterfall of Ruadh). This annotation is in Modern Irish, and the only waterfalls bearing the name Eas Ruaidh from the *Onomasticon Goedelicum* (E. Hogan 1910) are on the Erne in Donegal, and at the head of Killery Bay in Galway.

4. Along with Máelán, another of the five sons of Sinill from *CGSH*.

5. "In the Irish tradition Lugh is portrayed as a shining god of light." (Green 1992:135).

6. Corcomroe is an Anglicization of Corcu MoDruad.

7. The *Annals of Ulster* identifies the chieftain simply as mac Talamhnaigh. Aithechdai appears in the Corcu Baiscind genealogy. Aithechdai would be an unusual name for an aristocrat, as it means "vassal." It therefore seems to be a placeholder inserted by a victorious chiefdom.

8. I should acknowledge contrary evidence, however, that Senán and Crónán appear as ancestor-deities in the genealogy of the Corcu MoDruad in Rawl. B 502, but not in the Corcu Baiscind genealogy. It is possible that the Corcu Baiscind genealogy had been more extensively altered as a result of their declining political fortunes.

9. Bishop Ercc of the Cíarraige figures prominently in the hagiography of several saints of the southwest of Ireland. He may be a euhemerized ancestor deity of this group.

10. Plummer lays out the hypothesis based on how the saint's name is spelled in other contexts that the saint's nickname *Creiche* (plunder) may have originally been *Criche* (border) (Plummer 1925:11–12).

11. The townland Craggenboy in Rath parish in Inchiquin Barony, may also bear the name of this personage (e.g., *Creagán Báeth* [Báeth's Rocky Hill]).

12. It was also perhaps *Cathair Fhionnúirach* in the twelfth-century *Book of Rights* (Westropp 1902:121). Caherballykinvarga would have been *Cathair Baile Cinn Mharga*, which could be translated as "The Dwelling Place of the District of the Boundary's End." The name as it applies to the district containing the cashel is first attested in the fourteenth-century O'Brien's Rental (Hardiman 1828). That this place-name originated following the Early Middle Ages is indicated by the fact that *marga* is a loan word from Old Norse related to "march," and most likely refers to the site's proximity to the barony boundary between Corcomroe and Burren. This boundary originated with the partition of the Corcu MoDruad chiefdom in the twelfth century. The place-name element *baile*, reserved

usually for a chieftain's demesne territory, hints at the site's former aristocratic status (Gibson 2008b).

13. Farther to the south of Caherballykinvarga are two townlands and a rath site named Tullagh (*tulach* [mound or cairn]). This place-name usually designates an inauguration site. Though there is a hill, there does not seem to be any mound or cairn.

14. They were located in the vicinity of modern Killarney. The boundaries of their chiefdom became fossilized in the diocese of Aghadoe.

15. The name of a river, and currently the name of a parish.

16. Mo-Báeth is a hypochoristic name created by adjoining the first-person singular possessive pronoun to the name Báeth. This practice was common for the names of early Irish clerics.

17. Westropp states that Cluain Fhionnabhair was "probably Clooney in Kilfenora" (1900:110). If he means Clooney parish in the diocese of Kilfenora (Corcomroe Barony), the parish church here was dedicated to Lonan (ibid.:109, 138).

Chapter 4. An Early Medieval Chiefdom of Northern Clare: Archaeological Investigations

1. The "modern" stone boundary walls of the Burren (those in current use) range from 90 cm to 2 m in height, and probably average 110 cm in height.

Chapter 5. Reconstructing the Social Order of Irish Chiefdoms through Settlement

1. A souterrain is a manmade underground passage, often accompanied by chambers, constructed from the LIA IIc period on in Ireland.

2. For a more complete inventory, see Lynn 1978, Table 4.

3. *Rath* (gs. *raith*) is the capital given to a client by a patron, usually in the form of livestock. According to the Royal Irish Academy dictionary, *turchluide* is "stock granted by a lord to his client, apparently in addition to *turchrecc* and *rath* and equal in value to a client's honor price" (*DIL* 1983 (T):387). By my interpretation, *turchrecc* is the payment in purchase of the honor-price of a base client (*daerceile*). Indeed, by selling his honor-price to his lord, he becomes a *daerceile* (see Gibson 1982:62–65). By this interpretation this payment seems superfluous. It is more likely that *turchluide* is simply a linguistic variant of *turchrecc*.

4. Charles-Edwards proposes that during the seventh century, this unit was reduced in size to include only the male descendants of a common grandfather, what earlier had been termed the

gelfine (1972:15–17). He cites no textual evidence in support of this claim.

5. Unfortunately, the wall section that was recorded at this site was not wide enough for a chronological estimate to be made.

6. The estimate for the volume of stone incorporated into Caherballykinvarga includes the *chevaux-de-fris*. The volume of stone in the *chevaux-de-fris* was estimated on the assumption of a solid band of stone 40 cm thick and as wide as the present distribution of slabs, surrounding the site, to approximate the thickly placed slabs, which, from my recollection, are 1.5–2 m long.

Chapter 6. Of Settlements and Boundaries: Reconstructing the Chiefdom of Tulach Commáin

1. Moher is the English spelling for the Clare Irish dialect word *mothar*, meaning a stone enclosure or ruined cashel site.

2. The boundary incorporates the southwestern circumference of the enclosure wall of C-298, leaving the interior of the cashel in Burren Barony.

3. There are perhaps two relevant bits of information that may (or may not) tie in here. According to Robinson's map, there is some folklore surrounding the servant of St. Colmán Mac Duach. There is a church attributed to the saint in Keelhilla townland in the extreme northeastern corner of Carran parish. The servant's grave is indicated near this church, which is 6.5 km from the pass at Deelin. The name of the small cashel to the north of Cahercommaun, C-43, is Cahereenmoyle, which in Irish is *Cathairín Moil* (the Dwelling of Maol). This could also be a folk attribution by which the servant to the chieftain at Cahercommaun was believed to have lived in the small cashel.

4. One suspects that Tulach Commáin was once greater in extent to the east and west, due to Caherconnell's location adjacent to the western border, and to the curious extensions of this part of Drumcreehy parish here to the northeast and southwest parallel to the reconstructed border. On the other hand, the demesne land of Cahercommaun ends nearly at the western boundary of the chiefdom. Perhaps what was in the Middle Ages Uí Flanchadha (what is now Kilkeedy parish) was formerly a part of, or allied with, Tulach Commáin.

Chapter 7. The Rulers of Tulach Commáin

1. In the seventeenth century, the territory of *Gleann Chuinn* took in the entire valley, as one would imagine from the name alone. The *Books of Survey and Distribution* lists the present townlands of this valley as subunits of "Gleankeene" (1967:519).

2. Conchobur Ruad was contesting his brother Donnchad Cairprech for the office of paramount chieftain of Thomond.

3. This 16.6-year mean regnal generation length is at great variance from the 33.38-year figure arrived at by Diarmuid Ó Murchadha from his study of the genealogies (2004:319). I think that the 16.6-year estimate is acceptable when one takes into account that Ó Murchadha's figure was arrived at through the analysis of "early genealogies," whereas the Clann hIffernáin genealogy dates to the latter two stages of the Early Middle Ages. The 33.38-year figure would also seem way too high for real generation lengths in an era when few would expect to see their fiftieth birthday, and so must reflect the regular omission of chieftains from the lists.

4. In the genealogy, Colmán is a son of Conall [35].

Chapter 8. The World of Brian Bóroimhe

1. The territories of Thomond of the Middle Ages had names derived from the names of the present or former inhabitants, or rather, the ramages that dominated them. Uí Toirdhealbhaigh (the descendants of Toirdhealbhach) was named after a maximal ramage named for their ancestor Toirdhealbhach. Ó Corráin renders the name Toirdhealbhach as Tairdelbach. Though I am no expert in Irish, I imagine that the first version is late Middle Irish or Modern Irish, while the latter version is Old Irish.

2. At least that is how they are presented in the saga. This may have been a device by the author to vilify their chieftain Donnabhán mac Cathal, whom Brian killed (Todd 1965:103).

3. Máel Muad mac Bran, the *rí* of Caisel, died in battle against Brian in 978 AD. Brian is referred to as the *rí Caisil* in the Annals of Ulster in 999 AD. The first reference to Cenn Coradh is in 1010 AD in the *Annals of Innisfallen*.

4. "It is conceivable that the predecessors of the Dalcassians held sacred the grave of some chief, and that their later conquerors marked their victory by using it as a place of inauguration for their own princes, from the fifth to sixteenth century" (Westropp 1896a:58).

5. Its replacement was cut down by Áed Uí Concobhair of Connaught in 1051 AD (Westropp 1896a:59).

6. For example, *Coibnes Uisci Thairidne* "nemed cille no dúin, no (a) maigen f[e]irt" ("sacred [land] of a

church or of a chieftain's residence, or of the place of a grave mound").

7. Capital of the Connachta in Co. Galway.

8. Two sons of Dub-dá-crích [49] were named Óengus, by some genealogies. It is possible that at one time, Clann hIffernáin and the Aes Iar Forgus claimed a linkage with the Corcu MoDruad genealogy through these names.

Chapter 9. The World of *Caithréim Thoirdhealbhaigh*

1. I have followed the convention of the saga in calling this faction Clann Toirdhealbhaich. Aoife Nic Ghiollamhaith refers to this faction as Clann Taidc, after a reference in fragmentary annals from the West of Ireland (Gwynn 1924–1927:151).

2. Thomas de Clare was following a conventional pattern of Irish politics that existed prior to the arrival of the Anglo-Normans. Outside powers frequently took advantage of succession struggles to impose their will upon a chiefdom.

3. *Tríocha céad* translates literally as "thirty hundred," and in medieval times stood for what in earlier ages would be the territory of a *túath*. Its use probably implies the growing territorialization of these units – certainly significant in respect to the O'Deas who only inhabited half of the *tricha céd uachtarach*, or "upper *tríocha céad*" (Frost 1978:128; J. Hogan 1929; Macnamara 1901:204; for the use of the term *tríocha céad* in Caithréim Toirdhealbhaigh see O'Grady 1929 26:4). In CT *tricha céd uachtarach* would seem to refer also to the Burren (O'Grady 1929 27:5).

4. According to Westropp, Tuathglae included parts of the parishes of Clooney, Kilfenora, and Killaspuglonane in Corcomroe Barony (1900:119).

5. The *rechtaire* was the linguistic ancestor of the *maor*, or "steward" discussed above – one of the most ancient offices of record in Ireland.

6. In the Irish *Life of Mac Creiche*, St. Blathmac seems to have been the principal saint of Cenél Fearmaic (Plummer 1925). A church and rath-type settlement associated with him is in nearby Rath parish, and so this may have been an earlier capital of the O'Deas.

7. According to Westropp, Tully O'Dea does not match the physical description of the hill in the text. He preferred the hill of Cahernalough as the location of the battle (1903:154). He would attribute the misidentification to the more restricted application of the place-name in modern times. However, without contradicting him, I would prefer to see the transfer of the battle's location to Tully O'Dea as the effect of

the attraction that this auspicious spot held for the siting of important events for poets, who were, after all, the remaining fonts of Celtic religious culture and belief.

Chapter 10. The Political Topography of Late Medieval Clare

1. Frost also cites data from a list contained in a Trinity manuscript that he claims dates from 1580 (1978:1–2). He did not, however, publish this tract and so it is impossible for me to check it against the published list.

2. In the fourteenth-century saga *Caithréim Thoirdhealbhaigh* it is named *Tulach na nEspog* (modern Irish *Tulach na nEaspag*), "Hill of the Bishop."

3. This figure may be somewhat conservative. The surnames of a number of the castle proprietors are not given and I have combed the genealogical and historical sources to identify only two of these (Teig and Donough mac Murrough O'Brien).

4. It must be kept in mind, however, that the list is probably not complete, giving only the principal aristocratic lineage capitals. This fact will be brought out in subsequent analysis.

5. The word *sliocht* (pl. *sleachta*) in modern Irish can mean a mark, track, or trace, or offspring or progeny. From its use in the texts, it is clear that it refers to an aristocratic lineage, probably descended from a former *rí* (chieftain).

6. In fact, the establishment of O'Brien political supremacy in Inchiquin occurred several centuries prior to the creation of formal baronies by the English. It is, moreover, clear that the usurpation of the lordship of Corcomroe was in fact a usurpation from an examination of a deed from 1582 which lists the surviving and numerous O'Conor aristocrats (White 1893:393).

7. Feargus mac Conchubair meic Maoilsechlainn [Uí Conchubair] suffered the theft, and the fine resulting from the theft was paid to Taodhg mac Feidhleme Uí Conchubair, with a lesser amount to his son Taodhg Og. The names of these individuals do not turn up in any other text but the *Annals of the Four Masters* record the slaying of a Feidhleme Uí Conchubair in 1482. A Conchubair Uí Conchubair was slain in 1471 (Frost 1978:94–95). If Taodgh was a son of this Feidhleme, the theft could have occurred around 1500 AD.

8. For the most part I have retained James Hardiman's translation. Here I have made small changes to the translation in order to render it more literal. The names are rendered as they

occur in the Irish text except, for instance, where a surname occurs in the genitive form. In those cases I have given the Anglicized version of the name.

9. It is also probable that the victim died during the raid, since a lone woman, Moir Ini Domnallain, is designated to receive the smallest portion of the fine. This circumstance would make all the proceedings more credible.

10. "agus a tabairt uadha aris...."

11. Also spelt Ennistymon.

12. "an baile do ghabil do Toirdhealbhac, agus an baile do chongbáil aige, acus gan cóir na ceart na cunradh do bhedh aca an mbaile acht a ndearnadar fein don da ghabhail sin de mithoil muintire an baile."

13. The origins of this text are not given by White. It is introduced in the appendix by the catalogue(?) number 2603.

14. This covenant has been translated by both Frost and White from the original text in Irish, but they give differing years for its origin. The original has not been published (Frost 1978:20–21; White 1893:392–393).

15. Máire Ní Loingsigh noted this tendency in her data in her study of the location of castles in Late Medieval North Donegal (1994).

16. Tromroe, the O'Brien center in Ibrackan, was not a major political center in Tudor times. The ramage at this castle had authority over Ibrackan and the Aran Islands (Frost 1978:148).

17. The barony name is given as "Gregans" in the list, and baronies are often called after their capitals.

18. The chieftain's name is rendered corruptly in several Tudor documents. It is actually Uaithne, and so appears in a mortgage or "pledging" deed of 1562 (Hardiman 1828:70). Owney is probably the closest phonetic English equivalent. He died in 1591.

19. "AD 1590. O'Lochlainn – Uaithne mac Maoileachlainn mic Rudhraighe mic Ana – died, and his son Rosa, and his grandson Uaithne were contending with each other for his place." (Annals of the Four Masters)

20. If this is true, then Rossa's father would have been Ruaidhrí, as one brother was Uaithne mac Rossa mac Ruaidhrí. This would make Rossa a brother of Uaithne, and not a son, as Uaithne's father was Ruaidhrí. As a caution against this interpretation, it must be remembered that the same names were used repeatedly by aristocratic lineages, and the O'Lochlainn genealogy was replete with Uaithnes and Rossas.

21. One is reminded of Donnell O'Brien being bought off of his claims on the paramountcy of Thomond (Clare) in 1564 after protracted fighting with his nephew, who was installed by the Earl of Sussex. He was made paramount over Corcomroe by the treaty, which lies in the northwestern periphery of the province (Nicholls 1972:158).

22. The inquisition is interesting, for apparently O'Davoren was sitting on a jury convened in Ennis with other Brehons for the purpose of establishing the territorial divisions of Thomond for the English crown. This would demonstrate that the Brehons were thought to be most knowledgeable as a class with respect to political and property divisions – not surprising, since it was they who were most frequently called upon to arbitrate disputes over land.

23. The earliest reference I can find to this family is an entry from 1364 AD in the *Annals of Connacht.* "1364 8. Gilla na Naem Uí Duib da Boirenn, *ollam* (master) in Brehon Law of Corcumruadh, died this year." This man's first name translates as "Boy-servant of the Saint."

24. The place-name Carrowilliam, which appears in the book and on the Down Map, is probably today preserved as the place-name Carrownanweelaun (*Ceathrú na Faoileán*, the Quarter of the Seagull) in Ballvelaghan townland.

25. This fact is also corroborated for Finavarra in a conveyance deed of 1612 (Hardiman 1828:91).

26. In his descriptions of the ancient settlements of the Late Iron Age, Westropp frequently referred to "cahers." In his time, and in the modern English vernacular of Co. Clare, the term connotes the dwellings with circular stone enclosure walls, known in the vernacular of Irish archaeology as cashels. This is because so many of the cashels have Caher as a part of their place-name. It is possible that in the dialect of the region, *cathair* had a more specific meaning than it generally did in the Irish language, and referred chiefly to the homesteads of stone.

27. The first mention of a church at Kilfennora is in the *Annals of Innisfallen* in an entry of 1055 AD: "[1055] Murchad Ua Briain was attacked in Corcu Mruad, and Tairdelbach (Ua Briain) inflicted a great slaughter upon him. Two kings of Corcu Bascinn, namely Ua Baiscind and the son of Assíd mac Domnall, with other nobles, were slain therein." The stone church of *Cell Fhinnabrach* was completely burned.

28. The Down map and *Books of Survey and Distribution* would seem to indicate that the townland of Polquilicka was a part of this block, and together with Sheshymore equaled one quarter. However, a writ of 1683 identifies Polquilicka with Balleyganner, which lies to the west of Shehymore

(Ainsworth 1961: no. 1198). The *Books of Survey and Distribution* states that the Earl of Thomond owned all of Sheshymore, which came to two-thirds quarter. Polquilicka would then account for the remaining third. It was owned jointly by Connor O'Lochlainn and Donnough mac Rossa O'Lochlainn (1967:459). A sizable portion of this land behind the castle is enclosed by huge coursed stone walls. These have not been surveyed.

29. Lisduane might be identified with the site of *Cathair Lios na nDrom*, which is located in Poulnaborne townland, just to the north of Caherconnell.

Chapter 11. An Overview of the Social and Political Systems of Thomond

1. Even then, the O'Lochlainn and O'Davoren aristocrats managed to hold onto their lands following the Restoration. Turlough O'Lochlainn married the Protestant Mayor of Galway's daughter and assumed her last name of Martyn. They continued to own the lands at the center of the former chiefdom into the twentieth century (Cunningham 1978).

2. I don't follow Mac Airt's translation exactly as I have amended the social terminology.

Glossary of Irish Terms

áighe fine The "pillar of the family." The head of a *derbfine*.

baile The district immediately surrounding an aristocrat's residence and, in the Middle Ages, the largest territorial subdivision of the *tríocha céd*.

carn "cairn" – a heap of stones.

caiseal "cashel" – a habitation site with concentric stone walls.

cashel See *caiseal*.

cathair "caher" – a dwelling place. In modern Clare vernacular, a circular stone fort.

cedhramrum "quarter" – an Irish land unit.

céile "companion" – a client.

cenél "race, family, or descendants" – collective term connoting an aristocratic ramage.

cell, cill "church."

clann "children (of)" – collective term connoting an aristocratic ramage or faction thereof.

crannóg a chiefly residence established on an artifical island in a lake or marsh.

daer "unfree, base, or servile."

derbfine "true family" – the old Irish intermediate *ramage* consisting of the common male descendants of a great grandfather.

dún A chieftain's residence.

gelfine The senior sublineage of the *derbfine*.

ingen "daughter (of)."

mac "son (of)."

maor Early Modern Irish term for a steward.

maersecht The administration of a steward.

muintir "people (of)" see clann or cenél.

mór thúath "great *túath*" – a composite chiefdom or chiefdom confederacy.

óg "(the) younger."

ráth Habitation encircled by concentric earthen banks and ditches.

rí (dat. pl. *rígaib*) Chieftain.

rí ruirech Paramount chieftain.

seiseach "plowland" a subdivision or land unit.

saer "free, noble."

sliocht Multilineage aristocratic kin group.

tánaiste "second" – in theory, the designated successor to an Irish chieftain but often his most powerful rival who has been bought off.

tearmann The demesne lands of a church.

tríocha céd "thirty hundred" – a primary chiefdom in Medieval period times.

túath A chiefdom of the Early Middle Ages.

tulach A mound or low hill.

Uí, Ua, í "grandson(s) or descendant(s) (of)" – most frequently a collective term denoting an aristocratic ramage.

References

Ainsworth, John F. 1961. *The Inchiquin Manuscripts.* Irish Manuscripts Commission. Dublin: Stationery Office.

1865–1901. *The Ancient Laws and Institutes of Ireland.* Commissioners for Publishing the Ancient Laws and Institutes of Ireland. 6 volumes, edited by W. N. Hancock and others, John O'Donovan and Eugene O'Currey translators. Dublin: HMSO.

1896. *The Annals of Clonmacnoise.* Connell Mageoghagan (trans.), edited by Denis Murphy. Dublin: Extra volume of the *RSAI* for 1893–5.

1944. *Annála Connacht.* The Annals of Connacht, (A.D. 1224–1554), edited by A. Martin Freeman. Dublin: Dublin Institute for Advanced Studies.

1848–51. *The Annals of the Kingdom of Ireland by the Four Masters* (7 vols.), edited by John O'Donovan. Dublin: B. Geraghty.

1988 (1944). *The Annals of Innisfallen,* edited by Seán Mac Airt. Dublin: The Dublin Institute for Advanced Studies.

1887–1901. *Annála Uladh.* The Annals of Ulster (4 vols.), edited by W. M. Hennessy and B. MacCarthy. Dublin: HMSO.

1983. *Annals of Ulster.* (2 vols.), edited by Seán Mac Airt and Gearóid Mac Niocaill. Dublin: Dublin Institute for Advanced Studies.

Anderson, David G. 1994. *The Savannah River Chiefdoms.* Tuscaloosa: The University of Alabama Press.

1996a. Chiefly cycling and large-scale abandonments as viewed from the Savannah River basin. In John F. Scarry (ed.), 150–191.

1996b. Fluctuations between simple and complex chiefdoms: Cycling in the Late Prehistoric Southeast. In John F. Scarry (ed.), 231–252.

Anderson, David G., David W., Stahle, and Malcolm K. Cleaveland. 1995. Paleoclimate and the potential food reserves of Mississippian societies: a case study from the Savannah River Valley. *American Antiquity* 60:259–286.

Anthony, David W. 2007. *The Horse, the Wheel, and Language.* Princeton: Princeton University Press.

Applebaum, Shimon. 1954. The agriculture of the British Iron Age as exemplified at Figheldean Down, Wiltshire. *Proceedings of the Prehistoric Society* 20:103–114.

Arbuthnot, Sharon 2005. Cóir Anmann: A Late Middle Irish Treatise on Personal Names. *Irish Texts Society,* vol. 59. London.

Arensberg, Conrad and Solon Kimball. 1940. *Family and Community in Ireland.* Cambridge, MA: Harvard University Press.

Arnold, Jeanne E. and Anabel Ford. 1980. A statistical examination of settlement patterns at Tikal, Guatemala. *American Antiquity* 45 (4): 713–726.

Barker, Tom and Graeme Rasmussen. 1998. *The Etruscans.* Oxford: Blackwell Publishers.

Beck, Lois. 1986. *The Qashqa'I of Iran.* New Haven, CT: Yale University Press.

Bennett, Isabel and Eoin Grogan. 1993. Excavations at Mooghaun South, Co. Clare. Preliminary report on the 1992 season. *Discovery Programme Reports* 1:39–43.

Berger, Rainer. 1995. Radiocarbon dating of Early Medieval Irish monuments. *PRIA* 95C:159–174.

Berry, Walter E. 1987. Southern Burgundy in Late Antiquity and the Middle Ages. In *Regional Dynamics,* edited by Carole L. Crumley and William H. Marquardt, 447–607. San Diego: Academic Press.

Bhreathnach, Edel. 1999. The construction of the stone fort at Cahercommaun: a historical hypothesis. In *Discovery Programme Reports* 5:83–91. Dublin: Royal Irish Academy/Discovery Programme.

Binchy, Daniel. 1941. *Críth Gablach.* Dublin: Dublin Institute for Advanced Studies.

1954. Secular institutions. In *Early Irish Society,* edited by Myles Dillon, 52–65. Cork: Mercier Press for the Cultural Relations Committee.

1955. Irish law-tracts reedited. *Ériu* 17:52–85.

1958. The date and provenance of the Uraicecht Becc. *Ériu* 18:44–54.

1970. *Celtic and Anglo-Saxon Kingship.* Oxford: Clarendon Press.

1978. *Corpus Iuris Hibernici.* 5 vols.: Dublin: Institiúd Ard-Léinn.

Blitz, John H. 1993. *Ancient Chiefdoms of the Tombigbee.* Tuscaloosa: The University of Alabama Press.

Bogucki, Peter. 1999. *The Origins of Human Society.* Oxford: Blackwell.

Bradley, John. 1998. The monastic town of Clonmacnoise. In *Clonmacnoise Studies*, Vol. 1, edited by Heather King, 42–56. Dublin: Dúchas.

Bradley, Richard. 1984. *The Social Foundations of Prehistoric Europe.* London: Longman.

2007. *The Prehistory of Britain and Ireland.* Cambridge: Cambridge University Press.

Bugge, Alexander. 1905. *Caithréim Cellacháin Caisil.* Det Norske Historiske Kildeskriftfond. Christiania: J. Chr. Gundersens Bogtrykkeri.

Buxton, Jean. 1963. *Chiefs and Strangers: a study of political assimilation among the Mandari.* Clarendon Press: Oxford.

Byock, Jesse L. 1988. *Medieval Iceland.* Berkeley: University of California Press.

2001. *Viking Age Iceland.* London: Penguin Books.

Byrne, Francis John. 2001 (1973). *Irish Kings and High Kings.* Dublin: Four Courts Press.

Carneiro, Robert L. 1970. A theory of the origin of the state. *Science* 169:733–738.

1981. The chiefdom: precursor of the state. In *The Transition to Statehood in the New World*, edited by G. Jones and R. Krautz, 37–79. Cambridge: Cambridge University Press.

Carney, James (ed.). 1943. *Topographical Poems by Seaán Mór Ó Dubhagain and Giolla-na-Naomh Ó Huidhrín.* Dublin: Dublin Institute for Advanced Studies.

Charles-Edwards, T. M. 1971. The heir-apparent in Irish and Welsh law. *Celtica* 9:180–190.

1972. Kinship, status and the origins of the hide. *Past and Present* 56:3–33.

1976. Boundaries in Irish law. In *Medieval Settlement: Continuity and Change*, edited by P. H. Sawyer, 83–87. London: Edward Arnold.

1993. *Early Irish and Welsh Kinship.* Oxford: Clarendon Press.

2000. *Early Christian Ireland.* Cambridge: Cambridge University Press

Clinton, Mark. 2001. *The Souterrains of Ireland.* Bray: Wordwell.

Colin, J. 1998. The emergence of private property in land and the dynamics of agricultural production: A case study from the Ivory Coast. In *Property in Economic Context*, edited by A. C. Hunt and A. Gilman, 317–349. Lantham: University Press of America.

Collins, A. E. P. 1955. Excavations in Lough Faughan crannog, Co. Down, 1951–1952. *UJA* 18:45–82.

Collis, John. 1984. *The European Iron Age.* New York: Schocken Books.

Comber, M. and G. Hull. 2010. Excavations at Caherconnell cashel, Burren, Co. Clare: Implications for ringfort chronology and Gaelic settlement.' *Proceedings of the Royal Irish Academy* 110C:133–171.

Condit, Tom and Eoin Grogan. 2005. Mooghaun South: general site description. In *The North Munster Project, Vol. 1, The Later Prehistoric Landscape of South-East Clare*, edited by Eoin Grogan, 103–130. Discovery Programme Monograph No. 6. Bray: Wordwell.

Cotter, Claire. 1995. Western Stone Fort Project, interim report. In *Discovery Programme Reports* 2:1–11. Dublin: Royal Irish Academy/Discovery Programme.

1996a. Dún Aonghasa, Kilmurvey, Inis Mór. In I. Bennett (ed.) *Excavations 1995.* Bray: Wordwell.

1996b. Western Stone Fort Project, interim report. In *Discovery Programme Reports* 4: 1–14. Dublin: Royal Irish Academy/Discovery Programme.

1999. Western Stone Forts Project: Cahercommaun Fort, Co. Clare: a reassessment of its cultural context. *Discovery Programme Reports* 5: 41–95. Dublin: Royal Irish Academy/Discovery Programme.

Crabtree, Keith. 1982. Evidence for the Burren's forest cover. In *Archaeological Aspects of Woodland Ecology*, edited by Susan Limbrey and Martin Bell, 105–113. Symposia of the Association for Environmental Archaeology no. 2. Oxford: BAR International series no. 146.

Crumley, Carole. 1979. Three locational models: an epistemological assessment for anthropology and archaeology. In *Advances in Archaeological Method and Theory*, vol. 2, edited by Michael Schiffer, 141–173. New York: Academic Press.

Crumley, Carole and William Marquardt (eds.). 1987. *Regional Dynamics: Burgundian landscapes in historical perspective.* New York: Academic Press.

Cunningham, George. 1978. *Burren Journey.* Limerick: Shannonside Mid Western Regional Tourism Organisation.

Dahl, Gudrun and Anders Hjort. 1976. *Having Herds.* University of Stockholm: *Stockholm Studies in Social Anthropology 2*.

D'Altroy, Terence and T. K. Earle. 1985. Staple finance, wealth finance, and storage in the Inka political economy. *Current Anthropology* 26:187–206.

Davies, Wendy. 1993. Celtic kingships in the Early Middle Ages. In *Kings and Kingship in Medieval Europe*, edited by Anne J. Duggan, 101–124. London: King's College Centre for Late Antique and Medieval Studies.

de Paor, Máire and Liam. 1978. *Early Christian Ireland*. London: Thames and Hudson.

de Valera, Ruadhrí and Seán Ó Nualláin. 1961. *Survey of the Megalithic Tombs of Ireland*, vol. 1, Co. Clare. Dublin: Stationery Office.

Dodgshon, Robert. 1987. *The European Past*. London: Macmillan Education.

Doherty, Charles. 1985. The monastic town in early medieval Ireland. In *The Comparative History of Urban Origins in Non-Roman Europe*, edited by H. B. Clarke and A. Simms, 45–75. Oxford: British Archaeological Reports, International Series 255(i).

Drennan, Robert D. 1987. Regional demography in chiefdoms. In *Chiefdoms in the Americas*, edited by R. Drennan and C. Uribe, 307–323. Lanham: University Press of America.

Drew, David. 1982. Environmental archaeology and karstic terrains: the Burren, County Clare, Ireland. In *Archaeological Aspects of Woodland Ecology*, edited by S. Limbrey and M. Bell, 115–127. Oxford: BAR International Series no. 146.

1983. Accelerated soil erosion in a Karst area: the Burren, western Ireland. *Journal of Hydrology* 61:113–124.

Duffy, P. J. 1981. The territorial organisation of Gaelic land ownership and its transformation in Co. Monaghan 1591–1640. *Irish Geography* 14:1–26.

2001. Social and spatial order in the MacMahon lordship of Airghialla in the late sixteenth century. In *Gaelic Ireland*, edited by P. J. Duffy, D. Edwards, and E. FitzPatrick, 115–137. Dublin: Four Courts Press.

Duffy, Sean. 1997. *Ireland in the Middle Ages*. London: Macmillan Press.

Dwyer, Philip. 1878. *The Diocese of Killaloe from the Reformation to the Close of the Eighteenth Century*. Dublin: Hodges and Figgis.

Earle, Timothy K. 1978. Economic and social organization of a complex chiefdom: the Halelea District, Kaua'i, Hawaii. Ann Arbor: *University of Michigan Anthropological Papers no.63*.

1987. Chiefdoms in archaeological and ethnohistorical perspective. *Annual Review of Anthropology*:270–308.

1997. *How Chiefs Come to Power*. Stanford: Stanford University Press.

Earle, Timothy and Terrence N. D'Altroy. 1982. Storage facilities and state finance in the upper Mantaro Valley, Peru. In *Contexts for Prehistoric Exchange*, edited by Jonathon E. Ericson and T. K. Earle, 265–290. New York: Academic Press.

Edwards, Nancy. 1990. *The Archaeology of Early Medieval Ireland*. Philadelphia: University of Pennsylvania Press.

2005. The archaeology of Early Medieval Ireland, c. 400–1169: settlement and economy. In Dáibhí Ó Cróinín (ed.), 235–296.

Eogan, George. 1968. Excavations at Knowth, Co. Meath, 1962–1965. *PRIA* 66C:299–382.

1974. Report on the excavations of some passage graves, unprotected inhumation burials and a settlement site at Knowth, Co. Meath. *PRIA* 74C:11–112.

1977. The Iron Age – Early Christian Settlement at Knowth, Co. Meath, Ireland. In *Ancient Europe and the Mediterranean*, edited by Vladimir Markotic, 68–76. Warminister: Aris and Phillips Ltd.

1983. *The Hoards of the Irish Later Bronze Age*. Dublin: University College Dublin.

Evans-Pritchard, E. E. 1969 (1940). *The Nuer*. New York: Oxford University Press.

Fanning, Thomas. 1981. Excavation of an Early Christian cemetery and settlement at Reask, County Kerry. *PRIA* 81C (3): 67–172.

Feinman, Gary and Jill Neitzel. 1984. Too many types: an overview of sedentary prestate societies in the Americas. In *Advances in Archaeological Method and Theory*, vol. 7, edited by Michael Schiffer, 39–102. New York: Academic Press.

Finch, T. F. 1971. *Soils of County Clare*. National Soil Survey of Ireland, Soil Survey Bulletin no. 23. Dublin: An Foras Talúntais.

Firth, Raymond. 1929. *The Primitive Economics of the New Zealand Maori*. London: George Routledge and Sons.

1963 (1936). *We, the Tikopia*. Boston: Beacon Press.

1965. *Primitive Polynesian Economy*. New York: Norton.

FitzPatrick, Elizabeth. 2004. *Royal Inauguration in Gaelic Ireland, c. 1100–1600*. Woolbridge, Suffolk: The Boydell Press.

Fitzpatrick, Martin. 2001. Cahermore stone fort, Co. Clare: Survey and excavation. *North Munster Antiquarian Journal* 41:45–64.

Flannery, Kent. 1995. Prehistoric social evolution. In *Research Frontiers in Anthropology*, edited by C. Ember and M. Ember, 1–26. Englewood, New Jersey: Prentice Hall.

1998. The ground plans of archaic states. In *Archaic States*, edited by Gary M. Feinman and Joyce Marcus, 14–57. Santa Fe: School of American Research Press.

1999. Process and agency in early state formation. *Cambridge Archaeological Journal* 9:1, 3–21.

Foster, Sally M. 1989. Spatial patterns in the Scottish Iron Age. *Antiquity* 63:40–50.

Frankenstein, Susan and M. J. Rowlands. 1978. The internal structure and regional context of Early Iron Age society in southwestern Germany. *Institute of Archaeology Bulletin* 15:73–112.

Freeman, Phillip. 2001. *Ireland and the Classical World.* Austin: University of Texas Press.

Frost, James. 1978 (1893). *The History and Topography of the County of Clare.* Dublin: The Mercier Press.

Gallivan, Martin D. 2003. *James River Chiefdoms: The Rise of Social Inequality in the Chesapeake.* Lincoln: The University of Nebraska Press.

Gerriets, Marilyn. 1983. Economy and society: clientship according to the Irish laws. *Cambridge Medieval Celtic Studies* 6:43–61.

Gibson, D. Blair. 1982. *Craft Production and Consumption in Ireland 200–1200 A.D.* Unpublished master's thesis on file at University College, Dublin.

1988. Agro-pastoralism and regional social organization in early Ireland. In *Tribe and Polity in Late Prehistoric Europe,* edited by D. Blair Gibson and Michael N. Geselowitz, 41–68. New York: Plenum.

1990. *Tulach Commáin: A view of an Irish chiefdom.* Ph.D. Dissertation. Ann Arbor: University Microfilms International.

1995. Chiefdoms, confederacies, and statehood in early Ireland. In *Celtic Chiefdom, Celtic State,* edited by B. Arnold and D. B. Gibson, 116–128. Cambridge: Cambridge University Press.

2000. Nearer, my chieftain, to thee: central place theory and chiefdoms, revisited. In *Hierarchies in Action, Cui Bono?* edited by Michael W. Diehl, 241–263. Carbondale: Southern Illinois University Press.

2004. Scale and its discontents. In *Exploring the Role of Analytical Scale in Archaeological Interpretation,* edited by James R. Mathieu and Rachel E. Scott, 27–44. Oxford: BAR International Series 1261.

2008a. The hill-slope enclosures of the Burren, Co. Clare. *PRIA* 107C:1–29.

2008b. Chiefdoms and the emergence of private property in land. *Journal of Anthropological Archaeology* 27:46–62.

2010. Celtic democracy. In *Proceedings of the Harvard Celtic Colloquium* 28, edited by K. Conley, E. Lehman-Shriver, and S. Zeiser, 40–62. Cambridge: Harvard University Press.

2011. Chiefdom confederacies and state origins. *Journal of Social Evolution and History.* 10(1): 215–233.

Gibson, D. B. and Michael N. Geselowitz. 1988. The evolution of complex society in late prehistoric Europe: toward a paradigm. In *Tribe and Polity in Late Prehistoric Europe,* edited by D. B. Gibson and M. N. Geselowitz, 3–37. New York: Plenum.

Gifford, E.W. 1929. *Tongan Society.* Honolulu: Bernice P. Bishop Museum Bulletin 8.

Giraldus Cambrensis. 1982. *The History and Topography of Ireland,* translated by John J. O'Meara. Penguin Books.

Goldman, Irving. 1955. Status rivalry and cultural evolution in Polynesia. *American Anthropologist* 57: 680–697.

1970. *Ancient Polynesian Society.* Chicago: The University of Chicago Press.

Gowen, Margaret and Georgina Scally. 1996. *A Summary Report on Excavations at Exchange Street Upper/Parliament Street Dublin.* Temple Bar Archaeology Collections 4. Dublin: Temple Bar Properties.

Graham, J. M. 1970. Rural society in Connaught 1600–1640. In *Irish Geographical Studies,* edited by N. Stephens and R. E. Glasscock, 192–208. Belfast: Department of Geography, Queens University.

Grant, Alexander. 2000. The construction of the early Scottish state. In *The Medieval State,* edited by J. R. Maddicott and D. M. Palliser, 47–71. London: The Hambledon Press.

Grant, Christine. 1995. Mapping a Bronze Age Burren landscape. *Archaeology Ireland* 9 (1): 31–33.

Green, Miranda J. 1992. *Dictionary of Celtic Myth and Legend.* London: Thames and Hudson.

Grogan, Eoin. 1995. Excavations at Mooghaun South, 1993. Interim report. *Discovery Programme Reports* 2, 57–61. Dublin: Royal Irish Academy/ Discovery Programme.

1996a. North Munster Project. In *Discovery Programme Reports* 4, 26–46. Dublin: Royal Irish Academy/Discovery Programme.

1996b. Excavations at Mooghaun South, 1994. Interim report. *Discovery Programme Reports* 4, 47–57. Dublin: Royal Irish Academy/Discovery Programme.

2005. *The North Munster Project, Vol. 1, The Later Prehistoric Landscape of South-East Clare,* 63–77. Discovery Programme Monograph No. 6. Bray: Wordwell.

Grogan, Eoin, T. Condit, F. O'Carroll, and A. O'Sullivan. 1995. A preliminary assessment of the prehistoric landscape of the Mooghaun study area. In *Discovery Programme Reports* 2, 47–56. Dublin: Royal Irish Academy/Discovery Programme.

Gwynn, Aubrey and D. Gleeson. 1962. *A History of the Diocese of Killaloe.* Dublin: M. H. Gill.

Hardiman, James. 1828. Ancient Irish deeds and writings, chiefly relating to landed property, from the twelfth to seventeenth century. *TRIA* 15:3–95.

Heider, Karl. 1991. *Grand Valley Dani.* Fort Worth: Holt, Rinehart and Winston.

Heist, W. W. 1965. *Vitae Sanctorum Hiberniae.* Brussels: Société des Bollandistes.

Irish Manuscripts Commission. 1967. Books of Survey and Distribution: being abstracts of various surveys and instruments of title, 1636–1703, vol.

IV County of Clare. Introductions by R. C. Simington, Index of persons, places and subjects by Breandan Mac Giolla Choille.

Hencken, Hugh O'Neill. 1935. A cairn at Poulawack, County Clare (with a report on the human remains by Hallam L. Movius Jr). *JRSAI* 65:191–222.

——— 1938. *Cahercommaun: A stone fort in County Clare.* Extra volume of the *JRSAI.* Dublin: Hodges and Figgis.

——— 1950. Lagore Crannog: an Irish royal residence of the 7th to 10th centuries A.D. *PRIA* 53C:1–247.

Herity, Michael and George Eogan. 1977. *Ireland in Prehistory.* London: Routledge & Kegan Paul.

Hogan, Edmund. 1910. *Onomasticon Goedelicum.* Dublin: Hodges and Figgis.

Hogan, James. 1929. Tricha cét and related land measures. *PRIA* 38C(7): 148–235.

——— 1932 The Irish law of kingship, with special reference to Ailech and Cenél Eoghain. *PRIA* 40(3) C: 186–254.

Hooton, E. A. 1940. Stature, head form, and pigmentation of adult male Irish. *American Journal of Physical Anthropology* 26:229–249.

Hooton, E. A. and C. W. Dupertuis. 1955. *The Physical Anthropology of Ireland. Peabody Museum Papers* vol. 30, nos. 1, 2. Cambridge, MA: Harvard Peabody Museum.

Hull, Graham and Michelle Comber. 2008. Caherconnell cashel, Caherconnell, Carron, Co. Clare: Final excavation report. Ms. submitted to the Office of Public Works, Ireland, and posted online at www.archaeology.burrenforts.ie.

Jaski, Bart. 2000. *Early Kingship and Succession.* Dublin: Four Courts Press.

Johnson, Allen and T. K. Earle. 1987. *The Evolution of Human Societies.* Palo Alto, CA: Stanford University Press.

Johnson, Gregory. 1978. Information sources and the development of decision-making organizations. In *Social Archaeology: Beyond Subsistence and Dating,* edited by C. Redman, M. Bergman, E. Curtis, W. Langhorne, N. Veraggi, J. Warner, 87–112. New York: Academic Press.

Jones, Carleton. 1997. Final Neolithic/Early Bronze Age occupation of the Burren, a brief review of the evidence. *The Other Clare* 21:36–39.

——— 1998. The discovery and dating of the prehistoric landscape of Roughan Hill in Co. Clare. *The Journal of Irish Archaeology* 9:27–43.

——— 2004. *The Burren and the Aran Islands.* Cork: The Collins Press.

Jones, Carleton and Paul Walsh. 1996. Recent discoveries on Roughan Hill, County Clare. *JRSAI* 126:87–107

Jones, G. R. J. 1976. Multiple estates and early settlement. In *Medieval Settlement: Continuity and Change,* edited by P. H. Sawyer, pp. 17–40. London: Edward Arnold.

Karugire, Samwiri R. 1971. *A History of the Kingdom of Nkore in Western Uganda to 1896.* Oxford: Clarendon Press.

Kehoe, Alice B. 2004. When theoretical models trump empirical validity, real people suffer. *Anthropology News* 45(4): 10.

Kelly, Fergus. 1976. *Audacht Morainn.* Dublin: Dublin Institute for Advanced Studies.

——— 1988. *A Guide to Early Irish Law.* Early Irish Law Series vol. III. Dublin: Dublin Institute for Advanced Studies.

——— 2000. *Early Irish Farming.* Dublin: Dublin Institute for Advanced Studies.

Kelly, Raymond. 1985. *The Nuer Conquest.* Ann Arbor: The University of Michigan Press.

Kilbride-Jones, H. E. 1937. The evolution of penannular brooches with zoomorphic terminals in Great Britain and Ireland. *PRIA* 43C:379–454.

——— 1980. Zoomorphic penannular brooches. The Society of Antiquaries of London, *Reports of the Research Committee no. 39.*

Kintz, E. R. 1983a. Class structure in a Classic Maya city. In *Coba: a Maya Metropolis,* edited by William J. Folan, Ellen R. Kintz, and Loraine Fletcher, 161–177. New York: Academic Press.

——— 1983b. Neighborhoods and Wards in a Classic Maya Metropolis. In *Coba: a Maya Metropolis,* edited by William J. Folan, Ellen R. Kintz, and Loraine Fletcher, 179–190. New York: Academic Press

Kirch, Patrick V. 1984. *The Evolution of Polynesian Chiefdoms.* Cambridge: Cambridge University Press.

Kirchoff, Paul. 1955. The principles of clanship in human society. *Davidson Journal of Anthropology* 1:1–11.

Knight, Vernon James, and Vincas P. Steponaitis (eds.). 1998. *The Archaeology of the Moundville Chiefdom.* Washington D.C.: Smithsonian Institution Press.

Kristiansen, Kristian. 1982. The formation of tribal systems in later European prehistory: northern Europe 4000–500 B.C. In *Theory and Explanation in Archaeology,* edited by C. Renfrew, M. J. Rowlands, and B. A. Seagraves, 241–280. New York: Academic Press.

——— 1991. Chiefdoms, states, and systems of social evolution. In *Chiefdoms: Power, Economy, and Ideology,* edited by Timothy Earle, 16–43. Cambridge: Cambridge University Press.

Lawlor, H. C. 1925. *The Monastery of Saint Mochaoi of Nendrum.* Belfast: The Belfast Natural History & Philosophical Society.

Leask, Harold G. 1955. *Irish Churches and Monastic Buildings. vol. 1, The first phases and the Romanesque.* Dundalk: Dundalgen Press.

Lekson, Stephen H. 1984. Great pueblo architecture of Chaco Canyon, New Mexico. Albuquerque: National Park Service, *Publications in Archaeology 18B, Chaco Canyon Studies.*

Lopinot, N. H. and W. I. Woods. 1993. Wood overexploitation and the collapse of Cahokia. In *Foraging and Farming in the Eastern Woodlands,* edited by C. M. Scarry, 206–321. Gainesville: University Press of Florida.

Lucas, A. T. 1989. *Cattle in Ancient Ireland.* Kilkenny: Boethius Press.

Lynn, C. J. 1977. Trial excavations at the King's Stables, Tray townland, Co. Armagh. *UJA* 40:42–62.

1978. Early Christian period domestic structures: a change from round to rectangular plans? *Irish Archaeological Research Forum* 5:29–45.

1982. The excavation of Rathmullan, a raised rath and motte in County Down. *UJA* 44 & 45:65–171.

1997. Comparisons and interpretations. In Dudley M. Waterman, 209–230. Belfast: The Stationery Office.

Macalister, R. A. S. and R. Lloyd Praeger. 1928. Report on the excavation of Uisneach, Co. Westmeath. *PRIA* 38C:69–127.

MacAnany, Patricia. 1995. *Living with the Ancestors.* Austin: University of Texas Press.

Mac an Bhaird, Alan. 1993. Ptolemy revisited. *Ainm* 5:1–20.

McCone, Kim. 1998. "King" and "queen" in Celtic and Indo-European. *Ériu* 49:1–12.

McErlean, T. 1983. The Irish townland system of landscape organisation. In *Landscape Archaeology in Ireland,* edited by T. Reeves-Smyth and F. Hammond, 315–340. Oxford: BAR British Series no. 116.

McLeod, Neil. 1992. *Early Irish Contract Law.* Sydney: Centre for Celtic Studies, University of Sydney. 2000. Kinship. *Ériu* 51:1–22.

McManus, Damian. 1991. *A Guide to Ogam.* Maynooth: An Sagart.

Macnamara, George U. 1901. Inchiquin, County Clare, Part I. *JRSAI* 31:204–227.

1907. Kilnaboy (*recte, Cill Inghin-Bháith*) County Clare. *JRSAI* 37:406.

Mac Neill, Eóin. 1923. Ancient Irish law: The law of status or franchise. *PRIA* 36:265–316.

1911–1912. Early Irish population groups. *Proceedings of the Royal Irish Academy* 29C:59–114.

1981 (1921). *Celtic Ireland.* Dublin: The Academy Press.

Mac Néill, Máire. 1982 (1962). *The Festival of Lughnasa.* Dundalk: Dundalgen Press for Comhairle Bhéaloideas Éireann.

Mac Niocaill, Gearóid. 1968. The 'heir designate' in Early Medieval Ireland. *The Irish Jurist* 3:326–329.

1970. Seven documents from the Inchiquin archives. *Analecta Hibernica* 26:47–67.

1972. *Ireland before the Vikings.* Dublin: Gill and Macmillan.

Mallory, James P. 1988. Trial excavations at Haughey's Fort. *Emania* 4:5–20.

1989. *In Search of the Indo-Europeans.* London: Thames and Hudson.

1997. *Emain Macha* and Naven Fort. In Dudley Waterman, 197–207. Belfast: The Stationery Office.

Mallory, James P. and T. E. Mac Neill. 1991. *The Archaeology of Ulster from Colonization to Plantation.* Belfast: Institute of Irish Studies, The Queens University of Belfast.

Marcus, Joyce and Gary Feinman. 1998. Introduction. In *Archaic States,* edited by Gary N. Feinman and Joyce Marcus, 1–13. Santa Fe: School of American Research Press.

Marquardt, William H. and Carole L. Crumley. 1987. Theoretical issues in the analysis of spatial patterning. In Crumley and Marquardt (eds.), 1–18.

Marshall, Jenny White and Claire Walsh. 2005. *Illaunloughan Island: an Early Medieval Monastery in County Kerry.* Bray: Wordwell.

Meyer, Kuno. 1912. The Laud genealogies and tribal histories from Laud 610, fol. 75 a 1. *Zeitschrift für Celtische Philologie* 8:291–338.

Milisauskas, Sarunas. 1978. *European Prehistory.* New York: Academic Press.

Milisauskas, S. and J. Kruk. 1984. Settlement organization and the appearance of low-level hierarchical societies during the Neolithic in the Bronocice microregion, southeastern Poland. *Germania* 62:1–30.

Milner, George R. 1990. The late prehistoric Cahokia cultural system of the Mississippi River Valley: foundations, florescence, and fragmentation. *Journal of World Prehistory* 4:1–43.

1998. *The Cahokia Chiefdom.* Washington D.C.: Simithsonian Institution Press.

Mitchell, Frank. 1976. *The Irish Landscape.* London: Collins.

Mitchell, William J., B. Aran, and S. Liggett. 1982. The application of statistical pattern recognition techniques in dating ancient architectural construction. *Graduate School of Architecture and Urban Planning Discussion Papers no. 168.* Los Angeles: UCLA.

Monk, Michael A. 1988. Excavations at Lisleagh ringfort, North Cork. *Archaeology Ireland* 2 (2):57–60.

1995. A tale of two ringforts: Lisleagh I and II. *Journal of the Cork Historical and Archaeological Society* 100:105–116.

1998. Early Medieval secular and ecclesiastical settlement in Munster. In Michael A. Monk and John Sheehan (eds.), 33–52.

Monk, Michael A. and John Sheehan (eds.). 1998. *Early Medieval Munster.* Cork: Cork University Press.

Monk, Michael A., John Tierney, and Michael Hannon. 1998. Archeobotanical studies and Early Medieval Munster. In Michael A. Monk and John Sheehan (eds.), 65–75.

Morgan, Lewis Henry. (1969) 1887. *Ancient Society.* Cleveland: Meridian Books.

Movius, Halam Jr. 1942. The Irish stone age, its chronology, development & relationships. Cambridge (Eng.): The University Press.

Mytum, Harold Clive. 1982. The location of early churches in northern Co. Clare. In *The Early Church in Western Britain and Ireland*, edited by S. M. Pearce, 351–361. Oxford: British Archaeological Reports International Series 102.

Nic Ghiollamhaith, Aoife. 1981. Dynastic warfare and historical writing in North Munster 1276–1350. *Cambridge Medieval Studies* 2:73–89.

1995. Kings and vassals in Later Medieval Ireland: the Uí Bhriain and the MicConmara in the fourteenth century. In *Colony and Frontier in Medieval Ireland*, edited by T. B. Barry, Robin Frame, and Katharine Simms, 201–216. London: The Hambledon Press.

Nicholls, Kenneth W. 1972. *Gaelic and Gaelicised Ireland in the Middle Ages.* Dublin: Gill and Macmillan.

1976. *Land, Law and Society in Sixteenth-Century Ireland.* O'Donnell Lecture. National University of Ireland

Ní Ghabhláin, Sinéad. 1995a. *Church, Parish, and Polity: the Medieval Diocese of Kilfenora.* Ph.D. dissertation, University of California, Los Angeles. Ann Arbor: University Microfilms.

1995b. Church and community in Medieval Ireland: the diocese of Kilfenora. *JRSAI* 125:61–84.

1996. The origin of Medieval parishes in Gaelic Ireland: the evidence from Kilfenora. *JRSAI* 126:37–61.

2006. Late twelfth-century church construction. Evidence of parish formation? In *The Parish in Medieval and Early Modern Ireland*, Elizabeth FitzPatrick and Raymond Gillespie, 147–167. Dublin: The Fourcourts Press for the Study of Irish Historical Settlement.

Ní Loingsigh, Máire. 1994. An assessment of castles and landownership in Late Medieval North Donegal. *UJA* 57:145–158.

Nugent, Pat. 2000. The dynamics of the clan system in fourteenth century Clare. In *County Clare Studies*, edited by Ciarán Ó Murchadha, 55–71. Ennis: Clare Archaeological and Historical Society.

Oberg, K. 1955. Types of social structure among the lowland tribes of South and Central America. *American Anthropologist* 57(3): 472–487.

1978 (1940). The kingdom of Ankole in Uganda. In *African Political Systems*, edited by M. Fortes and E. E. Evans-Pritchard, 121–162. Oxford: Oxford University Press.

O'Brien, M. A. 1976. *Corpus Genealogiarum Hiberniae.* Dublin: Dublin Institute for Advanced Studies.

Ó Buachalla, Liam. 1952. Contributions towards the political history of Munster. *Journal of the Cork Historical and Archaeological Society* 57:67–86.

Ó Cathasaigh, Tómas. 1977. *The Heroic Biography of Cormac Mac Airt.* Dublin: Dublin Insitute for Advanced Studies.

Ó Corráin, Donnchadh. 1971. Irish regnal succession: a reappraisal. *Studia Hibernica* 11:7–39.

1972. *Ireland before the Normans.* Dublin: Gill and Macmillan.

1973. Dál Cais – church and dynasty. *Ériu* 24:52–63.

1975. The families of Corcumroe. *NMAJ* 17:21–29.

1978. Nationality and kingship in pre-Norman Ireland. In *Nationality and the Pursuit of National Independence*, edited by T. W. Moody, 1–35. Belfast: The Appletree Press.

2005. Ireland c. 800; aspects of society. In Dáibhí Ó Cróinín (ed.), 545–607.

Ó Cróinín, Dáibhí. 1995. *Early Medieval Ireland 400–1200.* London: Longman.

2005. Ireland, 400–800 AD. In Dáibhí Ó Cróinín (ed.), 182–233.

Ó Cróinín, Dáibhí (ed.). 2005. *A New History of Ireland. Volume 1: Prehistoric and Early Ireland.* Oxford: Oxford University Press.

Ó Dónaill, Niall. 1977. *Foclóir Gaeilge-Béarla.* Baile Átha Cliath (Dublin): Oifig an tSoláthair.

O'Donnchadha, Tadhg (ed.). 1940. *An Leabhar Muimhneach* (The Book of Munster). Dublin: Coimisiún Láimhscríbhinní Na hÉireann D'Oifig Díolta Foillseacháin Rialtais.

O'Donovan, John (ed. and trans.). 1862. *Topographical Poems of John O'Dubhagain and Giolla Na Naomh O'Huidhrin.* Irish Archaeological and Celtic Society.

Ó Floinn, Raghnall. 1999. The date of some metalwork from Cahercommaun reassessed. In Cahercommaun Fort, Co. Clare: A reassessment of its cultural context. In *Discovery Programme Reports 5*, edited by Claire Cotter, 73–82. Dublin: The Discovery Programme/Royal Irish Academy.

O'Grady, Standish Hayes. 1929. Caithréim Thoirdhealbhaigh. *Irish Texts Society*, vols. 26 & 27, London.

Ó hÓgáin, Dáithí. 1999. *The Sacred Isle: Belief and Religion in Pre-Christian Ireland.* Woodbridge: The Boydell Press.

2002. *The Celts: A History.* Woodbridge: The Boydell Press.

References

Ó hÓgáin, Seán. 1938. *Conntae an Cláir: A Triocha agus a Tuatha.* Baile átha Cliath: Offig an tSoláthair.

O'Keeffe, Tadhg. 1991. *The Irish Romanesque.* Ph.D. Thesis. University College Dublin.

2003. *Romanesque Ireland.* Dublin: Four Courts Press.

O'Kelly, Michael J. 1951. An Early Bonze Age ringfort at Carrigillihy, Co. Cork. *JCHAS* 56:69–86.

Ó Murchadha, Diarmuid. 2004. Rawlinson B. 502: dating the genealogies. In *Cín Chille Cúile Texts, Saints and Places: Essays in Honour of Pádraig Ó Riain*, edited by John Carey, Máire Herbert, and Kevin Murray, 316–333. Aberystwyth: Celtic Studies Publications.

O'Rahilly, Thomas F. 1999 (1946). *Early Irish History and Mythology.* Dublin: Dublin Institute for Advanced Studies.

Ó Riain, Pádraig. 1972. Boundary association in early Irish society. *Studia Celtica* 7:12–29.

1985. *Corpus Genealogiarum Sanctorum Hiberniae.* Dublin: Dublin Institute for Advanced Studies.

Ó Ríordáin, A. B. 1971. Excavations at High Street and Winetavern Street. *Medieval Archaeology* 15:73–85.

Ó Ríordáin, Seán P. 1939–40. Excavations at Cush, Co. Limerick. *PRIA* 45C:83–181.

1949. Lough Gur excavations: Carraig Aille and the "spectacles." *PRIA* 52C:39–111.

1955. A burial with faience beads at Tara. *Proceedings of the Prehistoric Society* 21:163–173.

1979. *Antiquities of the Irish Countryside*, 5th ed. Revised by Ruaidhrí de Valera. London: Methuen.

Ó Ríordáin, Seán P. and J. B. Foy. 1941. The excavation of Leacanabuaile stone fort near Caherciveen, Co. Kerry. *JCHAS* 46:85–91.

Ó Ríordáin, Seán P. and J. Hunt. 1942. Medieval dwellings at Caherguillamore, Co. Limerick. *JRSAI* 72:37–63.

O'Sullivan, Aidan. 1998. *The Archaeology of Lake Settlement in Ireland.* Discovery Programme Monographs 4. Dublin: Discovery Programme/ Royal Irish Academy.

Palmer, R. 1984. *Danebury: An Iron Age Hillfort in Hampshire; an aerial photographic interpretation of its environs.* Royal Commission on Historical Monuments, Supplementary Series 6.

Patterson, Nerys. 1981. Material and symbolic exchange in early Irish clientship. *Proceedings of the Harvard Celtic Colloquium* 1:53–61.

1985. Kinship law or number symbolism? Models of distributive justice in Old Irish law. *Proceedings of the Harvard Celtic Colloquium* 5:49–86.

1994. *Cattle-Lords and Clansmen.* Notre Dame: The University of Notre Dame Press.

Pauketat, Timothy R. 2004. *Ancient Cahokia and the Mississippians.* Cambridge: Cambridge University Press.

2009. *Cahokia: Ancient America's Great City on the Mississippi.* New York: Viking-Penguin.

Pearson, G. W., J. R. Pilcher, M. G. Baille, D. M. Corbett and F. Qua, 1986. *Radiocarbon*, 28: 911–934.

Peebles, Christopher S. and S. M. Kus. 1977. Some archaeological correlates of ranked societies. *American Antiquity* 42:421–448.

Petty, Sir William. 1685(?). *Down Survey map of County Clare.* Reprinted in *IMC* 1967.

Plummer, Charles. 1925. *Miscellanea Hagiographica Hibernica.* Brussels: Société des Bollandistes.

Plunkett Dillon, Emma. 1983. Karren analysis as an archaeological technique. In *Landscape Archaeology in Ireland*, edited by T. Reeves-Smyth and F. Hammond, 81–94. Oxford: BAR British series no. 116.

1985. *The Field Boundaries of the Burren, Co. Clare.* Unpublished Ph.D. dissertation, Department of Geography, Trinity College, Dublin.

Polanyi, Karl. 1968. *Primitive, Archaic and Modern Economies: Essays of Karl Polanyi*, edited by George Dalton. Garden Grove N.J.: Anchor Books.

1971 (1957). The economy as an instituted process. In *Trade and Market in the Early Empires*, edited by K. Polanyi, C. M. Arensberg, and H. W. Pearson, 239–270. Chicago: Gateway Edition.

Possehl, Gregory L. 1998. Sociocultural complexity without the state. In *Archaic States*, edited by Gary M. Feinman and Joyce Marcus, 261–291. Santa Fe: School of American Research.

Power, D., E. Byrne, S. Lane, and M. Sleeman. 1997. *Archaeological Inventory of County Cork, Vol. 3: Mid-Cork.* Dublin: The Stationery Office.

Proudfoot, V. B. 1961. The economy of the Irish rath. *Medieval Archaeology* 6:94–122.

Pryor, F. M. M. 1987. Earlier Neolithic organized landscapes and ceremonial in lowland Britain. In *The Archaeology of Neolithic and Bronze Age: Recent Trends*, edited by I. A. Kines and J. Barrett, 63–72. Sheffield: Sheffield University Department of Prehistory and Archaeology.

2001. *Seahenge.* London: HarperCollins.

Quin, E. G. (ed.) *Dictionary of the Irish Language, Compact Edition.* 1983. Dublin: Royal Irish Academy.

Radner, Joan N. 1978. *Fragmentary Annals of Ireland.* Dublin: Dublin Institute for Advanced Studies.

Raftery, Barry. 1972. Irish hill-forts. In *The Iron Age in the Irish Sea Province*, edited by C. Thomas, 37–58. Council for British Archaeology, Research Report 9. London.

Raftery, Joseph. 1944. The Turoe Stone and the Rath of Feerwore. *JRSAI* 74:23–52.

Redman, Charles. 1974. Archaeological sampling strategies. *An Addison-Wesley Module in Anthropology no. 55.* Reading, Mass.

Renfrew, Colin. 1973. Monument, mobilization and social organization in Neolithic Wessex. In *The*

Explanation of Culture Change, edited by C. Renfrew, 539–558. London: Duckworth.

1974. Beyond a subsistence economy, the evolution of social organization in prehistoric Europe. In *Reconstructing Complex Societies*, edited by C. B. Moore. *Bulletin of the American School of Oriental Research* 20:69–95.

1979. *Investigations in Orkney*. London: The Society of Antiquaries.

Robinson, T. D. 1977. *The Burren: a map of the uplands of North-West Clare, Éire*. Galway.

Roche, Helen. 1997. Excavations at Ráith na Ríg, Tara, Co. Meath. Discovery Programme Reports 6, 19–82, Dublin: Royal Irish Academy.

Rosman, Abraham and P. K. Rubel. 1978. Exchange as structure, or why everyone doesn't eat his own pigs. *Research in Economic Anthropology* 1:105–130.

Rowlett, Ralph M. 1991. Western "Old European" response to early Indo-European chiefdoms. *Journal of Indo-European Studies* 19:93–122.

Roymans, Nico. 1990. *Tribal Societies in Northern Gaul: An Anthropological Perspective*. Amsterdam: Cingula.

Ryan, John. 1943. The Dalcassians. *NMAJ* 3(4):189–202.

Sagan, Eli. 1985. *At the Dawn of Tyranny*. New York: Alfred A. Knopf.

Sahlins, Marshall D. 1958. *Social Stratification in Polynesia*. Seattle: The American Ethnological Society, University of Washington Press.

1963. Poor man, rich man, big-man, chief: political types in Melanesia and Polynesia. *Comparative Studies in Society and History* 5:285–303.

1972. *Stone Age Economics*. New York: Aldine.

Scarry, John F. (ed.). 1996. *Political Structure and Change in the Prehistoric Southeastern United States*. Gainesville: University Press of Florida.

Scott, Brian G. 1976. *Ancient Ironworking in Ireland: Industrial and Technological Development to the End of the 14th century A.D.* Unpublished Ph.D. thesis, Queen's University, Belfast.

Scupin, Raymond. 1998. *Cultural Anthropology: A Global Perspective*, third ed. Upper Saddle River, N.J.: Prentice Hall.

Service, Elman. 1971 (1962). *Primitive Social Organization*. New York: Random House.

1975. *Origins of the State and Civilization*. New York: Norton.

Sexton, Regina. 1998. Porridges, gruels, and breads: the cereal foodstuffs of Early Medieval Ireland. In Michael A. Monk and John Sheehan (eds.), 76–86.

Sharpe, Richard. 1991. *Medieval Saints' Lives: An Introduction to Vitae Sanctorum Hiberniae*. Oxford: Clarendon Press.

Sheehan, John. 1982. The Early Historic church-sites of North Clare. *North Munster Antiquarian Journal* 26:29–45.

Shennan, Stephan. 1982. Ideology, change and the European Early Bronze Age. In *Symbolic and Structural Archaeology*, edited by Ian Hodder, 155–161. Cambridge: Cambridge University Press.

Simms, Katharine. 1998. The contents of later commentaries on the brehon law tracts. *Ériu* 49:23–40.

Simpson, Linzi. 1999. *Temple Bar West: Director's Findings*. Temple Bar Archaeological Reports 5. Dublin: Temple Bar Properties.

Smith, Kevin P. 2004. Patterns in time and the tempo of change: a North Atlantic perspective on the evolution of complex societies. In *Exploring the Role of Analytical Scale in Archaeological Interpretation*, edited by James R. Mathieu and Rachel E. Scott, BAR International Series 1261, 83–99. Oxford: Archaeopress.

Smith, Marvin T. 1998. *Coosa: The Rise and Fall of a Southwestern Mississippian Chiefdom*. Gainesville: University Press of Florida.

Smythe, Alfred. 1982. *Celtic Leinster: towards an historical geography of early Irish civilization A.D. 500–1600*. Blackrock (Ireland): Irish Academic Press.

Soderberg, John. Distinguishing the local from the regional: Irish perspectives on urbanization in Early Medieval Europe. In *Exploring the Role of Analytical Scale in Archaeological Interpretation*, edited by James R. Mathieu and Rachel E. Scott, BAR International Series 1261, 67–82. Oxford: Archaeopress.

Sproule, David. 1984. Origins of the Éoganachta. *Ériu* 35:31–37.

Start, Laura E. 1950. The Textiles. In Lagore Crannog: an Irish royal residence of the 7th to 10th centuries AD. *PRIA* 53C:1–247.

Steponaitis, Vincas. 1978. Location theory and complex chiefdoms, a Mississippian example. In *Mississippian Settlement Patterns*, edited by Bruce Smith, 417–452. New York: Academic Press.

1981. Settlement hierarchies and political complexity in nonmarket societies: the Formative period of the Valley of Mexico. *American Anthropologist* 83:320–363.

Steward, Julian. 1979 (1955). *Theory of Culture Change: the methodology of multilinear evolution*. Urbana: University of Illinois Press.

Stuiver, Minze and G. W. Pearson. 1986. *Radiocarbon*, 28, 805–838.

1986. High-precision calibration of the radiocarbon time scale, 500–2500 BC. *Radiocarbon* 28(2B): 839–862.

Sweetman, H. S. and G. F. Handcock. 1886. *Calendar of Documents Relating to Ireland, 1302–1307*. London: Public Records Office.

Todd, James H. (ed. and trans.). (1867) 1965. *Cogadh Gaedhel re Gallaibh*. Wiesbaden: Kraus Reprint Ltd.

Twohig, Dermot. 1990. Excavation of three ring-forts at Lisduggan North, County Cork. *PRIA* 90C:1–32.

Upham, Steadman. 1987. A theoretical consideration of middle range societies. In *Chiefdoms in the Americas*, edited by R. Drennan and C. Uribe, 345–368. Lanham: University Press of America.

Van de Velde, Pieter. 1979. *On Bandkeramik Social Structure.* Analecta Praehistorica Leidensia XII. The Hague: Leiden University Press.

Wailes, Bernard. 1976. Dún Ailinne: an interim report. In *Hillforts: Later Prehistoric Earthworks in Britain and Ireland*, edited by D. W. Harding, 319–338. London: Academic Press.

— 1990. Dún Ailinne: a summary excavation report. *Emania* 7:10–21.

Wallace, Patrick. 1992. *The Viking Age Buildings from Dublin*, Medieval Dublin Excavations 1962–1981. Dublin: Royal Irish Academy.

Warner, R. B. 1997. The radiocarbon chronology of the Navan excavations. In Dudley M. Waterman, 173–196.

Waterman, Dudley M. 1956. The excavation of a house and souterrain at White Fort, Drumaroad, Co. Down. *UJA* 19:73–86.

— 1971. A marshland habitation site near Larne, Co. Antrim. *UJA* 34:65–76.

— (C. J. Lynn ed.). 1997. *Excavations at Navan Fort 1961–71.* Northern Ireland Archaeological Monographs no. 3. Belfast: The Stationery Office.

Webster, Gary. 1990. Labor control and emergent stratification in prehistoric Europe. *Current Anthropology* 31 (4):337–366.

Welch, Paul D. 1991. *Moundville's Economy.* Tuscaloosa: The University of Alabama Press.

Westropp, Thomas J. 1895. The cow legend of Corofin, Co. Clare. *JRSAI* 25:227–229.

— 1896a. Magh Adhair, Co. Clare. The place of inauguration of the Dalcassian kings. *PRIA* 4 (1): 55–60.

— 1896b. Prehistoric stone forts of northern Clare – Part 1, Inchiquin Barony. *JRSAI* 26:142–157.

— 1897. Prehistoric stone forts of northern Clare – Part III, The border of Burren. *JRSAI* 27:116–127.

— 1899. Notes on the lesser castles or "Peel Towers" of the County Clare. *PRIA* 20:348–365.

— 1900. The churches of Co. Clare, and the origin of the ecclesiastical divisions in that county. *PRIA* 6:100–180.

— 1901a. Prehistoric remains of northwestern Clare. *JRSAI* 31(1): 1–17, (3): 273–291.

— 1901b. The cahers of County Clare: their names, features, and bibliography. *PRIA* 6:415–33.

— 1902. *The Ancient Forts of Ireland.* Reprinted from the *TRIA* 31 (14). Dublin: The University Press.

— 1903. On the external evidences bearing on the historic character of the "Wars of Torlough,"
by John son of Rory Macgrath. *TRIA* 32C Part II:132–197.

— 1905. Prehistoric remains (forts and dolmens) along the borders of Burren, in the County of Clare. *JRSAI* 35 Part I:205–229, Part II:343–361.

— 1907–8a. Types of the ring-forts and similar structures remaining in eastern Clare (The Newmarket Group). *PRIA* 27C no. 8:217–233.

— 1907–8b. Types of the ring-forts remaining in eastern Clare (Quin, Tulla and Bodyke). *PRIA* 27C no. 16:371–400.

— 1909a. The Termon Cross of Kilnaboy, County Clare. *JRSAI* 39:85–88.

— 1909b. Ring-forts in the barony of Moyarta, County Clare, and their legends – Part II Kilkee to Carrigaholt. *JRSAI* 39:113–126.

— 1911 (1912). Prehistoric remains (forts and Dolmens) in the Burren, Co. Clare. *JRSAI* 41:343–367.

— 1915. Prehistoric remains in the Burren and its south western border, Co. Clare. *JRSAI* 45:45–62, (4): 249–274.

White, P. 1893. *History of Clare and the Dalcassian Clans of Tipperary, Limerick, and Galway.* Dublin: M. H. Gill and Son.

Wright, Henry T. 1984. Prestate political formations. In *On the Evolution of Complex Societies: Essays in Honor of Harry Hoijer, 1982*, edited by Timothy K. Earle, 43–77. Malibu: Undena.

Ziegler, Sabine. 1994. *Die Sprache der Altirischen Ogam–Inschriften.* Göttingen: Vandenhoeck & Ruprecht.

Zvelebil, M., J. M. Moore, S. W. Green, and D. Henson. 1987. Regional survey and analysis of lithic scatters: a case study from south-east Ireland. In *Mesolithic Northwest Europe: recent trends*, edited by P. Rowley-Conway, M. Zvelebil, and H. P. Blankhorm, 9–32. Sheffield: Department of Archaeology and Prehistory, University of Sheffield.

Index